# *More Adventures with Britannia*

# MORE ADVENTURES WITH

# *B*RITANNIA

*Personalities, Politics and Culture in Britain*

## Edited by Wm. Roger Louis

University of Texas Press
*Austin*

I.B.Tauris Publishers
*London*

Published in 1998 by

University of Texas Press
P.O. Box 7819
Austin, TX 78713-7819
ISBN 0-292-74708-X, hardcover
ISBN 0-292-74709-8, paperback

and

I.B.Tauris & Co Ltd
Victoria House, Bloomsbury Square
London WC1B 4DZ
United Kingdom
ISBN 1-86064-287-X, hardcover
ISBN 1-86064-293-4, paperback

♾ The paper used in this publication meets the minimum requirements of
American National Standard for Information Sciences—
Permanence of Paper for Printed Library Materials,
ANSI Z39.48-1984

Library of Congress Catalog Card Number 98-61464

For reasons of economy and speed this volume has been printed from camera-
ready copy furnished by the editor, who assumes full responsibility for its contents.

# Table of Contents

# List of Authors

Paul Addison earned his D.Phil. at Oxford, where he studied under A. J. P. Taylor. He is the author of *The Road to 1945* (1975) and *Churchill on the Home Front, 1900–1955* (1992) and editor, with Angus Calder, of *Time to Kill: The Soldier's Experience of War in the West* (1997). He is Director of the Centre for Second World War Studies at the University of Edinburgh.

Noel Annan was Provost of King's College, Cambridge (1955–1966), moved to London to become Provost of University College (1968–1978), and was elected the first full-time Vice-Chancellor of the University of London (1978–1981). His books include *Leslie Stephen* (1951; revised edn. 1984), *Our Age* (1990), and *Changing Enemies: The Defeat and Regeneration of Germany* (1995).

Walter L. Arnstein is Professor of History and Jubilee Professor of the Liberal Arts and Sciences at the University of Illinois. He is the author or editor of six books including *Britain Yesterday and Today: 1830 to the Present* (7th edn., 1996) and *The Bradlaugh Case* (1965) as well as the author of more than thirty scholarly articles, six of them on Queen Victoria.

Samuel H. Beer is Eaton Professor Emeritus of the Science of Government at Harvard University. A former President of the American Political Science Association, his books include *Modern British Politics* (3rd edn. 1982). His lecture in this book is part of an introduction to his collected essays to be published by the University of Chicago Press, *Encounters with Modernity*.

John W. Cell is Professor of History at Duke University, where he teaches courses on world history as well as on the history of the British Empire. His books include *British Colonial Administration in the Mid-Nineteenth Century* (1970), *By Kenya Possessed* (1976), *The Highest State of White Supremacy* (1982), and *Hailey: A Study in British Imperialism 1872–1969* (1992).

Linda Colley is Leverhulne Research Professor and School Professor in History at the London School of Economics. She is the author of *In Defiance of Oligarchy: The Tory Party, 1714–1760* (1982), *Namier* (1989), and *Britons: Forging the Nation, 1707–1837* (1992), which won the Wolfson History Prize.

Bernard Crick is Emeritus Professor of Politics at London University, an Honorary Fellow of the University of Edinburgh, and a former editor of the *Political Quarterly*. His books include *In Defence of Politics* (1962), *George Orwell: A Life* (1980), and *Essays on Politics and Literature* (1989). He is working on a history of the United Kingdom as a multi-national state.

Jack P. Greene is Andrew W. Mellon Professor, The Johns Hopkins University, and a former Harmsworth Professor, Oxford University. His books include *Great Britain and the American Colonies* (1970), *All Men Are Created Equal* (1976), *Peripheries and Center* (1987), *Pursuits of Happiness* (1988), and *Understanding the American Revolution* (1995).

John Grigg is a biographer of Lloyd George. His volumes on this subject include *The Young Lloyd George* (1973), *Lloyd George: The People's Champion* (1978), and *Lloyd George: From Peace to War, 1912–1916* (1985). His lecture in this book is an adapted version of the Nehru Memorial Lecture which he delivered at Cambridge in November 1994.

Joanna Hitchcock is Director of the University of Texas Press and Past President of the Association of American University Presses. Before coming to Texas in 1992, she had worked in both Oxford and Princeton university presses and then as an editor at Princeton, where she went on to become Executive Editor for the Humanities and Assistant Director.

Antony Hopkins is the Smuts Professor of Commonwealth History and a Fellow of Pembroke College, Cambridge University. He is the author of *An Economic History of West Africa* (1973) and, with Peter Cain, a two-volume work entitled *British Imperialism* (1993). He has served as editor of both the *Economic History Review* and the *Journal of African History*.

Warren F. Kimball is Robert Treat Professor of History at Rutgers University at Newark. He has served as President of the Society for Historians of American Foreign Relations. He has edited *Churchill and Roosevelt: The Complete Correspondence* (3 vols., 1984). His other books include *The Juggler: Franklin Roosevelt as Wartime Statesman* (1991) and *Forged in War* (1997).

Mark Kinkead-Weekes is Professor Emeritus of the University of Kent at Canterbury, having taken early retirement to work on the *Cambridge Biography of D. H. Lawrence*, his volume of which, *Triumph to*

*Exile, 1912–1922,* came out in 1996. He was the Cambridge Editor of *The Rainbow* (1989). His critical books include *Samuel Richardson* (1973) and *William Golding: A Critical Study* (1984).

R. W. B. Lewis is the author of *The Jameses: A Family Narrative* (1991), and, among many other books, *The Presence of Walt Whitman* (1962), *Malraux* (1964), and *Edith Wharton: A Biography* (1975). A Pulitzer Prize winner for biography, he is Professor Emeritus of English and American Studies at Yale University.

Thomas Pinney is editor of *The Letters of Rudyard Kipling.* He has also published a collection of Kipling's earliest work, his newspaper stories from India, *Kipling's India* (1986), and an edition of Kipling's final work, the autobiography *Something of Myself* (1990). He is William M. Keck Distinguished Service Professor of English at Pomona College, Claremont, California.

John Ramsden is Professor of Modern History, University of London. In 1995–96 he was Robertson Visiting Professor of British History at Westminster College, Fulton, Missouri. He has written all three twentieth-century volumes in the Longman *History of the Conservative Party*, the most recent of which was *The Winds of Change: Macmillan to Heath 1957–1975* (1996).

S. P. Rosenbaum is Professor Emeritus of English Literature at the University of Toronto and a Fellow of the Royal Society of Canada. Among the books on the Bloomsbury Group that he has edited or written are *Victorian Bloomsbury* (1987) and *Edwardian Bloomsbury* (1994), which are the first two volumes of a literary history of the Bloomsbury Group.

Reba Soffer is Professor of History at California State University, Northridge, and a former President of the North American Conference on British Studies. Her work includes *Ethics and Society in England: The Revolution in the Social Sciences, 1870–1914* (1978) and *Discipline and Power: The University History and the Making of an English Elite, 1870–1930* (1995).

Peter Stansky is the Frances and Charles Field Professor of History at Stanford University. He has written extensively on modern Britain, including, with William Abrahams, two studies of George Orwell, *The Unknown Orwell* (1972) and *Orwell: The Transformation* (1979). He has also written *On or About December 1910: Early Bloomsbury and Its Intimate History* (1996).

Philip Ziegler has served in the British Foreign Service and as Editor-in-Chief at the publishing house of William Collins. His books include *Diana Cooper* (1981), *Mountbatten: The Official Biography* (1985), and *The Sixth Power: Barings, 1762–1929* (1988). His most recent biography is *Wilson: The Authorised Life of Lord Wilson of Rievaulx* (1993).

*The Editor* Wm. Roger Louis is Kerr Professor of English History and Culture at The University of Texas at Austin, and Fellow of St. Antony's College, Oxford. His books include *Imperialism at Bay* (1976) and *The British Empire in the Middle East* (1984). He is the Editor-in-Chief of the *Oxford History of the British Empire*.

*More Adventures with Britannia*

# Introduction

## WM. ROGER LOUIS

I n introducing a successor volume to *Adventures with Britannia,* I am reminded of the Cambridge mathematician G. H. Hardy, who once wrote that the pain of having to repeat himself was so excruciating that he decided to end the agony by offering no apology. Perhaps it is best not to alter language so carefully wrought on a previous occasion. I thus begin by stating that this book consists of a representative selection of lectures given to the British Studies seminar at the University of Texas at Austin mainly in the years 1995–1998.

Lectures fall within a slightly different genre from that of essays or scholarly articles. A lecture presumes an audience rather than a reader and usually has a more conversational tone. It allows more freedom in the expression of personal or subjective views. It invites and permits greater candor. It is sometimes informally entertaining as well as anecdotally instructive. In this volume, the lecture often represents intellectual autobiography—the relating of how the lecturer has come to grips with a significant topic in the field of British Studies, which broadly defined means things "British" throughout the world as well as things that happen to be English, Irish, Scottish, or Welsh. The scope of British Studies includes all disciplines in the social sciences and humanities including the history of science. Most of the lectures in this collection fall within the fields of history, politics, and literature, though the dominant theme here as previously is historical. The full sweep of the lectures given before the seminar will be apparent from the list at the end of the book, which is again reproduced in its entirety to give a comprehensive idea of the seminar's substance.

The British Studies seminar at the University of Texas is a remarkable institution, and it may be of general interest to retrace

briefly its history. For those at other universities or colleges who feel
trapped within the narrow confines of a single field or discipline,
the experience here may offer inspiration. What makes a seminar
successful is the willingness of its participants to meet on a regular
basis for discussion of work-in-progress, whether their own or that
of visitors. The circumstances for the founding of the seminar at
the University of Texas were exceptionally favorable because of the
Humanities Research Center, now known as the Harry Ransom
Humanities Research Center. Harry Ransom was the founder of the
HRC, a Professor of English and later Chancellor of the University,
a collector of rare books and a rare man of humane vision. Through
his administrative and financial genius, the HRC has developed into
a great literary archive with substantial collections in English literature. Ransom thought a weekly seminar might provide the opportunity to learn of the original research being conducted at the HRC
and coincidentally to create a common bond of intellectual interest
in a congenial setting of overstuffed armchairs, Persian carpets, and
generous libations of sherry. This was an ingenious idea. The seminar was launched in the fall semester 1975 by William S. Livingston
(now Senior Vice-President), Warren Roberts (the first Director of
the HRC), and myself. It had the dual purpose of providing a fo-
rum for visiting scholars engaged in research at the HRC and of
enabling the members of the seminar to discuss their own work-in-
progress.

In the fall semester 1998, the seminar entered its twenty-fourth
year. In the life of any institution, especially one based on voluntary
participation, there comes a time for renewal of effort and regeneration of purpose. The test for the British Studies seminar came at
the end of two decades, when the participants congratulated themselves on, in their view, the heroic achievement of twenty years of
intellectual adventure. But, in a collective sense of shock, they recognized that the faces around the seminar table were essentially the
same ones, twenty years older. Could it be that the seminar might
grow old and stale? Where were the younger faces, the fresh blood
needed to keep this or any comparable institution alive and well,
flourishing in new ideas and prospering from the intellects of young
and brash junior faculty members?

The seminar now has some two dozen Junior Fellows, assistant
professors or instructors of comparable rank, appointed over the
last three years along with about ten undergraduates who hold British Studies Scholarships. We are immensely grateful to the Dean of
Liberal Arts, Sheldon Ekland-Olson, for providing the funds necessary to implement this new program. Each Junior Fellow receives a
modest research grant and each British Studies Scholar a stipend to

offset the cost of tuition. The Junior Fellows are concentrated in English and History, but other departments include Anthropology, Government, Philosophy, Sociology, Law, Art History, Theater, Music, Architecture, Middle Eastern Studies, Asian Studies, Library Science, Radio-Television-Film, and even Finance. The impact of the Junior Fellows on the proceedings of the seminar in Round Table discussions and in individual presentations will be apparent from the list of lectures at the end of the book. The intellectual vitality and range of interests of the Junior Fellows, individually and collectively, has been the saving grace of the seminar.

The sherry at the Friday seminar sessions continues to symbolize the attitude. The seminar meets to examine in a civilized way whatever happens to be on the agenda, Scottish or Indian, Canadian or Jamaican, English or Australian. When Oscar Wilde said that England and America were two great countries divided by a common language, he understated the case. The interaction of British and other societies is an endlessly fascinating subject on which points of view do not often converge. The discussion is civil, but diverse preconceptions, which are tempered by different disciplines, help to sustain controversy, not to end it. What makes the ongoing debate in British Studies engaging is the clash of different perspectives as well as the nuance of cultural interpretation. Though the printed page cannot recreate the atmosphere of engaged discussion, the following lectures do offer the opportunity to savor the result of wide-ranging research and reflection.

The seminar has been the beneficiary of generous gifts by Baine and Mildred Kerr of Houston, by Becky Gale and the late Edwin Gale of Beaumont, by Creekmore and Adele Fath, by Charles and Custis Wright, and by William Braisted as well as by numerous yearly contributions by members of the seminar. I wish to extend warmest thanks to Sam Jamot Brown and Sherry Brown for establishing an endowment to further the seminar's purposes. As a result of the Brown Endowment the seminar is now able to sponsor a British Studies Research Fellowship at the HRC, to offer undergraduate and graduate scholarships, to carry forward our publication program, and to sponsor the Junior Fellows in British Studies.

The chapters are presented in chronological order, though a few are linked in pairs to emphasize recurrent seminar themes: for example, the two lectures on India, the two on Orwell, and the two on Churchill.

The first lecture, Linda Colley's "The Significance of the Frontier in British History," raises broad issues in both American and

British historical consciousness of how events on the frontier influenced national development. In a bold and memorable argument, Frederick Jackson Turner held in 1893 that new opportunities in the American West and the encounters with the Indians shaped the American character. Turner had been influenced by an earlier work: Sir John Seeley's *The Expansion of England* published in 1883. For late-Victorian and Edwardian imperialists such as Seeley, it was axiomatic that an expanding frontier was a crucial determinant in the shaping of British "national character." How valid was that belief? Did the troubled frontiers of colonies in Asia and Africa play a part in British national life comparable to the opening of the West? Might the idea of the frontier be used in a metaphorical sense to express the divide between Protestant and Catholic? In this lecture, Linda Colley explores the extent to which imaginary as well as real frontiers have shaped and complicated the evolution of British identity.

Jack Greene on the American revolution as a *British* revolution is also concerned with the question of British identity. The English who settled in America were devoted to the principles of law and liberty. They did not regard themselves as inferior in any sense to those who remained in Britain. They claimed their rights as equals, and they regarded liberty as the essence of "Britishness." These views were not reflected in British legislation. At a profound level, the American revolution occurred because of British subordination of the colonies that called into question the colonists' claims to be British. In that sense the creation of the American nation was the unintended consequence of colonial determination to gain metropolitan recognition of fundamental British rights. What came to be known as the American revolution was in fact, Jack Greene argues, a British revolution in America.

Ireland is a subject of standing interest in the British Studies seminar. One theme to emerge from "Queen Victoria's Other Island" by Walter Arnstein is that there was nothing inevitable about the course of Irish history during Queen Victoria's long reign 1837–1901. Notwithstanding surface inconsistencies in attitude, the Queen remained steadfast in her assumptions about Ireland's proper place in the political world of Victorian Britain. Though she spent only five weeks in Ireland in a reign of sixty-three years, she did consistently believe that her duty was to uphold civil order, thereby enabling the Irish people to share in the increasing prosperity enjoyed by a United Kingdom of the English, the Scots, the Welsh, and, in her view, not least the Irish. The Irish would not merely advance economically but would gain religious liberty and equality. "I am their Queen, and I must look after them," she summed up her duty. This is a revisionist account, all the more interesting because of the lecturer's sympathy for both the Irish and the Queen.

Reba Soffer inquires into the Catholic church and the issue of loyalty to the British state. She is concerned above all with the question of free will, a subject that comes into focus in the mid-nineteenth century and extends to the Catholic historians of the 1950s. The Jacobite legacy of Catholicism as treason was sustained in the nineteenth century by the identification of Catholicism with Irish civil disruption. Catholics themselves were discouraged by the Church from pursuing historical issues. How could Catholic historians reconcile the doctrines of the Church with empirical inquiry as well as with the necessity to draw conclusions freely? It was as late as 1940 that a work by a Catholic historian won the general respect of the scholarly community in Britain. The book was *The Monastic Order in England* by Dom David Knowles, a Benedictine monk. Knowles became Regius Professor of Modern History at Cambridge in 1954. Even in Knowles, the most outstanding of the Catholic historians, there was tension between conscience and authority. Though Reba Soffer's lecture is concerned mainly with historical issues, it also throws light on literature, for example, on the problem of evil as it appeared to Evelyn Waugh in 1928 when he published *Decline and Fall.*

R. W. B. Lewis relates how in 1869 the young and impressionable Henry James began exploring literary London as an "observant outsider." James was twenty-four years old when he met the "magnificently ugly—deliciously hideous" George Eliot. He later reviewed *Middlemarch,* which, in the view of R. W. B. Lewis, may well be the finest novel ever written in English. James's review of it marked a critical stage in the search for his own literary identity and the beginning of his quest to lead English literature into a new era. How did James view the influence on his writing of Dickens, Thackeray, and Trollope? What was his reaction to later writers such as Meredith and Hardy, Conrad and H. G. Wells, who once wrote that James's novels resembled a church lit but without a congregation, with an altar on which one could observe, "very reverently placed," a dead kitten, an egg shell and a piece of string? This then is a lecture that assesses the views of British writers on James as well as James's impressions of such writers as Kipling, whom he characterized as "the most complete man of genius (as distinguished from 'fine' intelligence) that I have ever known."

Although Rudyard Kipling is frequently described as an "Imperialist" poet, Thomas Pinney argues that he possessed three qualities that are to be found simultaneously only in the greatest of poets: abundance, variety, and all-round stylistic competence. Kipling's

Indian writings are known throughout the world, but his short stories, his journalism, his historical works, his speeches, his comic verse
and parodies, and his epitaphs all have a range that extends from
antiquity to the contemporary and virtually to all continents of the
world. Can Kipling still be read with continued pleasure and discovery? Though he could express violence and outrage, he was also
genuinely modest and aware of the limitations of human achievement. He saw that defeat of human endeavor was certain but that
the spirit is indomitable. The conclusion drawn by Thomas Pinney
is deeply at variance with the popular view: Kipling was not a racist
or a jingo but a tolerant and sympathetic poet of highest stature.

In 1917 Leonard and Virginia Woolf bought a small printing press.
He was thirty-seven, she two years younger. In his lecture on the two
Woolfs at the Hogarth Press, S. P. Rosenbaum argues that an understanding of their publishing experience gives insight into the work
of Virginia Woolf and the Bloomsbury Group as well as the history
of the book in English modernism. Part of the reason for the success of the Hogarth Press can be found in Leonard Woolf's colonial
service in Ceylon, where he had been trained to be rigorously efficient. The Hogarth Press amounted to what today would be called
an alternative press run with little overhead and a small staff. For
Leonard as well as for Virginia it was worth the effort because they
gained the freedom to produce their own work without the pressure exerted by editors and other publishers. In 1922 they published
Virginia's first modernist novel, *Jacob's Room*, which carried a post-
impressionist dust jacket by Vanessa Bell. Conveying a casual or
amateur approach with printer's errors and jagged format, they
upheld the principle that the content of the book was always more
important than its printed form. They also refused to publish something merely because it would sell. We now live in different times,
but S. P. Rosenbaum poses the question: do the Woolfs' values continue to have a bearing on the publishing world of today?

There have been so many gossipy anecdotes and so much speculation about D. H. Lawrence's sex life that it is often easy to forget,
according to Mark Kinkead-Weekes, that he was "the greatest English writer of this century." His work came directly out of his life
experience. His writing was his most intense way both of living and
of coming to grips with his feelings and his day-to-day problems.
How can a biographer who is also a critic and a scholar find the
right relationship or the right boundaries between life and art? Mark
Kinkead-Weekes addresses the question by studying the affair between Lawrence and Rosalind Baynes, the daughter of a well-known
English sculptor, in Italy in 1920. Lawrence was thirty-five and married tempestuously to Frieda. Rosalind was in the throes of a di-

vorce. Constance in *Lady Chatterley's Lover* in some ways resembles her. But that is a minor point. The episode with Rosalind is touching, indeed tender, and traces of it can be found in Lawrence's poetry as well as his novels. It would be reductionist, however, to view his artistic renditions as autobiographical. Mark Kinkead-Weekes draws a firm conclusion: Lawrence's poetry and novels never lose their own autonomy as works of art.

Orwell is a subject of enduring interest in the British Studies seminar, and two lectures are devoted to him in this book. In the first lecture on Orwell, Bernard Crick is preeminently concerned with the question of evidence in the writing of political biography. Biographers, like historians, are or should be limited to what can be said on the basis of evidence, which of course comes in different shapes and sizes and degrees of reliability. In investigating Orwell many writers have commonly assumed, in a point similar to the one made by Mark Kinkead-Weekes about Lawrence, that what Orwell wrote was autobiographical. Where is the evidence, Bernard Crick asks, for believing that Orwell actually shot an elephant? Extensive research failed to produce credible evidence, circumstantial or otherwise. This by no means diminishes the quality of Orwell's writing. It merely suggests that the use of "the fictive I" must be approached with caution. Orwell's stories cannot be reduced to true confessions. He deliberately evolved a plain and pugnacious style, which had the paradoxical effect of conveying what he regarded as the truth but of confusing the extent to which his writing was or was not autobiographical. Much biographical writing on Orwell has been eulogistic because it assumes the truth of the "fictive I" and elevates Orwell to an almost godlike position.

In the second lecture on Orwell, Peter Stansky inquires into the reasons for the lasting ideological echo of *Nineteen Eighty-Four*, now in the 96th American paperback edition. A clue lies in the era the book was written and in the title, which Orwell devised simply by reversing the last two digits of the year of publication, 1948, at the height of the cold war. The ideas on confrontation with totalitarian power are at once so basic and universal yet so sophisticated that they continue to have meaning in the post–cold war era. Orwell was above all concerned with the problem of the individual and the state. One of the themes of *Nineteen Eighty-Four* is corruption of language as well as corruption of power and the consequences. Peter Stansky's lecture explains the episodes in Orwell's past, especially the Spanish civil war, that shaped his vision. The lecture is no less concerned with the development of technology and the ideological manipulation of our lives that have just as much terrifying potential today as they did in 1948. Orwell emerges from this lecture less as a

prophet than as a critic of authoritarian tendencies of his own time
and their implications for the future.

In the first of the two lectures on India, Philip Ziegler reflects on
recent evidence on the partition of the subcontinent in 1947 and
the part played by the last Viceroy, Lord Mountbatten. Philip Ziegler
published *Mountbatten: The Official Biography* in 1985. Since then
Mountbatten's historical reputation has been battered, notably by
Andrew Roberts in a collection of essays called *Eminent Churchillians.*
One piece of new evidence is especially controversial. Christopher
Beaumont, the secretary to the boundary commission that delim-
ited the frontiers between India and Pakistan in 1947, decided to
publish a memorandum that he had drawn up a few years earlier.
He stated that Mountbatten attempted to persuade the boundary
commissioner, Lord Radcliffe, to alter the boundary in India's favor in the Gurdaspur district, thus securing India direct road access
to Kashmir. If true, this would do serious damage to Mountbatten's
claim to absolute neutrality. What does Philip Ziegler make of it?
How does it change the account in his biography? How do historians or biographers respond when confronted with new evidence at
variance with their published accounts? This lecture is filled with
many small surprises on issues of large magnitude: Mountbatten's racial attitudes, the problem of the boundaries in relation to the massacres in the Punjab, and, not least, Mountbatten's stature as a statesman.

In the second lecture on India, "Myths about the Approach to
Indian Independence," John Grigg agrees with Philip Ziegler that
Mountbatten was the right man for the job of transferring power in
1947 even though he could not avert the greatest of India's trag-
edies, in Gandhi's phrase, the "vivisection" of the country. John Grigg
is out to demythologize certain sacred subjects including, on the
Indian side, Gandhi and Nehru, and, on the British, the belief that
they intended from early on to progress step by step toward the
granting of Indian independence within the Commonwealth. As in
Philip Ziegler's lecture, there are significant surprises in interpretation: for example, Muhammad Ali Jinnah, the founder of Pakistan
who appears in many Indian and British accounts as a villain, appears here more favorably and "not always a wrecker." Gandhi
emerges ambiguously because of his complex attitude toward Britain and because he was a Hindu revivalist as well as the leader of the
Indian nationalist movement. Gandhi's political enemies, including Churchill, believed that an Indian Raj would be a Hindu Raj.
Nehru by comparison was a more radical and certainly more modernizing nationalist. These intricate themes are woven together at
the end of the lecture in a counterfactual interpretation: could the
story have been different? In small compass here is a systematic and

radical critique of Britain's failure to achieve an independent and united India.

Churchill is the subject of a further pair of lectures. In "A Victorian Tory" Warren Kimball states as prelude that all Englishmen know that the United States played a part in the collapse of the British Empire. Churchill held diehard views on empire while Franklin Delano Roosevelt believed that the antiquated system of colonial rule needed to be abolished. Roosevelt pursued his goal of liquidating the British Empire just as tenaciously as Churchill resisted it, but Warren Kimball points out that a closer look at the evidence proves that despite their divergent attitudes they worked together toward the creation of a stable post-war world. Ultimately the debate transcended the colonial controversy. How did Churchill view the future of China? The Soviet Union? The creation of a United Nations organization? What in turn was Roosevelt's response to what he regarded as Churchillian obstruction on the colonial issue? Roosevelt could not prevent the European reoccupation of the Asian colonies, but he never ceased to believe that a smooth, non-violent transition from empire to independence was a key to creating a peaceful world. How did the two of them manage to reconcile their views in their common quest for a stable post-war order? Or did they?

In "Churchill as His Own Historian," John Ramsden points out that in a poll of heads of state in 1968 asking for the name of "the most admired man in history" Churchill ran ahead of Gandhi (though Churchill came in second; the winner was Abraham Lincoln). After Churchill's death in 1965, *Life* magazine's cover had carried his picture and the caption "Giant of the Century." No one would have anticipated such spectacular future public esteem in 1945, the year of Churchill's stunning electoral defeat at the end of the war. John Ramsden asks the simple question, how did Churchill create his own mythic image? The answer lies principally in Churchill's literary as well as political genius in constructing his war memoirs as an autobiographical account. He knew what he was doing, and he did it superbly well. One of Churchill's biographers, John Connell, summed up the main point: "The memoirs . . . give a one-sided picture of the war's conduct and administration, but as [Churchill] himself would have said, *some side*." John Ramsden's lecture not only helps to explain Churchill's mythic image but also the reason why the war memoirs remain one of the great historical accounts of the twentieth century.

Paul Addison's lecture on the debate over the "post-war consensus" raises a critical issue in understanding British history since 1945. In the contemporary view, and until recently the view espoused by most historians, during the wartime years members of all political parties worked together toward the creation of the welfare state, toward a mixed economy, and toward full employment. British politicians favored an expansion in the role of the state to prevent a return to the economic and social conditions of the 1930s. Much later, in the 1980s, younger historians began to argue that no consensus had existed at all. In their view the conflicts between Conservative and Labour governments remained unresolved. British historians under the age of forty grew up in a society polarized by ideology and strife and in a nation that seemed to be in danger of losing its identity. They believe indeed that national unity never existed. Does each generation interpret its own history according to its own times? This lecture will be influential in future historical debate about Britain in the years after the Second World War.

Astonished, delighted, and alarmed, Noel Annan reflects on his book *Our Age*, a study in the history of ideas and a portrait of British intellectuals who grew up between the wars and ruled Britain after 1945. Lord Annan was astonished at the request to reassess his own work, delighted to accept the invitation to present his ideas before the British Studies seminar, and alarmed that further discussion might provoke further criticism. Could there be any truth in one of the far-reaching critiques of the book, that there were two authors— the young intellectual iconoclast of the 1940s and the wizened bureaucrat of later decades? Had he betrayed the life of the mind? He acknowledges that there are certain key questions, among others, to which he would address himself if he were rewriting the book today. How, on reflection, does the critical decade of the 1960s now appear at the end of the century? What of the continued consequences of Labour's mismanagement of the economy and the subsequent dismantling of the welfare state? What is one to make of national unity in view of Scottish and Welsh devolution? What of the dubious achievement of Margaret Thatcher, who challenged all the assumptions of her generation? Did she turn the country around? The lecture concludes: "The jury is still out on that issue," as it is on Tony Blair.

In a sense the themes in the previous two lectures by Addison and Annan are sustained by Samuel Beer. "The Rise and Fall of Party Government in Britain and the United States" inquires into the reasons for the collapse of stable, competitive two-party systems that existed in both countries until the 1960s, when a series of government failures resulted in a loss of control over the economy. In Britain the collapse of control has often been attributed to long-run economic decline, but Samuel Beer believes a far greater influence was the cultural revolution of the 1960s. Attacking authority in every sphere including dress, music, education, sex, work, religion, and especially politics, this revolution, in both Britain and the United States, eroded the sense of community and gravely weakened the power of government to control the economy. Distrust of politics and dissatisfaction with government now run deeply in both countries. Yet the restoration of a civic culture of trust may be possible. Despite an underlying sense of despair at what has happened since the 1960s, the lecture ends on a note of hope by defining in specific ways how public order and coherence in public policy may be possible in both countries.

Slightly out of chronological sequence, the lectures by John Cell and Antony Hopkins deal with the British Empire and the consequences of its dissolution. In "Who Ran the British Empire?" John Cell points out that on the eve of the Second World War the British had only 125 administrative officers in the Sudan, a country twice the size of Texas. In India there were only 1,250 members of the Indian Civil Service for a population of 353 million. How did so few manage to rule so many? Part of the answer lies in the phrase "Indirect Rule," the British colonial philosophy expounded by the proconsul Frederick Lugard and given academic credibility by the Oxford don Margery Perham. Lugard was an autocrat and an inefficient administrator but an effective propagandist. He faced no alternative but to enter into alliances with African rulers who already exerted an authoritarian chain of command. Indirect rule had the practical effect of freezing African societies rather than modernizing them. How then did Margery Perham, who was an intelligent woman and in John Cell's view a force for good, come to view indirect rule as a justification and rationale for enlightened British administration? From today's vantage point, was it better to have retained traditional customs and institutions, modifying them slowly and cautiously, rather than plunging Africa and other places into the modern world? In John Cell's lecture there emerges a lingering admiration for the officers of the British colonial service, however muddled in retrospect their mission might seem.

Antony Hopkins in "From Africa to Empire" deals with the academic repercussions of the end of the British Empire, though the consequences extend far beyond the ivory tower. In a theme that connects with other lectures in this book, the critical era was the decade of the 1960s, when "Area Studies" began to flourish with centers, journals, and monograph series. The end of empire brought down with it the old style of British colonial history. The inspiration behind the new study of Asian and African societies was not entirely academic. This was the era of the cold war in an intense phase of competitive co-existence. There was an outpouring of good will associated with anti-colonialism and with the prospects for assisting newly independent countries to achieve their aspirations. Antony Hopkins offers gentle yet incisive criticism that trends in American cultural studies and history reflect to the present day an urge to shape the world in America's image: "the projection abroad of an implicit concern with the American soul and the American destiny." The lecturer traces his own experience as he progressed from specialized studies in African history to the magnificent work of synthesis and general analysis, *British Imperialism*. How, he asks, can the balance be struck between, on the one hand, detailed studies by specialists writing for other specialists and, on the other, more general works that can be read by an intelligent, general reading public?

In the last lecture, "British and North American University Presses," Joanna Hitchcock is concerned with precisely the same themes of specialized and general publishing. Historically the purpose of a university press has been, and continues to be, the publication of scholarly works that are not commercially viable. What are the major differences in university presses in Britain and America? This useful lecture, one of the very few attempts to address the subject directly, establishes that the distinction in Britain between a "university press" and a commercial house is much more blurred or ambiguous than in the United States and Canada. In America a university press usually has a procedure that guarantees standards of scholarly excellence. In Britain there may or may not be a comparable review process, and some of the smaller British "university presses" may in fact be more similar to American academic publishers out for profit. In Britain the academic publishing community is dominated by the two giants, the Oxford and Cambridge university presses, which not only prosper financially, to the benefit of the two universities, but may also prove to be the salvation of that endangered species, the scholarly monograph. What of the technological revolution of electronic publishing and how will it affect university presses? Will they have the resilience not merely to save the scholarly monograph but to broaden the appeal and marketability of their books while fulfilling the primary mission to scholarship?

1

# The Significance of the Frontier in British History

## LINDA COLLEY

I t is a very great pleasure to be invited to deliver one of the lectures in British Studies here at the University of Texas. But you may well wonder why someone so honored should want to echo in her title the most famous, even notorious interpretation ever advanced of the history of the American West. It was just over a century ago—on the evening of July 12, 1893—that Frederick Jackson Turner, then a young assistant professor at the University of Wisconsin, set out for the very first time "The Significance of the Frontier in American History." His central thesis will doubtless be familiar to you. "Up to our own day," he argued:

> American history has been in a large degree the history of the colonization of the Great West. The existence of an area of free land, its continuous recession, and the advance of American settlement westward, explain American development . . . This expansion westward with its new opportunities, its continuous touch with the simplicity of primitive society, furnish the forces dominating American character.[1]

From this turbulent, westwards movement of successive generations of hardy and venturesome individuals had sprung a less Europeanized kind of American, and a distinctive brand of American democracy.

It is a daunting thought that there were those among Turner's first audience who slept as he spoke, and that his lecture elicited no questions whatsoever. Indeed, for all its subsequent massive fame, Turner's thesis has almost always received a rough ride from critics. Among recent historians of the American West, in particular, it has

become common to castigate Turner for the geographical impreci-
sion of his notion of the Frontier, and for his erroneous assumption
that it was necessarily conducive to fledgling democracy or even to
marked autonomy from the center. Angry revisionists like Patricia
Limerick have insisted that the American West was not "free" or
empty or primitive: the "meeting point between savagery and civilization" as Turner so sweepingly styled it. Interpreting the frontier
in this fashion, these scholars argue, glossed over those millions of
Indians and Chicanos who were driven under by American westwards Imperialism, just as it obscured—by its concentration on heroic pioneer virility—the often very different western experience
of women, servants and blacks.[2]

Such objections are valid enough, of course. But more subtle
scholars have looked beyond the imperfect knowledge and tenden-
tiousness undoubtedly present in Turner's thesis to its irreducible
originality and broad and enduring value. Whether we like it or
not, Turner, as William Cronon points out, "gave American history
its central and most persistent story," the essence of one of this
country's most enduring and popular myths.[3] As such, reading
Turner is indispensable if we want to understand late nineteenth-
and twentieth-century American nationalism. Moreover, the frontier remains a vital and legitimate site for historical inquiry—even if
not for the precise reasons that Turner himself formulated. A frontier, John Mack Faragher reminds us, is a "region of encounter . . .
an area of contest but also of consort between cultures": and consequently a crucial point at which to investigate the content of those
different cultures.[4] Such "intersections" between different peoples
and differing customs, Stephen Aron insists, are often in real life
zones of danger: but they "make the most interesting history."[5]

But where does all this leave British history? Part of the answer
was suggested by a one-time member of this very University, Walter
Prescott Webb. In a 1952 book entitled *The Great Frontier,* he argued
that the Imperial frontiers of the various European colonial powers
in the seventeenth, eighteenth and nineteenth centuries should be
focussed on and analysed as the American frontier had been: "The
fact that [this Imperial] . . . frontier was scattered geographically,"
Webb remarked, "should not obscure its common characteristics
and the unity of the force it exerted."[6]

Audacious for its time, this was in fact a restatement of what,
back in the later nineteenth century, had been a fairly standard
observation. Then, it had been common enough in Germany,
France, as well as in Britain, to draw comparisons between European overseas expansion and America's expansion westwards. The
future Liberal Unionist, Goldwin Smith, for instance, remarked *en*

*passant* in 1866 that "If America has an outlet in the West, England [too] has outlets—her Colonies."[7] But it was of course the Cambridge historian Sir John Seeley who developed this claim most famously and in detail. In 1883, exactly a decade before Turner launched his own thesis, Seeley's *The Expansion of England* attacked his peers for concentrating so remorselessly on domestic, constitutional history. "Good or bad," he argued, the "great fact of modern English history" was relentless expansion overseas: "The history of England is not in England but in America and Asia."[8]

It is possible that Frederick Jackson Turner read Seeley's work at Wisconsin in advance of formulating his own theories of the frontier. And it is certain that leading British Imperialists and nationalists in the late Victorian and early Edwardian eras read and relished both Seeley and Turner. In a lecture delivered in Oxford in 1907, for example, Lord Curzon, former Viceroy of India, drew an explicit parallel between the nation-building impact of the American frontier experience and the invigorating effect on British youth of what he styled the "savage, chivalrous, desperate, adventurous, alluring" life to be found "in this larger atmosphere, on the outskirts of empire, where the machine is relatively impotent and the individual is strong." In this same lecture, Curzon went on to stress the historical significance of the internal frontiers of the British Isles:

> In our own country how much has turned upon the border conflict between England and Scotland and between England and Wales. In Ireland the ceaseless struggles between those within and those without the Pale has left an ineffaceable mark on the history and character of the people.[9]

Because men like Seeley and Curzon, and their many imitators, belonged to a late stage of British Imperialist and nationalist assertion which has long since passed away, their more abstract and apolitical remarks on the importance of frontiers for a proper understanding of the history of the British Isles have tended to be forgotten or dismissed as mere ephemeral and chauvinistic punditry. The year that witnessed the crisis over Suez and the hollowness of Britain's remaining Imperial pretensions—1956—was also the year in which Seeley's *Expansion of England* was allowed, for the very first time, to go out of print.[10] Now that the dust has settled, however, it is surely time to disinter some—only some—of his perspectives. Today, I want to argue for a modified revival and re-appraisal of the significance of the frontier—broadly interpreted—in British history.

First, because Seeley was of course right to insist that a great deal of early modern and modern English, and later British history took place not at home, but in America, Asia, and Africa. As Salman

Rushdie has recently quipped, the trouble with the British is that so much of their history "happened overseas, so that they don't know what it means."[11] Even Imperial historians (whose subject is rightly now undergoing both revision and renaissance) too often focus their researches *either* on the colonizing metropolis (as P. J. Cain and A. G. Hopkins have done in their recent blockbuster) *or* on the autonomous development of what John S. Galbraith once called the "Turbulent Frontier."[12] By contrast, I would argue that, in Britain's case, developments and ideas at the edge of empire often had an impact on and were inter-connected with those in the metropolis. In particular, unless we know how different Britons experienced the frontiers of their changing Empire abroad, we shall never fully understand how they viewed the frontiers of their identities at home.

But there is a second fundamental point. In recent years, historians of Continental European nationalism such as Peter Sahlins have urged us to look again not just at the ways that political and "natural" frontiers delimit nations, but at how such frontiers can contribute to the *symbolic* construction of different nations.[13] Historians of the British archipelago are only just beginning to attempt this. In the main, English historians—particularly historians of modern England—still concentrate overwhelmingly on England, Scottish historians on Scotland, and so on. Yet exploring how these different peoples both clashed and intermixed at the real and imagined frontiers between them can be deeply revealing, not least if we want to understand the limits and the extent of Britishness and the British state.

In the rest of this lecture, then, I want to suggest briefly, and I hope provocatively, three ways in which examining different kinds of frontiers can illuminate but also problematize the question of British identities—and I use the plural form deliberately. First, I want to glance at these islands' internal frontiers. Second, I shall say something about the absolutely crucial frontier—which could be both a function of prejudice and a matter of geography—between Protestantism and Catholicism. Finally, I want to return to the question of how the English, the Scottish, the Welsh and the Irish made contact with the Imperial frontier overseas.

Modern British historians—especially historians of England—have been slow to address the question of their own frontiers, in part from a lingering assumption that there is no question to address. Back in the 1930s, Lewis Namier summed up this complacency very well:

> The historical development of England is based upon the fact
> that her frontiers are drawn by Nature and cannot be the subject
> of dispute . . . In short, a great deal of what is peculiar in English
> history is due to the obvious fact that Great Britain is an island.[14]

Other nations have frontier problems: Great Britain is defined by
God and the sea. As Namier's own slippage from *English* history to
*Great Britain* bears witness, this is a glib and strictly retrospective
interpretation. It is certainly the case that by the sixteenth century
(perhaps as early as the twelfth century), a sense of privileged
islandhood was part of the identity of some educated Englishmen.
(Think of some of Shakespeare's imagery: a "precious stone set in a
silver sea.") But, at this early stage, such references to splendid insu-
larity were obviously as much an expression of English internal colonialism as English patriotism. The view from Scotland and Wales
was naturally very different. Even within England itself—at least until
Britannia really did rule the waves—the sea could seem less a symbol and guardian of national identity, than the means by which invasion from without might come. Keith Thomas reminds us that
some English coastal villages continued commemorating Viking
invasions as late as the seventeenth century.[15] We badly need, I think,
a kind of Braudelian exploration of when and to what extent the
sea came to be viewed by the British as a decisive, "natural" frontier.[16]

What is clear is that in all three parts of Great Britain, a sense of
the paramountcy of inland frontiers—using that term to mean that
which stands face to a real or imagined enemy, or at least to something that is considered alien in part—persisted long after the Acts
of Union of 1536 and 1707. Military expeditions from Scotland into
England, and from England into Scotland, continued, after all, until
1746. When George IV made the first Hanoverian state visit to Scotland in 1822, he was careful to come by sea so as not to revive unhappy memories of that earlier, overland, and violent cross-border
incursion by his ancestor, William, Duke of Cumberland. As for
persistent Anglo-Welsh border tensions, I have an anecdote of my
own. My parents live in a small village called Farndon which is on
the border between the English county of Cheshire and the north
Welsh village of Holt. The border is marked by the River Dee and
an ancient stone bridge. The oldest villagers on both sides of the
river still claim to remember the time when, every Sunday evening,
scores of thirsty Welshmen would pour over the bridge into Farndon
—where the pub opening hours were more generous than in
Wales—and how, sometimes, drunken Englishmen and Welshmen
would mark the end of the sabbath holiday by beating each other
up in a half-friendly, half-unfriendly fashion. Accurate or not, this

folk memory—which seems in fact to go back to Victorian times—makes the point that frontiers are often the place where different identities are acted or invented, the place where people determine who to include as "us" and who to exclude as "them."

In addition to Welsh, Scottish, and English border tensions, there was, and is, the complication of John Bull's other island. In recent years, revisionist historians have argued, to my mind convincingly, that much of our traditional emphasis on the dichotomies between Irish and British, and Irish and English history, is exaggerated. In Roy Foster's words: "the Irish presence in . . . British life" has been an "infinitely more complex, stratified and influential sector than is often realised."[17] Nonetheless, it seemed to me when I was writing *Britons*—as it seems to me still—that, as far as British lower and middle class civilians at home were concerned (upper class Britons, and Britons in the armed forces and overseas empire were, as we shall see, sometimes a different matter), the Irish *were* more likely to be perceived as alien, than the English, Welsh, and Scottish were by the early nineteenth century to see each other as alien. This was partly because of religion, a point to which I will return, partly because of language and geography, but mainly perhaps because a disproportionate number of Irish immigrants to Britain in the eighteenth and nineteenth centuries were extremely poor and illiterate. So, prejudices based on class reinforced, as they often do, prejudices based on nationality.

Let me give you just one telling example. It dates from 1803 when every mainland British county was organizing volunteer corps to repel Napoleon's threatened invasion. An enterprising insurance company sprang up in the south of England which undertook, in return for a fee, to supply any town or village unable to raise its proper quota of men with the necessary manpower. Communities were specifically asked whether they would be willing to accept (I quote) "foreigners or Irishmen." Two things strike me here. First, the insurance company clearly felt that there was no need to enquire whether Scots or Welshmen would be acceptable substitutes, even though Welsh and Scottish migrants in search of work were common enough in southern England at this time. The company just assumed that such men—unlike the Irish—would be acceptable. Second, the compiler of this insurance company clearly felt that the Irish were *sui generis*. They were not quite foreign. But neither—and despite the recent Act of Union with Ireland—could Irishmen, especially poor ones, be accepted as reliable fellow Britons to the degree that the Welsh and the Scots now were. The recent Irish "rebellion" in 1798 explains part of this sense of difference and distrust: but only part. I stress again, though, that this particular mental frontier could usually in practice be surmounted by the rich, the talented and the warlike. Presumably, no southern English volunteer corps in 1803 would have objected to being joined by Arthur Wellesley, future Commander-in-Chief of the British army and 1st Duke of Wellington, who was of course himself an Irishman.

Careers like Wellington's remind us that in the eighteenth, nineteenth, and for much of the twentieth century (among the elite, perhaps even earlier), British, English, Scottish, Welsh, and Irish national identities often in practice co-existed, jostling for space in peoples' minds and habits. Robert Burns, for example, wrote some verses celebrating past Scottish victories over the English. But after the outbreak of war in 1793, he also wrote a song for his volunteer company explicitly invoking collective British defiance of the French enemy. And here is another, particularly piquant example of dual national identities dating from the 1880s. It concerns Lady Frances Campbell, who was among other things a fierce Scottish patriot. Her daughter described how she imposed a ritual on her children every time they crossed the ancient border between England and Scotland:

> At last the train slowed down on the curve before Berwick bridge, and weariness was temporarily forgotten as the great moment approached. Rigid I sat, with eyes fixed upon Mamma, waiting for her signal that we were exactly half-way across [the] Tweed. Then we all cheered. On the south-bound journey [back to England] we hissed like serpents at this point.[18]

Should we interpret this behaviour as an expression of unabashed Scottish separatism? Scarcely. Because we have to ask: why were Lady Frances and her brood crossing the Tweed into England so regularly? The answer is that her father, the 8th Duke of Argyll, was a British cabinet minister, while her brother-in-law, Arthur Balfour, would later be British Prime Minister. Lady Frances was a fervent Scot, but also an equally fervent member of the British establishment. And, typically, it was at the old frontier that the tensions between her dual nationalities, gut Scottishness and self-interested Britishness, sought expression.

My second point, the divide between Protestant and Catholic, might seem a purely metaphorical frontier, a matter of intense faith, myth and memories only. But this divide was frequently lent more material substance by the recurrent conflicts that occurred between Britain and Catholic Continental powers, first Spain and then France. These military, dynastic, and increasingly colonial conflicts drew on and reinforced acute and longstanding fears about the Catholic presence within.[19]

As a result, Catholics inside Britain were often viewed not just as alien in religious terms, but in a more thoroughgoing sense. In the seventeenth and eighteenth centuries, one finds English Protestants referring to Catholics as "outlandish"—as if, in some fundamental way, they were not really part of the land. And language was used to de-naturalize Catholics in other ways as well. Even today, we still employ the term "beyond the pale," without, perhaps, thinking very hard about what it means. But "the Pale," of course, was the term applied to that part of Ireland controlled from Protestant London. To be beyond the pale is to be unacceptable—just as it originally meant to be among those who were literally out of bounds: those who, in large part because of their faith, were "them" not "us."

Some reviewers of *Britons* have argued that my concentration on the tensions between Catholics and Protestants is too glib: what about the often very violent disputes between different kinds of British Protestants? Let me say, once and for all, that I readily acknowledge them. One has only got to read, say, Anthony Trollope's *Barchester Chronicles* to be reminded of the enduring fractures between Anglicanism and English dissent; the gulf between Scottish Presbyterianism and the Church of England was obviously much greater still. Nonetheless, I remain convinced that, after 1688, the significance of the Catholic-Protestant divide was greater than the barriers separating different kinds of Protestants from each other. This was particularly so among the lower classes. Britain's governors became more relaxed in their official treatment of Catholics after the final scotching of the Jacobite threat in 1746. Lower down the social spectrum, however, anti-Catholic prejudice was largely unalloyed, and remained so in most areas until this century.

Compare, for instance, the Sacheverell riots of 1710, London's biggest anti-dissenting riots in the Hanoverian era, with the Gordon riots of 1780, the capital's biggest anti-Catholic riot. On the former occasion, two people were killed: one by falling masonry. On the latter occasion, the usual body-count given is 300—and this is almost certainly an under-estimate. Or compare the number of petitions dispatched to Parliament protesting against the formal admission of all Protestants to full citizenship in 1828, with the petitioning campaign against Roman Catholic emancipation the following year. Just twenty-eight petitions condemned the former concession; well over 3,000 petitions were submitted against the second. Anti-dissenting prejudices certainly co-existed with anti-Catholicism. But the quality of the latter was substantially different precisely because it was caught up with British identity in a unique way.

Indeed, anti-Catholicism arguably served much the same self-defining function in England, Wales, and Scotland—and of course in parts of Ireland—as anti-semitism did in parts of Eastern and Western Europe. Anti-semitism, Tony Judt has suggested, "is as much a way of talking about 'them' and 'us' as it is a device for singling out Jews in particular."[20] So it was with anti-Catholicism in much of the British Isles between the late sixteenth and early twentieth centuries; and in Ireland for longer still.[21]

In prejudiced, Protestant eyes, Catholicism was more than an alien and dangerously proselytizing religion. It was associated by many educated and most uneducated Britons alike with a string of other, often contradictory, failings: lax sexual morality and idleness on the one hand, arbitrary rule and aggression on the other; mindless conformity but also excessive cunning. Condemning Catholicism—and consequently these vices—was a way for Protestants to vaunt by contrast their own religious and national virtues. From the late seventeenth century onwards, France, in particular, was used as a coat-peg for prejudice in this way, with results that can still be seen in present-day British-French relations. In July 1992, a London tabloid, the *Daily Express*, quoted a recent European Union poll on national alignments within its member states. It may not surprise you that the French were reported as having nominated Britain as the EU country they most distrusted. But it may, just, surprise you that, as far as the British who were polled were concerned (and it was not specified who these were), France was the nation they trusted least in the world, less than Russia, Germany, Japan. Who, according to this same survey, did the British trust the most? The Danes and the Dutch, small, unthreatening countries, but also countries which are perceived (however erroneously in the case of the Netherlands) as being predominently Protestant. It is a nice example of how traditional mental boundaries endure long after the religious culture that fed them has lost much of its force.

From here it is a small step to one of the best-known icons of British Imperialism: the picture, which could be found in countless late-nineteenth-century homes, schools and text-books, of Queen Victoria bestowing a copy of the Bible on a black man as the secret of Britain's greatness. Here, classically, are the British represented as the Protestant Israel, given benevolent sway over huge portions of the globe by a God who was usually on their side. It is a painting which seems to lend vivid reinforcement to the argument set out by Sir John Seeley and his kind: that developments on Britain's Imperial frontiers were not autonomous and extraneous, but rather inextricably caught up with the work of British self-imagining. And this is my third and last point: how far in fact should British colonial frontiers be explored by historians, not just for their own sake—for what they can tell us about North America, or Australia, or South Africa, or India, or wherever—but for what they can also reveal about the colonizing metropolis and its diverse peoples?

It is clearly the case, as Peter Marshall has recently stated, that:

> Assessment of the impact [of empire] on Britain's sense of iden-
> tity has to face the obvious problems that the British had and
> have many senses of identity and that empire, even as a system of
> rule, could be interpreted in different ways to fulfill differing
> aspirations to identity.[22]

This said, the expanding British Imperial frontier did serve both to forge and to endorse attitudes and assumptions in the metropolis. We have already seen, for instance, that empire could cater to what was already a deeply entrenched Protestant triumphalism. One thinks of that truly astonishing passage in John Ruskin's Slade lectures in 1870 where Britain's colonies are described as "motionless churches . . . ruled by pilots on the Gallilean lake of all the world."[23] In addition, the democratic progress of the so-called "white" colonies in the later nineteenth century—New Zealand, Canada, Australia, even perhaps that lapsed colony, the United States—reassured many Britons that their civilization was the cradle of right constitutional liberties, the mother of parliaments. Most vividly, perhaps—and as Lord Curzon pointed out—accounts of the real or imaginary exploits of their soldiers, officials, missionaries and settlers on the colonial frontier could serve to reassure the British that they were indeed a plucky and manly lot. At one and the same time, they could congratulate themselves on their marked technological and industrial advance at home, while priding themselves—as so many nineteenth century Americans also did—that contact with "the primitive" on the frontier would preserve them from becoming over-cultivated and soft. As one of the leading British proponents of emigration to the colonies, Edward Wakefield, argued in 1849: "By colonization nations are able to retrieve the past . . . [it] supplies at critical periods a *tabula rasa*," a new frontier.[24]

But how were those at home to learn about the edges of Empire? In recent years, cultural critics such as Edward Said and Sara Suleri have written a great deal about the Imperial content in eighteenth-nineteenth- and twentieth-century European, and especially English literature: the novels of Jane Austen, W. M. Thackeray, Charles Dickens, Wilkie Collins, Rudyard Kipling, and E. M. Forster have all, been scrutinized in this way. Yet, of course, the vast majority of Britons in the past only rarely had access to these kind of fairly expensive and medium-brow works. Instead, scholars interested in the transmission of knowledge and prejudice about the colonies could usefully investigate two very different kinds of texts: on the one hand, manuscript letters; on the other, the memoirs, apologias, and reports produced by frontiersmen of different kinds which, from the mid-eighteenth century onwards, were made increasingly available in cheap, printed form.

When the French Saint-Simonian, Gustave D'Eichthal, toured Britain in 1828, it seemed to him that there was "hardly a family . . . which does not have someone overseas."[25] A large proportion of these absent family members will have been in the colonies, either as soldiers or settlers. And many of them must have written home at least once in their lives and said something about their new surroundings. Yet, apart from Charlotte Erickson's pioneering work on the letters of working-class English emigrants to the United States in the nineteenth century, very little systematic analysis has ever been done on what must have been one of the main and most vivid sources of information about the empire for many ordinary families.[26] More educated actors on the colonial frontier, particularly those operating on its most dangerous edges who wanted celebrity and cash, regularly committed their experiences of new scenery, new ecology, new customs and new races to print. And one can explore this particular literary genre right down to the young Winston Churchill's account of his adventures on the north-west frontier of India, *The Story of the Malakand Field Force* (1898) and beyond. It should go without saying that many of these accounts—including Churchill's—are studded with errors and fabrications, but they often achieved a wide circulation, and made a major and still unexplored contribution to how different Britons at home perceived their Empire.

Let me give you two examples from the Seven Years War. The first concerns one of the most notorious British Imperial legends, the "Black Hole of Calcutta." For those of you who do not know, in June 1756, after the fall of the East India Company's base in Calcutta to Siraj-ud-Daulah, an unknown number of Europeans were imprisoned in a small, airless room and many suffocated. An initial account of this by an East India Company official called John Zephaniah Holwell first appeared in the London press in June 1757. It was promptly reproduced by all of the influential monthlies, like the *Gentleman's Magazine*. And by the end of the month this saga, with its inflated total of British casualties, tales of British fortitude under stress, and allusions to Indian sadism and depravity, had been regurgitated by the English provincial press, and by the Scottish and Dublin newspapers.[27] Holwell subsequently published a still more lurid account as a pamphlet, which was again widely extracted by the press. By 1772, a witness before the House of Commons could say confidently that "The circumstances of the Black Hole affair, with all the horrors of that night, are so well known . . . that I shall say no more upon that subject."[28]

Scalping provided an analogous and equally well-publicized atrocity image from the North American theatre of this same war. These kind of atrocity stories had of course been common in the American colonies from the beginning of settlement. But their wide circulation in the British Isles (and indeed Continental Europe) only seems to have commenced after 1754.[29] Once again, the British and Irish press reproduced lurid accounts of massacres by Canadian and American Indians, many drawn from the letters and reports of soldiers fighting on the front. This conflict's quite unprecedented slew of military memoirs, works like the Irishman John Knox's trilogy on the Canadian campaign, almost invariably contained one or more scalping set-pieces as well.[30] By the 1760s, allusions to hatchets, scalps, and Indian braves crop up in British parliamentary debates, in magazines such as Samuel Johnson's *Idler*, in pub and coffee house signs, and in fashionable masquerades.

It should be obvious that such references often served to deepen an already pronounced sense of moral and cultural superiority to the indigenous peoples of North America. But their impact was almost certainly broader than this. British army officers serving in America were hypocritical about scalping. They (like their French opponents) regularly ordered their Indian allies to take enemy scalps, usually with a caveat that women and children were not to be mutilated in this way. And the British often commented that white American rangers and some New England regulars also took scalps. But they claimed, falsely, that British troops themselves did not behave in this manner. One Highland Scottish officer wrote in 1759, for example, that "such inhumanity" could only stem from that "cowardice and barbarity which seems so natural to a native of America, whether of Indian or European extraction."[31] I stress this kind of reaction in the light of an argument advanced by many historians of colonial America: namely, that the experience of fighting side by side with an unprecedented number of British soldiers and officers in the Seven Years War served to convince many American soldiers that they were not really British after all.[32] This was doubtless the case. But, by the same token, fighting on the American frontier seems also to have convinced many Britons that the colonials were indeed un-British, representatives of the Other, not their own.

The Scottish Highlander's complacent assertion of his own superior humanity in the face of American difference, which I have just quoted, points to one of the most important domestic consequences of British Imperial expansion. Joint participation in the business and—among the elite and enterprising—in the profits of empire helped to cover over some of the profound differences between the English, Welsh, Scots and Irish, and so cement the Union. Even many Irish Home Rulers in the late nineteenth century would for a long time be diffident about attacking the Empire as a whole precisely because its armed forces and bureaucracy employed so many of their own countrymen. It is worth remembering that the full name of the eponymous hero of Rudyard Kipling's Imperial classic *Kim* is Kimball O'Hara. Transparently he's an Irishman.

To this extent, then, the British Imperial frontier—like the American Western frontier—served as something of a safety valve: a safety valve not just in the sense that the colonies absorbed some of the surplus population of the British Isles, but also in that they eased its internal cultural and ethnic fractures. This said, it needs to be stressed that different kinds of Britons often responded to the Empire in very different ways. As William Cronon, George Miles, and Jay Gitlin have written of the American West:

> The various communities in a frontier area sometimes succeeded in blending ethnic traditions, but as often as not they displayed a fierce loyalty to the places they had fled. The very opportunity that frontiers offered people to abandon their old ways often put a premium on maintaining them.[33]

So it was that some Scots and Irish, in particular, reacted to contact with a new, Imperial frontier, by an assertion of their own discrete identity. Occasionally, such assertions took a dramatic form. During the Napoleonic Wars, for example, some Scottish soldiers under English officer command reacted to being sent to put down a West Indian slave revolt by deserting and joining forces with the slaves. A more typical pattern of behaviour is set out in a recent article by Cliff Cumming which shows how early nineteenth century Scottish settlers in Australia continued to celebrate a distinctive Scottish and Presbyterian identity: the menfolk, for example, insisting on establishing their own Masonic lodges in rivalry with the English lodges in the colony.[34]

Or consider the case of Sir John Pope Hennessy, Irish Catholic Governor of Hong Kong from 1877 to 1882, and the model for Anthony Trollope's literary hero Phineas Finn. Hennessy was a committed Imperialist and an efficient one. But, throughout his governorship, he found himself increasingly at odds with Hong Kong's colonial elite, which was predominantly Anglo-Scottish and Protes-

tant. So great were the disagreements that, on the day he formally
left his posting, almost every influential British colonist was absent
from the ceremony. By contrast, the colony's harbor was crowded
with members of the Chinese and Portuguese Catholic communities to see him off; and the Irish army band saluted him with its
traditional battle tune "The Minstrel Boy." Exposure to this Imperial frontier had made Hennessy far more conscious of his Irishness,
not less.[35]

Hennessy was something of an exceptional case. But reacting to
the challenge of new, Imperial frontiers—Greater Britain as Sir
Charles Dilke and Seeley both called it—by seeking refuge instead
in older, more established identities was common enough. So,
among many men and women in the different parts of the British
Isles, was a considerable unconcern about matters Imperial. For
while I have wanted in this lecture to draw attention to ways in which
the Imperial frontier was important: I do not want to exaggerate
that importance. We should always remember that one of Seeley's
chief complaints in *The Expansion of England* in 1883 was that the
British (and despite his title, it was often the British that he meant)
had acquired their vast Empire in a fit of absence of mind. "We have
never accustomed our imaginations to the thought of Greater Britain," he wrote.[36] Curzon, too, was appalled at how insular many of
his countrymen remained. "We have by now the greatest extent of
territorial frontier of any dominion in the globe," he said in 1907:
"Not much is heard of this astonishing development in Parliament."[37]

Why were many Britons never wholeheartedly caught up in an
Imperial identity? There are obviously many different reasons which
apply at different times. But one of the most important influences,
in this as in so much else, may have been Protestantism. British
Imperialism, both in terms of its outrageous extent, and in terms of
the ambiguous responses it often evoked at home, can surely usefully be viewed in the light of this culture's dominant Protestantism.
The Calvinist belief in the concept of the elect led some Britons to
argue that, since they were the best, it was right and pre-ordained
that they should rule over as much of the world as possible. But this
sense of privileged, Protestant election could lead other Britons to
regard contact with abroad, whether this meant Africa, or India, or
Catholic Europe, as a contamination which must be avoided as much
as possible. There was always a tension between those, especially
perhaps those English, who thought about the frontier primarily in
terms of that which protected what was within, and those intent on
expanding the frontier of British dominion overseas.

These, of course, are mighty and contentious areas of debate. My intention, manifestly, has not been to supply you with ready-made or comprehensive answers. Rather, I wanted to throw out some issues, approaches and connections which seem to me to have thus far been insufficiently addressed by British historians.

Let me end with an anecdote. I first delivered a version of this lecture in the city of Montreal, Canada. Just before I gave it, I walked to the heart of Old Montreal, to the Place Jacques-Cartier. To my surprise, I saw there a large pillar which had been raised to the memory of Horatio Nelson in 1809, the first such monument to Nelson ever built. Round its base were bas-reliefs celebrating Nelson's various naval triumphs over the French. But why was the monument there, on one of the great sites of French, as distinct from British, Canada? It is there because a group of ambitious Scottish merchants in Montreal and London paid to have it there. And they did this of course because Montreal in the early nineteenth century was a frontier town, deeply challenged by the divide between its French past and its current British rulers. Celebrating Nelson in stone was a way for the Scots to remind their French mercantile peers of who was now in charge. Some 160 years after this statue was raised—in 1967—General De Gaulle stood on the balcony of the Hotel de Ville, close to Nelson, and made his famous salute "Vive Quebec Libre." It is one more vivid reminder of just how important frontiers are as sites where different cultures meet, and where identities of different kinds are acted out.

Spring Semester 1995

1. Frederick Jackson Turner, *The Frontier in American History* (New York, 1958), pp. 1–2. The text of the present lecture contains themes and arguments which I extended in the Trevelyan Lectures at the University of Cambridge in 1997.

2. For an incisive and sympathetic analysis of Turner's thesis and its successive critical reception, see John Mack Faragher, *Rereading Frederick Jackson Turner* (New York, 1994), pp. 1–10, 225–41.

3. "Revisiting the Vanishing Frontier: The Legacy of Frederick Jackson Turner," *Western Historical Quarterly*, 18 (1987), p. 176.

4. *Rereading Frederick Jackson Turner*, p. 239.

5. Ibid., p. 241.

6. Walter Prescott Webb, *The Great Frontier* (New York, 1964 edn.), p. 11. For a critique of Webb's ambitious thesis, see J. H. Elliott, *The Old World and the New, 1492–1650* (Cambridge, rev edn., 1992), pp. 57–59.

7. Quoted in Raymond F. Betts, "Immense Dimensions: The Impact of the American West on Late Nineteenth-Century European Thought about Expansion," *Western Historical Quarterly*, 10 (1979), p. 151 n.

8. *The Expansion of England: Two Courses of Lectures* (Boston, 1883 edn.), pp. 9 and 12.

9. *Frontiers* (Oxford, 1907), pp. 8 and 55 *et passim.*

10. Deborah Wormell, *Sir John Seeley and the Uses of History* (Cambridge, 1980), p. 154.

11. Quoted in Bruce Robbins, "Colonial Discourse: A Paradigm and Its Discontents," *Victorian Studies* (Winter 1992), p. 213.

12. P. J. Cain and A. G. Hopkins, *British Imperialism: Innovation and Expansion, 1688–1914* (London, 1993); John S. Galbraith, "The 'Turbulent Frontier' as a Factor in British Expansion," *Comparative Studies in Society and History*, II (1959–60).

13. See his *Boundaries: The Making of France and Spain in the Pyrenees* (Berkeley, 1989), and particularly his "Natural Frontiers Revisited: France's Boundaries since the Seventeenth Century," *American Historical Review*, 95 (1990), pp. 1423–51.

14. Quoted in Hugh Kearney, *The British Isles: A History of Four Nations* (Cambridge, 1989), p. 2.

15. See his *The Perception of the Past in Early Modern England* (London, 1983).

16. The only, and somewhat unsatisfactory, attempt to address this (one would think mainline) topic is Cynthia F. Behrman, *Victorian Myths of the Sea* (Athens, 1977).

17. "Paddy and Mr. Punch," *Journal of Newspaper and Periodical History* (1991), p. 34.

18. Blanche E. C. Dugdale, *Family Homespun* (London, 1940), p. 65.

19. This paragraph, like the next three paragraphs, draws on material in my *Britons: Forging the Nation, 1707–1837* (New Haven, 1992).

20. In an unpublished paper "The Past Is Another Country: Myth, Memory and National Identity in Post-War Europe," delivered at a colloquium at Oxford University in 1992.

21. For an early example, see the introductory epistle to the reader in Richard Cox, *Hibernia Anglicana: or, The History of Ireland, from the Conquest thereof, to the Present Time* (London, 1689): "If the most ancient natural Irish-man be a Protestant, no man takes him for other than an English-man; and if a cockney be papist, he is reckoned, in Ireland, as much as an Irishman as if he was born on Slevelogher." Note the emphasis: it is religious allegiance, rather than ethnicity, that matters.

22. In his unpublished paper: "An Agenda for the History of Imperial Britain."

23. Quoted in Edward W. Said, *Culture and Imperialism* (New York, 1993), p. 124.

24. *A View of the Art of Colonization* (London, 1849), p. 54.

25. Barrie M. Ratcliffe and W. H. Chaloner (eds.), *A French Sociologist Looks at Britain* (Manchester, 1977), p. 65.

26.  Charlotte Erickson, *Invisible Immigrants: The Adaption of English and Scottish Immigrants in Nineteenth-century America* (Leicester, 1972); and see David Fitzpatrick (ed.), *Oceans of Consolation: Personal Accounts of Irish Migration to Australia* (Ithaca, 1994).

27.  See S. C. Hill (ed.), *Bengal in 1756–1757,* 3 vols. (London, 1905), III, p. 69 *et seq.*

28.  Ibid., p. 302.

29.  On the surge in British publications on the American colonies in general, and native Americans in particular, after 1754, see Richard C. Simmons, "Americana in British Books, 1621–1760," in Karen Ordahl Kupperman (ed.), *America in European Consciousness 1493–1750* (Chapel Hill, N.C., 1995), pp. 367–74.

30.  See John Knox, *An Historical Journal of the Campaigns in North America,* Arthur G. Doughty (ed.), 3 vols. (Toronto, 1914), *passim.*

31.  "The Capture of Quebec: A Manuscript Journal Relating to the Operations before Quebec from 8th May, 1759, to 17th May, 1760. Kept by Colonel Malcolm Fraser," *Journal of the Society for Army Historical Research,* 18 (1939), p. 142.

32.  For a classic exposition of this thesis, see Fred Anderson, *A People's Army: Massachusetts Soldiers and Society in the Seven Years' War* (Chapel Hill, 1984).

33.  "Becoming West: Toward a New Meaning for Western History," in William Cronon, George Miles, and Jay Gitlin (eds.), *Under an Open Sky: Re-thinking America's Western Past* (New York, 1992), p. 19.

34.  "Scottish National Identity in an Australian Colony," *Scottish Historical Review* LXXII (1993), pp. 22–38.

35.  Kate Lowe and Eugene McLaughlin, "Sir John Pope Hennessy and the 'Native Race Craze': Colonial Government in Hong Kong, 1877–1882," *Journal of Imperial and Commonwealth History* 20 (1992), pp. 223–47.

36.  Seeley, *Expansion of England,* pp. 306 and 308.

37.  *Frontiers,* pp. 8–9.

# 2

# The *British* Revolution in America

## JACK P. GREENE

In the United States, historians and the broader public have, for most of the past two centuries, looked at the American Revolution principally as the first step in the creation of the American nation.[1] They have stressed the process of nation building epitomized by the creation of a republican political regime in each state and the establishment of a federal system for the distribution of power between the states and the nation. They have emphasized the centrality of the drive for national self-realization that, beginning during the Revolutionary era, provided the foundation for the construction of an American national identity. From the national-state perspective that has shaped the writing of United States history, such an emphasis makes sense. For developing an understanding of *why* a revolution occurred in America during the late eighteenth century, however, it is seriously deficient. In particular, it obscures the extraordinary extent to which the American Revolution was very much a *British* Revolution. If we hope to understand that revolution, we need to examine it from the perspective of not the republican national state to which it led but the larger British imperial world in which it happened.

Beginning in the early decades of the seventeenth century, immigrants, at first mostly from England but later and increasingly from elsewhere in the British Isles, began to establish settlement societies in North America and the West Indies. Like other European immigrants to America during the early modern era, they carried with them explicit and deeply held claims to the culture they left behind and to the identities implicit in that culture. In extreme climates, under primitive conditions and with limited resources in people and money, they endeavored to reorder existing physical and cultural landscapes along English lines, implanting in them

English patterns of land occupation, economic and social organization, cultural practices, and religious, political, and legal systems
and making the English language the language of authority in their
new homes. Their great physical distances from England; the social
and cultural contrasts, especially during their earlier decades, between the simple and crude societies they were building and the
complex and infinitely more polite society from which they came;
their situation on the outermost edges of English civilization, in the
midst of populations who to them appeared to be pagan, barba-
rous, and savage; the presence, if not the preponderance, in their
societies of aliens, in the form of Amerindians and later Africans;
their frequent reliance upon new institutions, such as plantations
and chattel, race-based slavery; and metropolitan reluctance to acknowledge their Englishness—all these were conditions that both
rendered settler claims to Englishness problematic and enhanced
the urgency of such claims among immigrants and their creole
descendants.

In their efforts to imprint Englishness upon colonial landscapes,
the legal systems by which they defined the new social spaces they
were creating were critical. During the second wave of European
imperialism in the nineteenth and early twentieth century, European law would serve the conquerors as an instrument of domination and control. In that later phase of European expansion, a
(usually) relatively small group of *colonizers*, acting as agents of European states and as the self-appointed bearers of European cultures, would seek with varying degrees of success to subject the
*colonized*, an often vast population with ancient and complex legal
systems of their own, to European legal traditions and institutions.

During the first wave of European imperialism, however, when
Europeans established their many settler societies in America, law
functioned as the principal instrument of cultural transplantation.
Intending to create offshoots of the Old World in the New, the large
numbers of emigrants to the colonies insisted upon taking their law
with them and making it the primary foundation for the new societies they sought to establish. For these societies, European law was
"not a tool of imperialism," a device to dominate whatever indigenous populations remained in their midsts, "but a concomitant of
emigration. It was not imposed upon settlers but claimed by them."
To "live under European law," Jorg Fisch has recently and correctly
noted, "was a privilege, usually not to be granted to the indigenous
people,"[2] a vivid and symbolically powerful signifier of the emigrants'
deepest aspirations to retain in their new places of abode their identities as members of the European societies to which they were attached, identities that, in their eyes, both established their superiority

over and sharply distinguished them from the seemingly rude and uncivilized peoples they were seeking to dispossess.

The English settlements established in North America and the West Indies provide a striking case study of the way this process worked. Among the main components of the emerging identity of English people in early modern England, the Protestantism and, increasingly during the eighteenth century, the slowly expanding commercial and maritime superiority of the English nation were both important. Far more significant, however, was the system of law and liberty that, contemporary English and many foreign observers seemed to agree, distinguished English people from all other peoples on the face of the globe. The proud boast of the English was that, through a variety of conquests and upheavals, they had been able, in marked contrast to most other political societies in Europe, to retain their identity as a free people who had secured their liberty through their dedication to—and insistence upon— what later analysts would call the rule of law.

As elaborated by a long series of writers from Sir John Fortescue in the fourteenth century to Sir William Blackstone in the 1760s and 1770s, the English jurisprudential tradition held that the happy capacity of English people to preserve this liberty rested largely upon two institutions for determining and making law: juries and Parliaments. Throughout English history, Parliaments and juries, those "two grand Pillars of *English* Liberty" through which "the Birth-right of Englishmen" had always shone "most conspicuously," had functioned effectively to ensure that in England "the law" would continue, as Sir Edward Coke said during the early years of the seventeenth century, to be "the surest sanctuary, that a man can take" and "the best Birth-right of the Subject." "A greater Inheritance descends to us from the Laws, than from our Progenitors," wrote the Whig popularizer Henry Care in paraphrasing Coke in the 1680s. By protecting every subject in his "Goods, Lands, Wife and Children, his Body, Life, Honour and Estimation," and his liberties, the law had been the principal device through which English people had managed to remain "more free and happy than any other People in the World."

For Englishmen, freedom, or liberty, was thus, according to the powerful English jurisprudential and liberal political traditions, not just a condition enforced by law but the very essence of their national identity. In most early modern countries, noted the radical Whig theorists John Trenchard and Thomas Gordon quoting the republican Algernon Sidney during the early eighteenth century, rulers "*use[d] their Subjects like Asses and Mastiff Dogs, to work and to fight, to be oppressed and killed for them,*" considering "their People as

Cattle, and" using "them worse, as they fear[ed] them more. Thus"
had "most of Mankind" become "wretched Slaves" who maintained
"their haughty Masters like Gods," while "their haughty Masters often use[d] them like Dogs." Only in England were "the Lives and
Fortunes" of the people not subject to the "Wills (or rather Lusts)"
of "Arbitrary" tyrants. Only in England did the monarchs, in
Fortescue's words, have "*two-Superiours, God and the Law.*" Only in
England was "the Commonality . . . so guarded in their Persons and
Properties by the Sense of Law, as" to be rendered "Free-men, not
Slaves." Only in England did law require the consent of those who
lived under it. Only in England was "the Law . . . both the Measure
and the Bond of every Subject's Duty and Allegiance, each Man
having a fixed fundamental Right born with him, as to Freedom of
his Person, and Property in his Estate, which he cannot be deprived
of, but either by his Consent, or some Crimes for which the Law has
impos'd such Penalty or Forfeiture." Few early modern English
people had any doubt, as Care put it, that the "Constitution of our
English Government" was "the best in the World."

More than any other component of English life or character,
possession of this unique system of law and liberty was the most
distinctive and important marker of the English people during the
early modern period. Together, England's status as the palladium
of liberty and the English people's profound devotion to law and
liberty were the principal badges of Englishness, the essential—the
most deeply defining—hallmarks of English identity.

For English people migrating overseas to establish new communities of settlement, the capacity to enjoy—to possess—the English
system of law and liberty was thus crucial to their ability to maintain
their identity as English people and to continue to think of themselves and to be thought of by those who remained in England as
English. For that reason as well as because they regarded English
legal arrangements as the very best way to preserve the properties
they hoped to acquire in their new homes, it is scarcely surprising
that, in establishing local enclaves of power and authority during
the first years of colonization, English settlers all over America made
every effort to construct them on English legal foundations.

Several developments during the early stages of the colonizing
process encouraged this attempt. To entice settlers, colonial orga-
nizers early found that they not only had to offer them property in
land but also to guarantee them the property in rights by which
English people had traditionally secured their real and material
possessions. Thus, in 1619 the Virginia Company of London found
it necessary to establish a polity that included a representative assembly through which the settlers could, in the time-honored fash-

ion of the English, make—and formally consent to—the laws under which they would live. Directed by company leaders "to imitate
and follow the policy of the form of government, laws, customs,
and manner of trial; and other administration of justice, used in
the realm of England," the new assembly immediately claimed the
right to consent to all taxes levied on the inhabitants of Virginia.

The legal instruments of English colonization—letters patent,
charters, proclamations—encouraged this attempt in three ways.
First, they often specified that the settlers and their progeny should
be treated as "natural born subjects of England" and thereby strongly
suggested that there would be no legal distinctions between English people who lived in the home islands and those who resided
in the colonies. Second, they required that colonies operate under
no laws that were repugnant to "Laws, Statutes, Customs, and Rights
of our Kingdom of England" and thereby powerfully implied that
the laws of England were to provide the model, and the standard,
for all colonial laws. Third, beginning with the charter to Maryland
in 1632, they also stipulated that colonists should use and enjoy "all
Privileges, Franchises and Liberties of this our Kingdom of England,
freely, quietly, and peaceably to have and possess . . . in the same
manner as our Liege-Men born, or to be born within our said Kingdom of England, without Impediment, Molestation, Vexation, Im-
peachment, or Grievance," and that no laws be passed without the
consent of the freemen of the colony.

Everywhere in the colonies, the early assemblies followed the lead
of the first Virginia Assembly and asserted the claims of their con-
stituents to all the rights and legal safeguards enjoyed by English
people at home. The result of these efforts was the creation in
America of several local systems of authority modeled on that of the
English. Although, beginning in the 1650s and continuing in recurrent phases for the next half century, London officials sought to
impose metropolitan authority upon these local centers of power,
metropolitan intrusions into colonial affairs everywhere provoked
a profound mistrust of central authority among the colonists and
intensified the determination of property holders within the expanding colonies to secure both their new estates and their claims
to an English identity by obtaining metropolitan recognition that,
as English people or the descendants of English people, they were
entitled to enjoy all the rights and legal protections of English people
in the home island. This determination stimulated an extensive
constitutional discussion intended to identify explicit legal defenses
that would put their claims to English rights and legal protections
on a solid foundation and thereby protect the colonies from such
wholesale intrusions of metropolitan power.

In these discussions, colonial spokesmen articulated an elaborate argument to strengthen their early claims to what they thought of as their inherited rights as English people. According to this argument, the original settlers and their descendants were all equally "honest free-born Subjects of England," who, with authorization from the English monarchy, had voluntarily left their "native country" for "a waste and howling wilderness." "*With great danger to our persons, and with very great charge and trouble,*" they said, they had turned that wilderness into thriving and well-inhabited settlements and had thereby, at little or no cost to the English government, significantly "enlarged the *English* Trade and Empire" and brought "*England* . . . its greatest Riches and Prosperity." While they were thus creating the new and valuable "*English* Empire in *America*," they retained their English identity and remained, as a Barbadian declared in 1698, "no other but *English* Men: . . . your Countrey-Men, your Kindred and Relations," who, said another, "pretended to have as good *English* Bloud in our Veins, as some of those that we have left behind us." It followed that their continuing identity as English people entitled them to all the "hereditary Rights" of English subjects, rights that they could not lose merely "by Transporting themselves" to America, rights, moreover, that had been confirmed to them by their charters and were secured by their respective civil governments—governments which, they pointed out, had been formed on their own initiative on "the nearest model of conformity to that under which our predecessors of the English nation have lived and flourished for above a thousand years." To be in any way diminished in their rights simply because of their "great Distance . . . from the Fountain of Justice" in England, they believed, would deprive them of "their Birthright and the Benefits of the Laws and Priviledges of English Men" and reduce them to a species of "slavery far exceeding all that [any of] the *English* nation hath yet suffered."

The effort to secure these rights against the claims of the crown was continuous from 1660 to 1760. In general, colonial leaders pursued this quest along two parallel lines. First, they sought explicit guarantees of the rights of the colonists to English laws. Second, they sought to enhance the authority of their elected assemblies. In the colonies, no less than in the metropolis, they hoped that law and parliaments would be the bulwarks of the people's liberties and properties.

Among the liberties inherited by and confirmed to these distant colonies, colonists considered none more essential to their identities as British people than the rights, in the words of New York justice William Smith, "*to choose the Laws by which we will be Governed*" and *"to be Governed only by such Laws."* Colonial writers were fond of quoting Sir William Jones, attorney general under Charles II, that the king "could no more grant a commission to levy money on his subjects in the plantations, without their consent by an assembly, than they could discharge themselves from their allegiance." If the colonial legislatures thus existed by virtue not of royal charters or commissions but of the colonists' "right to participate in the legislative power," it followed that because their distance prevented them from being represented in the British Parliament and having "Laws made for them . . . from Home" they "must therefore have new Laws from a legislature of their own." Both law and necessity thus dictated that the colonies should have "a perfect *internal* Liberty, as to the Choice of their own Laws, and in all other Matters that" were *"purely* provincial." "What . . . may be done by the Legislature there," declared a Jamaican in the mid-1740s, "may be done by the Legislature here."

This position implied a conception of colonies as extensions of Britain overseas and of colonists as Britons living "abroad and consequently the brethren of those at home," virtual "mirror images" of those who still resided in Britain.[3] This conception, as Benedict Anderson has pointed out, implied that the colonies were societies *"parallel and comparable* to those in" Britain and that, in their lives, colonists were "proceeding along the same trajectory" as those who remained in the British Isles.[4] From this perspective, held by many people in Britain, the British Empire was "a free and virtuous empire, founded in consent and nurtured in liberty and trade"[5] and colonists were "fellow-subjects" who, though "living in different parts of the world," together with those who resided in Britain formed, as the political economist Arthur Young remarked in 1772, "one nation, united under one sovereign, speaking the same language and enjoying the same liberty."

For those who viewed the Empire in this *expansive* way, the transfer of English liberties to the colonies was precisely the characteristic that distinguished the British Empire from others. Just as Britain was the home of liberty in Europe, so also was the British Empire in America. "Without freedom," Edmund Burke remarked in 1766, the empire "would not be the British Empire." In America, said Young, "Spain, Portugal and France, have planted despotisms; only Britain liberty." "Look, Sir, into the history of the provinces of other states, of the Roman provinces in ancient time; of the French, Spanish, Dutch and Turkish provinces of more modern date," George Dempster advised the House of Commons in 1775, "and you will find every page stained with acts of oppressive violence, of cruelty, injustice and peculation."

As those of similar persuasion thought more deeply about the
nature of the empire, they began to suggest that liberty not only
"distinguish[ed]" the "British colonists . . . from the colonists of
other nations," but was responsible for the Empire's extraordinary
success. In their two-volume *Account of the European Settlements in
America,* Edmund and William Burke expressed their confidence
that colonial commerce had flourished as it had because "of the
freedom every man has of pursuing it according to his own ideas,
and directing his life according to his own fashion." As they surveyed the extraordinary growth and development of the British
colonies, analysts such as John Campbell and Adam Smith concluded
that, as Campbell wrote, "in their very Nature Colonies require Ease
and Freedom" and that colonization was "not very compatible with
the Maxims that prevail in despotic Governments." To Adam Smith,
the experience of the British colonies seemed conclusive proof that,
along with plenty of good land, extensive liberty, permitting wide
latitude in self-direction, was one of "the two great causes of the
prosperity of new colonies."

If "notions of consent and liberty" were indeed "central" to one
contemporary conceptualization of the Empire, there was an alternative and, in Britain, more pervasive view of colonies and colonists. This competing view saw the colonies less as societies of Britons
overseas "populated with free white British subjects"[6] than as outposts of British economic or strategic power. In this *restrictive* conception, explicit in the Navigation Acts and other Restoration
colonial measures, the colonies were, principally, workshops employed in raising certain specified and enumerated commodities,
"solely for the use of the trade and manufactures of the mother-
country." Increasingly after 1740, and especially during and after
the Seven Years' War, this view gave way to a complementary emphasis upon the colonies as instruments of British national or imperial power. Between 1745 and 1763, intensifying rivalries with
France and Spain and the growing populations and wealth of the
colonies produced, for the first time among metropolitan analysts,
an intensive discussion about the nature and workings of the empire.

Most of the contributors to this discussion started from the assumption that the very "word 'colony,'" as Charles Townshend subsequently declared, implied, not equality, but "subordination."
Contending that the colonies had been initiated, established, and
succored by the metropolitan state for the purpose of furthering
state policy, they argued that the colonies always had to be considered in terms of "power and dominion, as well as trade." In this
view, the original purpose of colonization was to "add Strength to
the State by extending its Dominions," and emigrants to the colo-

nies had always been "subject to, and under the power and Dominion, of the Kingdom" whence they came. So far, then, from being in any sense equal to the parent state, colonies were nothing more than "Provincial Governments . . . subordinate to the Chief State."

Such conceptions of the colonies suggested that colonists were something less than full Britons; not, as Benjamin Franklin put it in 1768, "fellow subjects, but subjects of subjects." They also reinforced longstanding metropolitan views of colonists as people of "vulgar descent" and unfortunate histories, the miserable outcasts of Britain and Europe. During the Stamp Act crisis of 1765–66, Franklin, who throughout much of the period from the mid-1750s to the mid-1770s resided in London and acted as a self-appointed cultural broker for the colonies, was dismayed to see metropolitan newspaper writers dismiss the colonists with the "gentle terms of *republican race, mixed rabble of Scotch, Irish and foreign vagabonds, descendents of convicts, ungrateful rebels &c.*," language that, he objected, conveyed only the most violent "contempt, and abuse." By "lumping all the Americans under the general Character of 'House-breakers and Felons'" and by "raving" against them "as 'diggers of pits for this country,' 'lunaticks,' 'sworn enemies,' 'false,' and 'ungrateful' . . . 'cut-throats,'" Franklin protested during the decade after 1765, metropolitans had repeatedly branded the colonists as a people who, though "descended from British Ancestors," had "degenerated to such a Degree" as to become the "lowest of Mankind, and almost of a different Species from the English of Britain," a people who were "unworthy the name of Englishmen, and fit only to be snubb'd, curb'd, shackled and plundered." Such language identified colonists as a category of others, "foreigners" who, however much they might aspire to be English, could never actually achieve those aspirations and who on the scale of civilization were only slightly above the native Amerindian.

The expansion of British activities in India and the massive employment of enslaved Africans and their descendants throughout the British American colonies strongly reinforced this image in Britain. The more Britons learned about India, the more convinced they became that, as Dempster remarked in Parliament, the "eastern species of government" and society was replete with "rapines and cruelties." Beginning in the late 1750s, the transactions of Robert Clive and others persuaded many Britons that, in their rapacious efforts to line their own pockets, their countrymen in India had themselves often turned plunderers and been guilty of "Crimes scarce inferior to the Conquerors of *Mexico* and *Peru*." Already by the late 1760s, the term *nabob*, initially a title of rank for Indians, had become, as a contemporary complained, "a general term of reproach, indiscriminately applied to every individual who has served the East India Company in Asia" and "implying, that the persons to whom it is applied, have obtained their fortunes by grievously oppressing the natives of India." Published in 1768, the dramatist Samuel Foote's *The Nabob* was only the most prominent of many works that presented a "scathing indictment of the moral corrosiveness of empire in India."[7]

Throughout the latter half of the eighteenth century, the rapidly growing antislavery movement more and more focused attention on the association of racial slavery with the colonies and fostered the conviction in Britain that "no People upon Earth" were such "Enemies to Liberty, such absolute Tyrants," as the American colonists. With "so little Dislike of Despotism and Tyranny, that they do not scruple to exercise them with unbounded Rigour over their miserable Slaves," colonists were obviously "unworthy" of claims to a British identity or to the liberty that was central to that identity. No less than the image of the nabob, that of the dissolute "creolean planter"—a despot schooled by slavery in "ferocity, cruelty, and brutal barbarity," whose "head-long Violence" was wholly unlike the "national" temperament of the "native genuine English"—shaped contemporary metropolitan conceptions of colonists through dramatic works such as Richard Cumberland's *The West Indian*, in 1772, or George Colman Jr.'s *Inkle and Yarico*, in 1787.

The images presented in these works and in the antislavery literature suggested that no people who consorted with the corrupt and despotic regimes of the East or held slaves in the American colonies could be true-born Britons, who, above all, loved liberty. To reassure themselves that Britain actually was the land of freedom, metropolitan Britons had to distance themselves from such people and Britain from such places. "In *Asia's* realms let slavery be bound," demanded one anonymous poet in 1773,

> Let not her foot defile this sacred ground,
> Where Freedom, Science, Valour fix'd their seat,
> And taught all Nations how they should be great.

In the same spirit, some polemical writers called for measures to "preserve the race of Britons from [the] stain and contamination" of American settler despotism.

The long debate that preceded the American Revolution provided colonists and their advocates in Britain with an opportunity to combat this negative image. In protesting that the extensive free colonial populations were mostly "descendents of Englishmen" or Britons, and in trying to define of what their "ancestral Englishness"[8] consisted, colonial protagonists penetrated to the essence of

Englishness and Britishness as contemporaries understood it. What distinguished them from the colonists of other nations—and identified them with Britons at home—was not principally, they insisted, their Protestantism or their economic and social success, but their political and legal inheritance. *Modern* colonists, in James Otis's view, were *the noble discoverers and settlers of a new world,* from whence as from an endless source, *wealth* and *plenty,* the means of *power, grandeur,* and *glory,* in a degree unknown to the hungry chiefs of former ages, have been pouring in to *Europe* for 300 years past; in return for which those colonists have received from the several states of *Europe,* except from *Great Britain* only since the Revolution, nothing but ill-usage, slavery, and chains, as fast as the riches of *their own* earning could furnish the means of forging them. Not just the Catholic and despotic Spanish, Portuguese, and French had been so guilty, but even the Protestant and free Dutch, who shamelessly admitted that the liberty of Dutchmen was confined to Holland and was never intended for provincials in America or anywhere else. If British America had thus long been "distinguished from the slavish colonies around about it as the fortunate Britons have been from most of their neighbours on the continent of Europe," colonial advocates argued powerfully, Britain's colonies should "be ever thus distinguished."

To colonial protagonists in the 1760s and 1770s, the colonists' claims to share in this central component of British identity seemed unassailable. "To the infinite advantage and emolument of the mother state," the colonists, as the Providence merchant Stephen Hopkins announced in 1764 in echoing several earlier generations of colonial theorists, had "left the delights of their native country, parted from their homes and all their conveniences, [and] . . . searched out . . . and subdued a foreign country with the most amazing travail and fortitude." They had undertaken these Herculean tasks on the assumption "that they and their successors forever should be free, should be partakers and sharers in all the privileges and advantages of the then English, now British constitution," and should enjoy "all the rights and privileges of freeborn Englishmen." Exulting in their identity as Britons, colonists took pride in having come "out from a kingdom renowned for liberty[,] from a constitution founded on compact, from a people of all the sons of men the most tenacious of freedom." They expressed their happiness that, unlike the inhabitants of most other polities, they were not "governed at the will of another, or of others, and" that they were not "in the miserable condition of slaves" whose property could "be taken from them by taxes or otherwise without their own consent and against their will." Rather, they militantly asserted, they lived, like Britons in the home islands, under a "beneficent compact" by which, as British subjects, they could "be governed only agreeable to laws to which themselves [they] have some way consented, and are not to be compelled to part with their property but as it is called for by the authority of such laws."

This assertion that the colonists enjoyed "the Liberty & Privileges of Englishmen, in the same Degree, as if we had still continued among our Brethren in Great Britain" was a reiteration of the colonists' longstanding demand for metropolitan recognition of their identities as Britons. Not just "Our Language, . . . our Inter-marriages, & other Connections, our constant Intercourse, and above all our Interest[s]," they cried, but also, and infinitely more important, "Our Laws [and] . . . our Principles of Government," those preeminent characteristics of true Britons, identified colonists as Britons who, "descended from the same Stock" as their "fellow-Subjects in Great Britain" and "nurtured in the same Principles of Freedom; which we have both suck'd in with our Mother's Milk," were "the same People with them, in every Respect."

Vociferously, then, the colonists objected to being taxed or governed in their internal affairs without their consent because such actions subjected them to a form of governance that was at once contrary to the rights and legal protections traditionally enjoyed by Britons and, on the very deepest level, denied their very identity as a British people. To be thus governed without consent was to be treated not like the freeborn Britons they had always claimed to be, but like a "conquered people"; not like the independent proprietors so many of them were, people who "possessed . . . property" that could be "called" their "own" and were therefore not dependent "upon the will of another," but like "miserable . . . slaves" who could "neither dispose of person or goods, but" enjoyed "all at the will of" their "master[s]"; and certainly not like people with similar amounts of property in Britain, as "*free agent[s] in a political view*" with full rights of civic participation, but like those many people in the home islands who had little or no property, people who were "*in so mean a situation,* that they" were "supposed to have no will of their own" and were therefore ineligible even to vote. "Unless every *free agent* in America be permitted to enjoy the same privilege[s]" as those exercised by similarly free agents in Britain, the young Alexander Hamilton declared in 1775, the colonists would be "entirely stripped of the benefits of the [British] constitution," deprived of their status as British peoples, "and precipitated into an abyss of slavery."

That such was the return made by metropolitan leaders to the colonists "for braving the danger of the deep—for planting a wilderness, inhabited only by savage man and savage beasts—for extending the dominions of the British crown—for increasing the trade of British merchants—for augmenting the rents of the British land-lords—[and] for heightening the wages of British artificers" seemed to colonists to be understandable only as an act of "Tyranny and Oppression" intended to deny colonial Britons an equality of status with metropolitan Britons by "destroy[ing] the very existence of law and liberty in the colonies." Only by exercising their inherited right, a right "secured to them both by the letter and the spirit of the British constitution," to employ force to defend their "British liberties" against such "Violence & Injustice," only by actively "resist[ing] such force—force acting without authority—force employed contrary to law," they decided in 1775–76, could they manage to "transmit" their British heritage "unimpaired to" their "Posterity" and to make good their own claims to be worthy of a British identity.

The insistence with which colonial protagonists adumbrated these themes persuasively testifies to the fact that, at the time of the American Revolution, Britons, in the far peripheries as well as at the center of the British Empire, still regarded liberty as the essence of Britishness. Once the actions of the metropolitan government seemed aggressively to contest their claims to a British identity, colonists made every effort to articulate and secure metropolitan acknowledgment of those claims, to make clear, as Burke said, that they were "not only devoted to liberty, but to liberty according to English ideas and on English principles."

On a deep, perhaps even on the very deepest, level, the American Revolution was thus the direct outgrowth of metropolitan measures that seemed to call into question colonial claims to a British identity. Colonial resistance to those measures needs to be understood, in the first instance, as a movement by colonial Britons to establish their entitlement to such an identity and not as a drive by incipient Americans to realize a latent American selfhood—well before there was any formal political entity known as America, an interpretation that is anachronistic and that contemporary colonial resistance leaders would have found both wrong and deeply disturbing. Before the winter of 1775–76 when sentiment for independence became widespread, union among the colonies was principally a means to this end. In its earliest stages, then, the creation of the American nation was an unintended consequence of colonial determination to gain metropolitan recognition of the Britishness of colonial British America. In this sense what came to be known as the American Revolution was very much a British Revolution in America.

Spring Semester 1996

1.  Citations in this lecture are only to secondary sources. Citations to many of the primary sources will be published in "Empire and Identity from the Glorious Revolution to the American Revolution," in P. J. Marshall (ed.), *The Oxford History of the British Empire, II* (Oxford, 1998).

2.  Jorg Fisch, "Law as a Means and as an End: Some Remarks on the Function of European and Non-European Law in the Process of European Expansion," in W. J. Mommsen and J. A. De Moor (eds.), *European Expansion and Law: The Encounter of European and Indigenous Law in 19th- and 20th-Century Africa and Asia* (Oxford, 1992), 21.

3.  Linda Colley, *Britons* (New Haven, 1992), pp. 105, 135.

4.  Benedict Anderson, *Imagined Communities: Reflections on the Origin and Spread of Nationalism* (London, 1983), pp. 188, 192.

5.  Kathleen Wilson, *The Sense of the People: Politics, Culture and Imperialism in England, 1715–1785* (Cambridge, 1995), p. 277.

6.  Ibid., p. 24.

7.  Kathleen Wilson, "Empire of Virtue: The Imperial Project and Hanoverian Culture c. 1720–1785," in Lawrence Stone (ed.), *The Imperial State at War* (London, 1994), p. 153.

8.  Anderson, *Imagined Communities*, p. 145.

# 3

# Queen Victoria's Other Island

## WALTER L. ARNSTEIN

T he Act of Union that in 1800 was intended permanently to unite all of Ireland with Great Britain lasted only one hundred and twenty-one years, and for more than half of that time Victoria reigned as Queen of that United Kingdom. And yet, during an era in which biographies of Queen Victoria continue to pour from the presses and in which the nineteenth-century Irish nationalist movement and its leaders have been assessed and reassessed several times over, it seems remarkable how little attention has been allotted to Victoria's role as Queen of Ireland, the monarch's other island. Her more recent biographers appear to have become far more absorbed by the peculiarities of the Queen's personality and by her role as a symbol either of anti-feminism or of unwitting proto-feminism. Therefore, they have failed to take seriously the very genuine political influence that she could and did exercise on diplomatic, military, and episcopal appointments as well as on particular acts of legislation.

In 1902, her first comprehensive biographer, Sidney Lee, did pay attention, highly censorious attention. He noted that she had spent seven years of her reign in Scotland and but five weeks in Ireland. That contrast, Lee concluded, "emphasized the errors of feeling and of judgment which made her almost a complete stranger to her Irish subjects in their own land. . . ."[1] Three decades later, G. M. Young observed that early in her reign the Queen had won great acclaim in Ireland. According to Young, "her failure to draw on this fund of loyalty was the gravest error of her life."[2]

I shall make no attempt to argue that the verdict of Lee and Young ought to be set aside as without merit. I shall argue, however, that the Queen's approach to Ireland involved more than a fatal compound of ignorance and blindness and that, indeed, it changed significantly over time. Secondly, I shall remind you that the resolution of the nineteenth-century "Irish Question" was not preordained and that the emergence of an independent sovereign Irish nation-state was not the only possible outcome. After all, Giuseppe Mazzini, the great prophet of nineteenth-century European nationalisms, did not think that the Irish truly qualified. He believed, in Douglas Hyde's words, that "we ought to be content as an integral part of the United Kingdom because we have lost the notes of nationality, our language and customs."[3]

When Queen Victoria ascended to the throne in June 1837, the state of Ireland was relatively quiescent, and—under the terms of the so-called Lichfield House compact of 1835—Daniel O'Connell's Irish party helped keep Lord Melbourne's Whig ministry in power during the six years that followed. Melbourne freed Irish peasants from the duty of having to pay a tithe to an alien Protestant church, and he began the process of setting up elected councils in Irish towns. More controversially, in 1838 he also extended to Ireland a Poor Law system like that of England. At the same time O'Connell acquired a powerful influence over ministerial appointments in both England and Ireland, and, for the first time in modern British history, professing Roman Catholics received such appointments.

Victoria was herself fascinated by "the Liberator," and, when she met him at one of her levees, she found him "very tall, rather large," and displaying "a remarkably good-humoured countenance." O'Connell, in turn, was chivalrously prepared to rush to the defense of "the Queen of the Whigs" when Tories criticized her publicly—as they did on the occasion of her engagement to Prince Albert. "Oh! if I be not greatly mistaken," O'Connell declared, "I'd get, in one day, 500,000 brave Irishmen to defend the life, the honour, and the person of the beloved young lady by whom England's Throne is now filled."[4]

In 1841 Melbourne's Whigs gave way to a Conservative government led by Sir Robert Peel, and it was Peel's ministry that found itself compelled to use troops and confiscate cattle in Ireland in order to collect the taxes to pay for the new Poor Law there. The ministry's actions strengthened Daniel O'Connell's revitalized movement to repeal the Act of Union of 1800. Once again, the most vocal leader of Irish opinion was an opponent rather than an ally of Britain's government. Although Peel strongly opposed the restoration of an autonomous Irish Parliament, it had not been his intention to alienate Irish opinion. Thus, he was fully prepared to reform higher education in the Emerald Isle so that a new Irish University, with constituent colleges at Belfast, Cork, and Galway, would be open to all academically qualified applicants without regard to religious affiliation. Higher education in Ireland was no longer to be monopolized by the established Protestant Church of Ireland. Victoria and Albert strongly favored Peel's proposed reform. They also supported Peel's plan to triple the amount and to make permanent the annual government grant to Maynooth, the Roman Catholic seminary near Dublin that educated two-thirds of Ireland's priests.

The youthful royal couple came deeply to admire the courageous manner in which Peel carried the controversial Maynooth bill through to ultimate triumph. As the Queen reported privately during the spring of 1845:

> Here we are in a great state of agitation about one of the greatest measures ever proposed; I am sure poor Peel ought to be *blessed* by all Catholics for the manly and noble ways in which he stands forth to protect and do good to poor Ireland. But the bigotry, the wicked and blind passions it brings forth is quite dreadful and I blush for Protestantism! . . . The Protestant Establishment in Ireland must remain untouched, but let the Roman Catholic Clergy be well and handsomely educated. . . . [5]

During the early 1840s, the years during which Queen Victoria first discovered Scotland and the Isle of Wight and the European continent, there was preliminary talk also about an official royal visit to Ireland—the first such visit since that of King George IV to Dublin back in 1821 and, prospectively, only the second monarchical state visit to Ireland since the reign of King Richard II (1377–1399). The Lord-Lieutenant of Ireland strongly urged such a sojourn, and early in 1845 the mayor and the corporation of Dublin assured the Queen that "the mere rumour of your intentions has filled every Irish heart with gladness."[6]

In the course of the summer of 1845, however, the potato blight first afflicted the foodstuff that took up less than one-tenth of the island's arable land but that nourished at least one-half of Ireland's eight million people. Within the next four years, the greater part of a million Irish men and women were to fall victim to diseases spawned by famine and a comparable number was to seek refuge in the United States, Canada, Australia, Scotland, and England. In order to open Irish ports to food from abroad, Sir Robert Peel pushed through Parliament the repeal of the Corn Law, a step that divided his party and that led to the downfall of his ministry in the summer of 1846. Although some historians have accused the ministry that succeeded, the Whig government (1846–1852) of Lord John Russell, of deliberate "genocide,"[7] most concede that, within the limits of the economic understanding and the administrative capabilities of the early

Victorian state, it made significant efforts to keep the Irish alive: soup kitchens fed as many as three million people a day in 1847, and hundreds of thousands earned income from public work projects.[8] At the same time, Russell's government tended to exaggerate the wealth of Irish landlords and their ability to support the famine-stricken by means of the Irish Poor Law system. When economic depression hit Great Britain itself in 1848 and tax revenues fell sharply, British efforts to relieve Ireland's apparently unending crisis became stingier. Prime Minister Russell found Irish M.P.s adamantly opposed to an additional increase in the Irish Poor Rate. English M.P.s were equally reluctant to add to the appropriations that had already been voted and the loans that they had already extended to Ireland.

Both in her private conversations and in her semi-annual speeches to Parliament, Queen Victoria showed herself deeply sympathetic to the plight of the Irish peasants, whose sufferings "were really too terrible to think of." Her private journal includes entry after entry reporting that "the people are starving & the landlords are ruined, & there does not seem to be a ray of hope, as to matters improving." At her side, Albert drafted memorandum after private memorandum assessing official and unofficial reports from Ireland and outlining possible ameliorative measures.

At the same time, the Queen insisted that her governments were doing all that lay within their power to help. In 1847 she cordially approved "of the Acts of large and liberal Bounty by which you have assuaged the Sufferings of My *Irish* Subjects." A year later, she took comfort in the thought that the "Distress in Ireland consequent upon successive Failures in the Production of Food has been mitigated by the Application of the Law for the Relief of the Poor, and by the Amount of charitable Contributions raised in other Parts of the United Kingdom." British and American Quakers had set up a Central Relief Committee in 1846, and early in 1847 Baron Lionel de Rothschild and other London bankers and merchants organized "The British Association for the relief of the extreme distress in the remote parishes of Ireland and Scotland," to distribute food, clothing, and fuel to "the multitudes who are suffering under the present awful calamity."

Queen Victoria headed the list of patrons with a pledge of £2,000 from her privy purse, and Prince Albert followed her with a pledge of £500. According to one estimate, at that time a single pound coin could feed eight families of five for a week. The royal couple's pledge was therefore the equivalent in 1996 of approximately $300,000.[9] By the spring of 1849, destitution in Ireland was as severe as ever, however. The land was afflicted by cholera, fever, and dysentery;

250,000 people lived in workhouses and more than 750,000 subsisted on "outdoor relief." Russell's ministry was so shaken by such reports that each member of the cabinet privately contributed £100 to a new private subscription; Victoria once again headed the list with a donation of £500 (worth about $62,500 today).

Victoria's concern was not limited to public speeches to Parliament and private contributions to charity. Thus, in February 1847, she attended an opera performance of which the proceeds were given to "the Distressed Irish & Scotch." Every few weeks thereafter she and Albert patronized yet another charity event designed to aid the deeply afflicted Irish. In the meantime, Victoria was happy to go along with Prime Minister Russell's request that she provide the "authority of a Queen's Letter for collections in all the Churches for the destitute in remote districts of Ireland and Scotland. . . ." The Queen was rather more reluctant to agree to the fixing of March 24, 1847, as "a Fast Day in connection with the distress in Ireland." Admittedly she and Albert attended the service on the appointed day at Windsor, with its twelve special prayers and with a sermon preached by Samuel Wilberforce, the youthful Bishop of Oxford. The Queen felt distinctly uncomfortable, however, with the manner in which the bishop "stamped the famine as a punishment for our sins." "We all recognize that we are sinful," Victoria admitted, but she thought that Britain's people had become less sinful in the course of the previous half century, and she was far from persuaded that the deity had imposed a famine because of "the heedless & improvident way in which the poor Irish [had] long lived" and because of "the wicked agitators . . . and the deeds of violence" that they had long tolerated.[10] The fast day of 1847 proved to be one of the last such ritualist occasions in which the Queen acquiesced. A decade later she helped bring the custom to a permanent end.

Whereas during 1846 and 1847 Albert's and Victoria's correspondence with their chief ministers had focused on the best ways of relieving the famine, in the course of the year 1848 their attention was concentrated on the revolutions that had broken out first in France and then elsewhere in Europe, on Chartist agitation in England, and on the scattered outbursts of revolt in the Emerald Isle led by Smith O'Brien and the other leaders of "Young Ireland." In April, Albert warned Russell that his ministry ought not only suppress the rebels but must also express its readiness "to listen to any complaint & to take any proposition for the amelioration of Ireland into the most serious consideration. . . ." The famine years had brought in their train a quadrupling in the rate of murder, of cattle-stealing, highway robbery, and other "outrages of every kind." Ireland was also beset by the mismanagement of relief supplies and by inflammatory proclamations by Roman Catholic Archbishop John MacHale, who alternately accused the British government of failing to feed the hungry and of seeking to convert them to Protestantism by handing out free soup.[11]

Albert's own long-range plans included a Roman Catholic clergy whose salaries were paid by the British government—at an expected cost of £350,000 per year to the British taxpayer—and the abolition of the post of Lord-Lieutenant. Now that it had become possible to travel from London to Dublin in only fourteen hours—by a combination of steam railway and steamship—Ireland should no longer be governed as a separate province; rather it should be elevated to complete "equality with England & Scotland." As a substitute for the Lord-Lieutenant and his Dublin court, Albert recommended regular visits by the Queen. Russell and Lord Clarendon, the astute new Lord-Lieutenant, were strongly sympathetic to both plans, but they regarded as premature, in the midst of famine and rebellion, the plan to abolish the lord-lieutenancy. As Clarendon also wrote in disgust to Russell—"to pay the [Roman Catholic] Clergy is, I suppose impossible in the present state of English and Scotch Bigotry" and of Treasury stinginess. Clarendon strongly supported the notion of regular royal visits, however: "whatever may be the political feelings or animosities of the Irish, their devotion to the Queen is unquestionable. . . ."

Clarendon was compelled to concede, however, that a significant number of Irishmen had responded to aid with rebellion rather than with gratitude. "England is their Scapegoat," he noted, "and is held responsible for all the evils that afflict this country, & the misgovernment of former days does unfortunately afford some justification for this now erroneous notion." Although the Irish were still "prepared to view with distrust every measure of the Gov[ernmen]t or of Parliament & to seek in it some fresh cause or excuse for their long-standing state of malaise," even he could take satisfaction in the ten million pounds (approximately one billion 1996 dollars) that the British government had spent in Ireland in the course of 1847. "Whatever may have been the faults of the system," Clarendon told Russell, "it has beyond all question been a noble work of humanity. It has preserved human life and checked the progress of pestilence. . . ." Somewhat smugly, *The Times* publicly concurred: "England & Scotland . . . have not hesitated to take their poor sister by the hand, and raise her from her calamitous prostration and inveterate squalor." "When Englishmen are charged with indifference to the calamities of Ireland, we think the history of the last five years may furnish a very satisfactory reply."

As late as October 1848, Queen Victoria wrote privately of "Ireland quivering in our grasp, and ready to throw off her allegiance at any moment . . . ," but by then the Irish insurrection was largely over. The leaders had been captured, tried, and exiled to Australia. In May of 1849, Victoria became herself directly involved in Irish violence when a young man shot at the Queen while she was driving in a carriage in London; he turned out to be an unemployed Irishman from County Limerick. By then, however, Ireland's Lord-Lieutenant felt assured that in Ireland "agitation is extinct." O'Connell was dead. His Repeal movement was passé. The seditious associations had all been shut down.

Clearly, the time had come for the Queen to make her oft-postponed first visit to Ireland. In the light of the country's continued state of distress, it seemed sensible to make modest plans. Even modest preparations might stimulate the depressed economy, however. In the words of one Dublin merchant, the visit would prove "a great godsend to raise the country from its present deplorable condition."[12] In the course of July, therefore, an army of Dublin workmen repaired and decorated the Castle, the Vice-Regal Lodge, and St. Patrick's Hall, while regular army troops rehearsed their parade drill in Phoenix Park.

On August 1, the royal yacht, the *Victoria and Albert*, steamed into the harbor of Cove, which the monarch honored by renaming Queenstown—in emulation of her uncle King George IV, who a generation earlier had renamed the town of Dun Laoghaire as Kingstown. On board a smaller vessel, the *Fairy*, the Queen swept into Cork, where she received a triumphant reception. Cannons boomed, flags flew, and thousands of onlookers cheered. Having knighted the city's mayor, the royal couple then toured Cork in an open carriage amidst a crowd that Victoria described as "noisy, excitable, but very good-humoured . . . running and pushing about, and laughing, talking and shrieking." Many of the banners were inscribed with the words: "Hail Victoria, Ireland's Hope and England's Glory."[13]

The next day the *Victoria and Albert* continued to steam along Ireland's southeast coast. The vessel anchored for the night near Waterford, but, unlike her husband and her two eldest sons, Victoria felt too seasick to go ashore. On Sunday, August 5, a flotilla escorted the royal vessel into Kingstown harbor. There, thousands of enthusiastic spectators welcomed the royal couple and their four oldest children. As Victoria and her family disembarked the next morning, a stout old woman shouted, "Ah, Queen dear, make one of them Prince Patrick and Ireland will die for you."

In Dublin the enthusiasm of the citizens seemed to grow by the day, and Victoria was deeply impressed by the beauty of the city and its surroundings—Sackville Street and Merrion Square, Trinity College and the old Parliament House. With its attractive parks and its riverside, the city resembled Paris, and the apparent joy of the people in seeing their Queen in person was "a wonderful and striking spectacle." On the one hand, she was shaken by the poverty of the masses. As she noted in her private journal, "The raggedness of the people is beyond belief, man & boy having really hardly any covering, for they never mend anything." On the other hand, she was struck by the attractive appearance of even the poorest women; they had "such beautiful black eyes and hair and such fine colour and teeth."

In the course of the next several days, the Queen drove about the city informally, and she visited the botanical gardens, the Bank of Ireland, a model school, a hospital for army veterans, and numerous other sites. At Trinity College the royal pair inspected the early medieval Book of Kells. "I gladly share with you the hope," she told assembled Dubliners,

> that the heavy visitation with which Providence has recently visited large numbers of people in this country is passing away. I have felt deeply for their sufferings, and it will be a source of heartfelt satisfaction to me if I am permitted to witness the future and lasting prosperity of this portion of the United Kingdom.

On August 8, in the magnificent Throne Room of Dublin Castle, two thousand people were individually presented to the monarch in the course of a four-and-a-half-hour levee. At a formal state dinner that evening, Victoria wore a dress of green Irish poplin lavishly embroidered with gold shamrocks and adorned by the blue ribbon and star of St. Patrick. By then she could do no wrong in the eyes of Dubliners. "The enthusiasm and loyalty were beyond everything," Victoria noted privately, and the O'Connellite *Freeman's Journal* readily acknowledged that "the more the citizens of Dublin see Queen Victoria the more she wins their affections." In the meantime Prince Albert made visits to the Royal Irish Academy, the Royal College of Surgeons, and the Royal Dublin Society. He strongly urged his hosts to make their prize cattle and their agricultural implements "the harbinger of a termination to those sufferings under which the people have so lamentably, yet with such exemplary patience, laboured."

While in Dublin, one of the Queen's purposes was to meet the leaders of Ireland's three major churches, the (Protestant) Church of Ireland, the Presbyterian Church, and the Roman Catholic Church. Among the last-named, she was impressed most favorably by Bishop Dennors, "an excellent and moderate man," and by the venerable Archbishop Daniel Murray of Dublin. The octogenarian patriarch was a strong supporter of Ireland's non-sectarian national schools (established by Lord Grey's Whig Ministry in 1831). In such schools Protestant and Roman Catholic children were educated side by side, and Murray supported such a policy, the Queen noted, "against the bigoted opposition of others of his creed." In the course of the next two decades, Murray's successor, Cardinal Paul Cullen, was on a *de facto* basis to resegregate primary school education in Ireland on the basis of religion, a policy that was approved by many Protestant clerics as well. For the time being, however, Prince Albert could take comfort in the thought that—contrary to his earlier fears—"the Catholic clergy are quite as loyal as the Anglicans, the Presbyterians, and the Quakers."

The last two days of the Queen's visit involved a gigantic military review of six thousand men in Phoenix Park. At a drawing room in Dublin Castle that evening, some 1,700 Irish men and women were personally presented to the monarch. On the next day came a visit to the home of Ireland's only duke, the Duke of Leinster, whose estate was located west of Dublin. The royals took the train to Maynooth, where the Roman Catholic seminary students cheered them. Another gigantic crowd surrounded Victoria when she returned to Dublin and drove through the city to Westland Row railway station. There she took the train to Kingstown and reembarked on her yacht amidst a crowd so dense that the *Dublin Evening Mail* reporter could not figure out where all the people had come from. He did take note, however, of the "tremendous enthusiasm" that was manifested by the people on the pier as the Queen and her party waved for an hour from the paddle-box atop the *Victoria and Albert* as it drifted slowly into the Irish Sea. A brief but successful visit to Belfast followed before the yacht sailed on to Glasgow, Scotland; from there the Queen went overland to Balmoral, her "dear Highland home." As a parting gift, the Queen divided £1,000 among the hospitals and charitable institutions of Cork, Dublin, and Belfast.

All observers were in agreement that the 1849 visit to Ireland constituted one of the great ceremonial success stories of the early Victorian monarchy. The often cynical Viceroy, Lord Clarendon, reported to London that "all classes and all parties" in Ireland had become "enchanted" by a monarch who in her punctuality, her neatness, her apparent child-rearing ability, and her kindliness served as a model for all womankind. Ireland's people were also pleased with themselves for having behaved so well in public and for having therefore risen in "the eyes of the world." Victoria in turn took comfort in the hope that the visit would "promote among all her faithful subjects in Ireland that union of heart and affection, which is essential to the prosperity of their common country." In the immediate aftermath of the visit, the Queen formally created her eldest son, then seven, the Earl of Dublin, and when her third son was born on May 1, 1850, he was christened Arthur William Patrick Albert—"Arthur" for the Duke of Wellington, "William" after the Crown Prince of Prussia, and "Patrick," wrote Albert, "for the Irish to show our gratitude for their friendly reception of us last year." In the meantime in London *The Times* exultantly described the royal visit as "the concluding chapter of the history of the Irish rebellion."

Although some of her Irish subjects had expressed the hope that Queen Victoria would henceforth make annual visits to her "other island," four years elapsed before the second journey. The occasion was "Ireland's Crystal Palace," the first Irish attempt to play host to an international exhibition of the wonders of modern technology and industry. It was analogous to the exhibition that during the summer of 1851 had brought hundreds of exhibits and hundreds of thousands of visitors to London's Hyde Park (as well as renown to Prince Albert).[14] The chief sponsor of the Dublin exhibition was William Dargan, Ireland's most successful railway magnate and in1853 also Lord Mayor of Dublin. It was his hope, as it was Albert's, that a Dublin "Crystal Palace" would inspire a new burst of industry in the Emerald Isle during this post-famine decade.

In effect, the exhibition taught a rather different lesson: that the products of labor-intensive Irish handicraft workshops were continuing to give way to manufactured imports from England, Scotland, and the continent. Irish exhibitors remained far more successful in designing "costly furniture fitted only for the mansions of the great" than in making chairs and tables for the lowly. In the words of one Irish observer, "ornamentation more than utility formed the basis of every exhibitor's endeavour." Queen Victoria took enormous satisfaction in the thought that Dargan, a man who had begun life as a mere "labouring man," had succeeded in accumulating an immense fortune while remaining in demeanor so "touchingly modest & simple" as to turn down the baronetcy that she offered him. His spirit of enterprise ought to have provided a splendid example to his countrymen, but the Queen came away from Dublin with a large purchase of handmade Irish lace and with no evidence that— except for Belfast and vicinity—large scale industrialization was now under way on her other island.

Popular enthusiasm for the royal visit on the part of what the Queen called "the warmhearted though unwashed Dublin populace" was as great, however, in 1853 as it had been in 1849. The Queen could also take comfort in the reflection that "the state of the country generally ha[d] wonderfully improved . . ." and that there was now "an entire absence of political excitement & religious dissension."

Eight years elapsed before Queen Victoria and Prince Albert set foot in Ireland again. Their eldest son at the age of nineteen had been granted permission, after several months at Cambridge University, to spend ten weeks with the Grenadier Guards at the army camp at Curragh, not far from Dublin. There, he was expected to master the duties of every military rank from ensign up to general and to acquire all the social graces of an officer and a gentleman. By the time his parents and three of his siblings were able to watch him in action on the Curragh parade ground, however, the prince's military superiors had privately concluded that young Bertie possessed neither the will nor the energy ever to make a successful soldier.[15]

Queen Victoria herself seemed pleased to be in Ireland again, and she was impressed favorably by the military review, by the "most friendly and enthusiastic" people in the streets of Dublin, and by the enormous crowds that cheered her at every stop on the train trip to the Lakes of Killarney. Her memories of this third visit were to be marred, however, by reports that their eldest son's stay at the Curragh camp had been afflicted by scandal as well as by incompetence. His fellow officers had smuggled a young actress into the Prince's bed, and Nellie Clifden proved to be "a vivacious, cheerfully promiscuous and amusing girl who was also unfortunately most indiscreet." In Victoria's eyes, his son's misdeeds had hastened Prince Albert's death only three-and-a-half months later. Victoria was not to set foot in Ireland again for more than thirty-eight years.[16]

The death of her beloved husband opened a new and distinct chapter in Queen Victoria's life. She retained a keen interest in Britain's relations with its continental neighbors, in the prospective marriages of her children, and in the appointment of bishops, ambassadors, and cabinet members, but for at least a decade-and-a-half she avoided all but a handful of public ceremonial occasions. This was the first and the most obvious reason why she contemplated no further state or semi-state visits to Ireland, but there were other reasons also. She came increasingly to look on such public appearances as rewards to be bestowed on well-behaved subjects only. As she phrased the matter in 1868, "if the Irish behave properly," then she was fully prepared to provide visits by herself or her children. Unfortunately, "the more one does for the Irish the more unruly and ungrateful they seem to be."[17]

The Irish men and women whose behavior the Queen deplored were increasingly likely to be identified with the Roman Catholic religion. As I have suggested elsewhere,[18] the later 1860s and early

1870s was the time during which the Queen was most likely to describe herself (privately) as "very anti-Catholic." The Queen was also alienated from Ireland by the Fenians, the members of the Irish Republican Brotherhood who launched an abortive invasion of Canada in 1866 and who two years later blew up London's Clerkenwell prison, thereby killing twelve Londoners and severely wounding thirty others. Supposed Fenian plots to kidnap the Queen did not materialize, but one Fenian sympathizer attempted to assassinate—and did succeed in wounding—her son Prince Alfred during a visit to Australia. In 1872, yet other Fenians sought (with only partial success) to blow up a statue of Prince Albert newly erected in Dublin.

The same spirit of Fenianism that for many years soured Queen Victoria on the Irish inspired William Ewart Gladstone, when invited to become Prime Minister in 1868, to remark: "My mission is to pacify Ireland." In the course of the next two decades, the Queen showed mild sympathy with Gladstone's Irish Land Acts of 1870 and 1881 but virtually none with his successful attempt to disestablish and in part to disendow the Protestant Church of Ireland, the sister to the Church of England and the spiritual home of at most one Irish person in eight.[19]

Gladstone's conversion in 1886 to the cause of Irish "Home Rule"—to the restoration of a separate Irish Parliament and Irish prime minister in Dublin—was not emulated by the Queen. She was convinced from the start that the plan would "tend towards the disruption of her Empire and the establishment of an impracticable form of Government."[20] She was delighted, therefore, when the House of Commons defeated Gladstone's first Home Rule measure in 1886 and when the House of Lords defeated his second such measure in 1893.

Queen Victoria was equally unsympathetic to the notion of setting up a royal summer residence in Dublin. The analogy drawn with her Scottish summer home, Balmoral Castle, was fallacious, the Queen insisted, because "for health and relaxation, no one would go to Ireland . . . but . . . thousands go to Scotland."[21] In response to the pleas of her prime ministers, Victoria did grudgingly permit her heir, the Prince of Wales, and his wife to visit Ireland on three occasions, and in 1868 the prince could happily report to his mother on "the cheering and enthusiasm" that he and Princess Alexandra had encountered in Dublin. They had also received "a wonderfully enthusiastic reception" at the Punchtown race course. Victoria was adamant, however, that the Prince of Wales not be employed permanently as Irish Viceroy, as ceremonial head of state in Dublin. The prince concurred. He had no desire to exile himself to Ireland for four or five months each year, while the Queen did not think him capable of undertaking such weighty responsibilities at a time when she continued to deny him access to secret cabinet and Foreign Office papers.

The most popular of all royal visitors to late-Victorian Ireland was the youthful Prince Arthur, who in Ireland was known as "Prince Pat" and who, in due course, was granted an Irish title, the Duke of Connaught. When he toured Ireland in 1869 and again in 1871, he received ovations at Londonderry, Belfast, Maynooth, and Trinity College. Even in Tipperary was he "most enthusiastically received, though," in the Queen's eyes, "it is the worst part of the whole of Ireland." Back in London, Arthur appropriately became a staunch patron of the Benevolent Society of St. Patrick, which provided education, clothing, and meals for five hundred children of Irish immigrants living in London. He was most anxious, the twenty-three-year-old prince told the group in 1873, "to benefit the poorer classes of Irishmen in London."[22] When his youngest child was born in 1886 on St. Patrick's Day, he happily named her Patricia. A few years later, "Prince Pat" was appointed the commanding general of the British Army in Ireland.

The late 1870s and the early 1880s were in Ireland a time of economic depression, agrarian agitation, and political militancy on the part of Charles Stuart Parnell's Irish Home Rule party. The Queen's prime concern, unlike Gladstone's, was not with additional social reform legislation, however, but with the need to keep order in her other island. She reminded one of Gladstone's cabinet colleagues that the open defiance of the law had to be met with "boldness and firmness," and in December 1881, she warned the prime minister directly:

> If there are not sufficient soldiers to perform the duties required of them, let more regiments be sent. If the law is powerless to punish wrong-doers, let increased powers be sought and . . . let no effort be spared for putting an end to a state of affairs which is a disgrace to any civilized country.[23]

Gladstone's assumption that he had been providentially appointed to resolve the Irish Question impressed his monarch as "a most unfortunate delusion." She much preferred the policy of "kindly firmness" imposed on Ireland by Gladstone's Conservative successor Lord Salisbury.[24]

Many of the opponents of parliamentary autonomy for Ireland feared that "Home Rule means Rome Rule," but Victoria's opposition was based on other concerns. By the 1890s, indeed, her relations with both Pope Leo XIII and the Roman Catholic hierarchy in

England had become remarkably cordial. When a strong Protestant protest arrived at Windsor, the Queen observed that the objectors

> entirely forget how many 1000 Catholic subjects the Queen has who cannot be ignored—And it is grievous to think that what w[oul]d be good for the peace of Ireland will probably be prevented by these well-meaning but fanatical Protestants.[25]

Although the Irish had not distinguished themselves in sending congratulations on the occasion of either Victoria's Golden Jubilee in 1887 or her Diamond Jubilee in 1897, they did distinguish themselves repeatedly in the conflict that broke out in South Africa in October 1899, the Anglo-Boer War. On a per capita basis, Irish volunteers were indeed overrepresented both in the late Victorian British army and among the casualties. Thus, when the Queen visited London's Herbert Hospital early in the year 1900, the Queen observed the presence of "a great number of Irish soldiers. . . . Some were very badly wounded."

By then Victoria was almost eighty-one years old, virtually blind, confined to a wheelchair, and largely dependent on the ministrations of her youngest daughter, the widowed Princess Beatrice. The vocal "Pro-Boer" sentiment that was being voiced in France and Italy seemed to argue against the Queen's customary late-winter sojourn to the French Riviera. At this very time she had become convinced that the Anglo-Boer war had confirmed the underlying loyalty of the Irish people to the cause of the British Empire and its head. And so early in March 1900, the Queen announced publicly that, for the first time since 1861, she was about to visit Ireland. Understandably enough, the announcement was not welcomed by the more ardent Irish Nationalists. A number of Irish municipal and district councils had actually passed resolutions of sympathy with the Boer cause, and the militant William O'Brien ridiculed the Queen as the "recruiting sergeant" of Joseph Chamberlain, the Colonial Secretary.[26]

Although Irish Nationalists strongly suspected that the old Queen was playing a "political game" at the behest of her ministers, those ministers well knew that Victoria was tone-deaf to any advice that they might give her about her public ceremonial role. It was on the advice of General Garnet Wolseley, the British Commander-in-Chief in South Africa, that the Queen authorized her Irish regiments to wear shamrocks on St. Patrick's Day and created a new regiment consisting of three battalions of Irish guards. The evidence seems conclusive, however, that the projected visit to Ireland was fundamentally a matter of royal initiative. As she confided to her favorite lady-in-waiting, "I know people will say I was *advised* to go to Ireland but it is *entirely* my own idea, and I must honestly confess it is *not* entirely to please the Irish, but partly because I expect to enjoy myself."[27]

At the port of Kingstown large crowds greeted her with renditions of "God Save the Queen" and "Soldiers of the Queen," and tens of thousands of people welcomed her to rain-drenched but elaborately decorated Dublin. There the banners read: "Blest for ever is she who relied/On Erin's honour and Erin's pride." As one of the Queen's equerries was to recall, "Although I had seen many visits of this kind, nothing had ever approached the enthusiasm and even frenzy displayed by the people of Dublin."[28]

For the next three weeks—her longest trip to Ireland by far—the Queen resided at the Viceregal Lodge. Every afternoon the Queen went for a twenty-mile drive in her carriage. Initially, a guard of thirteen accompanied the carriage, but when her courtiers discovered how warm a welcome Victoria was receiving in the villages surrounding Ireland's capital, the guard was reduced to only three men. Queen Victoria was able to contrast her sense of personal safety in the Emerald Isle with the horrifying experience that her eldest son and wife were undergoing at the very same time while on a state visit to Brussels. An assassin's bullet fired into their railway carriage missed them by inches.

The stay in Dublin involved a series of visits to schools, hospitals, factories, and convents on the part of the monarch and her accompanying children. The Queen also received innumerable addresses of welcome from civic officials and clergymen. The highlights of the stay were three, however. One was the Queen's visit with Cardinal Logue, the Archbishop of Armagh and Roman Catholic Primate of all Ireland. They chatted together happily for several hours, both surprised to find out how well they got on. According to her equerry, "The Queen went out of her way to make herself agreeable, while the Cardinal was quite captivated by her charm." The second highlight was the review of the troops in Phoenix Park with her son, the Duke of Connaught, in command. A quarter of a million people were present, and it was "a scene of unparalleled enthusiasm." Another highlight was a gathering in Phoenix Park of more than forty thousand school children from all over Ireland. The Queen, who found the children's enthusiasm "quite overpowering," was driven up and down the main road of the park, waving and smiling. Twin girls presented a handsome bouquet of flowers set in a basket of shamrocks. Inscribed on a white ribbon was the dedication: "To our beloved Queen, from the children of Ireland—Queen's Day, April 7th, 1900." When one child called out, "Sure, you're a nice old lady," the Queen laughed.[29]

On April 26, the Queen bid Ireland a warm farewell after thanking the Irish people for having provided her with "a most agreeable time" in "this charming place." Less than nine months later she was dead. Although Queen Victoria's final months were preoccupied with the Boer War, she did not forget her final visit to Ireland. Indeed she chastised her Prime Minister, Lord Salisbury, for failing to push through Parliament a bill that would have established a Roman Catholic University in Dublin. She "could not understand" why Conservative opponents of the project should prove so short-sighted. When latter-day Protestants criticized Victoria for what in her final years had become an outspoken sympathy for her Roman Catholic subjects, her response was succinct: "I am their Queen, and I must look after them."[30]

Almost one hundred years have passed since Queen Victoria's last visit to Ireland, and this lecture merits a few conclusions:

(1) Biographers of our day have paid scant systematic attention to Queen Victoria's connection with Ireland. They remember the monarch as a multi-faceted symbol and forget her as an important player in Victorian politics and diplomacy. If we wish to understand her relationship to Ireland in a manner that Victorians would have understood, then we ought at least in part return to the latter approach.

(2) "Poor Ireland," lamented Gladstone, "it holds but a small place in her heart." In one sense that would seem to be an obvious conclusion. After all, in a reign of sixty-three-and-a-half years, she spent only five weeks in Ireland. Admittedly, that was far more than the time spent there by her five Hanoverian predecessors added together. Curiously enough, that was significantly longer also than the amount of time that William Ewart Gladstone ever spent in Ireland—and he was the British statesman who courted political martyrdom on behalf of the Emerald Isle. What Gladstone really meant by his statement was that he and the Queen had drifted far apart as to how Irish matters should be dealt with by successive British ministries. His solution lay in reform—in the land system, in education, in religion, and in government—even if such reform meant the imposition of a federal legislative system on the United Kingdom. Her solution lay primarily in the preservation of civil order, an order that would enable the Irish people to share fully in the prosperity that economic growth within a single common market was gradually making possible for all the people of the United Kingdom—the English, the Scots,

the Welsh, *and* the Irish. In that United Kingdom per capita income quadrupled in the course of the nineteenth century, and the Irish could—to an increasing degree—claim not only parliamentary representation but also religious and economic liberty and equality under the law. Queen Victoria may have visited Ireland rarely, but does that mean that she took no interest in Irish matters? Forty-six large boxes of documents and letters in the Royal Archives at Windsor strongly suggest the contrary.

(3) One reason why biographers of recent decades, in contrast to those who wrote earlier in the century, are little interested in the subject of "Did Queen Victoria Lose Ireland?" is that, in defiance of the work of scores of Irish historical revisionists, for almost all American historians Irish nationalism remains a given. With regard to the Emerald Isle, the given is the inevitable establishment and persistence of a separate Irish Republic. The sole question that historians are therefore expected to ask of earlier centuries is: how and when can we first discern those republican nationalist acorns from which descended that sturdy Irish oak tree that stands today?

(4) The fact remains that during that century-and-a-quarter that links Wolf Tone with Eamon de Valera, nineteenth-century Ireland underwent at least four transformations that were related indirectly at best to the theme of Irish nationalism:

(a) a land of large estates owned in part by absentee landlords was transformed into a land of small family farms.

(b) a largely illiterate land was transformed into one in which illiteracy was virtually unknown.

(c) a land dominated by a "Protestant Ascendancy" was transformed into a land dominated by devout Roman Catholics.

(d) a land in which the electoral franchise was exercised by only one man in three thousand was transformed into a land in which most adults had the right to vote at the municipal, the county, and the parliamentary level. As former Conservative prime minister Arthur Balfour noted sardonically in the 1920s: "What was the Ireland that the Free State took over? It was the Ireland that we made."[31] It was the Ireland, in other words, that had been either fashioned or permitted to develop during the Victorian era by British ministries responsible to the parliament of the United Kingdom.

(5) Am I suggesting that Victorian Irish nationalist movements
should therefore be ignored altogether? Obviously not. The
point to remember, however, is that outright revolutionary
republicans in nineteenth-century Ireland constituted a small
and generally ineffectual minority. The Irish Home Rule Party
was, after all, pledged not to the establishment of an independent republic but to the creation of a federal United Kingdom over which a single monarch would continue to reign
and serve as focus of unity.

(6) For a time Queen Victoria herself seemed to accept the ultimate triumph of Irish nationalism as a given and to look on
every Irishman as an actual or potential rebel; but by the time
of her visit to Dublin in 1900, she had obviously changed her
mind. We know that the more ardent Irish Nationalists of
1900 felt deeply discouraged by the eagerness with which tens
of thousands of their countrymen took every available train
to Dublin so that they too might see and cheer their Queen.
Of course, some of the spectators were simply curious, others
merely hospitable; still others found in every celebration a
cause for high spirits. But nationalism is ultimately a state of
mind, and—when it is has not already materialized as a separate nation-state—it may well be a state of mind that has to
compete with numerous rival *foci* of allegiance. Doubtless,
the Queen was mistaken in not following the advice of Albert
in supporting a systematic and continual royal presence in
Ireland. Even so, the Ireland that she visited in 1900 was far
less on the verge of nationalist revolution than it had been
earlier in the century.

Had the First World War not plunged a saber through the entire
nineteenth-century world, the multi-ethnic Austro-Hungarian empire of Francis Joseph might not have broken up as it did. Had the
First World War not shattered the fundamentals of Victorian life,
then the United Kingdom of Queen Victoria's time might also, with
relatively gradual adjustment, have lasted well into our own century—and both the British and the Irish might have been spared
some of the evils of the Northern Ireland imbroglio that has afflicted our own time. In 1900 a majority of the people of Ireland
took pride in the courageous manner in which their boys were fighting in far-off South Africa. Queen Victoria took equal pride in these
"Soldiers of the Queen." In Dublin's St. Stephen's Green one may
still encounter a triumphal arch dedicated to "Ireland's Bravest Soldiers," victors in the Anglo-Boer War. Nowadays, Dublin's public
monument to Queen Victoria weeps quietly in a private courtyard.

Its demotion may impress us as readily explicable, but—from the vantage point of 1900—it was far from inevitable.[32]

Fall Semester 1996

1. *Queen Victoria* (London, 1902), p. 547.

2. G. M. Young, *Victorian England: Portrait of An Age*, 2nd ed. (London, 1936), p. 79.

3. Cited in Nicholas Mansergh, *The Irish Question, 1840–1921*, 3rd ed. (Toronto, 1975), p. 100.

4. Viscount Esher (ed.), *The Girlhood of Queen Victoria*, 2 vols. (London, 1912), 2:286.

5. *The Letters of Queen Victoria*, ed. A. C. Benson and Viscount Esher [First Series] 3 vols. (London, 1908), 2: pp. 36–37.

6. Royal Archives (Windsor), D14/140. This and subsequent citations from the Royal Archives—both the correspondence involving Irish affairs and the excerpts from Queen Victoria's (transcribed) journals—are quoted by the gracious permission of Her Majesty Queen Elizabeth II. I am most grateful to Lady Sheila de Bellaigue, the Registrar, and to Miss Pamela Clark, the Deputy Registrar of the Royal Archives, for their helpfulness.

7. E.g. in *Ireland: From Colony to Nation State* (Englewood Cliffs, 1979), Lawrence J. McCaffrey writes: "The Famine was the Irish holocaust. . . . the Irish were victims of ideological murder—no-popery and *laissez faire*," p. 73.

8. See Dominic O'Grada, *The Great Irish Famine* (Dublin, 1989) and Cecil Woodham-Smith, *The Great Hunger: Ireland 1845–1849* (New York, 1962) for many of the details.

9. Woodham-Smith, pp. 151–52, 164–65. The records of the association "disprove a legend, widely believed in Ireland" that the Queen had limited her contribution to £5. Curiously, neither Woodham-Smith nor any other historian has mentioned Albert's contribution. Rothschild and the Duke of Devonshire each gave £1,000, Lord John Russell £300, and Sir Robert Peel £200.

10. RA. Queen Victoria's Journal. Entries for March 9, 18, and 24, 1847.

11. RA. D15/68; D16/15, 69; D18/84.

12. Cited in Woodham-Smith, pp. 386. Pages 381–404 of that volume provide the fullest account of the royal visit of 1849.

13. Cited in ibid., p. 393.

14. The fullest account may be found in Alun C. Davies, "Ireland's Crystal Palace, 1853," in J. M. Goldstrom and L. A. Clarkson (eds.), *Irish Population, Economy, and Society: Essays in Honour of the Late K. H. Connell* (Oxford, 1981), pp. 249–270.

15. Christopher Hibbert, *The Royal Victorians: King Edward VII, His Family and Friends* (Philadelphia, 1976), pp. 45–46. For the third visit, see also Sir Theodore Martin, *The Life of His Royal Highness the Prince Consort*, 5 vols. (London, 1876–80), 5: pp. 376–85.

16. Roger Fulford (ed.), *Dearest Mama: Private Correspondence of Queen Victoria and the Crown Princess of Prussia, 1861–1864* (London, 1968), pp. 30–31.

17. *Letters of Queen Victoria*, 2nd ser., ed. G. E. Buckle, 3 vols. (London, 1924–26), 1:514; RA, D29/179. Queen Victoria to Earl Cowper, the Irish Viceroy, Dec. 5, 1880.

18. Walter L. Arnstein, "Queen Victoria and the Challenge of Roman Catholicism," *The Historian*, 58, 2 (Winter 1996), pp. 295–314.

19. *The Queen and Mr. Gladstone*, ed. Philip Guedalla, 2 vols. (London, 1933), 1:252. See also Roger Fulford, *Your Dear Letter: Private Correspondence of Queen Victoria and the Crown Princess of Prussia, 1865–1871* (London, 1871), p. 230.

20. Christopher Hibbert, *Queen Victoria in Her Letters and Journals* (Harmondsworth, 1985), p. 324.

21. *Letters of Queen Victoria*, 2nd ser. 1:512–14.

22. Cf. Court Circular, *The Times*, Mar. 17, 1873. For the prince's career see Noble Frankland, *Witness of a Century: The Life and Times of Prince Arthur Duke of Connaught, 1850–1942* (London, 1993).

23.  Hibbert, *Victoria*, pp. 266, 271.

24.  The phrase "kindly firmness" may be found in RA. Agatha Ramm MSS for 1891, p. 278; See also, *Beloved and Darling Child*, pp. 35, 144.

25.  Cited in Arthur Ponsonby, *Sir Henry Ponsonby, Queen Victoria's Private Secretary* (London, 1942), p. 50.

26.  Cited in William Butler Yeats, *Letters*, ed. Allan Wade (London, 1954), p. 336. I owe this reference and several others involving the Queen's visit of 1900 to Professor Thomas Connors of the University of Northern Iowa.

27.  Cited in *Life with Queen Victoria: Marie Mallet's Letters from Court, 1887–1901*, ed. Victor Mallet (Boston, 1968), p. 192.

28.  See Stanley Weintraub, *Queen Victoria: An Intimate Biography* (New York, 1987), p. 620, and Frederick Ponsonby, *Recollections of Three Reigns* (London, 1951), p. 63.

29.  *Letters*, 3rd ser., p. 524; Robert Wilson (ed.), *The Life and Times of Queen Victoria*, 2 vols. (London, 1900) 2:930; *Illustrated London News* (April 14, 1900), p. 502.

30.  Cited in Walter Walsh, *The Religious Life and Influence of Queen Victoria* (London, 1902), p. 261.

31.  Cited in D. George Boyce, "1916: Interpreting the Rising," in D. George Boyce and Alan O'Day (eds.), *The Making of Modern Irish History: Revisionism and the Revisionist Controversy* (London, 1996), p. 175.

32.  As John Wolffe points out in *God and Greater Britain: Religion and National Life in Britain and Ireland, 1843–1945* (London, 1994), when King George V and Queen Mary entered Dublin in 1911, they encountered "cheering and hospitable crowds . . . There was virtually no public sign of hostility to the royal party" (p. 153).

# 4

# Was It Possible to Be a Good Catholic, a Good Englishman, and a Good Historian?

## REBA SOFFER

While some historians approach their subject as ardent participants, others attempt to be interested but uninvolved observers. Which of these kinds of people make the most reliable historians? Can the historian whose passion informs his or her subject tell us more than one whose approach is tempered by deliberate neutrality? Does it really matter if the historian is an insider or an outsider? One of the historical fields where these questions have consistently mattered is the study of religions and especially of religious beliefs. Historians of religion are divided by these competing imperatives about how the history of their subject ought to be studied and written. In England, among the various religions existing historically, Catholicism has been the most problematic for historians because the meaning of texts, contexts, audiences and writers is confounded by the considerable gap between the insiders and the outsiders. A story about a recent ecumenical conference in which British religious leaders met to emphasize their common ground describes the conversation between a Methodist and his Catholic tablemate. "How marvelous," said the Methodist, "that we all manage to serve God." "Yes," his Catholic neighbor agreed, "You in your way and I in His."

When historians discuss English religion it is often within the context of political institutions or religious practice rather than as a matter of theological belief. But, from the late seventeenth century, Catholicism was effectively excluded from politics. The organization of the Catholic Church was of little national importance except for that rare occasion when Protestants suspected the foreign Papacy of interfering with English religious life. Catholicism was made even more peripheral because many of its religious practices had been adopted, with modifications, by the established Anglican Church. What was genuinely foreign about Catholicism was its theology. The Catholic system of belief rested upon ecclesiastical tradition, defined centrally and authoritatively and, until very recently, accepted in its entirety by the faithful. But, that ecclesiastical tradition carried within itself a legacy of conflicts whose reconciliation required Sisyphean effort, especially if a Catholic wanted additionally to be a historian. The most obvious and historically long-running conflict among the faithful was between freedom of thought and the authority of Rome. But there were other conflicts equally wrenching for the individual. The spiritual attraction of renunciation for the purpose of cultivating one's soul always had to be balanced against the pull of worldly obligations. The Catholic had to choose between personal piety and public good, between self improvement and the improvement of others, between individuality and submergence in the community, and between religious zeal and religious moderation. If Catholic historians had deliberately studied the historical contexts in which these dilemmas developed, they might have discovered their resolution, or abandoned them as problems, or at least have reached a better understanding of their origins in time. But, until Vatican II in the 1960s, with its historic and unprecedented Declaration of Religious Liberty, Catholics were largely discouraged from studying such historical issues.

In the absence of Catholic historians, were Jews, Protestants, agnostics and atheists, the outsiders, able to write fairly and accurately about the historical Catholic faith and its internal dissensions, or was it only the Catholic insider who felt and lived that faith able to correctly represent it? How have Catholics fared in the hands of historians with different religious backgrounds? Even a cursory survey of books written about Catholicism in England throughout the nineteenth century until today reveals that there are at least as many, if not more, written by non-Catholics on anti-Catholicism than by Catholics, or anyone else, on Catholicism itself. Conspicuous among the English non-Catholic authors is Edward Norman, whose *Anti-Catholicism in Victorian England* appeared in 1968 and *The English Catholic Church in the Nineteenth Century* in 1984. Norman also figures prominently as the specialist on Catholicism in several collections of essays about English Catholicism. An outsider to Catholicism, Norman is an insider in the established Anglican Church and may be, in Maurice Cowling's admiring phrase, the most bloody-minded of all Anglican apologists. It is not clear if that quality makes him the most perceptive student of nineteenth- and twentieth-century English Catholicism.

Concentration on anti-Catholicism is also evident in work such as Robert J. Klaus's *The Pope, the Protestants, and the Irish: Papal Aggression and Anti-Catholicism in Mid-Nineteenth-Century England* (1976) and in the most recent book on English Catholicism, D. G. Paz's *Popular Anti-Catholicism in Mid-Victorian England* (1992). Paz echoes Walter Arnstein's *Protestant versus Catholic in Mid-Victorian England*, written a decade ago, to argue that the English Catholics have been badly treated by non-Catholic historians because their behavior invited critical treatment. Although neither Arnstein nor Paz carries the argument forward recklessly, in less skilled and cautious hands it could conclude that the arrogant and provocative, especially when they wear scarlet dress, can be assumed to be whores who incite the abuse they receive. Even books ostensibly about Catholicism are often really about anti-Catholicism, as is Derek Holmes' *More Roman than Rome: English Catholicism in the Nineteenth Century* (1978). These writers are not combative religious warriors. It is rather that extensive evidence leads them to find anti-Catholicism historically more important in England than Catholicism.

Since the seventeenth century, it has been very difficult to be a Catholic in England and even more difficult to be a Catholic and a loyal English citizen. The perception of Catholicism as a discredited religion in England was so much a part of Protestant culture that every Protestant group treated Catholics with chronic suspicion. This distrust continued even after the laws excluding Catholics from full citizenship were repealed during the nineteenth century. Catholics remained at the center of political controversy, even though they were marginal in numbers and in influence. The Jacobite legacy of Catholicism as treason was strengthened by the continuing identification of Catholicism with Irish civil disruption. Existing Protestant distaste for Catholicism was heightened during the second half of the nineteenth century by a series of papal acts in 1864 that seemed to herald the papacy's contentious forays into English religious life. The result was a national outcry against "papal aggression." Then, in 1870, when the Vatican Council decided to support a doctrine of papal infallibility, William Ewert Gladstone, on his way towards becoming the Grand Old Man of English political life, asked whether it was possible to be both a good Catholic and a good Englishman.

Catholic isolation was confounded further by the Catholic hierarchy's considered decision to segregate the faithful from the main streams of intellectual life, which they found tainted because Protestant. But, the attempt to secure an autonomous, separate existence was very difficult for a minority church in a country where religion defined civil and other rights. Catholics in England could not afford political indifference, let alone neutrality, because of a practical need to secure legal status. Additionally, Catholics wanted to educate, continue, and increase their followers. Even so, the reasons for the English Catholic Church's failures do not rest entirely, or perhaps even largely, on the effects of papal intrusion, or aggressive doctrine, or separatism, or a discredited public image. Catholicism was diminished far more by a religious success over which they had no control—the ecumenical progress of the Anglican Church.

One of the grounds for excluding Catholics from English life was that there already was an established Church in England. The existence of the Catholic Church, with its centralized, hierarchical structure and its attempt to define and impose religious truth, was superfluous. The Established Church, its supporters maintained, was justified by English history and it embodied moral principles and spiritual goodness uniquely personified by the English. In 1913 Cosmo Lang, then Archbishop of York and in 1928 Archbishop of Canterbury, referred to his church as part of the corporate heart of national life.[1] That sentiment had already been imprinted upon national memory in the teaching of history and the preaching of Anglican doctrine. William Stubbs, as Regius Professor of Modern History at Oxford and then as Bishop of Oxford, had located the roots of the national Church in the early development of England's free institutions. According to Stubbs, the Anglican Church's historical evolution perpetuated and guaranteed national values. Stubbs's interpretation was taught in every school and university and echoed in the pulpits. It is not surprising that this celebration of an historically proven church left little sympathy for a competing church based on alien values and foreign historical traditions. The denominations were also excluded by the national Church, but they were, after all, "English," and by the early twentieth century there were systematic attempts by the Anglican hierarchy and the leaders of the other Protestant sects to act together, especially in responding to social problems. After the middle of the nineteenth century, another reason for the dismissal of Catholicism by most English Protestants was that the Tractarian Movement left a residue within the Anglican Church that defined itself as the "Catholic party." These Anglo-Catholics remained within the Church of England while stressing Catholic ideals and practices such as ritualism, liturgical traditionalism, religious aesthetics, and the definition of the faithful as those who took the sacraments.

As early as 1849, George Cornewall Lewis's *Essay on the Influence of Authority in Matters of Opinion* (1849) distinguished between the

Church of Rome and the Protestant Churches by pointing to the reliance of every Protestant Church on scripture and of the Catholics on "uninterrupted tradition in the true Church."[2] That definition was unaltered throughout the rest of the nineteenth century, even by the presence of Anglo-Catholics in the Anglican Church. Roman Catholics continued to rely on ecclesiastical tradition which contained its own authoritarian mechanisms to protect continuity. During the intellectually tumultuous second half of the nineteenth century, Anglicans and other Protestants, in sharp contrast to the Catholics, constantly examined and altered theology and worship. They were responding to the churchmen and chapelmen, armed with historical and scientific methods of textual criticism, who were examining the authority of the Bible.[3] Among Catholics, also, in response to the application of the genetic sciences to religious understanding, a short-lived liberal movement developed in an attempt to accommodate the Catholic Church to the new approaches of history and biology.

That movement was doomed, even before the hierarchy's opposition, by the nature of its leadership as well as by its doctrines. An important leader and the only Catholic historian to achieve reputation in England during the nineteenth century, was the then very young John Acton, whose ties to continental, and especially German thought, always remained more attractive to him than his understanding or appreciation of the English. The other leaders were Catholic intellectuals, generally converts, who formed the enthusiastic staffs of *Rambler* from the 1850s to the early 1860s and of *Home and Foreign Review* in the early 1860s. But, both publications were effectively opposed by the English Catholic hierarchy and, after a decade of trying to make themselves and their publications acceptable to Rome, their members succumbed, loyally, to the censure of the authorities. It is interesting and revealing that it was also converts, although not necessarily Catholic liberals, who provided Downside, the most distinguished Catholic Abbey and school, with monks, teachers, and students.

The distinction drawn by Lewis and maintained by Protestants and Catholics through the twentieth century also made it almost impossible to be a good Catholic and a good historian. Owen Chadwick has argued that in the 1860s and 1870s, "ultramontanes appeared to set the authority of the church above truth. If the doctrine of the church and the results of human inquiry disagreed, then human inquiry must give way."[4] But it was a far more complex issue. The intention of ultramontanism was to make the Church independent of all secular and political control by centralizing greater power in the papacy. That centralization has to be understood within a European, and especially a German context. After 1815, the Hapsburgs and the Wittelsbachs alike treated the Catholic Church as part of their civil service. For those Catholics living in the German world, ultramontanism was a promise of liberation from political domination. The issues become even more confusing because the debate over freedom and authority in the Catholic Church became part both of the German struggle for greater freedom of thought and of a movement for political constitutionalism.

Acton, consistently more German than English, felt compelled to defend ultramontanism in the pages of the *Home and Foreign Review* in 1863. But, he could only do that by redefining its meaning in a way that must have made the Papacy wish for a very different champion. To Acton, ultramontanism was "a habit of intellect carrying forward the inquiries and supplementing the work of authority. It implies the legitimate union of religion with science, and the conscious intelligible harmony of Catholicism with the system of secular truth. Its basis is authority, but its domain is liberty, and it reconciles the one with the other." Acton argued further that unless the Catholic undergoes a "struggle in his mind" between liberty and authority, science and religion, his "conscience has obtained no security against the necessity of sacrificing faith to truth or truth to faith, and no impulse to that reflection which recognizes the ultimate unity."[5] The Roman Catholic Church in the second half of the nineteenth century was not prepared to sacrifice "faith to truth" and the hierarchy decided for authority and against liberty. Although Acton accepted the dogma of the Church, he was not a favored son and his two German teachers of history were less fortunate. Johann von Dollinger died outside the Church and Lasaulx, the Rector of Munich University, had all his books placed on the Index.

Almost a century later, in 1955, Douglas Woodruff, a Catholic journalist, popular historian, and Downside graduate who had been President of the Oxford Union, tried to understand the internal struggle within Catholicism during Acton's time. When Woodruff introduced his edition of Acton's writings on church and state, he explained ultramontanism as a disaster for the Catholic Church. From Woodruff's twentieth-century view, ultramontanism was blamed for persuading Catholic intellectuals that it was irreverent to study what was the most obvious subject for them, their Church and its institutions. Beyond ultramontanism, Woodruff found two additional circumstances, unique to English Catholicism, that restricted all kinds of inquiry. These were the nervousness of a new hierarchy more authoritarian than it would be after it had matured into an institution; and, the emergence of Henry Edward Manning, a "narrow, masterful ecclesiastic" who succeeded Nicholas Patrick

Stephen Wiseman in 1864 as Cardinal. The same year as Manning's succession, the Pope issued a syllabus of errors, Galileo was condemned anew, and the argument over infallibility accelerated. Manning was convinced, Woodruff argues, that a better educated laity would come at too high a price.[6] Until his death in 1892, Manning remained a dominating Cardinal resolutely turned away from a new Catholic world that changed in spite of his best efforts to prevent it.[7] The effect of Manning's resistance was that the reforming pontificate of Leo XIII, far more liberal than that of his predecessor Pius IX, did not begin to affect English Catholics until the turn of the century.

While the nineteenth-century English Catholic hierarchy resolutely rejected attempts to combine history and theology, the Anglican Church saw the advantages of an historical theology. In Oxford, where vigilance was maintained against any further Oxford Movements, both theology and history were entrusted to sound Anglicans such as Stubbs. As Regius Professor of History for seventeen years, Stubbs gave an historical imprimatur to the idea of an ancient national church. When he retired from the Regius chair, he became an active Bishop of Oxford. Tractarians never established themselves in Cambridge, and Stubbs's contemporaries there, J. B. Lightfoot, B. F. Westcott, and F. J. A. Hort, studied theology through the new historical techniques of textual criticism. At the same time, the Historical Tripos included ecclesiastical history. The Dixie Chair of Ecclesiastical History, as well as the Norrisian Chair of Divinity, could be held by laymen although the first layman to be professor of Divinity was F. C. Burkitt in 1905, and there was no nonconformist in that chair until 1935 when it was filled by C. H. Dodd. The Cambridge degrees of bachelor and doctor of divinity were opened to any candidate from any religion in 1915. Roman Catholics could legally attend the universities from the 1870s, but the Roman Catholic hierarchy prohibited them from either Oxford or Cambridge, until the intervention of Pope Leo XIII in April, 1895, allowed Catholics to matriculate. Even then Catholic students lived separately in Catholic Halls and no Catholic priest or ordinand was allowed to study in schools of theology within Oxford and Cambridge. Catholic historical studies were given permission to proceed in 1883 by Leo XIII's assertion that "The first law for writing history demands that nothing false be said; furthermore that the truth not be hidden; and lastly that any suspicion of either favoritism or hostility to Rome be avoided."[8] But Pius X, Leo's successor in 1903, attempted to stop the threatening revolution in Catholic intellectual and spiritual thought. In 1907 he condemned as heretical "Catholic modernism," a movement that wanted to subordinate the centralizing power of the papacy to the early church ideal of an egalitarian community.

Was Woodruff correct in assuming that the history of the Church and its institutions were the obvious focus for a Catholic historian? Norman Cantor's *Inventing the Middle Ages* (1991) has pointed out that the focus of Catholic historical studies since 1907, whether liberal or absolutist in purpose, has tended to be the Middle Ages. Because of Catholic reliance upon the descent of tradition, the medieval period was seen as the predecessor of the twentieth-century church. Cantor argues that Catholic scholars who write about the medieval world have been compelled by their Catholicism to respond to the three "falls" in their historical work. The first is the fall of Adam and Eve, which left human beings sinful and dependent upon God's grace transmitted to the individual directly or through the Church. Cantor finds diametrically opposed responses within Catholicism to the fall from grace: one is that after the expulsion from Eden the church saved its corrupt and helpless members through the sacraments, and the other is that the expulsion proved that human nature is so corrupt as to be incapable of devising and maintaining good institutions, including the church.

Cantor's second obstacle to be faced by Catholic historians is the fall of the Roman empire. The traditional Catholic explanation was that the disintegration of the Roman Empire allowed the Church to carry out missionary and civilizing work that culminated in the religious world of the Middle Ages. But, an opposing interpretation argued instead that the authoritarianism and inequality of the Roman Empire was perpetuated through the organization and teaching of the early medieval church. The third fall, the *Glaubenspaltung*, the division of the faith, was the most difficult for Catholic illuminati because they had to account for those intellectuals who sided against Rome. Cantor concludes that when a Catholic historian studied Catholic medieval institutions, he was really engaged in a contemporary study with doctrinal as well as historical implications.[9] Cantor has concentrated on the study of the Middle Ages, but it is equally true that any study by Catholics of their own Church faces very similar problems.

Beyond Cantor's perceptive analysis of the difficulties facing Catholic historians, one might argue that for Catholics, more perhaps than for other faiths or for atheists, it is necessary to confront history. To make individual free will responsible for the existence of evil in the world, they have to prove that history is neither determined nor blindly fortuitous. In Stanley Elkin's novel *The Living End* (1979), God does not justify His ways, but He does explain them. He tells Heaven that interest in the sanctity of the human will or in goodness were irrelevant to His actions. He did what He did rather because "it makes a better story."[10]

An earlier and more serious twentieth-century treatment of the problem of evil occurs in Evelyn Waugh's *Decline and Fall* published in 1928 before Waugh's conversion to Catholicism. Mr. Prendergast, the former Church of England priest who leaves the ministry because of his "doubts" explains them by saying that it was not miracles, or religious mythology, or the abuses of power within the Church that weighed upon him. Instead, he confesses, "I couldn't understand why God has made the world at all."[11] The real problem for Prendergast was that if free will has been given to human beings by God, then why do people regularly choose evil? Within Catholicism, one tradition answered that God made the world and filled it with people able to choose freely between good or evil and then act upon their choice. An individual's character determined the choice they would make. While non-Catholic and especially Anglican historians in England studied national character, one might expect the understanding of individual character in historical time to be the most likely subject for a Catholic historian.

What did English Catholic historians actually choose to study in history? In order to answer that, it would be helpful to look at a Catholic historian whose motives were strongly and traditionally Catholic but who produced historical work widely accepted by scholars of every other faith. There were no such Catholics in either nineteenth- or twentieth-century England until Dom David Knowles, a Benedictine monk, published his *The Monastic Order in England* in 1940. Knowles was not the most "Catholic" of English Catholic historians or in any way the most representative. He was simply the only one who succeeded remarkably and uniquely as an historian in an intellectual world largely anti-Catholic.

Although Knowles lived and wrote in the twentieth century, he was more a nineteenth-century figure. Secluded as a child by overprotective parents and then educated in the abbey school of Downside, the most learned of the Benedictine monasteries in England, he entered the novitiate in his late adolescence. From then, he lived the spiritual life of a monk until his death, even when he was at Cambridge first as a teacher at Peterhouse, then as Professor of Medieval History and finally as Regius Professor of Modern History. As an undergraduate, he was sequestered in Benet Hall, the Catholic Hall in Cambridge. After Cambridge, he was sent to Rome for a year of theological study and then he returned to his monastery. Brief holidays with his family were largely spent visiting Catholic Churches, and from the 1930s, he cut himself off from travel, literature, and even the radio except for the rare news broadcast and the annual Christmas Carol performance from King's College. Indifferent to politics, unless they were internal Cambridge politics, and to those issues of contemporary life which were not specifically Catholic interests, he was an ascetic tourist who rarely visited his own century. He was most at home in the English monastic houses from about 940 to 1540, the centuries covered by his massive four-volume study of the English monasteries. He recognized and sympathized with the monks in those "bare ruined choirs" because they were part of his lived and intensely felt experience.

In the distinction between insiders and outsiders in the writing of history, there never was such an insider as Father David. When he reflected upon that distinction, as he did in 1929, Knowles rejected the writing of Protestant scholars, such as G. G. Coulton, about the Catholic Church. In a letter to a Downside friend, Dom Adrian Morey, Knowles recognized that it would be equally difficult for a Catholic to write about the Reformation because that "brings one too much across deep subjects . . . which we know no more about than Coulton does of Catholic spirituality."[12] Thirty-two years later, after spending twenty years as a Cambridge historian, he argued that it was possible for a Voltaire or a Marx "by reading and careful expression" to "give an account of the Christian doctrine of the Trinity," but they could not understand that doctrine unless they believed in it.[13] Knowles was far from endorsing outsiders, let alone nonbelievers, as competent to write about Catholicism. The account of a Voltaire or a Marx was worthless to Knowles because the doctrine of the Trinity was true and a lack of belief meant the impossibility of understanding.

Did Knowles's absolute commitment to the theology of Catholicism obstruct or enable his historical vision? That theology was embedded in his monastic sensibility and it may be that a monk's life allowed Knowles to bring an unusual intuition to his work. All historians are voyeurs of one kind or another, but their concentration upon observation is limited by the distraction of other responsibilities within the academy, the counting house, and the family. Knowles experienced far fewer distractions in his deliberately contemplative life. That life had as its essence a mystical knowledge of God, an experience of the divine presence in one's soul, a reality that was, as he put it in *The English Mystical Tradition* (1961), "wholly incommunicable, save as a bare statement." It was an experience of God's grace, which he believed few ever had, that allowed him to view himself and those from whom he was removed in time, if not in place, with a special knowledge that "was wholly distinct from the reasoning mind and its powers."[14] Whether one accepts or rejects the reality of such mystical experience, it may be that the believing mystic is in a position to look more closely at other mystics or near mystics because he is prepared to see what sceptics will miss.

At the same time, Knowles spent his formative years as a member of a relatively contained, traditional community where a practical daily life was rigorously ordered and supervised. In the monastery, where day to day existence was so uniform and repetitive, the uses and abuses of power stood out in greater relief than they might have in a more dynamic institution governed by less predictable forces and less restricted personalities. What Knowles combined, then, was an aspiration for other-worldly ends and the pragmatic life of a member of a miniature society whose problems of order, authority, and conflict were magnified because of the constancy of both its membership and the rule under which they lived in common. Knowles recognized that the effective operation of a monastery depended, above all, on the kind of people within it.

Knowles's four-volume study of the English monasteries, although it deals in some part with institutions, concentrates on analyses of character. Religious thought and life, which he treats with exceptional clarity, are presented as an extension of individual personality. When Knowles explains Erasmus, the great Christian humanist, his approach appears initially to be sympathetic: "the 'philosophy of Christ,' which he preaches . . . is one in which a wide culture and a humanistic moral outlook form the basis of a life modeled on the gospel teaching presented in a purely human fashion." But Erasmus was unacceptable to Knowles who saw him as a dangerous seducer because the Christian humanist never "adequately recognizes the wholly supernatural plane on which the life of Christ moved." The life of the Christian, he continued, "implies depths of love and wisdom and of redemptive suffering of which the unaided human mind could not dream and to which the unaided human will could not attempt to attain."[15] Erasmus failed Knowles's very personal test for the essential qualities that defined a true Christian.

Biographical studies of individuals in their relations to each other and to the larger spiritual culture of their time, especially in the Middle Ages, interested Knowles most. One of the reasons that the medieval centuries were so attractive to religious historians of all Christian denominations is because they could assume, as the Anglo-Catholic Congress did in 1923, that during that time societies organized their whole lives, "their politics, their economics, their social structure according to the mind of our Lord."[16] Other historians of the Middle Ages, especially in the growing emphasis upon social conscience prevalent among Protestants and Catholics before the Great War, idealized the uniquely Christian relationships of the medieval world as a model for religious responsibilities to the greater community.

But Knowles's study of the monasteries was critical enough to make him recognize that they were far from perfect institutions in a world far from Christian ideals. He was too much of a religious pessimist to believe that reforms succeeded in ways that really were substantive. Knowles's writings are filled with disappointment and sadness because the monks in the Middle Ages, just like those in contemporary Downside, and just like himself, had never maintained the religious purity that brought the individual to God. In his *The Monastic Order in England,* covering the tenth through the early thirteenth centuries, he lamented that "in almost every religious order the original period of intense fervour is relatively brief." Among the very few that endured with "their purity all but unimpaired" he found the Carthusians and the nuns of the Teresian reform whose success was due to their rigid observance of an unchanging rule and to their equally "rigid and exclusive selection and probation."[17]

What chronically troubled him were the barriers preventing his own mystical, elitist relationship with God. Herbert Butterfield, a lay Methodist preacher until 1935 and after the Second World War Regius Professor of Modern History at Cambridge, Vice-Chancellor of the University, and Master of Peterhouse College, was more responsible than anyone else for Knowles's career at Cambridge. They later fell out about the assignment of rooms at Peterhouse, a quarrel about entitlement to the peripheral comforts of the flesh rather than about the central teaching of the spirit. But there was no one at Cambridge who had been closer to Knowles. Butterfield felt that Knowles had always had an "unmistakable attitude not indeed of personal but of doctrinal superiority." In a letter to a colleague in December, 1935, Knowles had written: "In the last resort the mind can only obey TRUTH and this—the light par excellence—will be received by the mind (or rather re-received) according to its own purity . . . which is not—no by heavens—the same as saying that we all see different facets of the same truth." Beyond and above the monastic life and the abbot, he continued, "spiritual obedience" can only be given "to one more enlightened than oneself."[18] Knowles apparently never found such a person. Both his religious introspection and his flight from Downside, precipitated by his abbot's authoritarian zeal and by his own frustration at not being allowed to form a more spiritual religious community, may have contributed to his despondent strain of Catholicism. That strain is evident in his historical work, where he invariably found pessimism more historically and spiritually congenial than optimism.

When Knowles succeeded Butterfield as Regius Professor of Modern History at Cambridge in 1954, his famous inaugural on "The Historian and Character" attempted to explain his spiritual imperatives to a secular audience in secular language. It is worth listening to at some length because of its Catholic resonance and because it proposed a view of history from the inside that attempted to touch those who were outside. Knowles never conceded merit to non-Catholic religions, although he came close in his friendship for Butterfield, whose son became a convert to Catholicism. Only Catholicism was true and as such had to be inclusive. Knowles's concern for character was centered in that Catholic tradition that emphasized the exercise of free will. Because a "man has free will," he contended, "he can, indeed he must, exercise it. His nature with its characteristics remains recognizable, as do his features, but his aims, his ideals, his sense of values, and his directive strength of will may have changed entirely. The change is greatest when a moral or spiritual issue predominates in a man's life, as with St. Augustine and St. Francis and John Wesley, but the development is always there, even if gradual and unseen. No one remains the same in virtue or in love; not to go forward is to go back." Knowles believed that it was integral to Catholic teaching to admit that every person had the freedom to be good and that such willing goodness required enormous and unremitting effort. History demonstrated that abiding struggle and it demonstrated further that it was much easier to lose than to win.

The study of character, he told his ecumenical audience, "draws its strength from the centre of the personality, the final and most precious thing in man, his goodness of will, achieved by conscious and tenacious choice. That is of more significance than his natural characteristics or his intellectual gifts, or even the inspiration of genius." To Knowles, intellect was nothing in history compared to spirituality. What did that mean for the historian who attempted to explain human behavior in a particular place and period? Knowles was convinced that it was "impossible for us not to look for goodness and justice in a man," but he denied Acton's exhortation that the historian must be a moralist. Knowles urged historians to have sympathy but not to be a judge, "still less a hanging judge." Instead, the historian "watches the stream of events and the actions of men, and records them as best he may . . . he looks to see whether" a man during his life shows "any evidence of acting according to a divine or moral law outside of himself, whether he ever sacrifices his own profit or pleasure for the sake of a person or a principle; whether he shows evidence of loving other men . . . of wishing them well and doing well to them; whether he puts justice before expediency;

whether he is sincere and truthful. In so doing the historian is not trying the men and women of the past; he is contemplating them; he had to see them as in truth they were and to present them as such to others, and a man, as a man, cannot be seen truly unless his moral worth, his loveworthiness is seen."[19] It is difficult to see the distinction between Acton's hanging judge and Knowles's contemplation of character. When Knowles actually wrote about a particular person's character, moral worth rarely figured as prominently as moral inadequacy.

A problem faced by Knowles and other Catholic intellectuals was the intensely introspective quality of Catholicism that required an unrelenting test of one's own thought, emotions, and actions. Conflicts between conscience and authority, or religious obligations and personal inclination could not be put aside to be solved at some later time. Were it not for the confessional, these dichotomies might be almost impossible to bear. The insistence upon free will is not simply an argument for the right to choose freely. In Catholic tradition, free will meant accountability to a God who had expelled humans from Eden because they chose badly. Inevitably, in Catholic tradition, free will usually meant failure. For a Catholic historian the reality of a God-given free will required more than an explanation of Norman Cantor's three falls: Eden, the end of Christian Rome, and the Reformation. The Catholic historian had to explain the daily fall of individuals, both weak and powerful, whose characters were not sufficient to elevate their lives in conformity to the spiritual good that God required of them. Perhaps even more seriously, Catholic historians were prepared by their faith to find that the flaws in human character also prevented people from constructing institutions that could at least contain, if not remedy, evil. Every state, like all other human achievements, was inherently flawed and the role of the good citizen was problematic. Even more paradoxically, the fallibility of institutions called into question the very existence and authority of the Catholic Church itself. The burden of spiritual worthlessness, demonstrated historically in individual preference for evil and compounded by the frailty of human institutions, made it prohibitively difficult to be a good person, let alone a good historian, a good Catholic, and a good Englishman.

Fall Semester 1996

1. Cosmo Lang, *Hansard*, 5th ser., xiii, 1195 (Feb. 12, 1913), quoted in Edward Norman, *Church and Society in England, 1800–1970* (Oxford, 1976), p. 278.

2. George Cornewall Lewis, *An Essay on the Influence of Authority in Matters of Opinion* (London, 1849), p. 95.

3. Horton Davies, *Worship and Theology from Newman to Martin* (Princeton University Press, 1962), p. 10.

4. Owen Chadwick, *The Victorian Church*, II, *1860–1901*, 2nd. ed., (London, 1972), p. 416.

5. John Acton, "Utramontanism" (July 1863), in *Essays on Church and State* (New York, 1953), p. 40.

6. Douglas Woodruff, "Introduction" to Acton, *Essays,* pp. 7–8.

7. Lytton Strachey's "Cardinal Manning" in his attack on Victorian mythology, *Eminent Victorians* (London, 1918), is an acidic portrait of a calculating opportunist that reveals more about Strachey's revulsion towards religion, and especially Catholicism, than it does about Manning.

8. Quoted in Norman Cantor, *Inventing the Middle Ages* (New York, 1991), p. 288.

9. Cantor, *Inventing the Middle Ages*, ibid., pp. 292–96.

10. Stanley Elkin, *The Living End: A Triptych* (New York, 1979), pp. 136–144.

11. Evelyn Waugh, *Decline and Fall* (London, 1977), p. 27.

12. Oct. 24, 1929, in Adrian Morey, *David Knowles: A Memoir* (London, 1979), p. 120.

13. Knowles, *The English Mystical Tradition* (New York, 1961), p. 2.

14. Ibid., p. 3.

15. Knowles, *The Religious Orders in England*, III, *The Tudor Age* (Cambridge, 1959), p. 146.

16. *Report of the Anglo-Catholic Congress 1923* (London, 1923), p. 99.

17. Knowles, *The Monastic Order in England: A History of Its Development from the Times of St. Dunstan to the Fourth Lateran Council, 1216* (Cambridge, 1963, 2nd ed.), p. 224.

18. In a letter of Sept. 10, 1977, Adrian Morey had asked Butterfield to comment on Morey's manuscript about Knowles. Butterfield's response is in the Butterfield Papers, Cambridge University Library, Butt/239. The quotes appear on pp. 5 and 6.

19. Knowles, "The Historian and Character," An Inaugural Lecture as Regius Professor of Modern History, Nov. 17, 1954, in *The Historian and Character and Other Essays* (Cambridge University Press, 1963), pp. 7–14.

# 5

# Henry James: The Victorian Scene

## R. W. B. LEWIS

On a foggy, drizzly Christmas Eve in 1876, Henry James sat in his newfound lodgings on Bolton Street in London, trying to keep his spirits up, but half-admitting to his mother, in a letter, that he felt lonely and uncertain about his future. Not long after, however, he entered the English social and literary world— the Victorian world—with a rush: chatting with Robert Browning and the historian James Froude at a dinner-party, breakfasting one morning at the home of Lord Houghton, an old friend of Henry Adams, and on another at the home on the river (a "queer little house," James called it) of the American-born painter James Whistler. Before long, he was given guest privileges at the Atheneum Club on Pall Mall, and then made a member for life at the prestigious and exclusive Reform Club, where he happily observed Herbert Spencer taking an afternoon nap every day.

It was in the light of all this that Henry wrote his father, about London, that "*J'y suis, j'y reste,* forever and a day." And so he did. Towards the end of the year 1877, after a brief visit to Paris, James wrote his friend Grace Norton that he was returning to "London, whither I find I gravitate as towards the place in the world in which, on the whole, I feel most at home." It was the great decision in Henry James's career: the choice of England, and in particular of London, as his place of residence, of life and work. But if he spoke of being "at home" in London, he also had the strong sensation—an oddly energizing sense—of being an outsider in London: that is, in the Jamesian lexicon, of an *observer.* His role henceforth, he remarked, would be "that of an observer, in the place where there is most in the world to observe."

So, in 1876–77, Henry James, the observant outsider, was set to explore the Victorian scene, his home-to-be, just as, almost thirty years later, he would return to his old and actual home, especially New York and New England, and write about his re-discoveries in his book *The American Scene.* The two scenes are the main dimensions of his life.

This was anything but Henry James's first stay in England. He was scarcely six months old when his father, Henry James Senior, took the entire family to England. It was a visit that had extraordinary consequences for the father, but the younger Henry remembered nothing of it—though he did startle the family some years later by recalling in some detail the Place Vendôme in Paris, which he had seen near the end of that same European venture, at the age of less than two.

London made its first real impression on Henry James during the months the family spent there in 1855–56, when they occupied a comfortable house, with a garden, in St. John's Wood. William James would denounce this whole visit as a waste of time and educationally useless; he and Henry did nothing, William would say, but walk about together in their little high black hats and their gloves, gazing into shop windows, and occasionally entering one to buy watercolors and paintbrushes. Henry, in his memoirs, found in 1855 London something like the birth of his observing imagination:

> It was just the fact of our having so walked and dawdled and dodged [he wrote] that made the charm of memory; in addition to which what could one have asked more than to be steeped in a medium so dense that whole elements of it, forms of amusement, interest and wonder soaked through to some appreciative faculty and made one fail at the moment of nothing but one's lessons.

And, again recalling that time in another passage in his memoirs, Henry was revisited by the feeling that since "one was all eyes and the world, decidedly . . . all images," the experience simply "ministered to the panoramic."

But it was during the weeks Henry passed in London in March and April of 1869 that he might be said to have begun his literary associations with the English. Then, as later, London was dark and wintry, and Henry confessed to his mother that he felt "abjectly, fatally homesick." But, again as it would be on the subsequent visit, Henry was soon taken up socially and literarily. His sponsors were the American essayist and professor Charles Eliot Norton and his family; and through them he was soon encountering William Morris, John Ruskin, Charles Darwin, and Dante Gabriel Rosetti. But by far the highest point was on a Sunday afternoon in May, when Norton's sister Grace took Henry to a house in Regent's Park to call on George Eliot.

Henry James by 1869 had published four articles on George Eliot—two of them, in 1866, dealing respectively with the novel *Felix Holt* and with a collective edition of Eliot's novels. About *Felix Holt,* James wrote (in *The Nation*)—and if you want an example of Henry James the bright youthful critic (very bright, very youthful) this is it:

> Better perhaps than any of George Eliot's novels does "Felix Holt" illustrate her closely wedded talent and foibles. Her plots have always been artificial—clumsily artificial—the conduct of her story slow, and her style diffuse. Her conclusions have been signally weak, as the reader will admit who recalls Hetty's reprieve in "Adam Bede," the inundation of the Floss, and worse than either, the comfortable reconciliation of Romola and Tessa. The plot of "Felix Holt" is essentially made up, and its development is forced. The style is the same lingering slow-moving, expanding instrument which we already know. The termination is hasty, inconsiderate, and unsatisfactory . . . But if such are the faults of "Felix Holt" or some of them, we hasten to add that its merits are immense, and that a critic finds it no easy task to disengage himself from the spell of so much power, so much brilliancy, and so much discretion . . .

He goes on to speak of George Eliot's "firm and elaborate delineation of character," her "extensive human sympathy [and] easy understanding of character at large. . . . George Eliot's humanity colors all her other gifts—her humor, her morality, and her exquisite rhetoric."

Henry James was twenty-three years old when he wrote that; and he was only a few months older when he devoted an article in *The Atlantic Monthly* to "The Novels of George Eliot." He went through them one by one, with the young Jamesian mixture of admiration and severe if pained criticism, to end by saying that the strongest impression made on him by a reperusal of these novels was that "the author is in morals and aesthetics essentially a conservative." James entirely endorses Eliot's moral conservatism: "What moves her most," he suggests, "is the idea of a conscience harassed by the memory of slighted obligations." But James dissociates himself firmly from what he calls Eliot's aesthetic conservatism—"her inclination to compromise with the old tradition—and I use the word old *without* respect—which exacts that a serious story of manners shall close with the factitious happiness of a fairy-tale."

Needless to say, James, in thus appraising the work of another novelist, was seeking to understand his own fiction-writing ambitions, to clarify the reach and the boundaries of his own creative imagination. What James had to say about George Eliot's aesthetic conservatism was, so to say, illustrated, was virtually justified, by James's novel *The American* seven years later. In this novel, the wealthy retired American businessman Christopher Newman, arriving in Paris, becomes involved with the aristocratic de Bellegarde family. He hopes to marry the Marquise de Bellegarde's widowed daughter, Claire de Cintré; but the snobbish Marquise rejects the suit. Newman then comes into possession of a ghastly family secret, by means of which he could force the Marquise to yield to him. But Newman refuses to do so; and in the end, Claire is shut up in a convent, and Newman is last seen gazing up at the convent in pain and frustration.

The story began to run in the *Atlantic* in June 1876, and when he saw the final chapters, the magazine's editor, William Dean Howells, was completely dismayed. He begged James to reconsider, and write in a happy marital ending. The very request, James replied, made him tremble—tremble, one assumes, with aesthetic anxiety. The whole final point, James insisted, was exactly that of Newman losing the young woman, and so demonstrating the fundamental truth that tall stone walls divide all human beings one from another. So much for the traditional fairy-tale.

The meeting at the house in Regent's Park on that Sunday afternoon was, accordingly, a momentous one for Henry James. He responded to the living woman in a manner similar to his worked-up judgment of her books—deprecating, wondering, admiring, totally yielding. "She is magnificently ugly—deliciously hideous," he told his father the next day; but "in that vast ugliness resides a most powerful beauty which, in a very few minutes, steals forth and charms the mind, so that you end as I ended, falling in love with her." George Eliot's charm was extraordinary, and looking for the sources of it, James spoke of "a mingled sagacity and sweetness . . . a great feminine dignity and character . . . a hundred conflicting shades of consciousness and simpleness—shyness and frankness—graciousness and remote indifference." But, as James explained, the visit had to be cut short when the writer's twenty-four-year-old stepson collapsed on the floor with an attack of agonizing spinal pain.

Henry's devotion to George Eliot, whatever criticisms he might voice, was well enough known in the James family household, and sometimes elicited sibling counter-opinions. In 1877, after the appearance of Eliot's novel of inter-racial drama, *Daniel Deronda*, had appeared, Henry wrote warmly about it in letters home, to the point where his brother William evidently became fed up. In a review article of the book *Physical Basis of Mind* by G. H. Lewes (George Eliot's longtime companion), William went impishly out of his way to say: "Not since reading *Daniel Deronda* have we been so annoyed by a writer's redundancy, have we found ourselves so persistently seized by the button and moralized to when we were most impatient for the story to move along and for the author to effect something with his material."

And sister Alice James, after reading a volume of George Eliot's letters and journals in the summer of 1889, wrote severely in her own journal, in an expression of sisterly jealousy and jumping on the aspect that Henry had so often praised—"What a monument of ponderous dreariness is the book . . . Not one hint of joy, not one ray of humor, not one living breath . . ."

What is now generally regarded as George Eliot's masterpiece, *Middlemarch*, came out in 1873. In my own view, *Middlemarch* may well be the finest novel ever written in English. Henry James, reviewing it in the *Galaxy* in March 1873, was as usual mixed and even contradictory. He began by saying that *Middlemarch* "is at once one of the strongest and one of the weakest of English novels"; and went on to say that it was "a treasure-house of details, but an indifferent whole." It becomes increasingly evident that Henry James is arguing with himself; is, in effect, trying to *locate* himself—by relation to George Eliot and *Middlemarch*. Near the end of the review, he asserts forthrightly enough that "George Eliot seems to us among English romancers to stand alone." And then, a few sentences later: "[*Middlemarch*] sets a limit, we think, to the development of the old-fashioned English novel."

So: Henry James, approaching his thirtieth birthday, the author of one novella and a good many short stories (including, most recently, that first-class tale "A Passionate Pilgrim")—Henry James was going to move beyond the old-fashioned novel in his own fiction, was going to lead English-language fiction into a new era.

To describe how or to what extent James succeeded in that ambition would require a large-scale discussion of his literary development, and would pull us away somewhat from our theme. Perhaps a couple of instances, both deriving from *Roderick Hudson*, James's first accomplished full-length novel (it came out in 1876), can serve: one bearing on his habitual center of attention, one on his sense of narrative *design*. In his retrospective comments on *Roderick Hudson*, James declared that the real subject of the story was not the adventures of the title figure, the ill-fated sculptor from Northampton, Masasachusetts, who plunges to his death in Switzerland, after being defeated both as a lover and an artist, but much rather the view and experience of Roderick Hudson by his friend and mentor Rowland Mallett. "The center of interest throughout *Roderick Hudson* is in Rowland Mallett's consciousness, and the drama is the drama of that consciousness." That concept—the drama of consciousness—almost defines the new or post-Eliot mode of fiction.

In that same preface to the novel, in the early 1900s collective edition of his works, James spoke even more tellingly about the manner in which he had sought to round out the narrative. This is James moving carefully beyond the characteristic happy ending, the total tidying up, of the representative Victorian novel. "Really, universally," he writes, "relations stop nowhere, and the exquisite problem of the artist is to draw, by a geometry of his own, the circle within which they shall happily *appear* to do so." The novelist must be faithful to the truth of human experience—real, universal experience—which is that human relations never do get tidily wrapped up: but he must deploy his artistic skill to make the reader believe— as the shapely narrated design completes itself—that they have so ended in this particular case. Of all the actual endings in the novels of Henry James, perhaps that of *The Wings of the Dove* in 1904 most compellingly illustrates this post-Victorian aesthetic principle: an ending that is not an ending.

Merton Densher has been bequeathed an enormous fortune by the now deceased Milly Theale. He tells his lover Kate Croy that he will marry her, but only after giving up the money. This is the final dialogue:

> Kate: ". . . her memory's your love. You *want* no other."
>
> He heard her out in silence, watching her face but not moving.
> Then he only said, "I'll marry you, mind you, in an hour."
> "As we were?"
> "As we were."
> But she turned to the door, and her headshake was now the end. "We shall never be again as we were."

Henry James frequently rated Dickens, Thackeray, and George Eliot as the greatest of the Victorian novelists, with Trollope (as we shall see) just a cut below them. The inclusion of Thackeray is a trifle suspect, and may be due to certain family anecdotes, so often repeated. Thackeray had called on the James family home on 14th Street in New York in the 1850s, and had expressed astonishment at young Henry's jacket with its silver buttons; and later had dined with the Jameses in Paris and had exclaimed with mock horror at seven-year-old Alice's costume: "Crinoline!—I was suspecting it! So young and so depraved!" James wrote only sparsely about Thackeray, and never tackled a major novel; James's tone tended to be humorously affectionate rather than critically analytic.

But Charles Dickens was undoubtedly a Victorian literary giant for Henry James. His stature for James, indeed, may be measured by the extent to which James attempted to belittle him; for even more than with George Eliot, James's strictures on Dickens betray what Harold Bloom has taught us to recognize as the anxiety of influence—the anxious need of one writer to downgrade the achievement of a threatening predecessor and so to assert the creative self. Thus Henry James, in a review of *Our Mutual Friend* in *The Nation*, in December 1865:

> "Our Mutual Friend" is, to our perception, the poorest of Mr. Dickens's works. And it is poor with the poverty not of momentary embarrassment, but of permanent exhaustion. It is wanting in inspiration. For the last ten years it has seemed to us that Mr. Dickens has been unmistakeably forcing himself. "Bleak House" was forced; "Little Dorritt" was labored; the present work is dug out with a spade and pickaxe.

So spoke the twenty-two-year-old American critic, who had apparently been reading Dickens attentively since he was twelve. James did take note of a number of delightful Dickensian items in *Our Mutual Friend*, but concluded by declaring it "depressing and unprofitable."

Even so, having dismissed two of the greatest of all English novels in half a dozen words, Henry James was transfixed, a year later, by an actual encounter with Charles Dickens. Dickens was on his American tour, and in Boston was taken to dinner at the home of the Nortons—who kindly invited young James to come by after dinner for an introduction. Looking back on the occasion half a century later, Henry James—quite free now of authorial anxiety, and able to acknowledge the experience for what it was, though with certain fictional flourishes, as will be apparent—evoked the occasion in shimmering prose: "As a young person of twenty-four I took part, restrictedly yet exaltedly, in that occasion—and an immense privilege I held it to slip in at all—from after dinner on." It was impossible, James held, to explain to the present younger generation what it meant to a literarily aspiring youth of the 1860s to be in the presence of Charles Dickens.

> There has been since his extinction no corresponding case—as to the relation between benefactor and beneficiary, or debtor and creditor; no other debt in our time has been piled so high, for those carrying it, as the long, the purely "Victorian" pressure of that obligation. It was the pressure, the feeling, that made it . . . So that on the evening I speak of at Shady Hill, it was as a slim and shaken vessel of the feeling that one stood there—of the feeling in the first place diffused, public and universal, and in the second place all unfathomably, undemonstrably, unassistedly and, as it were, unrewardingly proper to one's self as an already groping and fumbling, already dreaming and yearning dabbler in the mystery [of creativity].

James recalled that he trembled in every limb; yet Dickens, facing him for a second in a doorway, was not a mere blur, but rather "shining with august particulars." James recorded an "extremely handsome face, the face of symmetry yet of formidable character . . . which met my dumb homage with an inscrutability, a merciless *military* eye . . . which at once indicated to me . . . a kind of economy of apprehension."

Henry James, we recognize, was never a more artful and luminous writer of fiction than when he was, allegedly, simply reminiscing. A further example of this nicely deceptive practice, and likewise with its Dickensian dimension, may be seen in his evocation—in the last and never completed portion of his autobiography, *The Middle Years*—of his wandering about Craven Street, a street just off the Strand, during his 1869 stay in London. What he recalled was an area that

> absolutely reeked to my fond fancy, with associations born of the particular ancient piety embodied in one's private altar to Dickens . . . The whole Dickens procession marched up and down, the whole Dickens world looked out of its queer, quiet sinister windows—for it was the socially sinister Dickens, I am afraid, rather than the socially encouraging or confoundingly comic who was still at that moment most apt to meet me with his reasons. Such a reason was just that look of the inscrutable riverward street, packed to blackness with accumulations of suffered experience . . .

What James has done there—to put the case with unJamesian directness and even reductiveness—is to cast back from 1915 to the London visit of 1869; and then to superimpose on that 1869 experience the atmosphere and coloration of his novel of 1885, *The Princess Casamassima*. *The Princess* is Henry James's most intensely Dickensian performance. It descends all openly from *Little Dorrit,* the novel James had once set aside as being too labored. It follows *Little Dorrit* in the character and stature of its diminutive protagonist, the young bookbinder Hyacinth Robinson; in its structure and some of its sequences; and most of all in its delineation of the city and the society of London. London is the overwhelming presence in *The Princess Casamassima* as it had been thirty years earlier in *Little Dorrit;* its twisting streets and overcast skies, its hurry and uproar, its bridges and shops and crowded pubs, its slum dwellings and Mayfair mansions, its speech. The whole Dickens procession, to borrow James's language in *The Middle Years*, marches up and down in it; the whole Dickens world looked out of its queer, quiet sinister windows—and it is, palpably, and to haunting effect the sinister Dickens world that we move through, as Hyacinth moves through the dark underworld of anarchist conspirators and assassination plotters, drawn to it yet alien to it. But it is a world begotten in large part by James's potent imagination, not the London Henry wrote happily home about in the actual months of late 1869 and early 1870.

When Anthony Trollope died in 1882, Henry James regarded the event as bringing to an end the great Victorian age in fiction: as a sign (so he put it in an article in the *Century*) "of the complete extinction of that group of admirable writers who, in England, during the preceding half century, had done so much to elevate the art of the novelist. The author of *The Warden, Barchester Towers*, of *Framley Parsonage*," James went on, "does not, to our mind, stand on the very same level as Dickens, Thackeray and George Eliot; for his talent was of a quality less fine than theirs. But he belonged to the same family—he had as much to tell us about English life, he was strong, genial and abundant."

James had not always spoken kindly of Trollope. In one of the first reviews he ever contrived, a comment on Trollope's *Miss Mackenzie* for *The Nation* in 1865, James described his liking of Trollope's fiction as a sort of amiable weakness. Citing *Can You Forgive Her?* to a friend, the same year, James said, "Yes, and I can forget her too": in his review, he let it be known that the novel "has nothing to teach us either about Mr. Trollope himself as a novelist, about English society as a theme for the novelist, or . . . about the complex human heart." After sitting next to Trollope at dinner in the winter of 1877, he depicted the English writer as "the dullest Briton of them all"; and reported to his brother that someone had described Trollope as "all gabble and glare." Nonetheless, he admittedly found Trollope, on other social occasions, most entertaining and enjoyable, good company; and in his critical retrospective, in 1883, he expressed an abiding admiration. Trollope's "great, his inestimable merit was a complete appreciation of the usual. . . . He felt all daily and immediate things as well as saw them, felt them in a simple, direct, salubrious way, with their sadness, their gladness, their charm, their comicality, all their obvious and measurable meanings."

That, it seems to me, is a very fair estimate of one part of Trollope's imaginative genius, though it hardly covers the whole of it; and it testifies—in this instance—to a talent (a complete appreciation of the usual) that James knew quite well that he personally lacked. But in one respect Henry James was appalled by Trollope—that is, by what he called Trollope's "suicidal satisfaction in reminding the reader that the story he was telling was only, after all, a make-believe." James deplored Trollope's habit of referring to the work in hand as a novel, and saying that it would all come out just as he, Trollope, wanted it to; that the reader need not worry about the happy ending and so on.

"It is impossible," James deposed, "to imagine what a novelist takes himself to be unless he regards himself as an historian. It is only as an historian that he has the smallest *locus standi*."

We may set beside those comments of 1883 James's ruminations at the end of his review of *Middlemarch* a decade earlier. Here he complained that, whatever the merits of the novel, "the author wishes to say too many things"; she wants "to recommend herself to a scientific audience," and in her diffuseness she writes more like an historian than a novelist. We see, here, Henry James marking out the delicate path, so to say, between imagination and reality; between the novelist's need to pretend that he is telling nothing but the truth about things, and his imaginative shape and rendering of his materials. James liked to say that a work of fiction was an impression of life; and from start to finish, he sought fidelity to both the impression (the artistic reshaping) and to the life (the actual).

Henry James could not of course know, or even guess, that Trollope's teasing habit of reminding his reader that the unfolding narrative was all pure make-believe would be a defining feature of American fiction in the 1960s and 1970s, when writers like John Barth—and Italo Calvino in Italy—would bring into the heart of their narrative speculations about such problems as the conventions of narrative and different ways of setting a story in motion.

Henry James's collected articles on English writers run to some 800 pages in the Library of America volume, published in 1984 and edited by Leon Edel. The volume also contains 500 pages of commentary on American writers, 37 of them (Emerson, Hawthorne, Howells, Parkman, Harriet Beecher Stowe, Catherine Fenimore Woolson, Whitman, and others). There are no less than 55 English writers addressed, mostly Victorian, though with Shakespeare at one end, so to speak, and at the other Rupert Brook (whom James greatly cherished, and whom he wrote about at length in 1916). This splendid and imposing volume contains 10 articles on George Eliot, amounting to 100 pages, 5 pieces and 43 pages on Trollope, 30 pages on Browning, and 40 pages on Robert Louis Stevenson. It is in its way—its quirky, shifting, often self-modifying way—a treasury of Victorian criticism.

James's more informal allusions to his London literary acquaintances are another kind of treasury. He spoke, for example, in 1869, of visiting the National Gallery, and having his eye caught by "a little man with an immense head dominating his small body and an extravagant mane of auburn hair, standing near him and talking 'with the greatest vivacity.'" It was Charles Algernon Swinburne, whom he recognized from a photograph. "To be admiring Titian, and to be admiring Swinburne, at the same time as Swinburne was admiring Titian, was bliss to the young author." (That passage comes from Fred Kaplan's very fine book *Henry James: The Imagination of Genius.*) And a little later, on the same visit, after being taken by the Nortons to dine at John Ruskin's house on Denmark Hill, James observed to his brother William that Ruskin seemed to be a man "scared back by the grim face of reality unto the world of unreason and illusion," where he "wanders without a compass or a guide—or any light save the fitful flashes of his beautiful genius."

On more than one occasion, James sat by and watched as Dante Gabriel Rosetti painted portrait after portrait of Jane Morris, now the wife of the poet and socialist William Morris, but formerly Rosetti's notoriously beautiful pre-Raphaelite mistress. Jane Morris, Henry informed his sister Alice, was "a tall lean woman in a long dress of some dead purple stuff . . . with a thin pale face, a pair of strange, sad, deep, dark Swinburnish eyes, with great thick black oblique brows, joined in the middle and tucking themselves away under her hair." William Morris, on the other hand, was "short, burly and corpulent, very careless and unfinished in his dress," a wonderful talker with "a very loud voice, and a nervous restless manner." One evening, while Jane lay back on a couch nursing a toothache, William Morris read to his guests parts of the not yet published sections of *The Earthly Paradise.*

It was probably Robert Browning whom Henry James most liked— plainly and simply liked—on the English literary scene. They encountered one another fairly often between 1870 and 1889, and James always had a good word for the poet—usually about a long intriguing conversation during dinner or after dinner. Browning and James shared a carriage to go to the Kental Green cemetery in the winter of 1888, to attend the funeral of their friend Adelaide Proctor. Browning was "infinitely talkative," James said later. He wrote a brief eloquent tribute to Browning after the poet's death in 1889, and in 1912, on the centenary of Browning's birth delivered a lengthy address on *The Ring and the Book* at the Royal Society of Literature in London. Henry James, great and original critic though he was, rarely wrote with any special discernment about poetry. He could—to make a James-like distinction—respond to the poetry of prose; but had relatively little sensibility for the poetry of poetry proper. If Browning's work proved the exception, it was because Browning was himself a master of narrative, in particular of dramatic monologue; and thus, as Fred Kaplan puts it, "had much to teach the novelist of relationships, of moral situations and discriminations, of the dramatic rendition of consciousness and human personality." Does any narrative stretch in Henry James provide a better example of the self-exposing narrator than the Duke of Ferrara in Browning's monologue "My Last Duchess"?

And beyond that, what James enjoyed and honored in Browning—as he said in the earlier tribute—was "the acceptance of life, the respect for its mysteries, the endurance of its changes . . . the validity of character, (and) the beauty of action."

Looking back from 1915 across fifty-five years to his teen-age school days in Switzerland, James remembered reading (mainly in the *Cornhill Magazine*, which Henry Senior sent on) writings by Thackeray, Dickens, George Eliot, and Trollope: those "various . . . deeper-toned strokes of the great Victorian clock," as he now thought them, which "were so many steps in the march of the age." The metaphor of Victorian culture, generally, as a clock—measuring and recording the successive beats of time and history—was an apt one; and with the death of Queen Victoria in January 1901, the clock stopped ticking. James surprised himself by the extent of his grief for the country's loss: "I mourn the safe and motherly old middle-class queen," he wrote William, "who held the nation warm under the fold of her big, hideous, Scotch-plaid shawl . . . I felt her death more than I should have expected; she was a sustaining symbol—and the wild waters are upon us now." The wild waters, that is, of the unpredictable twentieth century.

Two elderly survivors of the Victorian literary era might well be mentioned here: George Meredith, who was in his seventies at the time of the old Queen's death, and Thomas Hardy, who was entering his sixties. James found almost nothing to like about Hardy's novels, saying typically about *Far from the Madding Crowd* in 1874 that "the most genuine thing in [the] book . . . is a certain aroma of the meadows and lanes—a natural relish for harvesting and sheep-washing." But for George Meredith, his affection was strong and deep.

James never wrote a critical word about George Meredith, and we are indebted to Edith Wharton for a verbal picture of the two writers together. This was in 1908, when Meredith was eighty and almost completely deaf. James took Mrs. Wharton to Fox Hill to call on Meredith, and she, years later, recalled how, from her corner in the little sitting-room she watched

> the nobly confronted profiles of the two old friends: Meredith's so classically distinguished from the spring of the wavy hair to the line of the straight noses . . . and James's heavy Roman head so realistically and vigorously his own . . . As they sat there, James benignly listening, Meredith eloquently discoursing, and their

old deep regard for each other burning steadily through the surface eloquence and the surface attentiveness, I felt I was in great company and I was glad.

Among those wild waters, meanwhile, were a number of younger literary talents, on some of whom, at least, James kept a benevolent if always sharply observant eye. For Joseph Conrad, he entertained a healthy professional respect. When informed by Edmund Gosse in 1902 that Conrad was in dire financial straits, James at once rallied to the cause. "His production . . . has all been fine, rare & valid," he wrote the Royal Society, urging it to make Conrad a grant. ". . . His successive books have been real literature, of a distinguished sort." James singled out two works by Conrad for special praise: *The Nigger of the Narcissus* ("the very finest & strongest picture of sea & sea-life that our language possesses") and *Lord Jim* (which runs the earlier text "very close"). Half a dozen years later, perhaps after reading *The Secret Agent* (the case is not clear), James wrote a personal word to Conrad: "I read you as I listen to rare music—with deepest depths of surrender, and out of those depths I emerge slowly and reluctantly again, to acknowledge that I return to life." One does not feel, however, that James's own fiction-making imagination was in any way affected or challenged by his reading of Conrad. Perhaps by 1908, Henry James was beyond the state of being so affected.

With Rudyard Kipling, James clearly felt closer, as well as more intrigued and challenged. When the India-born writer came to England in 1890, at the age of twenty-five, James was persuaded to write an introduction to his collection of stories, *Mine Own People*, saying in it, among other things, that Kipling was "a bristling adventurer" in literature, and that Kipling was particularly attractive to the kind of critic (the right kind, James insisted) who wants to be challenged by a writer, who seeks "an appeal to interpretation, intelligence, ingenuity, to what is elastic in the critical mind." (Surely James had always sought to appeal in that very same way.) When he came to know Kipling, James characterized him as "the most complete man of genius (as distinguished from 'fine' intelligence) that I have ever known"; Kipling in fact was a prodigy, an "infant monster." And not long after that: Kipling was "the most curious—to me—of all literary phenomena; so exclusively a genius, as essentially one as a typewriter is a typewriter. I mean as inapt for anything out of his particular line as this machine to boil a potato."

That is strange and teasing language. It is tempting to speculate—Fred Kaplan hints at this in his tactful and sensitive manner—that Kipling's personality exerted a powerful attraction to Henry James, while at the same time warning James away from any sort of

deeper intimacy—intimacy of a sort that James did sometimes enjoy or seek, fastidiously and watchfully, with several other younger
writers.

Finally, there is the case of H. G. Wells.

James and Wells had known each other since 1898, and had exchanged a series of letters conveying praise and enthusiasm. James
wrote fulsomely, one letter after the other, about Wells's *The Time
Machine, Mankind in the Making,* and *A Modern Utopia;* and after reading the novel *Kipps* in 1905, he told "My dear Wells" that "you are,
for me, more than ever, the most interesting 'literary man' of your
generation—in fact, the only interesting one." He added—in a clear
tone of regard and amusement—that "In everything you do . . . it is
the quality of your intellect that obsesses me . . . to that degree that
even the colossal dimensions of your Cheek (pardon the term that
I don't in the least invidiously apply) fails to break the spell. Indeed
your Cheek is positively the very sign and stamp of your genius."

Wells evidently grew restive with such banter, mixed though it
might be with warmly laudatory comments. Then, in 1914, James
brought out a long two-part article in the *Times Literary Supplement*
called "The Younger Generation" (it was reprinted as a single essay
called "The New Novel"). Here James identified Conrad, Galsworthy,
Arnold Bennett, and Wells as comprising the now slightly older literary generation, with Hugh Walpole, Compton Mackenzie, and
D. H. Lawrence, among others, representing the younger breed. It
was, for James, a somewhat meandering piece; but he used it to sum
up his belated thought about the great Victorian period in fiction.
He characterized that age as essentially sentimental, romantic, and,
in his word, "dodgy": that is, given to steering clear of the meaner
and less inviting aspects of human life. "Who could pretend," he
asked, "that Dickens was anything but romantic, and even more romantic in his humour, if possible, than in his pathos. . . . Who could
pretend that Jane Austen didn't leave much more untold than told
about the aspects and manners even of the confined circle in which
her muse revolved?"

Wells and the others, so James argued, were resolutely realistic,
and they wanted to leave nothing out in their account of life. Their
technique, he kept repeating, was one of *saturation* (Tolstoy was the
leader and exemplar in this development); they wanted to tell us
everything they knew, and they knew an extraordinary amount. Literary *method,* James implied, was quite neglected in the interest of
novelistic *matter.* Wells was treated at great length and as the prime
figure in the English literary world.

Wells, however, took the whole thing as a sort of elitist literary
put-down, and resentment that had been simmering for some years

erupted in the savagely satirical Wellsian contrivance called *Boon,* which purported to be a selection from the literary remains of one George Boon. The fourth chapter was called "Of Art, of Literature, of Mr. Henry James," and contained an alleged conversation with and about the said James. In it (these passages have been quoted many a time), James is accused of being exactly the opposite of what James attributed to Wells and company. His besetting sin was that he left everything *out:* "In all of his novels you will find no people with defined political opinions, no people with religious opinions, none with clear partisanships or with lusts or whims. There are no poor people, people dominated by the imperatives of Saturday night and Monday morning. . . . All that much of humanity, he clears out before he begins his story."

And then, the deeper thrust: "The thing his novel is about is always there. . . . It is like a church lit but without a congregation to distract you, with every light and line focused on the high altar. And on the altar, very reverently placed, intensely there, is a dead kitten, an egg shell, a bit of string."

There was, of course, a certain real point to this witty mordant stabbing, with its Jamesian turn of phrase ("intensely there"). Some of James's own literary characters (the central consciousness in "The Beast in the Jungle" comes first to mind) eventually realize that a nothingness, an emptiness, a failure of response has comprised the essence of their lives. James, in any case, rallied after a bit to reply to Wells; and Wells, replying in turn, expressed contrition that he had not couched his disagreement with James in more gracious terms.

But even as James had defined his personal creative self by relation to—partially in opposition to, or extension beyond—the great Victorians, so now the conspicuous figure in the younger English generation was seeking to establish *his* creative self by opposition to James and what he took to be the dominant strain in literature and criticism. He recoiled, Wells said, from "dignity, finish and perfection in literature." "To you literature like painting is an end, to me literature like architecture is a means, it has a use. Your view was, I feel, too dominant in the world of criticism and I assailed it in terms of harsh antagonism."

James concluded this epochal exchange, on July 10, 1915, by identifying himself, as a literary practitioner, in the most vibrant phrasing he had ever hit upon. He believed most deeply, he said, that literature lived in the individual writer—"that is why I have always so admired your so free and strong application of it, the particular rich receptacle of intelligences and impressions emptied out with an energy of its own . . . Of course, for myself," James went on moving towards an identification that had been almost sixty years in the making, "I live, live intensely, I am fed by life, and my value, whatever it is, is in my own kind of expression of that." And then, finally, "It is art that makes life, makes interest, makes importance . . . and I know of no substitute for the force and beauty of the process."

Spring Semester 1996

# 6

# In Praise of Kipling

## THOMAS PINNEY

For many years I have taught a course in expository writing at
Pomona College. I follow the old-fashioned plan for such work,
assigning exercises in the description of a process, in comparison and contrast, division and classification, and so on. The final paper in the course is always a paper of praise, and this, I tell my
students, is not only the final paper but by far the hardest to write.
Praise does not seem to come easily to most of us, and though the
language is full of resource for insult and denigration, the vocabulary of praise—as anyone who has ever had to write a letter of recommendation knows very well—is comparatively meager. It is bland,
it is general, it is unpersuasive. The experience of Caliban, in
Shakespeare's *Tempest*, seems relevant. As he says to Prospero:

> You taught me language; and my profit on't
> Is, I know how to curse.

But I have now undertaken to do what, as I tell my students, it is
so very hard to do, that is, to write a paper of praise. I will try to be
something more than bland, general, and unpersuasive, but you
will, I hope, keep in mind the difficulty of the enterprise.

My job is made a little easier, before an American audience at
any rate, because for you I suspect that Kipling is largely an undiscovered country, and, like the early travelers in the New World, I
can say the most extravagant things without fear that anyone can
contradict me. Kipling is not read in the schools, and he is, so far as
my experience goes, practically invisible in our colleges and universities. The unexamined stock label of "Imperialist" that has been

stuck on Kipling seems to have been all that a politically correct
generation needed to know about him. And there has been another,
quite accidental, cause for the very limited notion of Kipling that
prevails in America. Kipling streaked like a rocket across the literary sky in 1890, when the Indian stories and *Barrack-Room Ballads*
appeared to astonish readers not just in England but wherever in
the world English was read. The earliest copyright agreement between England and the United States did not come into effect until
July of 1892, and until that time everything that Kipling wrote was
available for free to any American publisher who wished to exploit
the sensational fame of young Kipling. *Plain Tales from the Hills, Soldiers Three, The Phantom, 'Rickshaw, Under the Deodars, Wee Willie Winkie,
Barrack-Room Ballads*—all these, and more, the almost prodigal production of the young Kipling in the four years between 1888 and
1892, were reprinted, over and over again, by American publishers,
not just in the 1890s but steadily thereafter. Kipling, of course, went
on to a notably long and productive literary career after the international copyright agreement of 1892—the great bulk of his writing all comes after that date—but the American idea of Kipling
remains distorted by that accident of the uncopyrighted early
Kipling. Now that *all* of Kipling is out of copyright, the list of work
available to an American reader is really quite representative (though
one will look in vain for such books as *Rewards and Fairies*, or the late
masterpiece, *Debits and Credits*, among the reprints). But a glance at
the contents of such contemporary selections as *Kipling Stories* or
*The Best Short Stories of Rudyard Kipling*, books that we may suppose
express the currently prevailing notions, will invariably show that
the idea of what Kipling is all about is still dominated by those stories written by the young, uncopyrighted, Indian Kipling.

    Writing about Tennyson at a time when Tennyson was much de-
spised, T. S. Eliot observed that Tennyson has "three qualities which
are seldom found together except in the greatest poets: abundance,
variety, and complete competence." I think the same proposition
can fairly be made about Kipling, and I will, accordingly, divide my
sermon into those three heads: abundance, variety, and competence.
To take the matter of "abundance" first. Kipling did not have a very
long life: it conformed exactly to the Psalmist's measure of three
score years and ten, half of which was lived in the nineteenth and
half in the twentieth century. But he was a notably precocious writer,
and so a full fifty of those seventy years belong to his literary career.
He was not yet seventeen when he began work as a journalist in
Lahore. It took him only a few years to establish himself as a profes-

sional, one who could handle any kind of story, and only a short time after that to be recognized as a star of Indian journalism, one whose name had a following and who was allowed to go pretty much his own way. Much of what Kipling wrote in those few years in India was anonymous, so we won't ever have a complete record of it. But what we *can* identify is certainly impressive in quantity: Andrew Rutherford's recent collection of Kipling's uncollected early verse makes a stout volume of nearly 500 pages, and that was all written before Kipling had returned to England to make a name for himself. The tally of his anonymous Indian journalism has also been increased recently by several hundreds of new attributions. And there was of course that copious outpouring of stories, already spoken of as making up the dominant American idea of Kipling; these stories first appeared in the Indian newspapers and were collected in such volumes as *Soldiers Three* and *Under the Deodars.*

Kipling was never again so furiously productive as he had been towards the end of his Indian years, but his output was steady and full right down to the end of his life. He suffered no writer's block; he was never anxious about where the next story might come from, but was always besieged by ideas. He liked to write—he said that the covering of white paper with black ink was a sensuous pleasure to him—and he threw away far more than he ever published. And so he went on writing in unbroken productivity. When he died he left an unfinished autobiography that was published, but we can only guess at how much else that had not yet seen the light was destroyed by his defensive widow. There is no complete edition of Kipling, but as I count through his works, I estimate that, properly collected, it would run to at least fifty-five volumes. So I think that we may take the matter of copiousness as settled.

As to variety, I wonder whether Kipling can be matched by any modern English or American writer of reputation? On this point, it seems to me that most people are not very well informed—we hear so much about the Indian Kipling that we hardly think of any other kind of Kipling—so I would like to dwell at some length on how many different things Kipling managed to do as a writer. Between the unclassifiable *Jungle Books* and the densely allusive and sophisticated stories of the later period, all sorts of forms, subjects, and moods may be found. The stories in *The Jungle Books* and in *Just So Stories* show that he could write the best kind of children's literature, the kind that children and grown-ups both like to read, and that, like other classic works of the kind, enter into all sorts of cultural forms: *The Jungle Books* provide the symbolism and ritual of the

Cub Scout movement; they have recently been made into a play and an opera in England; and they survive their transformations at the hands of the Disney studio.

Another kind of children's story is in the two series of historical tales in *Puck of Pook's Hill* and *Rewards and Fairies*: these, too, may be read by both children and adults, but not, perhaps, in the same way as *The Jungle Books* and the *Just So Stories* can be. Kipling designed the history tales to speak to both audiences, grown-ups and children, but in different ways, according to the different experiences that each brought to them. Child and adult are, I think, equal before the *Just So Stories;* but their responses to "A Centurion of the Thirtieth" or "Marklake Witches" will differ widely according to their different knowledge.

Kipling even ventured into school-book history when he collaborated with the Oxford historian C. R. L. Fletcher in *A School History of England*. Nominally, Kipling contributed only the verses that punctuate the narrative at interesting points, but there is evidence that the collaboration was quite close and that Kipling had a hand in the narrative, as he certainly did in the general outlook and tendency of the book.

Kipling is, of course, the supreme short-story writer in English literature. Practically speaking, the form did not exist in English literature before Kipling appeared (American literature, in this respect, is a different story); after he left it, one could say that it hardly needed anything more done for it. The term "short story," in Kipling's case, conceals a great variety. There are historical short stories, like "The Church that Was at Antioch" or "The Eye of Allah"; there are stories that we would now call science fiction, like "With the Night Mail" and "As Easy as A.B.C."; there are many stories that invoke, in some way, the element of the "occult" or of inexplicable spiritual force, an element whose prominence in Kipling's work is perhaps not sufficiently recognized: these include stories as different as "They," or "A Madonna of the Trenches," or "The House Surgeon." The stories of India themselves run through a wide range of kinds. A few—only a few—might be called apologies for Empire—such stories as "The Tomb of His Ancestors," or "The Head of the District," or "William the Conqueror." These, however, bear no very high proportion to the whole. Much more common are the wryly amused, lightly satiric, ultimately admiring accounts of English administrators and soldiers at work down in the capital towns or at play, most often up in the hills at Simla. These are the prose equivalents of the verses in *Departmental Ditties*: stories such as "The Arrest of Lieutenant Golightly" or "Wressley of the Foreign Office," or any of those stories in which Mrs. Hauksbee figures. When Kipling ventures beyond the lines of the English settlement to look at native life, there is more than one kind of response. Sometimes the Englishman confronts the inexplicable and ultimately terrifying otherness of the Indian world—"Beyond the Pale," for example, or "The Mark of the Beast"; sometimes what one sees are simply interesting glimpses of native life, as in the stories about elephants; sometimes the view takes one far beyond the safety of the English quarter to places where the English presence seems strange and meaningless and only the native life makes any sense: such stories as "Without Benefit of Clergy," or "Lisbeth," or "On the City Wall." And to name just one more category, a very important category, from the rich array contained in the Indian stories, there are those that go well beyond the limits of the realistic sketch to reveal an imaginative understanding of the English in India, which includes an understanding of how precarious and transitory their position is: these stories include some of the most powerful that Kipling ever wrote: "The Man Who Would Be King," "The Strange Ride of Morrowbie Jukes," and "The Bridge-Builders."

India as a literary subject really occupied Kipling only for about a decade. It was at an end in about 1900. After that he was as likely to write about ancient Rome or neolithic Europe or revolutionary America as anything else. There is also a large body of specifically English stories. Kipling in some sense belonged to no country at all: he had been born in Bombay but was sent back to be schooled in England; when he returned to India, he spent part of his years there in Muslim Lahore and part in Hindu Allahabad. When he went back to England, it was only for a brief stay before he married an American wife, built a house outside Brattleboro, Vermont, and there began to raise a family. After he left America, he divided his life for almost a decade between summers in England and winters in South Africa. And in his later years, he almost preferred France to England. For him, then, England always kept something of the flavor of a foreign place: he liked to say that England was one of the great unknown countries, where one could discover layer after layer of unregarded history.

That was one reason Kipling became one of the first enthusiasts for motor travel in England: he had a car as early as 1899, and, though he never drove one, by that means was enabled to carry out what he called "the discovery of England." Here I would like to read at some length from one of Kipling's letters, this one written in 1904, because it seems to me particularly eloquent on the subject:

> But the chief end of my car, so far as I am concerned, is the discovery of England. To me it is a land full of stupefying marvels

and mysteries. . . . for instance, in six hours, I can go from the land of the *Ingoldsby Legends* by way of the Norman Conquest and Barons' War into Richard Jefferies' country, and so through the Regency, one of Arthur Young's less known tours, and *Celia's Arbour*, into Gilbert White's territory. Horses, after all, are only horses, but the car is a time-machine on which one can slide from one century to another at no more trouble than the pushing forward of a lever. On a morning I have seen the Assizes, javelin-men and all, come into a cathedral town; by noon I was skirting a new-built convent for expelled French nuns; before sundown I was watching the Channel Fleet off Selsea Bill, and after dark I nearly broke a fox's back on a Roman road. You who were born and bred in the land naturally take such trifles for granted, but to me it is still miraculous that if I want petrol in a hurry I must either pass the place where Sir John Lade lived or the garden where Jack Cade was killed. . . . in England the dead, twelve coffin deep, clutch hold of my wheels at every turn, till I sometimes wonder that the very road does not bleed (to Filson Young, April 1904).

But he did not neglect contemporary life: England, from the late Victorian through the Jazz Age, is richly represented in Kipling's stories, always with a sense of its long historical past felt in its present. There is rural Sussex in "Friendly Brook"; there is country-house England in the high Edwardian afternoon in "An Error in the Fourth Dimension"; there is the post-war England of radio sets and omnibus tours in "The Wish House." And this is only the beginning of the list that might be made. A special sub-category of Kipling's English stories is in *Stalky & Co.*, in which he took an existing genre of no particular artistic merit, the English schoolboy story, and reinvented it as the vehicle of ideas quite subversive of official school morality: what Kipling praised, in the words of Noel Annan, was "the underground code of the boys who, leading a life of debonair cribbing, smoking and drinking, learnt to harden their shell, to submit to being crammed if cramming enabled one to enter the army, to see facts as they were, never to expect fairness, not to betray their emotions or their comrades" (*The Headmaster*, p. 6).

Many of the stories are comic: Kipling is not usually thought of as a humorous writer, but *he* certainly thought that he was, and, towards the end of his career, published a large volume of his comic stories under the title of *Humorous Tales from Rudyard Kipling;* these include such things as "The Village That Voted the Earth Was Flat," "My Sunday at Home," and "The Puzzler." What is or is not funny is a very vexed question; but, as I have said that this talk will contain nothing but praise, I will say no more here about Kipling as humorist.

A small body of stories is made up of frankly non-realistic, symbolic fiction, quasi-allegories that depart wholly from the realistic conventions that dominate the short story: "The Children of the Zodiac," "The Enemies to Each Other," "The Bull That Thought." These remind us that Kipling was always drawn to the story as parable rather than the story as history.

There is a sort of cosmic division of artists into the class of putter-inners and the class of leaver-outers, and there can be no question that Kipling belongs in the second of these, the class of leaver-outers. All his artistic tendencies are towards compression, implication, the significant omission. He tells us that it was his practice to keep a fine-haired brush and a bottle of blackest India ink on his desk, and with this he would go over a finished story, lining out unnecessary words and phrases. He would then put the work aside to drain, as he said, after which the process of deletion would be repeated. He favored the highly wrought, the carefully designed, the thoughtfully revised composition rather than the contraries of these things. It is no wonder, we think, that the strong patterns of verse and the concentrated form of the short story are what attracted him as an artist. But, since my theme here is Kipling's variety, we must not forget that he wrote long fictions too. The first is the very early work called *The Light That Failed*; then followed *Captains Courageous*, the most ambitious work that came directly out of Kipling's American years; and finally *Kim*, an acknowledged masterpiece and Kipling's valedictory to his Indian experience. None of these long fictions fits the conventions of the nineteenth-century novel, but they are not the less interesting for that fact. If Kipling had written nothing else he would still be seen as a master.

Kipling began as a journalist, and despite all the varied work that he went on to, the taste for journalism never quite left him. It shows up in the considerable descriptive writing that he continued to do, long after his years of meeting newspaper deadlines were over. I wonder how many of you know such things as the virtuoso sketch called "Leaves from a Winter Note-Book," an account of winter as one experiences it in Vermont, or the series of articles written in 1927 called "Brazilian Sketches," or the brilliant descriptions of American scenes—San Francisco, the Columbia River, Yellowstone, Chicago, Niagara Falls, Chautauqua—sketches that the unknown journalist named Rudyard Kipling wrote for the Indian press in 1889? Some of his most characteristic things appear in these writings, and they remind us, too, of how much Kipling saw in his lifetime. He visited all of the continents, and it would be possible to do a whole array of books on the principle of one interesting collection recently published called *Kipling's Japan:* we might have Kipling's South Africa, Kipling's North Africa, Kipling's Mediterranean, Kipling's

United States, Kipling's Commonwealth, or Kipling's France—never mind Kipling's India—without any straining after material. I may add here that I have edited a collection called *Kipling's California,* and much had to be omitted from that.

A special category of Kipling's descriptive writing—what I have been calling his journalism, though that is hardly an adequate word—are his sketches of military operations, much of it about the navy, and most of it done as war-work. It includes such series as *A Fleet in Being,* on the state of the British navy at the end of the 19th century; *France at War,* sketches from the western front in 1915; *Tales of the Trade,* on submarine warfare; *The War among the Mountains,* on the Italian front; and *Destroyers at Jutland,* written after the naval battle of that name. All of these appeared originally in newspapers, and some were written under official sponsorship. They are all neglected titles now, but Kipling touched nothing that he did not adorn, and they are all eminently characteristic, readable, and interesting.

Kipling's only son, John, joined the Irish Guards on the outbreak of the war when he was barely seventeen, and was killed almost immediately upon reaching the front in 1915. For several years after the war Kipling devoted most of his time and energy to writing a long history of the war service of his son's regiment, a history called *The Irish Guards in the Great War;* an immensely detailed narrative published in two opulent volumes, it is, no doubt, a work of devotion, perhaps even of expiation, but it remains, if not the least-known, then almost certainly the least-read of all Kipling's major works.

I hope that by this point I have made Kipling seem Protean enough to you; but I have not done yet. There is another, now much-neglected, form in which Kipling excelled: he gave quite good speeches. Kipling lived into the age of film and radio—even to the earliest days of television—but he belonged to a time when the art of rhetorical performance before a living audience—the art of speech-making—was far from dead. Some of these speeches are collected in a volume called *A Book of Words,* and they show quite clearly that they belong not just to Kipling's biography but to Kipling's art. There are thirty-one speeches in the book, delivered over a period of 21 years, from 1906 to 1927 (a later edition extends the count to 37 speeches); they were delivered to medical societies, to military cadets, to South African businessmen, to the Royal Academy, to his son's public school literary society, to the faculty of the Sorbonne, to the Brazilian Academy of Letters, and to all sorts of other audiences on all sorts of occasions. Like all that Kipling did, his speeches are admirable compositions, and are quite often as vivid and as complex as his expression in other forms. I have, incidentally, made it a point of special interest in working over Kipling's letters, to identify as many of his speeches as I can, with rather surprising results. My current tally is 108 speeches, given over a period of almost fifty years. There are no texts for some of them—we know only that he gave them. But altogether they make a considerable addition to the Kipling canon. At least two of them were given as radio broadcasts which were recorded at the time; so it is still possible not just to read Kipling, but to hear him speak: an interesting experience. One may also add the footnote here that Kipling wrote a good many speeches for members of the royal family, a thing that he did not particularly enjoy doing but that he could hardly refuse.

The speeches that Kipling collected in *A Book of Words* are each prefaced with a motto or epigraph written by Kipling himself in imitation of the ancient texts that one finds in the Greek Anthology. This leads me to say a word on a final category in the list of Kipling's performances in the medium of prose. He was a distinguished writer of inscriptions and epitaphs, that most compressed and most difficult of public forms. He had some practice when the great memorial to Cecil Rhodes was being built on the slopes of Table Mountain in Cape Town: Kipling was one of the committee responsible for its design, and contributed three texts to be inscribed on the memorial. The great demand for inscriptions, however, came after the war, when the whole world was building memorials. Kipling had a central part in this work, for he was an original member of the Imperial War Graves Commission (now the Commonwealth War Graves Commission) when that body was formed in 1917, and he remained active on it until his death. The Commission was charged with the work of providing decent burial and memorial for the unprecedented numbers of war dead all over the world: this took the form of scores and hundreds of military cemeteries and even more memorials associated with them. Down to 1936, all of the inscriptions used on these memorials were either written by or approved by Kipling himself: his own inscriptions appear in, for example, the cemeteries at Baghdad, Dar-es-Salaam, and Thiepval. They may also be found on memorials in Melbourne, London, Edinburgh, Ottawa, and many other places. Some are for quite special categories: to the journalists who fell in the war, for example, in the offices of the Institute of Journalists in London, or to the dead actors, who have a memorial in the church at Stratford on Avon.

Some of these inscriptions are not in prose but in verse, and that takes me to my next illustration of Kipling's variety. For Kipling was not just one of the most fertile and various prose writers of his time but a great poet as well. It is typical of what might be called the Kipling problem in criticism that we speak almost invariably of Kipling's verse, not of his poetry. Kipling himself gave the lead for this practice, using very modest or even self-denigrating terms for his work: the very first independent book that he published was called *Departmental Ditties*—who else has ever chosen to appear before the public as a singer of "ditties"?—and many of his poems thereafter appeared as simple "ballads" or "songs." The collected edition of his poems put out shortly after Kipling's death has always been called *Rudyard Kipling's Verse: Definitive Edition.* It is, of course, anything but definitive. In his well-known essay on Kipling, published as a preface to *A Choice of Kipling's Verse,* T. S. Eliot wrestled with the question of whether Kipling was a poet or a versifier, with somewhat dubious results. I think we can be clear about the matter and conclude to call Kipling a poet, without further argument. He was copious—the so-called "definitive" edition runs to more than 800 pages; and he was various. He delighted in metrical experiment, he tried all the forms that might challenge the ingenuity of a poet, and he wrote poems in every tone and mood. This fact has been largely concealed by the over-familiarity of a few texts—especially "If" (recently voted the most popular poem in England), "Recessional," and "The White Man's Burden."

I am prepared to argue for the excellence of these poems, but the point here is simply that we hear them—or fragments of them—too often to be able to respond in an alert and perceptive way. Kipling always refused direct requests to write occasional verse, but he liked to write such things on his own motion, and there is no doubt that the results, the work of the "public" Kipling, are often hard for us to respond to sympathetically. They have too much of the Old Testament in their manner for us, though that cannot be a final judgment. Another age may be moved by them, as an earlier age was. The "public" poems also share in one of Kipling's distinguishing gifts, his power of inventing the striking and memorable phrases— "the white man's burden," "lest we forget," and "what should they know of England who only England know?" The current edition of the *Oxford Dictionary of Quotations* lists 202 items under Kipling's name: I don't know where that would rank him on the list of quotable poets, but his place would surely be high.

Whatever one may think of Kipling's humor in prose, he wrote delightful comic verse, and he had a remarkable gift for parody. One of his earliest works was a volume of verse, written in collaboration with his sister and published in India, called *Echoes.* The book consists of imitations of the standard poets applied incongruously to the daily life of the English in India, imitations carried out with high skill and with amusing results. They show how completely Kipling could enter into the form of another writer, and may make us regret that Kipling never allowed himself to publish any remark of any kind on any contemporary writer. At the other end of feeling, Kipling wrote poems of great lyric intensity on the eternal subjects of suffering, grief, and loss—"The Prayer of Miriam Cohen," "The Way through the Woods," "My Boy Jack." Verse and prose often went hand in hand for Kipling, and many of his finest poems were written to accompany his stories, sometimes as songs within the stories, but more often as chapter headings or tailpieces. This is a practice that goes back in English literature to Sir Walter Scott, but Kipling brought it to a new level of interest and complexity. As T. S. Eliot has said, the verse and the prose cannot be separated but combine together to make a third thing different from either. Another of Kipling's modes is the satiric, in which he showed, in my judgment, an almost unmatched power. The savagery of "Gehazi," which no editor would publish even when Kipling was at the height of his popularity and reputation, can still be immediately felt, even when the public scandal that provoked it has long passed out of memory. So, too, with "Cleared," or "The Islanders," the poem for whose lines about English sport ("the flannelled fools at the wicket or the muddied oafs at the goals") the English have not yet quite forgiven Kipling.

The strength of satire and the passion of lyric come together in the marvellous series of "Epitaphs of the War" that Kipling wrote during and after the Great War. Anyone who thinks that Kipling, as a poet, is merely the boisterous singer of a eupeptic expansionism need only to glance at these epitaphs to extinguish that idea at once and for ever. The fact is that Kipling, as a poet, carries even further the work that Craig Raine has described so well as one of the main motives of Kipling's prose, the work of giving voice to every kind of awareness. Henry James's outburst, provoked by reading Kipling's stories about railroad locomotives and steamships, is well-known: "He has come down steadily from the simple in subject to the more simple—from the Anglo-Indians to the natives, from the natives to the Tommies, from the Tommies to the quadrupeds, from the quadrupeds to the fish, and from the fish to the engines and screws." James is expressing his exasperation, but *we* might convert the remark into a part of the praise of Kipling, for it recognizes his power to give a voice to everything, whether it be in itself articulate or dumb, fluent or without any words or all.

It is remarkable how often—I do not say how successfully—but certainly how often, Kipling's poems have been set to music. There are not any reliable figures on such matters, but according to my sources some 400 musical settings of about 180 of Kipling's poems have been published. There is probably a critical fact of some importance in this, but I mention it only as a final remark on the subject of Kipling's variety. As an artist in words, he offers us the complete range of expression—spoken, written, and, through these many musical settings, sung.

After abundance and variety, the third of my heads is the matter of "complete competence." Kipling has always attracted the admiring interest of other writers, particularly of writers who themselves had a high regard for form and method—one need only mention Henry James, Joseph Conrad, James Joyce, T. S. Eliot, Hemingway, and, outside the English tradition, Jorge Luis Borges. As C. S. Lewis has argued, so long as a writer has one admirer among intelligent readers, that is a good writer; and with such an array of distinguished admirers, Kipling qualifies over and over again. But what was it that they admired? First—because most obvious—is the brilliant skill in description. Here, for a single instance, is a passage descriptive of sounds at sea. The narrator is falling asleep on a bunk in a torpedo boat, next to the "quivering steel wall" of the hull:

> The sea, sliding over 267's skin, worried me with importunate, half-caught confidences. It drummed tackily to gather my attention, coughed, spat, cleared its throat, and on the even of that portentous communication, retired up-stage as a multitude whispering. Anon I caught the tramp of armies afoot, the hum of crowded cities awaiting the event.

This is perhaps almost too rich, but it gives a hint of what Kipling can do. There is no point, however, in further illustration. It would be endless, and it would also be pointless, for such virtuosity is never indulged in for its own sake but is always subordinated to the design of the whole. Kipling, as I have already said, was a writer for whom every stroke counted. Yet this economy is allied with great richness of implication. He is a master of allusion, so that the words and phrases of his stories constantly set up connections with worlds of experience beyond their immediate limits. Such a combination of brevity with concentration means that the stories are, to use one of Henry James's favorite terms, thoroughly "done." Kipling's fellow artists were quick to recognize that quality.

Kipling, on the whole, was content to work within the conventions of realistic fiction that dominated European and American literature in the late-nineteenth century, when he was formed as a writer. The stories do not appear to present any remarkable formal experiments, but they are not therefore without their difficulties. The indirections and the omissions of some of the stories—"Mrs Bathurst" and "The Dog Hervey" are perhaps the most notorious instances, but there are many others—have baffled all readers, and there is hardly any story of Kipling's that will not merely profit from but almost seems to require the services of a commentator. He has, incidentally, one of the richest vocabularies among modern English writers, a vocabulary in part dialectal and in part exotic—Indian words, most obviously—but for the most part thoroughly English: he simply commanded a much wider repertoire than most of us enjoy, and he knew how to use it. In the second edition of the *Oxford English Dictionary,* Kipling is cited 2,601 times in illustration of English usage. I have tried to give an idea of the range of his diction in the list of unusual or out-of-the-way terms that I have handed out to you today. Such a list could no doubt be much extended, but this one will be enough to suggest to you what I mean.

Another sign of Kipling's care as an artist is the trouble that he took with his texts. He is not usually thought of as among the company of inveterate revisers—writers such as James, or Yeats, or Auden—but he was in fact constantly at work in polishing what he had written even after publication, as his work passed through magazine to book to collected edition. He is, by the way, perhaps the worst-edited of our major writers. That is partly Kipling's own fault. He gave away most of his manuscripts to institutional libraries—the British Library, the Bodleian, the Sorbonne, the National Library of Scotland, among others—always with the provision that they never be used for "purposes of collation." So, even though the text of a masterwork such as *Kim* bristles with deletions, additions, revisions and alterations, we are not permitted to publish the fact. But part of the fault is that of the people who ought to be doing such work, the academic scholars of literature, who do not seem yet to have grasped how much there is to be learned about Kipling in this way. I doubt that Kipling's text will ever be adequately studied: the job is probably too complex to be undertaken with any reasonable expectation of being completed, just as I doubt that there will ever be a really competent edition of his poems. But what opportunities they would present to editors!

I hope that we can agree by now that Kipling triumphantly meets all three of Eliot's standards—abundance, variety, and complete competence—but you will no doubt be thinking that more is required: what about vision, world-view, imaginative understanding? What compelling intellectual or emotional impulse, if any, operates through Kipling's work, and what should we think of it? It is not necessarily praise to say that a writer's deepest ideas resemble ours; but one does need to say about Kipling that there is, in his deepest

ideas, nothing that can offend ours. After some years of reading
Kipling with continued pleasure and continued discovery, I would
suggest these as among the main convictions behind his work.

There is first the modesty of the great artist. Despite all his care
as a practiced and scrupulous artist, attentive to every detail of his
work, Kipling knew that the sources of art are impersonal, communal, and anonymous. The artist, in Kipling's view as expressed directly and indirectly in many of his works, did not control the power
that worked through him but was merely its instrument. He did not
invent new things, but re-invented or renewed the magic, through
the gift that was given to him, in forms that had always been there.
In a similar way, the hero, in all the many shapes that he takes
throughout Kipling's work, is bound to do what the power that works
through him, and the conditions that surround him, demand: all
are servants of "the iron ring," and must, as Kipling said of his characters in *Rewards and Fairies*, do what the land that has bred them
compels them to do. The conditions of life are given, and must be
met, not evaded. As such ideas about the artist and the hero may
suggest, Kipling was deeply conservative: there was, for him, nothing new under the sun.

Yet at the same time he delighted in the variety of life. One of his
favorite sayings—he attributed it to the *Arabian Nights*—was "Praise
be Allah for the diversity of His creatures!" He used it for the title of
one of his collections of stories, and he frequently quotes it or adapts
it in his letters. Kipling was, in fact, not a racist, not a jingo, not any
of those things that are so often and so easily said about him, but a
widely tolerant, or one might better say, sympathetic man.

Here, however, I must do a little explaining. Kipling the individual, the man who lived at Bateman's and had an American wife,
and paid taxes, and travelled in a chauffeur-driven Rolls Royce—
that Kipling can certainly be charged with all sorts of unpleasant or
regrettable shortcomings. He was given to saying quite violent and
outrageous things about the Boers, or about labor leaders, or about
Germans, or about vulgar and violent Americans. There are many
things in his letters that I wish were not there: impatient and unfair
judgments, feelings of violence and hatred towards anything that
he saw as an enemy, and a disposition to see collusion and conspiracy where others would see only bad luck and muddle. Some of
this, I think, comes about because Kipling, in his personal utter-
ances, let words run away with him. And he mostly attacks groups,
rarely individuals. In his personal relations he was genuinely sympathetic and generous. I may say that I have, if anything, a higher
opinion of Kipling as a person now, after laboring over his letters
for many years, than I did when I began. But that is by the way. The

fact is that Kipling, the historical individual, participated fully in many of the prejudices of his time. Kipling the artist is a different story. "Trust the tale, not the teller," D. H. Lawrence has advised us, and though the formula may seem too glib and easy, I have no doubt that it is true in Kipling's case. If you try the experiment of reading his stories without any regard to your preconceptions about Kipling, I think you will see what I mean.

Kipling is, finally, like all the great writers that I know anything about, keenly aware of the limitations of human activity, and of the provisional, fragile character of all human achievement. He sees that defeat is certain, but that the spirit is indomitable. Let me give Kipling himself the last word, in the poem called "Cities and Thrones and Powers" from *Puck of Pook's Hill*:

> Cities and Thrones and Powers
>   Stand in Time's eye,
> Almost as long as flowers,
>   Which daily die:
> But, as new buds put forth
>   To glad new men,
> Out of the spent and unconsidered Earth
>   The Cities rise again.
>
> This season's Daffodil,
>   She never hears
> What change, what chance, what chill,
>   Cut down last year's;
> But with bold countenance,
>   And knowledge small,
> Esteems her seven days' continuance
>   To be perpetual.
>
> So Time that is o'er-kind
>   To all that be,
> Ordains us e'en as blind,
>   As bold as she:
> That in our very death,
>   And burial sure,
> Shadow to shadow, well persuaded, saith,
>   "See how our works endure!"

Spring Semester 1996

# 7

# Leonard and Virginia Woolf at the Hogarth Press

## S. P. ROSENBAUM

T he history of Leonard and Virginia Woolf's Hogarth Press is well documented. There is a fine checklist by Howard Woolmer of the 525 books that the Press published over a period of thirty years, and a detailed recent history of the Press has been written by J. H. Willis, Jr. John Lehmann, who was a manager and eventually a partner in the Hogarth Press, has told his story in several books; the title of the last—*Thrown to the Woolves*—sums up his view of the experience. Others have reminisced about their time working for Leonard and Virginia. But the best sources for our knowledge of the Press are Leonard Woolf's autobiographies which provide the basic information, supplemented by catalogues, ledgers, correspondence, and other records of the Press that have survived, together with the dozen volumes of Virginia Woolf's diaries and letters. These various accounts show certain aspects of the Hogarth Press that can contribute to British Studies and the history of the book as well as to our understanding of the work of Virginia Woolf and of the Bloomsbury Group. Before considering some of the most interesting of these aspects, however, it is useful to review briefly the development of the Hogarth Press.

In March 1917, Leonard, who was thirty-seven, and Virginia, who was two years younger, bought a small hand press, some type and the other paraphernalia of printing for £19.5s.5d. (Leonard kept very detailed accounts.) That is about $750 today. They had decided several years before to learn the art of printing. According to Leonard this was to be a recreation to take Virginia's mind off her writing. According to Virginia, however, printing was to deflect the influence of the Fabian socialists Beatrice and Sidney Webb on Leonard.

The Woolfs had originally wanted to take a course in printing but discovered, as Leonard said, "two middle-aged, middle-class persons" were ineligible because of union rules. So with the help of a friendly neighborhood printer Virginia and Leonard Woolf brought out in July 1917, Publication No. 1 of the Hogarth Press, which consisted of two stories, Virginia's well-known "The Mark on the Wall" and Leonard's now forgotten "Three Jews." Virginia set most of the type while Leonard did the machining. A congenital tremor of his hands that had kept him out of the First World War also prevented him from doing much of the typesetting, though he did do some. The pamphlet, which had four woodcuts by Carrington and a cover of Japanese paper, was sold by subscription, this method of distribution being a consequence of perhaps the most important early aim of the Hogarth Press: to print stories or poems that commercial publishers would not consider doing. The Hogarth Press thus began, we might say today, as an alternative press.

Profit on *Two Stories* was just over £7 or a little less than $150 today. Word of what the Woolfs were doing quickly got around, and Katherine Mansfield, a virtually unknown writer at this time, offered her important story "Prelude." It turned out to be too big a job, however, and after the Woolfs set the type it had to be machined by their neighborhood printer. Already with their second publication, then, Leonard and Virginia Woolf were forced beyond printing the Hogarth Press publications entirely by themselves. And before they had proceeded very far with Mansfield's story, they were brought the poems of Leonard Woolf's brother Cecil, who had been killed in action. These were privately printed and not even listed among the Hogarth publications. The distinction is revealing, for the Hogarth Press was never intended by the Woolfs to be a private press in this sense, and Cecil Woolf's poems was the only work the Hogarth Press printed privately.

Also while printing Mansfield the Woolfs were approached, at Roger Fry's suggestion, by James Joyce's patron Harriet Shaw Weaver, who asked them to consider publishing the unfinished *Ulysses*. The Woolfs did not much like the first four chapters she left with them, which includes Bloom's defecatory musings, but it was clearly a work worth publishing if they could get a printer to do it. The laws of the time made printers as well as publishers liable for obscene works, however, and the Woolfs knew they would not find a printer for it. *Ulysses* became, therefore, the first Hogarth Press rejection.

The Woolfs then printed Virginia's famous story *Kew Gardens* along with another work outside of Bloomsbury, T. S. Eliot's *Poems*.

(It may be worth noting that apart from their own work the Woolfs did not publish anything by a member of the Bloomsbury Group until E. M. Forster's *The Story of a Siren* in 1920, a work Forster had written years before but had been unable to publish.) Eliot's *Poems* together with *Kew Gardens* were the first review copies the Woolfs sent out, and, when the *Times Literary Supplement* published a favorable notice of *Kew Gardens,* the Woolfs found themselves swamped with orders and had to have a commercial printer do a second edition. Once again the Woolfs had fortuitously, Leonard recalled, to abandon the original intention of the Hogarth Press to print small books themselves. But they still considered the Press a hobby, a part-time activity to be done in the afternoons after their mornings of writing.

Two years after they started, the Woolfs bought a larger press and in 1920 engaged a paid employee. They then produced their first avowedly commercial publication, a translation of Maxim Gorky's recollections of Tolstoy which sold very well. Other Russian translations followed. The Woolfs continued to sell their books through subscription, however, until 1923—six years after the Press had begun—when they had become so successful that the subscriber system was given up and the Woolfs, in Leonard's words, became "more or less ordinary publishers selling our books mainly to booksellers at the usual discount." Yet Leonard and Virginia were hardly becoming ordinary publishers in terms of making money. After paying authors twenty-five percent of the gross profits, Leonard calculated the net profit of the Hogarth Press during its first four years at £90, or something under $1,500 today. This was possible because nothing was spent on overhead; the Woolfs ran the Press, including storage and distribution, from their home. While becoming ordinary, if not very profitable, publishers, who had professional printers doing their books that were then sold through bookshops, the Woolfs also continued to print books themselves until 1932. They hand-printed thirty-four in all, many of them poems, but some essays by the Woolfs, E. M. Forster, and others. A number of the volumes of poetry were by forgotten poets, but not all, for they included work by Robert Graves, Herbert Read, John Crowe Ransom, and Edwin Muir.

A crucial event in the evolution of the Hogarth Press was the publication of a full-length book in 1922, Virginia Woolf's first modernist novel, *Jacob's Room,* which was given a post-impressionist dustjacket by Vanessa Bell. The book was printed in Scotland by R. & R. Clark, who continued to print Virginia's novels for the Hogarth Press. The Press's profit from *Jacob's Room* was £42.4s.6d., or about $1,750 today. This was possible, Leonard Woolf noted, by having Virginia the publisher swindle Virginia the author—that is, she took part of the profits from the Press rather than a royalty. For her later books she was paid separately by Hogarth and by Harcourt Brace and Company, which published the American editions of her books.

As the Hogarth Press demanded more of their time—manuscripts had been pouring in since the beginning of the twenties—the Woolfs began to ask periodically if they wanted to continue with the Press. In 1922, just five years after they had started with their hand press, they were briefly tempted by an offer from William Heinemann Ltd. to take over the management of the Press, leaving the Woolfs with editorial autonomy. But Leonard and Virginia declined, fearing what would happen if they lost control of their enterprise. The demands of the Press were temporarily resolved by a series of young men and women who served as managing assistants.

In 1923 the Press expanded even further, publishing thirteen books instead of the previous year's six. The total capital invested in the Hogarth Press rose to £135.2s.3d. (or more than $4,000 today). A bigger press was put in the dining room where the other had been, until the Woolfs were warned it might fall through the floor into the kitchen below, so it had to be moved to the larder. "We printed in the larder," Leonard Woolf wrote in his autobiography, "bound books in the dining room, interviewed printers, binders, and authors in a sitting room." Among the books printed by the Woolfs in 1923 was that most famous of English modernist works, T. S. Eliot's *The Waste Land*, which Virginia set herself. What is the impact, one might wonder, on an author of a poem she not only reads but sets up in type? *The Waste Land* was originally advertized in the Hogarth Press catalogue as a long poem with notes and an introduction. Eliot commented that the notes had to be expanded because the poem was inconveniently short for printing, but of the intriguing introduction promised in the Hogarth catalogue, nothing more seems to be known.

In 1924 the Woolfs moved back to Bloomsbury, setting up the Hogarth Press in the basement of their place in Tavistock Square. Instead of just literature the Press now began to publish psychiatric and political works including Leonard's own books. (They also published in 1925 *Turbott Wolfe*, the first novel of a young unknown South African, William Plomer; the political and racial outrage it stirred up influenced the development of South African literature.) The most popular of the political offerings were pamphlets by the Woolf's Bloomsbury friend, John Maynard Keynes. One of the chief forms of publication by the Hogarth Press was the political or literary pamphlet. Booksellers did not like them, but the Hogarth Press kept trying to advance this literary form. The Woolfs started the series of

Hogarth Essay pamphlets in 1924 with Virginia Woolf's manifesto *Mr Bennett and Mrs Brown*. Essays by Leonard Woolf, Roger Fry, T. S. Eliot, Gertrude Stein, and others followed. Nearly twenty different series were published in all, including a Hogarth Living Poets sequence that was subsidized by Yeats's friend the poet Dorothy Wellesley. Though not nearly as remarkable as the poets Eliot was now publishing with his firm of Faber and Faber, the Living Poets did include Frances Cornford, Robinson Jeffers, Vita Sackville-West, C. Day Lewis, and Edward Arlington Robinson.

More important for the success of the Press than its political and literary pamphlets or its various series was the taking over of the International Psychoanalytic Library at James Strachey's suggestion in 1924. This entailed the publication of Freud's collected papers in four volumes. Eventually, *The Standard Edition of the Complete Psychological Works of Sigmund Freud,* translated from the German under the General Editorship of James Strachey, was published in 23 volumes. The Freud edition and the works of Virginia Woolf were the most outstanding contributions of the Hogarth Press to modern culture. But at the time there were dangers involved. Leonard Woolf was warned against publishing Freud and other psychoanalytic works: they would be unprofitable and there was the risk of being prosecuted under the obscenity laws. Woolf took the chance, invested £200 (over $7,000 now) for books that sold steadily and were more profitable than anything else except the writings of the Press's co-owner.

The big success of *Orlando* in 1928 was another turning point in the careers of Virginia Woolf and therefore the Hogarth Press. Then the Woolfs' first best-seller, Vita Sackville-West's *The Edwardians*, was published in 1930; it sold 30,000 copies. During the decade of the 1930s, the Hogarth Press was earning the Woolfs an average yearly income of more than £1000 each (around $20,000 each today). The Woolfs were now employing three typists, bookkeepers, or managing assistants and publishing twenty to thirty books a year that sold anywhere from 150 copies to Sackville-West's 30,000. Yet they continued to agonize over the Press's future. They still wanted to be just part-time publishers. The aim of publishing only worthwhile books appears to have been gradually modified. By 1933 the Press had lost its spring, Virginia Woolf felt, and she wanted to return to the old ideals with which they started in 1917. The assistants who had come to the Press to help the Woolfs manage it and maybe even become partners had all left. The latest was John Lehmann.

Unlike the others, Lehmann had some capital and was interested in becoming a professional publisher. But after two years as manager he left abruptly for Germany, angering the Woolfs. Yet in those years, Leonard noted, Lehmann brought to the Press some of his generation's best writers. In 1932, for example, Lehmann published the anthology *New Signatures*. Regarded as a kind of manifesto for the poets of the 1930s, it included poems by Lehmann, W. H. Auden, Julian Bell, C. Day Lewis, Richard Eberhart, William Empson, and Stephen Spender. Lehmann also introduced to the Press in 1932 the work of Christopher Isherwood, the most important novelist after Virginia Woolf that Hogarth would publish in the thirties.

John Lehmann reappeared and bought Virginia Woolf's half-ownership of the press in 1938 for £3000 (say $60,000 today). Lehmann was to run the Press as managing partner, while Leonard devoted about a quarter of his time to the publishing. The Press now employed seven assistants. Virginia remained, of course, as a Hogarth Press author and advisor, continuing to read manuscripts. It was also in 1938 that the Hogarth Press employed a salaried woman who was the first in the trade to sell their books to bookshops. Before then the Woolfs travelled with the books themselves or had their various assistants do so.

Lehmann continued to bring new authors and works to the Press, including the biannual *New Writing*. Then the war changed the Press completely. It was bombed out of Mecklenburgh Square, where the Woolfs had moved the year before, and transferred to the country location of one of the Press's printers. Paper rationing seriously curtailed the Press's offerings. There had been some disagreements—occasionally resolved by Virginia—between Leonard and John over what to publish (each partner had a veto). With Virginia's death in 1941, the incompatibilities of the two partners' literary tastes increased, exacerbated by their political disagreements. John Lehmann hoped to develop the Press in various ways; Leonard Woolf was unconvinced that expansion was necessary or desirable. Finally in 1946 Lehmann offered to buy Woolf's share of the Press, but Leonard chose instead to buy him out rather than giving up the Press. (In his posthumously published autobiography *The Journey Not the Arrival Matters*, Leonard Woolf wrote that Lehmann "shares to some extent the common tendency to megalomania, and it was this which made him leave the Hogarth Press." When Lehmann was shown the proofs of the volume, he insisted this passage be deleted and the current management of the Hogarth Press obliged.) Woolf was able to buy out his partner by selling Lehmann's half share to Chatto & Windus, which had a list similar in some respects to Hogarth's; they had published Lytton Strachey, Clive Bell, and Roger Fry, for example. The Hogarth Press now became a limited company and a subsidiary of Chatto & Windus, while retaining its editorial independence under the supervision of Leonard. The Press was to remain independent until his death, which occurred in 1969, two years after the Press's fiftieth anniversary. John Lehmann began his own publishing business, which lasted only seven years, to Woolf's grim satisfaction. The Hogarth Press imprint remains today, though its distinctive wolf's head logos are no longer used. The Press itself, however, was eventually swallowed up along with Chatto & Windus, Jonathan Cape (who tried for years to buy out Hogarth), and various other publishers by the conglomerate called Random House UK.

I have been recounting a familiar story in order to illustrate certain principles and procedures of the Hogarth Press's history that illuminate the work Virginia Woolf and the Bloomsbury Group as well as the history of the book in modern English literature. I shall first mention two predecessors that influenced the development of the Hogarth Press. Then I want to consider how the Press was shaped by what today we might call the management style of the Woolfs, especially Leonard, who was responsible for the daily operation of the Press. Finally I wish to say something about the implications of the Hogarth Press for Virginia Woolf's writing.

The Woolf's decision to start their own Press was influenced positively and negatively, I think, by two precursors. The first was the publishing firm that Virginia's half-brother started when she was sixteen. A great deal has been made about the effect of the Duckworth half-brothers, especially George, on Virginia Woolf's sexual development. The term incest has been loosely used in some accounts, but it has been known for a long time that there was what we now recognize as sexual abuse of Vanessa and Virginia Stephen by the elder brother George. It might be argued, however, that the younger, Gerald, was the more important figure in Virginia's life. It was Gerald Duckworth, she remembered in a late memoir, who traumatically explored her genitals when she was a child. It was also Gerald to whom Virginia Woolf later offered her first two novels.

Being Leslie Stephen's stepson had obvious advantages when it came to starting up a publishing firm. Among the books published by Gerald Duckworth in his first year were works by Stephen himself (whom the Hogarth Press would also later publish), by Stephen's friend Henry James, and by others such as Strindberg and Galsworthy. Books by W. H. Hudson, Charles M. Doughty, W. H. Davies, and Hilaire Belloc followed, as well as translations of Ibsen, Gorky, and Chekhov's stories (which were unknown in England at the time). Duckworth also started an influential series of books on art. Later writers published by him included Ford Madox Hueffer, D. H.

Lawrence, and Dorothy Richardson. Duckworth's distinguished list of modern books was largely owing to a publisher's reader of genius, Edward Garnett. But Gerald Duckworth and Co. Ltd. also published Elinor Glyn's forgettable but immensely popular romantic novels of passion on tiger-skin rugs. (It was rumored in the firm that she read each of her new novels to Gerald in the conservatory after lunch.) In later years the novelist Anthony Powell worked for Duckworth and encouraged the firm to publish Ronald Firbank, Evelyn Waugh, and the Sitwells. Powell thought it extraordinary that Duckworth had become a publisher at all, for "his interest in books anyway as a medium for reading, was as slender as that of any man I have ever encountered. . . ." Gerald Duckworth died in 1937 but his firm has continued as an independent publisher, controlled, they say, by their editors instead of their accountants.

The influence of Duckworth's firm on the development of the Hogarth Press could be viewed as both inspiring and depressing. As an inspiration, Virginia's half-brother had demonstrated what could be done by someone with some capital but little interest in books as a medium of reading. If Gerald Duckworth could start such a successful publishing business, the Woolfs could, and without the assistance of Elinor Glyn. Duckworth's Russian translations showed what kinds of modern things one might publish. As Virginia Woolf's own publisher, however, Gerald Duckworth exerted a depressing effect on her. To have to submit to Gerald again, and then wait for his approval, was there no way of avoiding this? It is clear that among the most important reasons for the Hogarth Press was the publication of Virginia Woolf's work. Wondering if the Press should be given up in 1926, the year after it had published *The Common Reader* and *Mrs Dalloway*, Virginia Woolf wrote revealingly in her diary, "speaking selfishly it has served my turn: given me a chance of writing off my own bat," and she doubted if publishers like Heinemann or Cape would now intimidate her. To be creatively free of intimidation, Virginia Woolf published her own books. Her third novel, *Jacob's Room*, the first that Hogarth printed, was much more experimental than the previous two published by Duckworth. The novel was in fact under option to Duckworth, but he generously released it to Hogarth and later allowed them to take over Virginia's two earlier novels as well, which lost his firm some considerable profit.

But the significance for Virginia Woolf of having her own press was not only a matter of personal antipathy or critical inhibitions. It was also clearly connected with her feminism, as she indicated in her manifesto of 1938, *Three Guineas*. Explaining to a woman of some economic independence how she might put into practice her opinions on protecting culture and intellectual liberty, the narrator tells her not to dream but to consider the facts of the actual world:

> the private printing press is an actual fact, and not beyond the reach of a moderate income. Typewriters and duplicators are actual facts and even cheaper. By using these cheap and so far unforbidden instruments you can at once rid yourself of the pressure of boards, policies, and editors. They will speak your own mind, in your own words, at your own time, at your own length, at your own bidding. And that, we are agreed, is our definition of "intellectual liberty."

A more immediate and influential predecessor of the Hogarth Press was not a press but a workshop—the Omega Workshops that Roger Fry started after his revolutionary exhibitions of post-impressionist paintings in 1910 and 1912. Around the time the Woolfs were thinking of learning to print, Fry issued the first of four small books illustrated with woodcuts from the Omega Workshops. All were designed but not printed in the Workshops. The last, a book of woodcuts, was originally to be published by the Hogarth Press, but disagreements between Leonard Woolf and Vanessa Bell over who would have final control of the book led to the Omega Workshops printing the book. It is, of course, not coincidental that the Woolfs used woodcuts in the early publications of the Hogarth Press, or that they went to considerable trouble with all their hand-printed books to find unusual colored papers for covers, which started a fashion in English publishing. Bright colours were characteristic of much post-impressionist art, and one of the two main purposes of the Omega Workshops was to bring post-impressionism into interior decoration, the other aim being to subsidize young artists by paying them to do part-time anonymous work at various crafts. A parallel with Virginia Woolf's working at the craft of printing as a relief from her art of writing has been noticed.

The inspiration of the Omega Workshops for the Hogarth Press is more than just a matter of woodcuts and decorative paper. The aesthetics of Fry and the Omega were to a considerable degree those of Bloomsbury and the Woolfs. The connection of Fry's Workshops with the English Arts and Crafts Movement of William Morris and others in the latter part of the nineteenth century has frequently been mentioned. Fry and his friends concurred with some of the aims of the Movement but not with its nostalgia for the past—which Fry characterized as lunatic medievalism. Fry objected, as Morris did, to the aesthetic hierarchy that divorced fine from decorative art; both wanted to blend the fine and decorative arts and bring them to bear on daily life. Yet, Fry had no socialist intentions, and he did not share Morris's antipathy toward the use of machines in art. He laughed at the affectations of craft in the Movement. Fry wanted to introduce spontaneity into the work of the Omega as well as the sense of formal design that post-impressionism had emphasized. With the Omega Fry hoped to produce brightly designed rooms, useful furniture and serviceable pottery. But Fry disliked the English worship of the mechanically perfect finish. The Omega artists were not as a whole very interested in becoming as skilled in their crafts as those in the Arts and Crafts Movement. The instability of Omega furniture has been exaggerated, but there is a sense in which Fry would have understood what Ralph Vaughan Williams meant when he once said about making music that anything worth doing was worth doing badly.

One important parallel of the Omega Workshops and the Hogarth Press appears in the Woolfs' aim to print literary works of art by young writers that could not be published in the regular way, just as the Omega Workshops had employed young artists who had not yet established themselves. Neither the Press nor the Omega was created for profit. The Hogarth Press refused to publish something just because it would sell. The Workshop's rejection of Arts and Crafts nostalgia for past art may also be reflected in the refusal of the Woolfs to republish classics, as they said in a fifth anniversary statement of the Press in 1922. In its avoiding highly crafted luxurious products and emphasizing utility, attractiveness, and spontaneity, the Omega's intention was analogous to the Hogarth Press's plan not to "embellish our books beyond what is necessary for ease of reading and decency of appearance." The aim was "cheapness and adequacy" rather than "high prices and typographical splendour," the fifth-anniversary proclamation of the Press continued. Leonard Woolf restated in his autobiography the Woolfs' purpose not to make the Hogarth Press into the kind of private press that published finely printed books which, he said,

> are meant not to be read, but to be looked at. We were interested primarily in the immaterial inside of a book, what the author had to say and how he said it; we had drifted into the business with the idea of publishing things which the commercial publisher could not or would not publish. We wanted our books to "look nice" and we had our own views of what nice looks in a book would be, but neither of us was interested in fine printing and fine binding. We also disliked the refinement and preciosity which are too often a kind of fungoid growth which culture breeds upon art and literature. . . .

In particular, Leonard went on, they did not want the Hogarth Press to turn into one like Kelmscott or Nonesuch, admirable though each was in its own way. This intention is fundamental to understanding the particular nature of the Hogarth Press. The "immaterial" content of a book was always more important than its printed form. The casualness and lack of finish in some of their printing was deliberate. In 1930 Virginia Woolf wrote a mock letter to an anonymous Hogarth customer about her pamphlet *On Being Ill*, which the Woolfs printed themselves. "I agree that the colour is uneven, the letters are not always clear, the spacing inaccurate, and the word 'campion' should read 'companion'." But, she explained, as they were not allowed to learn printing, it remained "a hobby carried on in the basement of a London house . . . in the intervals of lives that are otherwise engaged." Furthermore, her unsatisfied customer could sell his or her copy for more than it cost because the edition was oversubscribed.

The Hogarth Press did, however, produce some finely printed books—Vanessa Bell's decorated edition of Virginia's *Kew Gardens* is one example, Clive Bell's poem *The Legend of Monte Della Sibilla*, illustrated by Vanessa and Duncan Grant, is another. And of course there are the post-impressionist wrappers that Vanessa Bell designed for her sister's novels and other books published by the Hogarth Press. But the Woolfs' indifference to some aspects of the craft of printing led to a disagreement between them and the Bloomsbury artists Vanessa Bell and Duncan Grant. Two early Hogarth ghosts (books announced but not published) are volumes of original drawings by Vanessa Bell and Duncan Grant, although the Press did publish a handsome book of Fry's woodcuts.


In the end the Hogarth Press was more successful than the Omega Workshops, which lasted from 1913 to 1919. Fry was not much interested in marketing his products, and the war further hurt the Workshop's chances of survival. The Omega had originally announced, incidentally, that Leonard Woolf, who had served as secretary to the second post-impressionist exhibition, would help with the business side of the Omega, but there is no evidence he ever did. It might have been better for Fry if he had, for it was Woolf's acumen and determination that kept the Hogarth Press from going the way of so many other similar enterprises. Commentators on the Hogarth Press observe from time to time that it is not really very difficult to start a new press if you have young writers willing to contribute like Virginia Woolf, Katherine Mansfield, and T. S. Eliot. There is no doubt that the Hogarth Press had extraordinary good fortune in the quality of their early publications, but it was not simply a question of whom one knew. Katherine Mansfield and

Middleton Murry started their own press after they saw what the
Woolfs were doing; they had some of the same friends and some
others like D. H. Lawrence, but their endeavor went nowhere. When
Ralph Partridge, the first assistant of the Hogarth Press, left, he intended to set up a press with the backing of Lytton Strachey and
other Bloomsbury friends, but this project never even got started.
The success of the Hogarth Press depended on their contributors,
of course, but equally essential was Leonard Woolf's highly individual conception of how to develop a publishing business. Because
not enough attention has been paid to the practical, material conditions of publishing, Leonard Woolf's contribution to modern
English culture has been insufficiently appreciated.

It is quite remarkable that the Woolfs started their Press with no
experience in printing or publishing—and even more surprising,
with no working capital. For a contrast there is the successful career
of Jonathan Cape, who served for twenty years as a manager for
Gerald Duckworth before founding his own firm three years after
the Hogarth Press began with a partner and £12,000 of capital.
Leonard Woolf was able to make a go of the Hogarth Press, as he
said again and again, because he had no overhead and no staff. It
was a delusion, he insisted, to think you had to have an organization to be a successful publisher of, say, Freud's work. How did the
Hogarth Press succeed without the normal structure of a publishing business? The answer lies in the paradox that the Woolfs were
successful because they were not interested in the success of
their Press.

For years the Woolfs refused to publish anything they did not
think worth publishing for its own sake, even though it might make
money. The Press was never to be a way of livelihood for either Virginia or Leonard. In terms of Bloomsbury values, which derived
from the ethics of G. E. Moore, the Hogarth Press was an intrinsic
activity rather than an instrumental one, something done because
it was valuable in itself rather than being a means to something else
such as making money. Leonard Woolf asserted repeatedly in his
autobiographies that printing and publishing were to be only part-
time activities. (And in this it resembles again the Omega Workshops, which were also never a full-time occupation for Fry or the
other artists involved.) As a result of their determination to remain
part-time printers and publishers, however, the Woolfs eventually
found it necessary to employ someone to help them run the press.
Growth became inevitable, but Leonard insisted on keeping the Press
as small as he could. Only in this way, he said, could he steer the
business between the Scylla of being taken over by Heinemann or
whoever, and the Charybdis of bankruptcy from a too rapid expan-

sion. It was over the issue of expansion more than anything else
that Leonard Woolf and John Lehmann ended their partnership.

Leonard was able to keep the Hogarth Press small and manage-
able, he believed, because of his seven years' experience in the
Ceylon Civil Service where he was eventually put in charge of 100,000
Sinhalese. It is pleasant to think of the Hogarth Press as a by-
product of imperialism. Leonard Woolf was a rigorously efficient
colonial administrator, and he carried this habit over to the Hogarth
Press. He himself says he was allergic to fools. Because of the efficiency Leonard demanded of himself and his employees, more than
a few of them found themselves acting foolishly. There are a number of stories about conflicts between Leonard Woolf and his assistants, such as the one (there are different variants) where he quar-
rels with his manager over his being late to work; their watches differ and eventually in a rage they hire a taxi and drive to where they
can see Big Ben to determine whose watch is right. (Another version has Virginia Woolf poking her head around the corner in the
midst of the argument and asking innocently what time it was.)

In addition to appearing as a tyrant of efficiency, Leonard Woolf
has also been accused of being tight about money by Bloomsbury
friends, John Lehmann, and others associated with the Press. There
is a genteel anti-Semitism in some of these remarks, but Leonard
Woolf does seem to have carried economies pretty far at times. Visitors to both Tavistock Square and Monk's House in Sussex were
sometimes disconcerted to find galley proofs serving as toilet paper. Yet it is clear from the history of the Hogarth Press that Leonard
did not care about making money. On the other hand he was
damned if he was going to lose any, and that I believe is the key to
the finances of the Hogarth Press. The Woolfs would publish what
they thought was worth publishing—at least in the early years—but
only if they did not lose money by it. When Gertrude Stein offered
her 900-page manuscript of *The Making of Americans* to the Hogarth
Press, for example, Leonard offered to publish it on a commission
basis; Stein declined, but the Woolfs did publish her financially feasible pamphlet *Composition as Explanation*. Though the Hogarth Press
never had a year without profit, some of them were very lean. From
1924 to 1930 the Press averaged a profit of around £180—or two to
three thousand dollars a year. After that it was more prosperous,
bringing the Woolfs, as I said, about £1,000 or $20,000 a year. As
J. H. Willis points out in his history of the Hogarth Press, none of
the publishers comparable to Hogarth such as Jonathan Cape,
Chatto & Windus, Bodley Head, Faber and Faber or Gollancz could
have survived on the small profits that nourished the Hogarth Press.

Still there is a sense in which, despite Leonard Woolf's desire to neither make or lose much money, the Hogarth Press cost Virginia Woolf something. She wrote to Ethel Smyth in 1931, ". . . publishers told me to write what they liked. I said no. I'll publish myself and write what I like. Which I did, and for many years, owing to lack of organisation travellers etc. lost much money thereby." It was mainly in the 1920s that Virginia Woolf's books sold less than they might have with a more conventional publisher, assuming of course a conventional publisher would have taken them the way she wrote them. But it was a price Virginia was as glad as Leonard to pay for the freedom to write and publish as she wished, for she was no more interested in making money as a publisher than he was.

    The way in which Leonard and Virginia Woolf ran the Hogarth Press has other interesting ramifications besides profit for the works that they published. No overhead, no staff meant that the Press employed no publishers' readers, no designers or publicists, not even any editors. The Woolfs read or decided not to read almost all the manuscripts that were submitted. Occasionally when they disagreed or were uncertain they would ask someone like their friend the critic Raymond Mortimer for an opinion. (Poetry was the biggest problem and Leonard Woolf said if he were publishing in other times he might well have turned down Shakespeare and accepted the Victorian versifier Martin Tupper. When a friend complained to Virginia about the poetry they were publishing, she replied they could not manufacture genius and besides she should see the manuscripts they had refused.) For the books they printed themselves, the Woolfs controlled everything. In the midst of printing Mansfield's *Prelude*, for instance, Middleton Murry pointed out to the Woolfs that the running head was given incorrectly as "The Prelude" rather than just "Prelude." This was then corrected, but only for the pages not yet printed! The earlier pages are headed "The Prelude," the later ones just "Prelude." This was one way of controlling costs. Again, when Laura Riding's change in marital status required that her married name of Gottschalk now be deleted from the printed title page of her poem that the Woolfs were printing, Leonard in exasperation simply printed two thick (six point) black rules across her last name and let it stand rather than print the title page again. Not surprisingly, it was the last work of hers the Hogarth Press published. For books they published but did not print themselves, the Woolfs or their printers did whatever designing or editing was required.

    No editors meant that the Hogarth Press books were in effect never edited. Leonard and Virginia would read the manuscript, make what minor changes were necessary, and then send it to the printer. There was no "house-style" other than what the printers themselves imposed, and there does not seem to have been much of that. Manuscripts were not gone over carefully; they were accepted or rejected and that was it. No detailed criticism was offered. Leonard hated asking Hogarth Press authors for changes and seems to have done so only tentatively. (The publisher of his own two novels had required significant changes about which he was very unhappy.) When Vita Sackville-West's *The Edwardians* arrived, Virginia was so enthusiastic about it that Leonard sent the manuscript straight to the Scottish printers and read it only in proof. All he suggested was that Vita consider giving the chapters titles, which she did. Occasionally, however, Leonard Woolf's rare editorial advice was firmly rejected. In 1939 he wrote to a distinguished Austrian contributor to the Press who had submitted a book with a cumbersome title that "from a publishing point of view it is, I am sure, a great mistake to have the long title, for in England many people will be frightened by the word monotheism. Would you, therefore, agree to its appearing under the shorter title?" So confident of the persuasiveness of his judgement was he that Leonard listed in his Hogarth Press catalogue a forthcoming book by Sigmund Freud entitled simply *Moses*. Freud, however, was not persuaded, and the book, of course, appeared under its original title *Moses and Monotheism*. It does not seem to have frightened away English readers.

The way the Hogarth Press was managed, largely by Leonard, has a direct bearing on the works of both the Woolfs. Leonard had suffered from other publishers more than Virginia. His book *Co-operation and the Future of Industry* was originally written for the Home University Library series in 1915 but the publishers failed to bring it out. After two years Woolf threatened to sue, the original publishers cancelled his contract, and the book finally appeared with another publisher three years after it had been completed. For Virginia the most important aspect of publishing her own books was the freedom, the unself-consciousness it gave her, as she said, of writing off her own bat. But publishing her own books did not mean that Virginia was completely free of the pressures publishers exert on their authors. Leonard and George Rylands, an early assistant at the Press, started a series of lectures on literature in 1927 and persuaded Virginia to write one called "Phases of Fiction," partly in response to E. M. Forster's successful *Aspects of the Novel.* Her long essay was serialized in the United States and then announced for publication by Hogarth. She struggled with rewriting what she called her dullest and most hated book while writing another book on a similar subject, namely *A Room of One's Own.* Finally she decided that Rylands and her husband were wrong to push her into publishing the book, and "Phases of Fiction" became another Hogarth ghost.

Leonard was Virginia's only book editor, her only publisher's reader after she left Duckworth. And all that he did, he said in editing her posthumous essays, was to punctuate them where they needed it and correct verbal mistakes. It is noteworthy that the work of two of the greatest English prose modernists, James Joyce and Virginia Woolf, should have been published without the customary editorial interventions. Partly as a result of publishing her own books, Woolf at least avoided the bibliographical chaos that seems to envelop the printed work of Joyce. But this is not to say the situation of Woolf's texts is simple. The publication of her books in America by Harcourt Brace was on a take-it-or-leave-it basis. They always took them, setting their first American editions from the proofs of the Hogarth editions. Nevertheless, Virginia Woolf did not regard the Hogarth Press texts as definitive. In *Mrs Dalloway* and *To the Lighthouse*, for example, she made substantial changes in the wording of key passages in the American proofs of her novels. The absence of any editorial assistance also contributed to errors in the Hogarth editions that went unnoticed, such as the misnumbering of sections in the third part of the first English edition of *To the Lighthouse*.

The nature of the Hogarth Press operation is revealing in other ways for the study of Virginia Woolf's writing. Vanessa Bell's wrappers of her novels provide examples. They are, to borrow a phrase of Henry James's, "optical echoes" of the text. Yet they were done without Vanessa having read the books; Virginia would drop in and give her sister enough of an idea about the book for a cover. A number of these wrappers also had blurbs about the novel on their flaps. Given the small organization of the Hogarth Press, it is reasonable to assume that these blurbs were written by the author. And who wrote the copy for the Hogarth Press's catalogue announcements of the Woolfs' books? Again these descriptions can be considered authorial—or quasi-authorial, perhaps, if Leonard wrote them with Virginia's approval. As for other books Hogarth published, Richard Kennedy, in his irreverent account of a gofer in the basement of the Hogarth Press, describes Virginia Woolf writing a blurb for a novel on Spain, which the Press was publishing. How many unknown blurbs by Virginia Woolf are there in Hogarth's publication? Who knows, once the importance of the Hogarth Press for Woolf's writing has been fully recognized, we may have a thesis and perhaps a collected edition of Virginia's blurbs and catalogue announcements.

Virginia Woolf, of course, is the primary reason why we remain interested in the Hogarth Press today, and one of the most extraordinary aspects of the care that Leonard devoted to her—a care that ultimately made her writing possible—was his role in the creation of the Hogarth Press. But she is not the only substantial reason why the Press is part of the history of English modernism. John Lehmann has said the dazzling early promise of Hogarth as a modernist press was not sustained, except for her works. He is thinking only of literature, for surely the publication of the standard English translation of Freud is, by any standard, a great modernist achievement. It is true that the Woolfs did not find other writers of fiction like Katherine Mansfield or poets like T. S. Eliot to publish. They tried with E. M. Forster's help to publish a volume of C. P. Cavafy's translated poems; Cavafy was very grateful for the offer but did not finally commit himself to a volume of his poems in Greek, let alone English. He died in 1933, and it was not until 1951 that the Hogarth Press was finally able to bring out his poems in translation. The Press did succeed in publishing translations of modern Russian works as well as those of Rainer Maria Rilke and Italo Svevo. The Woolfs did publish their Russian translations as well as those of Rainer Maria Rilke and Italo Svevo. They brought out the first book on Proust in English, which was by Clive Bell. They drew attention to the new poets of the thirties and published Isherwood's Berlin stories. And they would have published Joyce's *Ulysses* and Stein's *The Making of Americans* if they had been able to. (They even offered to publish an early version of Wyndham Lewis's anti-Bloomsbury *The Apes of God!*) Virginia Woolf's derisive private comments on Joyce's work have often been cited. It is true she did not recognize his greatness in what she said, yet *Ulysses* had a profound influence on the writing of *Mrs Dalloway*. The important distinction here is between what the Woolfs liked and what they thought was worth publishing. They would have published *Ulysses* if the censorship laws of England had allowed them to find a printer who would do it. This no one was able to do. As for Gertrude Stein, Virginia Woolf was sceptical, again in private, about what she called her "dodge" of repeating a word "100 times over in different connections until at last you feel the force of it." Yet the Hogarth Press offered to publish first *The Making of Americans* and later another work on herself, Matisse, and Picasso if Stein would bear the cost, which she could have done. The Woolfs did reject in the thirties Ivy Compton-Burnett's third novel *Brothers and Sisters,* and regretted the mistake, for it does not appear that Virginia read the manuscript. Virginia Woolf always said she was not a good judge of her contemporaries' literary merit.

But was there another press in England at the time that had a better record? That this was partly a matter of luck, Leonard Woolf conceded. But it was also due to the Woolfs' realization that the publishing conditions of their time created the need for an alternative press. The historical moment of the Hogarth Press is passed; even if one could find another Virginia Woolf, it would not be possible for many reasons to do anything similar now to what they did nearly eighty years ago. But the example of their Press illuminates the history of the book in English modernism. Virginia and Leonard Woolf's Hogarth Press was a remarkable enterprise of book publishing—and not just for the works that they published, but for the ways in which they published them. The values by which they resisted becoming professional printers or commercial publishers still seem worth thinking about today.

Summer Semester 1995

*Bibliographical Note*

An earlier version of this talk was given for the University of Toronto Centre for the Book and the Friends of the Victoria College Library, which has one of the most complete collections of Hogarth Press books. Howard Woolmer's *A Checklist of The Hogarth Press: 1917–1946* (St Paul's Bibliographies, 1986) is the standard bibliography of the Press, and J. H. Willis, Jr.'s *Leonard and Virginia as Publishers: The Hogarth Press, 1917–41* (Charlottesville, 1992) a recent history. Leonard Woolf's autobiographical accounts of the Press are to be found in *Beginning Again, Downhill All the Way,* and *The Journey Not the Arrival Matters* (Hogarth Press, 1964, 1967, 1969) as well as his *Letters,* edited by Frederic Spotts (New York, 1989). Virginia Woolf's *Letters,* edited by Nigel Nicolson and Joanne Trautmann (Hogarth Press, 6 vols., 1975–80) and *Diary,* edited by Anne Olivier Bell and Andrew McNeillie (Hogarth Press, 5 vols., 1977–84) are the primary sources for the Woolfs on the Press. John Lehmann's last account of his Hogarth Press experiences is given in *Thrown to the Woolves* (London, 1978). Much of the correspondence between Leonard Woolf and John Lehmann is now at the Harry Ransom Humanities Research Center, University of Texas at Austin. (Lehmann's correspondence about Woolf's *The Journey Not the Arrival Matters* is in the Victoria College library, University of Toronto.) Richard Kennedy's *A Boy at the Hogarth Press* (Penguin Books, 1978) is an amusing account by an office boy in 1928 but written forty years afterwards. The archives of the Hogarth Press can be found at the universities of Reading and Sussex. Forster's and Cavafy's correspondence is at King's College, Cambridge. Anthony Powell's reminiscences of Duckworth and Company appear in *Messengers of Day,* vol. 2 of *To Keep the Ball Rolling* (London, 1978). Current currency values are derived from Dolf Mootham's 1990 Central Statistical Office figures in Jonathan Gathorne-Hardy's *The Interior Castle: A Life of Gerald Brenan* (London, 1992), p. 611. Examples of the differences between Virginia Woolf's English and American texts can be found in the Shakespeare Head Press editions of Virginia Woolf's works, particularly *To the Lighthouse,* edited by Susan Dick (Oxford, 1992).

# 8

# Beyond Gossip: D. H. Lawrence's Writing Life

## MARK KINKEAD-WEEKES

I believe someone once called biographers the dirty-laundrymen of literature. The late William Golding wrote a novel which begins with a noise outside a writer's door one night, which he thinks is a badger. It is no such thing. It is an academic, busy going through the novelist's trash-can. A biographer of Lawrence more-over—stormy petrel that he was—has to research and write about an embarrassing set of subjects, if only to clear away the crudities and falsehoods of bad biography, and try for something more accurate. The gossipy anecdotes and the speculation about Lawrence's sexuality, his amatory behaviour, and his possible affairs—let alone those of his wife—have been endless. Of course biography begins with gossip. (Well I *never*! Did you *ever*! What extraordinary people! Tell me more!) What is still the most indispensable biography of Lawrence, the so-called Composite Biography compiled by Edward Nehls, which snips out and stitches together into chronological or-der extracts from the flood of memoirs by Lawrence's contempo-raries, together with scholarly annotation, is what one might call the start of the higher gossip. That, however, is what I think most biographies of Lawrence have too often remained—with greater inclusiveness and, sometimes, greater understanding as we have learned more about him, if without that immediacy of experience that Nehls' sources had, writing about the Lawrence they knew—or thought they did.

Yet Lawrence was first and foremost a *writer*—the greatest En-glish writer of this century—and moreover a writer whose work came directly out of his life-experience, though it was never (even in works that might seem autobiographical) a transcript of that life, but always transformed by creative imagination and structuring. His writing was his most intense way both of living and of grappling with his problems—and I don't think we shall ever understand him unless we try to look over his shoulder, and discover how, and why, he came to write as he did, and how his work both came out of, and sought to comprehend, what was happening to the living man. That of course is no easy task. It involves going back to the manuscripts, the writing-at-the-time, behind the later and revised texts that we know—whereupon, however, links become clear among them, which one had never realized. It involves trying for sensitive critical reading of the works in their own proper terms, before trying to estimate their relevance to biography. So it involves trying to be scholar, critic, and biographer all at once—while trying also never to blur the proper boundaries between life and art.

Moreover, though literary biography remains hugely popular, it is a non-subject, according to much modern, or post-modern, critical theory. Not very long ago we were being confidently assured of the death of the author, of whom the text is now wholly independent. So, arduous effort to revive one might seem, to say the least, misconceived. It is true that reports of that death (like Twain's) have been somewhat exaggerated, and there have lately been louder and louder knockings from under the coffin-lid. But—more seriously—since critical theory was reacting against the crude old "The Man and His Work" studies which *did* blur the boundaries between literature and life (by crudely assuming that the one simply reflected the other) and was also seeking to liberate criticism from authoritative readings, it behoves serious literary biographers at least to ask themselves what they are doing, and to show a proper sense of limitation.

I am not, however, going to take you through a set of embarrassing subjects, nor engage in theoretical debate about the legitimacy of what I have been up to for the last five years through fever and fire—it's a bit late for that. Instead, I offer a case-study, to ask whether it is possible for a biography of Lawrence—while bound to peer into privacies which in daily life might decently seem none of one's business—so to discipline itself as to become not merely gossipy and intrusive but perhaps even illuminating about the work as well as the writer? This of course is to ask whether there are ways of connecting literature and life that do *not* intrude too crassly over the boundaries between biography and criticism—and that open up, rather than foreclose, more complex possibilities of reading both the man and the work of art.

What, for instance, is one as biographer (though also literary critic) to do with the first evidence, recently disclosed, of adultery by Lawrence—probably the only case in fact, for all the gossip—and with what moreover now seems a clear link with some of his finest poetry, written immediately afterwards? I speak of evidence since we have the lady's own word, in a memoir privately published by her daughter.[1] We can also date most of the spate of poems that Lawrence began to write, within days. How are these two happenings to be related?—since it would take a positive closing of the eyes to deny any connection. Can we hope to understand the biographical event and Lawrence's state of mind about it and his marriage in 1920, without the poetry? Conversely, is it possible to keep new knowledge about the man from changing (though not determining) one's reading of the poems? At the same time, how can we keep the boundaries of biography and criticism distinct enough to ensure that neither unduly interferes with, or blurs into, the other?

Some biographical background, first. Lawrence got to know Rosalind Baynes (née Thornycroft) only in 1919, though he had met her husband Godwin and her sister and brother-in-law Joan and Bertie Farjeon earlier. In 1919 Lawrence and Frieda had come to the village of Hermitage near Newbury in Berkshire. After being expelled from Cornwall by order of the military and losing their home, they had lived, impoverished, in an isolated mountain cottage in Derbyshire, paid for by Lawrence's sister. Because of the debacle of the banning of his great novel *The Rainbow* for obscenity, no publisher would look at *Women in Love*, which would have to wait until November 1920 before being privately published in America; and Lawrence found it very difficult to sell any work at all. At the beginning of 1919 he caught the lethal flu which had been ravaging Europe, and nearly died. He had to move somewhere warmer—and luckily they were able to borrow the cottage in Hermitage from friends. Bertie and Joan Farjeon had bought a holiday cottage nearby. Lawrence's friendship with them was renewed; and soon he met Rosalind too, and liked her even more.

She was married to Godwin Baynes, a doctor, who would later become Jung's close associate; but the marriage was about to break up. Godwin had "free and easy ways" with other women and Rosalind was jealous, but the breaking point came after he had been posted to Mesopotamia in October 1917, when she had gone to bed with an old flame, also about to embark for the front, and became pregnant. The child was born six months before Godwin's return. His parents had been told, and formal separation now seemed almost certain. Both sisters were artistic and intelligent—their father Sir Hamo Thornycroft was a well-known sculptor—and had been raised as free spirits. Rosalind seemed the quieter and less obviously intellectual, but her gentle manner and serene dark-haired rather pre-Raphaelite beauty disguised no less strong a mind and personality. With her three children, she took a house in Pangbourne on the Thames, only a few miles away, and at a trying time began to come often to the Farjeons. Soon she and the Lawrences had become very friendly. At the end of June 1919, however, the Hermitage cottage was needed and the Lawrences had to move again; but since Bertie and Joan were going away on holiday, Rosalind went to house-sit for them, and the Lawrences spent most of August in her house in Pangbourne by the Thames. At the end of the month she returned but asked them to stay on for a weekend to see Godwin, who had come to discuss the future. Either then or soon afterwards, Rosalind decided to allow herself to be divorced, in order (given attitudes at the time) not to damage Godwin's medical career. However, there was bound to be unpleasant publicity, and she and the girls had best be out of England when it happened.

The Lawrences had been wanting to leave England since the suppression of *The Rainbow*, but only now at long last—a year after the end of the war—could they get valid passports to go: Frieda to Germany to see her family, but Lawrence to Italy where she would join him later. Sir Hamo had written to an Italian who used to model for him but had now retired to his village in the Abruzzi mountains south of Rome to ask if Rosalind and the children could go there— and Lawrence offered to try it out first. So after a stay in Florence waiting for Frieda, to Picinisco he and Frieda went. It was a spectacular place in the mountains, but quite the wrong time of year as autumn gave way to winter and it became very cold. Conditions were primitive—not at all suitable for Rosalind and three little English girls—but Lawrence arranged for them to stay in Florence instead, and wrote long letters of advice. (He had also made warm coats for each of the children before he left).[2] And so Rosalind moved to Italy. It was a bold move for a woman so to strike out on her own, but she did, and soon had found a fine old house called La Canovaia in San Gervasio, near Fiesole.

Lawrence's attitude to his marriage had changed since 1916–17 and its twin literary celebrations: the story of Ursula and Birkin in *Women in Love*, and the dramatized sequence of poems *Look! We Have Come Through!* The change was complex, but its baldest shorthand would be that the last year in Cornwall had grown tense, both because of his relationship with a young farmer William Henry Hocking, of whom Frieda became very jealous; and because of her affair with the young composer Cecil Gray, which may have got as far as the bedroom though the evidence is not conclusive. In 1919 Lawrence began to feel that he was too dependent on her; and that his manhood demanded he learn to stand clear and alone, though married. (Always he had tried to balance commitment with single individuality—now the emphasis was beginning to tip towards the latter, though still within marriage.) His new short stories began to explore kinds of male assertion; and he began to renounce all talk of love as the essential basis for relationship. Frieda was an unsympathetic nurse, and he felt so angry at her failure to care for him in his dangerous illness that he threatened briefly to leave her. He didn't and couldn't, however, and as they moved to Picinisco, then Capri, and then to Taormina in Sicily in 1920, they were still very much together, though as quarrelsome as ever. In the summer of 1920 Frieda determined to see her mother again; but again Lawrence would not go with her. Instead, he went on a walking tour with a couple from Cornwall, and then decided to go to Florence by himself. As it happened, Rosalind's house La Canovaia had lost its windows owing to the explosion of an ammunition dump not far away, and Rosalind and the children had had to move to Fiesole; but Lawrence was happy to camp out in the windowless house, to work in its quiet garden—and to walk up to Fiesole to renew his friendship with Rosalind and the children. She told Edward Nehls (for publication) how she remembered Lawrence "climbing by a steep track up through the olives and along under the remains of Fiesole's Etruscan walls, and arriving rather jauntily, carrying something peculiar and humorous—a salamander or a little baby duck as a pet for the children," and staying for dinner, or to cook them an English Sunday roast.[3] But the private memoir, now published by her middle daughter Chloe, reveals how the relationship changed. Rosalind describes how, after a modest supper of mortadella and marsala on Thursday 9 September, two days before Lawrence's 35th birthday, they walked out beyond the cypress woods where there were the scents of thyme and marjoram, and the nightjar bird noises of the hillside.[4] They talked, a little edgily.

> Then he switched away and said: "How do you feel about yourself now without sex in your life?"
>
> I said I wanted it of course.
>
> "Well, why don't you have it?" says he.
>
> "Yes, why not? But one is so damned fastidious."
>
> "Yes, damned fastidious! Yes, most people one can hardly bear to come near, far less make love with," says he.
>
> "Yes," say I, "and it's no good just making love; there must be more to it than a few pretty words and then off to bed."
>
> "Yes there must be more in it than that, but God save us from the so-called Love—that most indecent kind of egoism and self-spreading. Let us think of love as a force outside and getting us. It is a force; a god . . . "

He didn't see any reason why they shouldn't have each other. Or was it too complicated?

This was all very off-hand and I liked that. I can't answer for a while. I am so astounded at my happiness.

"Yes, indeed I want it." I say at last.

Firenze and her lights twirled around and I felt off the world. He is so wonderful; my source of acceptable and exciting wisdom of a kind unheard of until he came. I said: "I had no idea you thought about me so."

He laughed. Heavens, had I instantly disappointed him? Was it, as I feared, a laugh of "Oh, they're all alike," plunging into personal slop for all her professions of something better, determined to make conscious the unconscious? I told him I guessed what he was thinking about me, but then went on somehow:

" . . . but nevertheless how do you account for the fastidiousness we have been talking about if there is no personalism in love?"

"Oh yes," says he, "there must be understanding of the god *together.*"

We were silent again. I pulled up the bramble plant.

"Che forza" says he. "Let's go back."

We stumble back over the stones in the darkness.

"Tonight you won't have me?"

"No," though I longed to dash into his arms.

In half an hour we are home, laughing on the way; and in the bright, ugly little hall passage we embrace and kiss our promise. Then he went off down the hill to San Gervasio.

The next day I spent in the greatest elation, and the next day Saturday he came again. Was this our day? But no. I tidied everything in my room to make it sweet for him; but not then. Sunday he came to lunch. We made the dinner together, quite an English Sunday one, beef and batter; and everything was fun. He laughed and played with my Nan and understood her—as he did with children—with delicate, amused perception. We walked out after the heat was over, up behind Fiesole town through the trees and passing the Sunday strollers. Italian girls in fluffy voile dresses along the country roads. We saw the black grapes—"black to make you stare." We saw the grand turkey cock (see poems). The spirit of America as it was in the Indian primitive America to which European America was inevitably trending. Place Psyches . . . We come down the long rather squalid village street. Sorb apples we buy—"Suck them and then spit out the skin!" and home with things to cook for our supper on the terrace, three hundred feet above Firenze.

"How good it is here. It is something quite special and lovely, the time, the place, the beloved."

My heart jumps with joy. We sit until it is quite dark, our hands held together in unison.
And so to bed.

Gossip or no, one feels grateful that this has survived, because it is revealing, is it not? They are remarkably careful of each other, fastidious about not rushing until sure of meaning what they do, therefore non-exploitative, and yet joyous. Rosalind is no mere acolyte despite her echoing of his ideas (including those of his latest essay). The question she asks on the Thursday is the pertinent and right one, and his answer a fudge, since her personality so clearly entered into his feeling for her, and his behavior now. Was he perhaps too careful—not passionately impulsive enough, for an advocate of the "blood"? Yet his carefulness shows how he would also have been with Esther Andrews (about whom Mabel Dodge Luhan passed on gossip), if it had ever come to that—let alone with William Henry Hocking—unlikely to have been carried away by an impulse of the moment. He had refused to leap into bed on Frieda's first invitation too. His wife had claimed her freedom several times; but in the manner of taking his, he shows that he is still serious enough about marriage not to breach it casually. And though this would not be as impulsive as one of Frieda's affairs, it would also mean more. Rosalind is clear that the poems that came out of the experience expressed its meaning for him, as her secret preservation of the joy of it did for her. As for all the speculation about him—she does not sound as though she had found him disappointing as a lover.

This emotional experience clearly lay behind, and indeed inspired, the poems which so quickly followed, and was bound to affect their significance—though not simply. Indeed the most obvious effects are probably the least interesting. It adds only a little to the reading of the sexiest of them, "Fig," to detect a private pun behind the salute to the "thorn in flower," "the brave, adventurous rosaceae."[5] Nor will it much increase the sexuality of the poem to know how it may have been heightened by recent experience. What does come into new focus, however, is the *relation* as well as the contrast—privately experienced in the *same* woman—between secret fig-sexuality ("The fissure, the yoni/The wonderful moist conductivity towards the centre") with the Rose-utterance "openly pledging heaven," of her blossoming consciousness. To concentrate too much on the genital element of the poem, moreover, is to underplay its part in satirizing blatant modern attitudes to sex; and above all, in exploring the deeper tensions between fruition and decay, love and transience, that run through the poems written in La Canovaia in the next few days.

Yet one does have a sharper sense, now, of the exultant and defiant tone of the "fruit" poems. These notes were always there, yet we can now "hear" them anew in their own time, whatever we make of them where the poems have to achieve existence for us, in ours. The "you" that is mockingly challenged in "Pomegranate" and "Peach"[6]—the supposedly higher "pale-face" consciousness which would repress the red-dark sexually suggestive fruitfulness everywhere beneath the surface, and disapprove of him for so exposing and enjoying it—can also be read with an additional sense of what is supposed to be "wrong," and even a reminder (in "Peach") that stoning was the biblical punishment for adultery. Yet to read biographically by no means explains the poems. For they have got along very well for seventy years on their own; and what was uppermost in the poet's mind as he wrote is only part of what the poem can be. The fissure in "Pomegranate," for example, is much more than merely sexual; it has also to do with splits between death and life; ripeness, decay and renewal, very different from those hinted at in colonial Syracuse and once-prosperous commercial Venice. And of course "Peach" also embodies a richer suggestiveness than the sexual alone can encompass, though it is hinted at in the difference between the sexual body and ideal, mental, lifeless shapes.[7] Where biography stops, the critic should have much more to say about the multiple and complex operation of the language. Moreover, if all the "San Gervasio" and "Fiesole" poems can reveal a new, secret "life," the biographer also needs to call in criticism, in order to speak adequately of the richness of Lawrence's response to what had happened. It takes far more complex reading than Rosalind's story—touching though that is—and it is continuously exploratory, so that the poems become a related series, though I haven't time to demonstrate that now.[8] They reveal themselves as an exploration coming out of life and held together by that origin—yet not at all reducible to autobiography, and for all their complex relation to living experience and to one another, never losing their autonomy as separate poems.

He sent several of the "Fruits" to his agent on 15 September, saying "don't be scared," and suggested that they be offered to *New Republic* from whose editorial department he had received a request for poetry.[9] Another poem was posted the following day. This may have been "Medlars and Sorb Apples," if only because that seems later, with its sense of the "taste" whose sweetness, now, already has the foretaste of decay: winter, the underworld of loss, yet the soul "distilled in separation."

A kiss, and a vivid spasm of farewell, a moment's orgasm of rup-
ture
Then along the damp road alone, till the next turning.
And there, another parting, a new partner, a new unfusing into
twain,
A new gasp, of isolation, intense,
A new pungency of loneliness, among the decaying, frost-cold
leaves;
Going down the road, more alone after each meeting,
The fibres of the heart parting one after the other,
And yet the soul continuing, naked-footed, ever more vividly
embodied,
Ever more exquisite, distilled in separation.

So in the strange retorts of medlars and sorb apples
The distilled potion of departure,
The exquisite fragrance of farewell. Jamque vale!
The secret of Orpheus and Hades.
Each soul departing in its own essence,
Never having known its own essence before.[10]

Perhaps there is previously undiscovered irony, now, in Louis
Untermeyer's having termed him lately in the *New Republic* the poet
of frustration; and new resonance in his own defiant acceptance of
conflict, in writing to Untermeyer on 13 September.[11] For although
he could not regret what he had so fastidiously and deliberately
chosen, it would be very awkward for both Rosalind and himself if it
developed. Yet he must have had conflicting feelings about that,
too. He could not want her to feel used, if he ran away. But was he,
having worried about her being frightened by Douglas scandal when
arranging for her to stay in the same pensione as Norman Douglas,
to risk involving her scandalously with himself, to add to the coming divorce hearing? The expatriate community, even in Florence,
was small and certainly gossipy enough for scandal to spread quickly.
Or again, as in "Medlars and Sorb Apples" he may have felt most
what the poem declares the "secret of Orpheus and Hades": the
hellish yet exquisite experience of renewed isolation, with increased
self-knowledge.

He began to haver. On the 17th he wrote an odd letter to John
Ellingham Brooks in Capri, saying that he didn't want to hang about
in Florence waiting for Frieda much longer, and was it possible to
share the house-sitting of Compton Mackenzie's Casa Solitaria for a
fortnight or so? This was, however, a little like St. Augustine's "Lord
make me chaste, but not yet," since he didn't propose to come for
another week or more. The very next day the problem was brought
to decision, by a letter from Frieda. She wanted him to come to

Baden-Baden, which she probably knew he would refuse; but she suggested as an alternative that they should meet with their young painter friends Juta and Insole in Venice on the 28th. He wrote an apologetic letter to Frieda's mother, of whom he was fond, pleading that it was too late in the year to come north now, though he would come next spring. But to Venice he would go.

There is no sign of how often or on what terms he saw Rosalind in the fortnight between their going to bed and his going back to his wife. There is however an extraordinary account of what it is to be imbued with the most new-born being-alone; or (conversely) to be filled with desire; or progressively "crucified in the flesh" (a term of Untermeyer's), between the two. This is displaced and transformed with extraordinary observation and great humor—but also (one sees now) with nicely adjusted fellow-feeling *and* self-distancing—in six poems about the tortoise family in the garden of La Canovaia. It is not that the poems about tortoises are really poems about Lawrence; but something far more interesting, and more unusual. The life of these poems required two conditions: exact observation and perception of tortoises and their sexuality, and the exclusion of what on that evening with Rosalind he had called "self-spreading." Yet the humor manifestly comes from a relationship between the man observing from his point of view, and the beasts intent on their non-human life, a relation that is both gulf and imaginative affinity.

He would write later of Van Gogh's most famous painting that its value lay neither in the rendering of sunflowers, nor in the rendering of the painter's feelings, but in the "perfected relation, at a certain moment, between a man and a sunflower," or more grandly, between "man and his circumambient universe."[12] If one may feel, reading the poems, an essence as it were of tortoise-ness caught there, that is because Lawrence so firmly kept his eye on the beasts and not on himself. And yet he "saw" with the sensibility he spontaneously brought to bear, and *that* had a great deal to do with the comedy and tragedy of sex that he had just re-experienced for himself, and which made for the tone that is also all-important in the poems. They are non-human but humanly observed; non-anthropomorphic in one sense, yet only the-man-Lawrence could have so created their humorous/ironic interplay with his humanity. Being "crucified in the flesh" is an idea, but the crosses on the tortoise-shell are "there" in both life and art—as is the male tortoise's soundless· orgasmic but also agonized cry, and the poet "seeing" and "hearing" in the language of the poems. Moreover, the relationship at a certain moment which they embody also implies, for both man and circumambulant beast, an unrelated and quite distinct being, *outside* the poems. Art can never be biography, nor biography explain any work of art. Life and art, and the differing disciplines that try to attend to each in their own proper terms, must retain their proper degree of autonomy. Yet it can perhaps help critics attend to what the poet—for Lawrence, "the whole man, wholly attending"—brought to the tortoises, at that moment, though it is the critic who must discover in its own detail what each poem then does, and what they do together.

Both the biographer and the critic should reinforce in each other the most significant point of all: the sequence of the poems in their process of interrelated exploration. The biographer must realize how the poems delicately, subtly, and extraordinarily balance the feelings of the man who had deliberately turned away from love and its dependence, determined to stand alone—but who now must know, fully, the combined ecstasy and torture of having succumbed again. The tiny "Baby Tortoise," alone without knowing it, is a living embodiment of what the Lawrence of 1919–20 said he wanted to be, single, an "invincible fore-runner," indomitable, self-sufficient. Embedded *in* the "Tortoise Shell" from the beginning, however, is the sign of the cross. And in "Tortoise Family Connections" and "Lui et Elle" there is the certainty that the baby tortoise's "arrogance" of being "all to himself" will be overcome by the imperative needs of sexual connection: the male driven, compelled to persist, doomed to make an intolerable fool of himself, forced continually to run after, snap at, pester, a female much bigger than he is—wicked comedy![13] Finally however, the full paradox of the opposite desires— the longing for singleness, the opposite longing for completion—is brought out in the tortoise's orgasmic cry: the cry of crucifixion in the flesh that is both paean and agony, death and birth, triumph and submission, self-laceration, abandonment, and fulfilment.

> Sex, which breaks up our integrity, our single inviolability, our deep silence
> Tearing a cry from us.

> Sex, which breaks us into voice, sets us calling across the deeps, calling, calling for the complement,
> Singing, and calling, and singing again, being answered, having found.

> Torn, to become whole again, after long seeking for what is lost,
> The same cry from the tortoise as from Christ, the Osiris-cry of abandonment,
> That which is whole, torn asunder,
> That which is in part, finding its whole again throughout the universe.

For the critic, the exploration of what each poem does in itself, in the detail of its language, and of what the poems in sequence do to one another, and together, can surely only be enriched by the realization of what they had to do with the "whole man, wholly attending"—though that does not explain the nature of their life as poetry, word by word, line by line, tone by tone, at which I have done no more than glance.

I think, moreover, that the experience with Rosalind Baynes played a part a year later in unblocking a novel, *Aaron's Rod*, that Lawrence had been unable to progress with, other than by jumping its protagonist picaresque, from Eastwood to London to Turin, to Florence. Aaron Sissons is a man who on a sudden impulse leaves his wife, out of a deep longing to be single-in-himself; but he is played off against Rawdon Lilly, a Lawrence-like figure, who has no intention of leaving his wife, though he has no more time than Aaron does for lovey-doveyness or for modern assertive womanhood. The novel had originally been started shortly after the Lawrences were expelled from Cornwall, but had never taken off and was abandoned. In Sicily eighteen months later, in July 1920, it was begun again. But by September, having been "jumped" chapter by chapter to just over half of what Lawrence wanted, it stuck once more. Then Frieda's mother fell ill in 1921, and Frieda had to go to Baden-Baden to take care of her—and this time Lawrence had to go with her. There, staying out of town in an inn in the village of Ebersteinburg, on the edge of the Black Forest, he went every morning to sit with his back to a pine tree and write—and there, the novel suddenly came unstuck and sped to its conclusion. I am confident that what made all the difference was the idea of having Aaron—who is a flautist, good enough to play professionally—have an affair with the American wife of an Italian Marchese, who has been a singer, but has a psychological inhibition against singing anymore. This becomes a decisive crisis, which precipitates the novel's ending when a bomb thrown into a cafe completes the split in Aaron (and his flute which is destroyed) and finally and dramatically poses his dilemma.

The Cambridge edition of *Aaron's Rod*[14] notes that the Marchesa "may have been suggested" by the American wife of the Marchese Carlo Torrigiani, to whom Lawrence had been introduced at one of her musical Sunday at-homes. However, though Lawrence often used apparently identifiable people as material, his re-creations were nonetheless fictive, free, and complex; and there is in fact little physical resemblance between his Marchesa and the large American woman who was studying singing to whom he introduced Catherine Carswell later in 1921.[15] If autobiographical material went into the imagining of Aaron's relationship with the Marchesa, it was surely the episode with Rosalind. But it should *not* be assumed that the 1921 fiction embodied DHL's true or final feelings about the experience of 1920. For to whatever extent he thought of himself and Rosalind, his imagination both transposed and selected for fictive purposes, and not merely for disguise. The idea of centering the whole episode on music, and therefore emphasizing one strand from the complex web of feeling and memory was, above all, thematic.

Now Aaron's flute—which had not budded like the one in the Bible—becomes a way of bringing about the major conflict within Aaron himself, and then of bringing his debate with Lilly the married man to a final question. Aaron has deeply not wanted a new sexual relationship. He has realized that he had never intended really to surrender himself to his wife, and therefore that his whole idea of himself as lover and husband has been a false mask. Now the flute—as opposed to the piano, let alone the orchestra—becomes a symbolic showing, both to himself and the woman, of what entire singleness of life would be like:

> It was a clear, sharp, lilted run-and-fall of notes, not a tune in any sense of the word, and yet a melody: a bright, quick sound of pure animation: a bright, quick animate noise, running and pausing . . . the notes followed clear and single one after another . . . a wild sound.

It has no artful form, yet is naturally harmonious. It is blessedly free from moral meaning or responsibility, and also from the burden of nervous emotion and consciousness. It liberates its hearer from consciousness of self, giving her freedom just to be. It needs no accompaniment or combination, and its notes are separate and single, unlike the piano's chords. It also embodies Lawrence's continual search for a language older than our present culture: mediaeval rather than Renaissance, but actually more archaic than mediaeval, indeed more ancient still, behind even Apollo to Marsyas and Pan, something wild rather than civilized—in our sense, that is. The Marchesa is able to sing again, while Aaron plays: the two singlenesses in one which an earlier Lawrence would have endorsed. But therein, and still more in the awakening, now, of desire through the music of singleness, there is a growing and ironic contradiction. The sexual budding of Aaron's rod now, with the Marchesa, not only exposes double meanings and contradictory powers—phallus as opposed to flute—but also begins to complicate what had seemed the primary contrast between Aaron and Lilly. It must have become clear that the debate between the longing for singleness and the belief in marriage (the contradiction in Lawrence himself) would need to be re-stated with greater complexity.

So, if Lawrence "used" his experience with Rosalind in imagining Aaron, what he chose to emphasize thematically, from among the many and complicated feelings in the poems, were those elements *alone* which would throw into the highest relief the challenge of sex to singleness and turn Aaron away in intense repudiation and a kind of agony—powerfully rendered in imaginative terms, drawn out of the self as all dramatizations are, but not on that account to be regarded as self-revelation by Lawrence. Aaron's experience with the Marchesa is the turning point in the novel which decisively separates out love (of any kind) from singleness, and reveals them as mutually exclusive, as far as Aaron is concerned. His sexual excitement robs him of his alertness, as of a single wild animal, so that he gets mugged in the street, his Being violated. Moreover, imagination concentrates and explores to an extreme the element in Lawrence that longed for singleness and non-dependence. Coition becomes a victimization of the god-in-Aaron; the ecstasy not a kind of death-and-rebirth (as in *The Rainbow*) but an extraction of his passionate power, "excruciating" as much as "gratifying," leaving him "blasted" and "withered." The child-woman on his chest becomes a clinging from which he finally recoils because it conceals *her* "strange and hateful power." Throughout, "there was all the time something hard and reckless and defiant, which stood apart."[16] Afterwards he feels *only* what "Medlars and Sorb Apples" in its revised version expresses—one feeling among many poems—"as the soul departing with its own isolation,/Strangest of all strange companions,/And best."[17] Aaron tells the Marchesa that he feels himself still married; but then writes a letter that is really to himself: renouncing all kinds of love and declaring his belief only "in the fight and nothing else," against woman, against the world, against "love which is of all things the most deadly to me."

Yet we forget at our peril that that "me" is a character in a novel—and a character moreover who the book shows to be unable to live alone. Aaron's feelings are not to be taken uncritically *in* the fiction—he himself is aware of his unfairness to the Marchesa—still less outside it, as supposedly summing up Lawrence's final verdict on the episode with Rosalind. Aaron is only part of D. H. Lawrence. Moreover the imagining of his repudiation of the Marchesa will force Lawrence to explore the contradiction between "Aaron" and the "Lilly" in himself at a deeper level. If Aaron won't have love, and can't live alone, what is his future? Furthermore, the bomb in the cafe shows the folly of imagining that one can live apart from society. The flute-as-singleness must be split asunder through internal and external contradiction. The complex imaginative exploration must go on.

Once more the biographer has to draw the line firm between biography and criticism, as well as, I hope, continuing to show the possibility of fruitful relationship, if one is careful enough. With my biographer's hat on, I maintain that both the poems and the novel must be crucial evidence, in their own proper complexity, of what the impact on Lawrence of his experience with Rosalind was—but only if we put on our critical hats as well, as best we can. Conversely, if I were to try to write critically on the novel now, I would regard it as humanly reductive to pretend that the episode with Rosalind had nothing to do with it, but I would also require sensitive and complex biography to show just how *different* Lawrence's exploratory imagining became.

Finally I will just mention, as a last proportioning, what may have been spotted, that an artist and his two "modern" daughters will appear in *Lady Chatterley's Lover*, and that in some respects the daughter called Constance is physically reminiscent of Rosalind—especially in the middle of the three versions of the novel.[18] But though this may perhaps suggest a lingering tenderness, I do not believe that Rosalind is usefully regarded as "the original" of the character (though she will have contributed along with others); or that "Hilda" reveals Lawrence's true feelings about her sister Joan—and Lawrence never met their father, who was very unlike Sir Malcolm Reid. I cannot find any significant ways in which biographical knowledge of what happened in Fiesole in 1920 affects one's reading of the developing fiction of 1926–28. There, the appropriate relation would seem to be a footnote.

Spring Semester 1995

1.  Rosalind Thornycroft, *Time Which Spaces Us Apart*, edited, completed, and privately published by Chloe Baynes (London, 1991).

2.  Thornycroft, *Time Which Spaces us Apart*, p. 66.

3.  Edward Nehls, *D. H. Lawrence: A Composite Biography*, II (Madison, 1958), pp. 49–50.

4.  Nehls, *D. H. Lawrence*, II, pp 49–50; Thornycroft, *Time Which Spaces us Apart*, pp. 78–79. Rosalind heads her account "September 11th 1920. D.H. Lawrence's birthday"; but the birthday was on Saturday, fitting neither the supper with which the account begins, nor the "And so to bed" with which it ends on Sunday. The most likely explanation is that she associated the experience with the birthday, but had forgotten on which of the days she describes it actually fell.

5.  This was acutely suggested some years ago, without knowing its full context, by Derek Britton, *Lady Chatterley: The Making of the Novel* (London, 1988), p. 83.

6.  "You tell me I am wrong./Who are you, who is anybody to tell me I am wrong?/I am not wrong." ("Pomegranate"). "Would you like to throw a stone at me?/Here, take all that's left of my peach" ("Peach"). "Look at them standing there in authority/The pale-faces,/As if it could have effect any more" ("The Revolutionary").

7.  "Why the groove?/Why the lovely, bivalve roundnesses?/Why the ripple down the sphere?/Why the suggestion of incision?/Why was not my peach round and finished like a billiard ball/It would have been if man had made it . . . "

8.  The private pun, for instance, suddenly acquires a much deeper resonance in the opposition between the "rose" and the "vine" in "Grapes" (adding a huge historical and psychic dimension to Lawrence's attitude towards the woman who embodied both); and in the further opposition between "pale-face" ethics, and the subversive "dark and moving hosts" in "The Revolutionary" and the underworld dark suggestiveness of "Etruscan Cypresses," to which the poet declares allegiance. The immediate connection of "Etruscan Cypresses" with the "fruit" poems and "The Revolutionary" has been obscured by its separation in *Birds, Beasts and Flowers* (London, 1923) into a different section of "Trees."

9.  James T. Boulton and Andrew Robertson (eds.), *The Letters of D. H. Lawrence*, vol. III (Cambridge, 1984), p. 596 and n. 2. The magazine printed "Medlars and Sorb Apples" and "The Revolutionary" in January 1921. "Pomegranate" came out in *Dial* in March.

10. Quoted from the original version published in the *New Republic*, Jan. 5, 1921. The poem ends with sorb apples "savored, perhaps with a sip of Marsala,/So that the withering, morbid grape can add its refrain to yours./Farewell, and farewell, and farewell."

11. "D. H. Lawrence," *New Republic*, XXIII (Aug. 11, 1920), reprinted in R. P. Draper (ed.), *The Critical Heritage* (London, 1970), pp. 132–35; and Lawrence's reply in Boulton and Robertson (eds.), *Letters* (Cambridge) III, p. 595.

12. "Morality and the Novel" (London, 1925) in Bruce Steele (ed.), *Study of Hardy and Other Essays* (Cambridge, 1985), p. 171.

13. Part of its wickedness is the way that looking at the tortoises—or the poems—tends immediately to precipitate an opposition of male and female sympathies.

14. Edited by Mara Kalnins (Cambridge, 1988), p. 325.

15. Nehls, *D. H. Lawrence*, II, p. 72; from *The Savage Pilgrimage* (London, 1932; reprinted Cambridge, 1981), p. 148.

16. Cambridge edition pp. 258–63, 272–74, and the cancelled passage p. 307.

17. *English Review*, July 1921, p. 81–82.

18.  To the "ruddy coloring and soft brown hair" of *The First Lady Chatterley* (Penguin, p. 17, and common to all versions) is added in *John Thomas and Lady Jane* (Penguin, p. 79) a "golden-ruddy" tone corresponding more closely to David Garnett's description of Constance as "a russeted apple in face." Parkin thinks of Constance as "a woman with a gentle, warm soul and a warm, soft desirous body," *The First Lady Chatterley*, p. 120. More specific still, Constance made quaint drawings and illustrations for old books "and got commissions for illustrating some children's book or some quaint little volume of verse . . . she really had a certain gift." (*John Thomas and Lady Jane*, pp. 14, 41). Rosalind studied at the Slade, and illustrated Eleanor Farjeon's *Nuts and May*, a book of verse and stories for children. As Britten once more was the first to point out, however, Rosalind's marriage and divorce are given to "Hilda," and it was Godwin, not she, who had studied music at Dresden. Does knowledge of these sources affect one's reading?

# 9

# Orwell and the Business of Biography

## BERNARD CRICK

Anyone can see that nowadays biography is big business.[1] If W. H. Auden were writing his *Phi Beta Kappa* poem today, he might alter one word in his immediate post-war lament that "enormous *novels* by Co-eds rain down on our defenceless heads . . ." If one reflected on why there seems an insatiable public demand for biographies of almost every kind at every level, one might conclude that, at a popular level, an indulgent curiosity in other people's lives, often involving vicarious fantasy, is fed heavily by the press and the habitual naturalism of television drama and soaps. But, more fundamentally, one would then conclude that part of modernism has long been a propensity to see all explanations in personal terms. People are more likely to read a life of Stalin than a history of the Soviet Union, a life of Mary Queen of Scots rather than an account of the Scottish politics she never understood, the life of a newspaper owner rather than a history of a great paper he has debased, or even a life of Freud rather than a critique of Freudianism. And that, they will think, is it. T. S. Eliot once called "personality" the "blasphemy of our times."

The word "biography" can create as many different expectations as the word "Orwell." There is Orwell as Orwellian—the gloomy prophet-pessimist of *Nineteen Eighty-Four*, so it is said, though I see the book as Swiftian satire, if only marginally more cheerful for that;[2] and there is Orwell as Orwell-like, the speculative essayist, humorist, humanist, lover of nature and of all small and curious things.[3] The word "biography" can mean a memorial or a panegyric; it can mean a hatchet job, or it can simply mean a good read. Now, of course, the hatchet job, whether literary journalism (stemming from Lytton Strachey) or political journalism (stemming from W. T. Stead in Britain or Lincoln Steffens in America), was itself partly reaction to both the pious monuments of the Victorian "lives and times" formula—the rolling down of a red carpet and the sweeping of all dross and dirt underneath; and also to the mercifully shorter celebratory lives, exemplary lives, of the *From Log Cabin to White House* ilk, or Samuel Smiles and Horatio Alger on the great entrepreneurs, explorers and inventors, often published in series well called "Popular Lives" or "Short Lives." This tradition has not died out, nor should it. "Let us now praise famous men," and women indeed: "There is a time and place for all things." I notice that Michael Foot now calls in its paperback edition his *Life of Aneurin Bevan*, "a polemical biography." Perhaps he is reacting to some criticism by pedantic historians that his book is just a wee bit partial. And so splendidly it is. There is a place in our culture for holding up certain lives as noble examples. I do not wish to say that these are not biography. They are precisely what many still mean by biography. Names are not sacred; only actions are good or bad.

Wyndham Lewis once said, disarmingly but perversely, that good biographies are like novels. Certainly, the common reader seldom looks for or follows up footnotes, and even scholarly biographers of famous figures are under great commercial pressure to lose or hide the footnotes; rather the reader welcomes a coherent, evenly flowing story and a clear portrait of a character. By and large, the truth of a text is either taken for granted or discrepancies are discussed not in terms of evidence but simply (post-modernists all) in terms of the different personal viewpoints of different authors or critics. And this kind of biography can exist for different levels of readership, just like novels.

So long as the difference is clear between popular and scholarly biography there is no need to label my sort legitimate and the rest bastard. Biographers, whose primary intent is not like a good historian to try by all means to discover and tell the truth (or truths), often fulfill, nonetheless, some useful, cultural role. But just let us not confuse the categories. I found some reviewers of my *George Orwell: A Life* who obviously expected me either to "put the case for Orwell" or to "cut him down to size at last," and were not merely disappointed when I didn't, but then accused me of doing just the other. Some old friends of his said that I evidently disliked him and most of his enemies said I was finding excuses for him, though they all conceded that I had provided a load of factual information that might one day be useful to someone else, to save someone more sensitive the sweat of working the streets like a detective-sergeant. Theoretically unfashionable attempts to be reasonably balanced and objective may more or less have worked when one is attacked from both sides at once. Epistemologically, I know that the position is now held to be absurd, even authoritarian, but a biographer cannot help feeling a bit smug when, nailed up there on one's own cross, the blood flows down from both cheeks.

Yet scholarly biographies have peculiar difficulties, some of which I discussed in the Introduction to *Orwell: A Life*. Michael Shelden in the Preface to his *Orwell: The Authorised Biography* (1992) mocked me for saying that "An honest biographer must be more dull than he could be." He professed to find that "the logic of this statement is still hard to grasp," yet saw it as typical of my "deliberately flat account of his life."[4] But my point was clear enough, and plainly Michael Shelden seems to share Wyndham Lewis's wild view that biographies should aspire to the novel. That certainly gives biographers more freedom and scope for effect, or do I mean "affect"? The novelist has a reasonable control over his or her characters, the plot, the length of chapters and the balance of one part of the narrative against another. And if he or she chooses to play modernist or post-modernist games with them, why so she and he can. But the scholarly biographer is sadly limited to what can be said truthfully by the availability of the evidence and the reliability of witnesses, however far beyond imagination might soar. And evidence, like witnesses, comes in all shapes and sizes and with all kinds of gaps: skill, patience and energy are necessary, but they are useless without luck, and they cannot recreate lost or destroyed papers, or reconstitute decayed memories or correct false memories. The final evidence can look very like that celebrated Irish description of a fishing net: a series of holes surrounded by string.

Sometimes one has more documentation than is needed or is easy to handle. Sometimes one has, as for the Burma period in Orwell's life, very little direct evidence. Nothing is rational, everything is accident. Orwell's letters to his agent, over almost thirty years, survive; but not his agent's letters to him. Two letters of George's to Sonia, his second wife, survive, and none from her to him. (Oh, I have my suspicions; but they are not evidence; and I could be wrong: either possibility to explain no letters implies presuming a motive: a reason for destruction by her, or simply indifference to him.) More mundanely, in writing a scholarly biography there is no way, without excessive speculation and padding, to ensure any proportionality between the length of chapters and the probable importance of various episodes of someone's life. I was not being foolishly modest or nervously defensive when I said in the Introduction that I could have produced a better book. I am not being modest at all. I will boast that I can write as well as most academic biographers and better than nearly all other social scientists. I actually enjoy writing. But if one's primary commitment is to truth based on evidence rather than to telling a good story based on intuition, then lumpiness and unevenness must be accepted. Literary facility can prove deadly if it tempts a biographer into lack of respect for the limitations of the evidence available. Publishers and agents may, however, understandably take the view that glibness is all. That is why I have never used an agent. I am not so righteous that I can take the risk of going for walks with the tempter.

Now of course I admit that this is not an all-or-nothing proposition. I am no advocate of that school of historical biography which dishes up documents raw and even uninterpreted on a scale only limited by the resources of university presses and foundation subsidies, or as Leon Edel said in his "A Manifesto" in the first issue of the journal *Biography*, "Like crushed cars in a car cemetery." Who are such historians writing for—themselves? Or there is the extreme, contrary response, as when the writer J. A. Symons chose to write the life of a notorious if talented liar, Frederick Rolfe, who moved among men to whom secrecy and duplicity were second nature, where documentation was destroyed, forged or scarce, and all living memory suspect for self-interest: therefore, he wrote his *Quest for Corvo* as an account of his quest and of his relationship with the witnesses, as if a novel. Decency, let alone the laws of libel, closed that door to me.

One of the main problems of a scholarly biographer is to define audience. If simply fellow scholars in "a field," that is easy, if sometimes sadly and unnecessarily limited. But if writing for the educated, general reader, then certain assumptions have to be made. Orwell reasonably (but mistakenly) assumed that *Animal Farm* would be read only by his existing small British readership who knew perfectly well what the satirist's own political position was; but after reading many of the American reviews, it was far less sensible for him to assume that American reviewers and readers of *Nineteen Eighty-Four* would realize that he was not throwing a comprehensive curse at all socialism, only at totalitarian varieties. In my life of Orwell, I presumed a serious but non-academic general reader, such as he himself wrote for, who had already read a good deal of him but who, even on my side of the great water, might need a little gentle reminding about historical events and socialist groupings between the two world wars, and, on the other shore, a little tactful information about the same (more than David Herbert Donald felt was needed writing on Lincoln for already convicted Civil War addicts, but far short of the "Life and Times" honored formula for filling pages).[5]

A biographer who presumes a serious readership, however, must present the evidence, must not merely have footnotes (which trade publishers and designers hate) but must bind himself or herself to saying nothing of importance that cannot be footnoted. But perhaps if the footnotes are detailed and sometimes long, as when one needs to discuss the reliability of evidence, and if they are tucked away at the back of the book, then the text can be kept reasonably clean and flowing. I tried to keep both scholars and general readers in mind. So the final result was, of course, as are most things in life, a compromise.

What is biography really about? I deliberately called my work a "Life" of Orwell because, as I argued in the Introduction, the word "biography" has since the time of Johnson and Boswell come to imply the portrait of a "character." The main business of a biographer has often been thought to be that of "getting inside" a subject, "grasping the inwardness," "knowing another person," or "revealing the true personality"—in a word, empathy. And this is why, presumably, Wyndham Lewis would prefer the novelist to the historian as biographer. Now I set out with this common view in mind, which I now hold to be romantic. For I gradually became impressed with the ambiguity of much of the evidence and even, in order to make good some well-established readings of Orwell's character, with the need to suppress contrary evidence. Critics are entitled to believe that in justifying an external, almost alienated approach, I was rationalizing a defeat. Several leading reviews, not merely by old friends of Orwell's, paid great tribute to my energy, industry, sense of period, and grasp of history, before saying either that I failed to paint a credible character, or that he was not as they remembered. But I'm unrepentant, and though, sentimentally, I would love to have met him—he feels like a lost lover whom I never knew—yet for the purposes of true biography I see advantages in having no personal memories. For while each of those reviewers was able to paint in a few paragraphs a more coherent picture of Orwell's character than I was able to do at great length, yet these miniatures were, while all life-like and beautiful, each quite different from the other and each fused with autobiography. Like so many of the obituaries of George Orwell, they were fine and noble writing but showed considerable diversity in characterization.

The point is an epistemological one: in the nature of knowing and being, can we really know the character even of people we are very close to, lovers, friends and family, in such a way that we can surmise accurately (as adolescents torture each other) "what are you really thinking"? Can we use such "knowledge" of character, such as it is, to entail facts: actually to fill gaps in the record of what some other was doing in the many years before, let us say, she remade our life, still less to be sure what her former motivations were? Surely not, or if so, only with the gravest truth warnings attached to the addictive packet. Yet English biographers, famous for their good judgement of people (which in itself may be a national stereotype, vice or collective delusion) commonly do just that. They follow the great Dr. Johnson in his *Lives of the English Poets* — "I knew that poor wretch, Savage," more intimately than he admitted, in fact; and even then he suppressed much and was cavalier about the need for documentation.[6] Enough that the Grand Cham said so and exercised his judgement. So a life is then inferred from a character. Now indeed, if we live with people or meet them intimately or often, we can build up a fair knowledge of their likes and dislikes, even of their probable behavior in response to past and future events—and different people's abilities will differ in all this, some are more empathetic than others. We can become fair judges of each other's probable behavior, allowing for a good many surprises and misunderstandings. But I am not a behaviorist. These things cannot be measured. Amid necessity there is human freedom. I suspect that most people who talk so confidently about the character of Orwell or anyone else do not really want to commit themselves to what Ernest Gellner once called *radical intuitionism*—the belief that you can have direct knowledge of somebody else's motives.

No names, no pack drill, but if I heard once on my trail, I heard a dozen times something like this: "I really didn't know Orwell awfully well; to tell the truth, Professor, we only met over lunch or drinks three or four times by way of business; but somehow we clicked at once . . ."

When, occasionally, this kind of claim could produce words and memories specific enough to be plausible, all I could do was to put it alongside other different revelations and puzzle: usually, I couldn't count them as evidence at all or only by default (and with warnings) if they related to some event in Orwell's life for which hard evidence was lacking. Why did he go to Burma? Why did he go to Spain? Why did he go to Jura? Why did he want a second marriage so badly? Only then did I think it right to trouble the reader with the speculative soft evidence of different opinions. As Brecht said of theatre: if people demand what *the true* interpretation of Hamlet is, don't satisfy them, refuse to over-interpret; better that each one of the audience make up his or her own mind differently (that's a tribute to the richness of the text) rather than that the actor and the producer should try to solve the enigma definitively and smooth it all out for them.

I think it is possible to give, as far as surviving evidence allows, a reasonably objective and reliable account of how someone led his or her life. Sometimes, the quantity of evidence may overwhelm one, so of course one makes judgements as to what was important. And to work on too large a scale may lose one's audience. In Orwell's case I chose (or rather I came to find myself choosing), not very surprisingly, to concentrate on his attempts to write and publish his books—as Marxists and structuralists would say, on his "literary production"; a useful enough phrase, on its own. But I note that if Malcolm Muggeridge had carried out his original commission to write a biography of Orwell, it would have been an account of the struggles of a Christian without God to find a cause; just as gentle and well-meaning Sir Richard Rees, who had known Orwell very well, did write a book about Orwell as "almost a saint."

If I concede that there is "character" in some unpretentious sense, then at least I must remind, in very friendly spirit, some good old friends of Orwell's, who said kind things about my book except that I missed his character, that they only knew him relatively late in his life. And that what he told each of them about his earlier life and states of mind is not conclusive evidence. Our own interpretations of our own past live and change; one reveals different things to different people; and if one never lies, as a German woman once said to me, one seldom sees need to tell the whole truth. Their own readings of his character—not surprisingly, thinking of their own diverse backgrounds, viewpoints and talents, and the fact that memory is not a passive filter—differed. Friends see friends as part of their own lives. Part of how we now see him is through the very diversity of the testimony of all who knew him well, quite as much as in the common ground. I presumed readers who might for once like being left alone with divergent testimonies to make up their own minds, not to be handed on plate a solution by some super-intelligent and super-empathetic biographer. The externalizing, the distancing, the "alienation effect," if you like, became deliberate: indeed I now think that that is the only proper stance for a biographer to take if the aim is to tell a true tale about a life and not the presumption of godlike last judgement on character and achievement. Too much English biography is an extended version of the Headmaster's report.

Preconceptions about character, even by those who knew the subject well, can actually end up contradicting the actual course of a life. Sonia Orwell was passionately convinced that it was not in his real character to be so political, and that in turning to her he was showing the dominance of his literary over his political self. Leaving aside whether this "politics" versus "literature" is not a false disjunction—he said that "above all else" he wanted to make "political writing into an art"—and leaving aside any speculations about other reasons why a man would turn to Sonia, her view involves a fallacy that I name "speculative teleology": what he should have done had he lived differently or longer, the logic of the "real character," not the contingent course of the actual life. Sonia wrote in her Introduction to the (so-called) *Collected Essays:*

> If political events had made less impact on him, he would have
> lived in the country, written a book—preferably a novel once a
> year, pursued his interest in the essay form and, when money was
> badly lacking, done straightforward book reviews which, he said,
> he enjoyed writing . . . War made him a political activist.

But if she meant the Second World War, he was by then already a political activist; and if she meant the Spanish War, that was a war that he chose to fight in, went out of his way actually to fight in, not simply to visit Spain for conferences like Connolly, Auden, and Spender. I quote this passage not so much to show that Sonia was wrong in her judgement of his "character," making it indeed an article of faith among her own friends that she would have saved him for Literature from politics; rather I quote it to show the danger of all such judgements based on the concept of "character." Since she was so clear what his real character was, several important or revealing political essays were discarded from the *Collected Essays, Journalism and Letters,* as being in her perspective inferior, not typical or repetitive.

So a "character study" cannot be the same as a "life." Arthur Koestler regretted that I failed in those laborious 473 pages to grasp Orwell's character as well as a Mr. Peter Lewis in a sprightly picture book. Perhaps so, but I was irritated that Koestler failed to notice why I was so openly skeptical of the concept of character. Let me try once more. I had interviewed Koestler once at length and more briefly talked twice in social occasions and had read most of his English works. From this I could have written a decent character sketch, certainly good enough for a *Times* obituary or an *Observer* profile; but this would have been as far from a life or a biography as Hyperion from a Satyr. Iain Hamilton wrote a biography of Koestler in his lifetime in which he did not trouble to look for any primary sources whatever (assuming that he had German, Russian, Hungarian and Spanish) for the first thirty-five years of Koestler's life, on the generous and convenient grounds that Koestler had himself written autobiographies covering that murky period.[7] But surely a prime duty of any biographer of a writer is to examine critically the relationship between the writer's own autobiographical writings and what actually happened? (He owes us a second edition now that many Communist archives are now open.) The distance between autobiography and biography may not discredit the man so much as enhance the writer. Both with Koestler and Orwell many critics and reviewers were naive to accept a professional writer's use of the first person as always an attestation of public truth.

Sonia Orwell, as is well known, was upset both by some of my judgements and by my "putting Orwell in the box," she said, as if it was wrong to doubt the literal truth of anything he wrote in the first person. She once shouted at me across a restaurant table, "Of course he shot a fucking elephant, he said so, didn't he!" "Short story, Sonia, short story!" I bellowed back (until a third bottle of wine restored temporary peace—there are practical difficulties in biography not covered in the manuals). Such skepticism seemed to me the elementary duty of any scholarly biographer. One of the practical difficulties of modern biography in general is with owners of the copyright in words (now unhappily extended in Europe), especially widows and sisters—for women live longer: Nietzsche, Wagner, Kipling, Eliot, Keynes, Orwell, and so on. To be fair to Sonia Orwell, when she asked me to do the biography, quite out of the blue, not knowing me nor I knowing her, she agreed to my firm condition that as well as complete access to the papers, I should have an absolute and prior waiver of copyright so that I could quote what I liked and write what I liked. These were hard terms, even if the only terms on which, I think, a scholar should and can take on a contemporary biography. It was courageous of her to meet them. That she signed such a contract (at the very last minute) should be a noble example to what she would often racily call "'the widows' union.'"[8]

That is only one of the special difficulties of contemporary biography. The obvious advantage of having living witnesses is partially balanced by the personal involvement of some of them, particularly if writers themselves, in the reputation of the subject. Also publication itself stimulates both new witnesses and unexpected reactions from old witnesses to the actual text. For instance George Mikes and Andre Deutch, no less, had been sitting on yet another authentic rejection of *Animal Farm* by a leading publisher. I had thought that Reg Groves was long dead. He had worked in the bookshop immediately before Orwell and was one of the original "Balham secession," the founding of British Trotskyism. His testimony strengthened the view that Orwell's conversion to socialism was far less sudden than he himself stated (presumably for dramatic effect), and that the socialists he knew best were far to the Left of main-stream Labour Party thinking. The British anarchists kindly sent me a collective review that added considerably to knowledge of his ambivalence and contacts with them in the *Animal Farm* period. I knew that Orwell's consultant physician for his tuberculosis at University College Hospital was long dead and medical records destroyed, so had given up that trail; but foolishly forgot (being then unfamiliar with hospitals) that a young houseman would do the day-to-day bedside work; but the houseman wrote to me after reading my first edition with important new evidence. Apparently Orwell didn't stand a chance: but they did not tell him nor did they tell Sonia, but neither did she ask about his chances. All this went into the 1992 edition.

Three things in Orwell's own writings and life raise particular difficulties for a biographer. Firstly, he was unusually secretive or perhaps simply private, liking to keep different groups of friends apart, for instance, and yet he let his pen name develop in the *Tribune* days into a public character—"good old George" or "that damned Orwell stirring it again." Secondly, his fame came late, but then came fast—therefore many writers, who only knew him well after the publication of *Animal Farm* (so if well, also relatively briefly), committed themselves to critical judgements in print about him long before it was possible to read his books and essays as a whole; and they also committed themselves to broad statements about his development in the 1920s and 1930s that were not based on either first-hand observation or adequate documentation. Thirdly, the nature of some of his best writings like "Shooting an Elephant" and "A Hanging" raise difficult problems of genre; are they fact or are they fiction? And does it matter? If one shows fictional elements in "Such, Such Were the Joys" or in *Down and Out in Paris and London*, is one to be accused of doubting the word of George Woodcock's "crystal spirit" (in a book of that name) and destroying his reputation for integrity and honesty? Or is one paying tribute to a craftsman less naive than some of his Chelsea and Bloomsbury literary friends of the days of his fame seemed, enthusiastically but patronizingly, to assume? A word on each of these problems.

Orwell valued privacy and was not given to self-revealing monologues, even to girl friends. Now, personally, I do not find anything psychologically abnormal about this. I suspect that more people are of that kind than those who must be telling all to everyone always, or who can't live without a *confidante;* and, certainly, when we do meet up with extreme cases of talkative people whose main sub-

ject is themselves, whether meeting as friends, teachers or as invol-
untary traveling companions, we don't need to be especially wise to
take what they say with a big grain of salt. Courts of law often are
rightly skeptical about convicting on uncorroborated confessions
and hearsay evidence. Orwell was simply not that type, and he had
no thought, until very close to the end, that he would be a household name throughout the world. To say that he was careless about
keeping "his papers" is pure hindsight, for why should he have had
any care? He was not born to the literary purple and while he wanted
to live by his novels, he showed no signs of thinking himself a great
man or a great writer. Some of the Bloomsbury group, for instance,
seem to have secreted papers and exuded letters even before their
first works were published in the calm expectation that one day
they would be useful, even valuable, to their family biographer. Not
so old George. If he became famous with *Animal Farm*, consider
that even though he had worked for the BBC and did scripts for
them even after *Animal Farm*, including a bad adaptation of it, nobody thought to record his voice. Old BBC hands told me that it
would have seemed a comic disproportion then. "Old George" was
simply one of the boys who had a lucky break with one book. "Luck"
sustained the self-esteem of all his colleagues and friends with unpublished manuscripts or with publications soon forgotten. Disc
recordings for the BBC archive were then only set up for the very
great, like Wells and Shaw, or for people thought to be assured of a
permanent place in the Pantheon, like Max Beerbohm and J. B.
Priestley.

Orwell's privacy was not pathological, it was perfectly normal,
even if it makes difficulties for a biographer. But he was not seeking
to help a biographer, nor expecting one until the last year of his life
when the reception of *Nineteen Eighty-Four* both impressed and worried him. Frankly, I do not think that the "Eric Blair–George Orwell"
disjunction need trouble one greatly. Even Stansky and Abrahams
had dropped it by their second volume. Their idea of a character
change when he adopted the pseudonym always seemed to me more
a formal excuse that they were not writing a biography about "George
Orwell" rather than a genuine and sustained psychological hypothesis.[9] Certainly, in the *Tribune* columns he produced a kind of ideal
image of himself: the plain, blunt, free-speaking man of common
sense and common decency. But this image was an extension of
part of himself, not a mask. If he was role-playing a bit, it was with
different proportions of genuine aspects of himself. I think of the
late Richard Hofstàdter's classic essay on Abraham Lincoln: how,
while an exceptionally honest and straightforward man, he could
say that "Honest Abe is useful to Abraham Lincoln." Similarly, Eric

Blair was always George Orwell for literary effect. Julian Symons has put this better than I did: there was no war of two selves, only a continual growth in his powers and range as a writer, and "'Orwell" was the writer's name. So compelling did the name become, almost an English institution, that Sonia Brownell, Mrs. Eric Blair, later for a while Mrs. Pitt-Rivers even, may have felt that she had no choice but to appear as Mrs. George Orwell in the London phone book.

The second problem peculiar to Orwell biography is that since his fame came late, many of those who wrote about him on the basis of personal acquaintance have been less than cautious at times in recalling precisely when it was they first got to know him. Perhaps because the man was so unusually private when writers are necessarily involved in self-publicity, and so irritatingly unwilling to talk about personal things, yet so interesting and provocative, that there was an unusual amount of rather dubious biographical interpretation of him, rather than of literary criticism, right from the first writings. And writers on Orwell have been apt to place great weight on their own diverse memories of him and, even more difficult for a biographer, on their memories of what he said to them about his memories of earlier periods of his life. Much of this evidence was difficult to use. Some people were surprised and a bit cross that I did not report some important anecdotes they told to me of what he said to them or did. But like a detective, the biographer must always seek corroboration and can never rest a case on hearsay alone. Rarely do people seek to deceive, even themselves. But is it to some a quite unholy thought that Orwell could have occasionally teased people who either pressed him too hard or ignored him completely by giving them deliberate pieces of misinformation?

This biographer must sadly report that he learned to be skeptical of memory unchecked by document or independent witness. I am sure I have suppressed some revealing incidents that did take place, more or less as stated. But I also heard several anecdotes as if at first hand which are in fact found in Orwell's own writings! It is not merely that over thirty or forty years memory can mature and grow as well as decay, but that memories of a famous man in his days of obscurity often become badly confused by reading and taking into memory subsequent writings on him or even by him. Memories are filtered through what one learns later. Memories are evidence, but of a difficult kind; they are not history in themselves. They are not even evidence of a state of mind at the time of the events, only of a narrator's state of mind at the time of narration.

Not only Cherokee chiefs read books on anthropology before being interviewed by anthropologists. Distinguished men of letters re-read their early essays on Orwell shortly before being interviewed and then recounted them to me with commendable accuracy, beguiling freshness and occasional grace notes thrown in. It is simply very difficult to get through to genuine remembrances or re-remembrances: people defend what they wrote long ago, however incomplete or inaccurate. Imagine trying to ask Proust on the one hand, or Richard Nixon on the other, "Come on, what really happened?" Their memories would be self-induced rationalizations, even if they were willing to tell all. Fred Warburg did not commission Orwell to go to Spain and write *Homage to Catalonia*, though he remembered doing so most vividly in his memoirs, even supplying a dialogue. When I produced a photocopy of a letter of his to prove that he did not meet Orwell until after Spain, he told me that secretaries often type the wrong year. "Look at page 231 of my book" (*An Occupation for Gentlemen*); and at least he had the page right. But then publishers' memories and memoirs are in a class of their own.[10]

The interviewer can only approach contradictions in the evidence, between what people once wrote and what is now known, with great delicacy. People don't like being contradicted in their own homes. And, thinking of some manuals that are from time to time written for research students, there is no such thing as "structured interview." If you impose it, you get very little beyond "'yes" or "no." When interviewed, most people enjoy talking at large and they turn attempted interrogation into discursive conversation. Then one is in the world of an English novel, not in the interrogation cells of Koestler's or Le Carré's novels. One or two points that are not already clear from the written record have to wait their turn in a long and patient process of digression and mutual exploration.

People who knew him well and had neither written about him nor been interviewed by the BBC were more rare and in some ways more precious to me, so then it was sometimes worth taking down every word (although normally I found that a verbatim record was not worth the risk of people being resistant to recording). But when every word was taken down, sometimes I discovered afterwards that precisely because Orwell had become such a popular writer, that they too, even the non-writers, had memories of Orwell or views about him that could only have been formed by a subsequent reading of his works or works about him. His sister, Avril, plainly only glanced at most of his works in his lifetime and did not like them. When I met her twenty years later, she had accepted that her brother's fame was justified, so famous were his friends. She had forgiven him, as she saw it, for letting the family down (his resignation from the Imperial Service, his tramping, his socialism, his friends, his poverty), and she had become a cultivated and sensitive reader of his works, really worth talking to on many points of

literary criticism. It was as if she had given herself an adult education course from her brother's books and the commentaries on
them. But this reading contaminated her memories of the past. Fortunately she was interviewed at length by the BBC not long after
her brother's death and those transcripts, while far less perceptive
about the writer, contain the more reliable, unreformed, family
memories.

Again I must point out that it was simply not possible for even
critics and scholars to make a proper assessment of Orwell until the
so-called *Collected Essays, Journalism and Letters* appeared in 1968; and
by then most people had committed themselves and continued to
defend entrenched positions.[11] A new edition is now near completion, a supreme scholarly editing by Peter Davison. It contains interesting and important matter not included in the earlier four volumes.
This will be the chance for fresh critical assessments.


The third peculiar difficulty for Orwell biographers is the genre
problem. Crudely, are some of his best writings fact or fiction? I
realized right from the beginning how complex was the relationship between his writings and his life, and the great danger of using
fictions as disguised autobiography. While the closeness of the relationship was generally appreciated, its complexity was less recognized, despite some clear warnings he himself made. In *The Road to
Wigan Pier*, he cautiously or artfully said of *Down and Out in Paris and
London* that "Nearly all the incidents described there actually happened, but they have been rearranged." That is why I could never
agree with Sonia when she said in her Introduction to *The Collected
Essays* that all his novels except *Animal Farm* and *Nineteen Eighty-Four*
"contain straight descriptions of himself" or that "a whole chapter
of *The Road to Wigan Pier* suddenly turns into straight autobiography." The man was straightforward, but the writer was neither naive
nor simply a reporter. Each of his autobiographical passages is
shaped for some particular literary and political purpose. Some of
his friends of the brief days of his fame typecast him as a kind of
Douanier Rousseau of English letters.

To distinguish between the autobiographical "I" and the story-
teller's "I" is never easy, and for Orwell it is damned hard. When
Penguin books reprinted *Down and Out in Paris and London* during
the war, the first printing was in the old orange fiction covers. It was
then reprinted in the famous non-fiction blue. Records have van-
ished. But I sympathize with what may simply have been a mistake
at a low administrative level. Did all those people who told the author such lurid tales in *Down and Out* really exist? There's no docu-

mentary evidence, but by a literary judgement on the text I would have bound the reissue in a bold candy-stripe of orange and blue. For *The Road to Wigan Pier* there is more evidence, which suggests that he did not invent, but that he did rearrange the order of events, touch up, heighten skillfully and elongate time-scales. As George Painter said in the Preface to his great life of Proust, "though he invented nothing, he altered everything." So a blue cover with a ruled orange surround would be appropriate for *Wigan Pier*. For *Homage to Catalonia* there is much more evidence, all of which supports the most literal veracity of what he described: so true-blue all through. I suppose that because he was writing the book as a polemic against false pictures of the war, he knew he must give his many opponents no possible opening to fault him on points of fact as distinct from "correct ideological perspective."

The sheer difficulty of how to use "Such, Such Were the Joys" as biographical evidence is still painful to me. Richard Hoggart in a sympathetic review nevertheless described me as circling around Orwell's account of his prep school days like a cat not sure its prey was dead, and, if so, which bits were fit to eat. Hilary Spurling thought that my caution was ludicrous and my "doubting his word" demeaning. The need to explore carefully its truth, since so much bad speculation about the genesis of *Nineteen Eight-Four* has been built on it, held up the telling of a story and made the opening of the book both hard to digest and contentious. But it had to be like that because so many critics (following a speculative lead by Antony West) seemed convinced that the psychological horror of *Nineteen Eighty-Four* could only have come from direct experience of an English private boarding school, not from reading about and talking to refugees from Hitlerism and Stalinism. Some English*men* are like that. Perhaps I should have simply ignored all those silly and arbitrary, infantile short-cuts to understanding, or simply referred them to Richard Ellmann's wise and trenchant essay on Freudian "Literary Biography" in his *Golden Codgers*. Nonetheless, I am unrepentant about the truth of the matter: if "Such, Such Were the Joys" had ever been printed by Penguin separately, there could well have been much blue on the cover, so long as there was a large and dramatic blob of fiction orange as well. I see it as a polemic against private schooling *based* on his own experiences, but with fictional supports to widen the attack, to bring out what he thought to be more general truths about English private education. Yet somehow the literal truth of it became an article of faith to some. Michael Shelden regards the writing as so gripping and authentic that he simply ignored my account of an interview with an old boy of the school who said that, indeed, a boy had been caned in front of the school for bed-wetting, but that it was *not* Eric Blair. My troubles with Mrs. Orwell began on this score.

From Burma Police manuals I could at least establish that someone in Blair's job would have had no business whatsoever to be at a hanging. But this kind of boring research is purely for the narrow purpose of recounting his life. It cannot affect our appreciation of his art. May I quote from David Lodge's essay on "A Hanging"?

> When I first read "A Hanging," I certainly assumed it was a true story. The more I studied it, the more I suspected that Orwell has added or altered some details for literary effect, but I did not doubt that the piece was essentially factual and historical. I think this is probably the response of most readers . . . [12]

But he then goes on to relate that Stansky and Abrahams in their biography found a lady whom Orwell had told that he never saw a hanging, despite subsequently claiming to have done so twice more in print; and I found (unknown to David Lodge) another such lady.

So there is at least an element of doubt about the eye-witness authenticity of "A Hanging," a possibility that it is a polemic—a double-barrel shot hitting both imperialism and capital punishment. It is very unlikely, at this date, that we shall ever be able to establish definitely whether Orwell attended a hanging or not. Certainly, the factuality of the elephant cannot be proved by saying of the prose, as Michael Shelden did, that it is "a riveting piece of work." So was Isherwood's "I Am a Camera," but no one really believed that he was in the room while Sally Bowles plied her time-honored trade. Orwell's essay may be completely factual, it may be partly fiction and partly based on experience, or on the reported experience of others, or wholly made-up—though the last possibility seems to me the least likely. I want to make the point, after all that, that it doesn't much matter. David Lodge reaches the same conclusion: "A Hanging" is, as a text, "self-sufficient and self-authenticating." Indeed, from the point of view of his art (as David Lodge also concludes), it does not matter. It does matter marginally from the point of view of biography, but even in using a sledgehammer to crack a nut, quite unsuccessfully in his case, the biographer cannot reduce the work of art to some other dimension.

Two patient helpers and I also wasted a lot of time trying to find from the *Rangoon Times* and the *Mandalay Gazette* whether or not he shot an elephant. To destroy a trained working elephant belonging to a timber company would be roughly the equivalent of the police destroying a modern building crane, so one might have expected some mention; but there was none. So I stuck to my guns, thinking of the row with Sonia on the elephant question, that "Shooting an

Elephant" is a brilliant, polemical fiction. But while I was preparing the revised edition of 1992 someone wholly reputable brought a tape-recording of an elderly relative into the Orwell Archive that brought the corporeal elephant back into play.[13] Interesting. I blush slightly, but my two points still stand: it is hard evidence, not the quality of the writing, that brings the elephant to life; and, in either case, it is the quality of the writing that counts.

Hugh Kenner offers a brilliant and cautionary discussion of Defoe's and Orwell's use of the fictive "I" in an essay, "The Politics of the Plain Style." He points out that the use of a plain style by a professional writer is as much a rhetorical device as the use of any other style, and that part of the skill of several of the best writings of both men is to leave the reader in doubt as to whether he or she reads fact or fiction.[14] Orwell in aiming his work at the common reader of his time, whom he took to be not the university educated but those whose education was through the free public libraries, evolved a plain style with a pugnacious colloquial syntax, vocabulary and tone. But his readers, as Kenner would imply, could too often believe that plain language guarantees truth; and Orwell sometimes seemed to deceive himself (in his essays on language and politics) that polysyllables always lie and monosyllables speak plain truth.[15]

How strange that some have honestly thought that one was diminishing Orwell if one pointed out that some of his essays in the first person are more like short stories than true confessions. His reputation must finally rest on being a writer, not simply as an exceptionally honest and decent human being. And despite his reputation as a writer, in the simple sense that ever so many people read him, some of his old friends, even Sonia Brownell, Cyril Connolly and Richard Rees, still felt so uneasy at the content of what he wrote and so dissatisfied with his formal qualities as a novelist that they made too much of the personal virtues rather than the literary craft of the man. Part of his literary craft was his use of his own virtues and, of course, his own experiences, which makes it very difficult to tell fact from fiction; certainly, I was not always sure which was which. But an artist deals in symbolic or speculative truths whereas a biographer must, Leon Edel has remarked citing Desmond MacCarthy, write as if under oath—however much at times that limits a good coherent narrative story and empathetic surmise. The commercial publisher and the honest biographer must ever have their differences.

Spring Semester 1996

1. This is, I firmly intend, the final version of a continuously revised reflection, of which an earlier version appeared as "On the Difficulties of Writing Biography and of Orwell's in Particular" in this author's *Essays on Politics and Literature* (Edinburgh, 1989), pp. 117–32.

2. As I argue in the heavy, scholarly Introduction and Notes to my Clarendon edition of Orwell's *Nineteen Eighty-Four* (Oxford, 1984), an edition unhappily not available in the United States.

3. The case that Orwell's lasting excellence and influence is as an essayist is put in my Introduction to *The Penguin Essays of George Orwell* (London, 1994 reprint).

4. And with even more polemical zest in the vulgarly and misleadingly titled "You Must Meet Eric to Understand George," *Weekend Telegraph* (London), Sept. 12, 1992, p. xvii. See also the exchange of civilities between Hilary Spurling, Julian Symons, Michael Shelden and myself in the *TLS* for the three weeks following Symons's review of Shelden's *Orwell*, Oct. 18, 1991.

5. David Herbert Donald, *Lincoln: A Life* (New York, 1995), p. 14.

6. See Richard Holmes's exemplary, *Dr Johnson and Mr Savage* (New York, 1994).

7. Ian Hamilton, *Koestler: A Biography* (New York, 1982), but the real point may be that it is impossible to write a *scholarly* biography of a living person, whether with or without his or her cooperation.

8. I have told the tale in, "On the Orwell Trail," *Granta* (Jan. 1985), a comic true essay reprinted in my *Essays on Politics and Literature*, pp. 215–17.

9. Peter Stansky and William Abrahams, *The Unknown Orwell* (London, 1972). I have sympathy with the problems they faced with Sonia Orwell when they decided to expand a study of Orwell in Spain into a full biography. She could not stop the book but capriciously refused to let them quote from any texts. It was a valuable first, serious and scholarly biography, even though I did not share its perspective and decided that there was still much to be discovered and something different to be said.

10. See Crick, *George Orwell*, rev. ed. (London, 1992), p. 339.

11. As Peter Marks of the University of Sydney has argued in his highly original Ph.D. thesis "Orwell's Essays" (Edinburgh, 1992).

12. In David Lodge, *The Modes of Modern Writing: Metaphor, Metonymy, and the Typology of Modern Literature* (London, 1977).

13. See Crick, *Orwell*, 1992 ed., pp. 586–89 with footnotes, p. 657.

14. Hugh Kenner, "The Politics of the Plain Style," in Robert Mulvihill (ed.), *Reflection on America, 1984: An Orwell Symposium* (Athens, Georgia, 1986).

15. This is discussed more fully both in my Introduction to *The Penguin Essays of George Orwell* and in the Clarendon edition of *Nineteen Eighty-Four*.

# 10

# *Nineteen Eighty-Four* Ten Years Later

## PETER STANKSY

In the last years of his life George Orwell, who had written so much of the past he knew, chose to write of the future he would never know. Doing so, he became in the eyes of some a kind of prophet; others have seen him, in my view more correctly, less as a prophet than as a critic of certain tendencies of his own time and what they might lead to. Either way, it is hard to believe he could have anticipated what the future held in store for his own work, how much attention would be paid to it, so that almost fifty years after his death he would still be the centerpiece of concentrated study by students and continue to enthrall millions of readers around the world. (The American paperback of *Nineteen Eighty-Four* is now in its 96th edition.)

*Animal Farm*, his brilliant fable about the perversion of socialism in Stalin's Russia, was published in 1945. Its non-stop popular success then and ever since transformed Orwell from a moderately recognized English literary figure into one of the best known writers in the world. His next book was *Nineteen Eighty-Four*, which he was writing in 1948, and he simply reversed those last two digits when searching for a title. Its publication in June 1949 added to his fame and his fortune. Unhappily he did not have long to enjoy his phenomenal success; he died in January 1950, of tuberculosis, at the age of 46.

The story of his early life is fairly well known, but I would like to indicate some elements in it that played crucial roles in shaping *Nineteen Eighty-Four*. There is an underlying sense of a betrayed society, an English world that had once been secure, a "Golden Land" that is glimpsed in the countryside where Winston and Julia make love.

Unusual in Orwell, certainly for someone who came to political maturity in the 1930s, was his combination of socialism and patriotism, a deep love of England. But it was always a rather paradoxical love, as suggested in the famous last paragraph of *Homage to Catalonia,* describing his return to peaceful England after he had fought on the side of the loyalists in the Spanish Civil War.

> And then England—southern England, probably the sleekest landscape in the world. Down here it was still the England I had known in my childhood: the railway-cutting smothered in wild flowers, the deep meadows where the great shining horses browse and meditate, the slow-moving streams bordered by willows, the green bosoms of the elms, the larkspurs in the cottage gardens; and then the huge peaceful wilderness of outer London, the barges on the miry river, the familiar streets, the posters telling of cricket matches and Royal weddings, the men in bowler hats, the pigeons in Trafalgar Square, the red buses, the blue policemen—all sleeping the deep, deep sleep of England, from which I sometimes fear that we shall never wake till we are jerked out of it by the roar of bombs.[1]

That sense of a lost paradise, even keener in *Animal Farm* than in *Nineteen Eighty-Four,* owes a great deal, I think, to the fact that the first eleven years of Orwell's life belong to the period before the First World War. As we all know, there were plenty of indications in that pre-war decade that the world was changing for the worse, that the securities of Britain, the greatest power in the world, were already being challenged, but such indications were not necessarily apparent to a child born in 1903 into the English establishment.

Allow me to digress for a moment about names. Orwell was born Eric Arthur Blair. He never changed his name legally—he told his friend Anthony Powell that if he did so he would have to find a new writing name. Although he was Eric Blair in private life, even after he had published his first works, he became known as George Orwell to friends that he made in the late 1930s and beyond, and signed letters to them as such. But his legal name remained Eric Arthur Blair, and he is buried under that name in the churchyard of the Oxfordshire village, Sutton Courtenay, near where he grew up in Henley. His declared reason for taking a pseudonym was that he was afraid that *Down and Out in Paris and London* might offend his family, and he offered three possibilities to his publisher: H. Lewis Allways, Kenneth Miles, or George Orwell. He admitted that he preferred Orwell and the publisher Victor Gollancz agreed with him. Later commentators have made much of the significance of the name—George, unlike Eric, the quintessence of an ordinary English name—and Orwell, the river in East Anglia near Southwold, where his family moved after several years in Henley. Both names are English through and through. So too, Winston Smith, in *Nineteen Eighty-Four*, can be seen as the epitome of an English name, Winston taken from Winston Churchill, the lion who had done so much to win the Second World War, at the time that Winston was born, and Smith standing for everyone. Is it too speculative to see O'Brien as deliberately not an English name for the betrayer in the novel, the authority figure that Blair himself had been trained to be and became in his early years? Ironically, it is Winston Smith, the minor functionary, whose position most resembled that held by Richard Blair, Orwell's father. In their different ways both were servants of empire and part of its ruling class, Blair in relation to the Bengali, Winston in relation to the proles.

Orwell's nostalgic ideal was to combine the security of his very first years—raised in India, where the lowliest British civil servant could lead an elegant life—with the decencies of an egalitarian society. His mother and sisters lived with him in England some years before his father retired to one of the idyllic spots of the home country, Henley, site of the annual regatta. In his childhood years, if it is not too psychoanalytical a point, Eric had the reassuring experience of being the one male in a household of women. That of course was in those unreconstructed days when it was accepted without question that males were the most important members of the household (despite the fact that his mother was quite a strong-minded lady).

The paradise was not to last. His father came home from India, and Eric, age eight, was sent away to boarding school—the English style for such families. As Orwell would later set out the paradox: he was part of the ruling class; at the same time, in that exact English way, in terms of family income, he would characterize himself as a member of the "lower-upper-middle class." At heart, it was a matter of status rather than of income, though lack of income would make status even more difficult to maintain. England is a land of accepted hierarchies. While the vast part of the population of the country was beneath him, to Orwell the significant difficulty came from those who were above. Such hierarchies were certainly to have a place in *Nineteen Eighty-Four*, transposed from pre-war England.

The boarding school to which he was sent in 1911 was one of the best in the country, St. Cyprian's, on the south coast on the Sussex Downs near the sea. The Blairs could not afford the fees but the proprietors of the school—the Vaughan Wilkes—and such private prep schools were and are profit-making institutions—took on some bright boys on reduced fees in the belief that they would win scholarships to grand "Public Schools" such as Eton and Wellington and enhance the reputation of the school. And so Orwell did.

Insecurity within security. He knew from his own experience the deeply insecure individual—Winston—who nevertheless tries to take a stand for the truth within a totalitarian system that is committed to arbitrary power, power apparently for its own sake. Mrs. Vaughan Wilkes was an O'Brien–Big Brother figure. The experience of the school was, at least to some degree, one of the formative influences in the making of *Nineteen Eighty-Four*. This was also true of the reading that he did at St. Cyprian's. Like most "advanced" schoolboys, he was a devotee of H. G. Wells and would stay up late at night reading his books with a flashlight under the bedclothes. Wells, as a leading science-fiction writer and inventor of utopias, proved a counter-influence in the shaping of Orwell's own great anti-utopia. It is a nice irony that the son of H. G. Wells and Rebecca West, the critic Anthony West, was the leading proponent of the theory that the world of *Nineteen Eighty-Four* is Orwell's revenge upon his society for forcing him to go to such a horrid school.

Orwell's memoir of the school—"Such, Such Were the Joys" (a line from William Blake)—was written in the late 1940s in the same half-decade as his two bitter fables. In that essay, he does present St. Cyprian's as a totalitarian system in which rewards and punishments were likely to depend on the whims of the Headmaster, and particularly of his wife. To a degree, this was a personal view; others have testified to the good education they received at the school. Its emphasis was upon facts, particularly historical facts, and their immutability. Orwell learned that lesson: that there was a firm past that should not be changed for the benefit of the ruling class. But he was aware, probably at the time and certainly in retrospect, that he was learning a set of facts designed to glorify the "island story" of Britain and the "world story" of the British Empire. It may seem minor, but this early experience in dealing with a capricious "total" system is, I agree with West, an important factor in shaping the nightmare vision of *Nineteen Eighty-Four*. Orwell also tells us that at this school he became convinced of his worthlessness—the sense of emptiness that Winston Smith was to experience.

On the other hand, it does not do to exaggerate, as West undeniably does. During these years Orwell was also well educated, and imbued with a love of England that never left him, the Golden Land, through his reading, and wandering over the downs of Sussex, experiencing the beauty of the south of England, that complacent powerful land. This was, of course, also the time of the First World War, and his earliest publications, when he was still at St. Cyprian's, were two poems in the Henley newspaper that echoed the patriotism of the war years. These roots of patriotism were extremely important for their contribution to that sense of the betrayed state at the heart of the two anti-utopias. In each, the individual, intrinsically good, is betrayed by the leaders of a state who are only interested in power. Orwell's two juvenile publications glorified the war: one, "Awake! Young Men of England" called upon young men to attack the Germans; the other mourned the death of Kitchener, the famous general who was Secretary of State for War. Although eventually Orwell became a socialist, he never lost this love of country and it inspired, in the autumn of 1940, his essay "My Country, Right or Left" as well as his polemic, *The Lion and the Unicorn*, in 1941. His love of England—and his fear that it might someday become a totalitarian system—was a driving force in the writing of his final novel.

What other elements in his life shaped the two books and their vision? His education accomplished a primary purpose: infusing him with a love of language and reinforcing that sense of authority imbued in the English upper classes. The elite form of English education appears committed to creating at one and the same time outward conformists and inward rebels. It would be hard, I believe, to find better definitions of Winston, O'Brien, and Julia, even though O'Brien is playing the role in order to ensnare—and as a result, Winston's and Julia's rebellions sadly crumble.

The education that the young Orwell received was also singularly committed to the "word," how to write it in order to secure good examination results, how to understand it through the exercise of translating it into Latin and Greek, how to revere it as the greatest English art form. It is particularly significant that Winston Smith's job is to rewrite the once canonical paper of England, *The Times*, so that it conforms to the party line of the moment. Orwell took an intense pleasure in language. Some of his more famous essays, most notably "Politics and the English Language," insist on the need to protect language from jargon, and the political power of language intentionally misused.

That concern culminates in the role of "Newspeak" in *Nineteen Eighty-Four*. Orwell would have understood the "linguistic turn" in present-day literary studies and history, although he probably would not have agreed with it. Syme, in the book, hopes by reducing language, by destroying words, to eliminate "thought-crime." One can sense Orwell's fascination with words and their power in the rather diabolical pleasure—parallel to Syme's—that he must have taken in writing the appendix, "The Principles of Newspeak," and its discussion of the definitive dictionary of the language, the Eleventh. This was no doubt a deliberate echo of the much revered edition of the *Encyclopedia Britannica*, the Eleventh, published in 1910, the summation of knowledge before the Western World moved towards great changes.

There is a certain compulsive literary quality in Winston Smith's work, as he uses language to pervert the truth. Orwell knew, and it is one of his most important contributions, that language was sacred to the preservation of truth and culture; that those who control the word can control the past, the present, and the future. In his novel he succeeded better than he might have wished. Even those who have not actually read *Nineteen Eighty-Four* are familiar with the terms Orwell has given the language—"Big Brother," "Newspeak," "doublethink," "Thought Police" among others—and are affected by them. There is an irony here, for these phrases—such brilliant examples of Orwell's fecundity and imagination—have almost become the sort of jargon terms which he, as a critic of language, so detested: they call up images in an automatic and easy way, and are short-cuts to thinking.

Orwell was different from many writers in that he had a more direct experience of the role of power in this world. The wielding of power by those who had previously been denied it frequently begins with an attempt to help those who are in need, and downtrodden. Presumably that was originally the message of Ingsoc, and might have been true in Russia at the time of the Revolution. It was also, with a radically different ideology, one of the major ways the British Empire thought of itself. Many of those who are in a powerful position in relation to others see themselves as benign improvers of the world, and end up, or certainly their successors do, having as their chief purpose the preservation of their power. Lord Acton's dictum is a cliché, but one that should frequently be repeated: "power corrupts and absolute power corrupts absolutely."

Orwell was wonderfully perceptive in realizing, as has happened in so many political situations in the world, in the past, in the present, and in the future, that it is not a question of there being "goodies" and "baddies." Rather, those with power run the danger of being "baddies" and those without power have goodness thrust upon them. It was a lesson that Orwell learned in the unusual step, for a member of his class, that he took after completing his secondary education at Eton.

He became a policeman, or rather a police officer, in Burma, the "Cinderella" province, in the command of the Indian Imperial Police. In a sense he was going into the "family" business and turning back to the modest attainments of his father, rather than the possibilities of university education and further advancement that his time at St. Cyprian's and Eton prepared him for. He was following the minor functionary style of a Winston Smith. But in the Empire,

as a police officer, he was powerful and he experienced the irrationality of power, the need to perform the ruling role—as when he
had to shoot an elephant which had gone amok, even though its fits
of madness had passed, in order to preserve the face of the Empire.
(He recorded the episode in one of the greatest essays in the language, "Shooting an Elephant," which is too often read for its style
rather than its historical content.) His imperial experience taught
him the need of the state for outward conformity—as in *Nineteen
Eighty-Four*—both on the part of the state's servants, as he had been
in Burma, and on the part of those who are ruled. The rulers themselves, the O'Briens, are caught in the same complicity.

Orwell's political experiences in the 1930s were to teach him the
dangers of inner conformity. Desperate world events conspired to
bring him—perhaps reluctantly—to politics, and he became one of
the most truthful political writers of the century. His earlier writings may be seen as political by implication; they depicted the classic novelistic situation of the individual against society, Flory in
*Burmese Days*, Dorothy Hare in *A Clergyman's Daughter*, Gordon
Comstock in *Keep the Aspidistra Flying*, George Bowling in *Coming Up
for Air*.

But in the last four years of the decade of the 1930s the events
and the man were well matched. (In a way his first book, *Down and
Out in Paris and London*, dealing with those at the very bottom of
society, in effect the homeless, was a reaction to the Depression, but
there was little sense in it that politics or economics had much to do
with the situation.) He became increasingly aware that the grimness of his literary vision was being matched by outside events: the
Depression and the rise of Fascism. Poverty was certainly a major
factor in his writings (and it remains in the sordidness of the world
of *Nineteen Eighty-Four*, reflecting the experience of the war itself,
and then, post-war austerity in Britain). But his first four novels had
been rather solipsistic, seen from the point of view of the particular
figure, a version of the author. His political experiences lifted him
out of himself so that he could create, in the character of Winston
Smith (who is hardly a "charm boat" but is nevertheless someone
who can stand for everyperson), someone who is trying to fight for
the truth that two and two equals four, that one has the right to love
apart from the state, that one should be able to think for oneself.

But in 1936, almost by chance, Orwell was exposed not to the
poverty of tramps but of those who would have worked if they could,
in his investigation of what the Depression meant for the North of
England. His publisher, Victor Gollancz, had formed the Left Book
Club, a highly successful and proselytizing publishing operation that
needed a constant flow of new books. He asked Orwell, a professed

socialist, to look into conditions in the North brought about by the Depression. The result was one of Orwell's most powerful books—*The Road to Wigan Pier*—an account of his journey, depicting both the desperate situation of the unemployed and the solid virtues of the English working class. (The proles in *Nineteen Eighty-Four* are a debased version, but even they still have some of the qualities that Orwell admired, as did Boxer in *Animal Farm.*) In the second part of the book, Orwell acted as the devil's advocate; he presented a fairly strong case against the English version of socialism while asserting his belief in it. Here too one sees a prefigurement of *Nineteen Eighty-Four*—the case for Socialism put in a negative way—by showing how it can go wrong, which has meant that the novel has frequently been taken, against Orwell's intention, as an anti-socialist tract.

But it was the events in Spain that made him truly a socialist and committed him to a vision of life that is then betrayed. The Spanish Civil War had broken out on July 18, 1936, while Orwell was in the midst of writing up his experiences in the North of England. When he was free, in December, he went to Spain and discovered in Barcelona what he regarded as a socialist paradise, a state for which he was happy to fight. This was a brief moment when he saw what an ideal world could be like. It unleashed his genius. Much of his best writings came after the Spanish experience: the great flowering of his essays, and their defense of democratic socialism "as I understand it"—and the two anti-utopias by which he is chiefly remembered. But in Spain he found that his vision of the ideal socialist society was being betrayed, by those elements on the Left who were primarily interested in power, and in serving a foreign policy, Russia's, that had little to do with the socialist aspirations of the Spaniards on the side of the Republic. This was done through the manipulation of the past, the truth, the press, by the Communists. He was appalled by their claim that the group with which he himself was fighting—the semi-Trotskyist Worker's Party of Marxist Unification—the POUM—were traitors rather than fighters for the cause. Orwell was dedicated—and it is a great English virtue and a theme in *Nineteen Eighty-Four*—to the importance of the individual: the man risking his life on the front line who, because he was a member of the POUM, might well be arrested and imprisoned as a Fascist in Barcelona. This is all discussed in his wonderful book of reportage, *Homage to Catalonia*. It is the vision there, of a socialist state and its betrayal, that provides the compelling force behind *Nineteen Eighty-Four.*

In the remaining years of his life were further experiences that he drew upon for the novel. Life in the British Broadcasting Corporation where he worked in the early years of the war provided much of the atmosphere and the language of the Ministry of Truth. The austerity made necessary by the war (and even its pleasures, so-called, such as Victory Gin), combined with the puritanism of Orwell and his wife, was drawn upon for the grimy atmosphere of the book. The war would reinforce the experience of Spain—he saw the honor and decency of ordinary people in their fight against Hitler. As in Spain he felt much more at one with them under wartime conditions. Too old to fight, and not particularly well, he mucked in with ordinary men in the Home Guard, and he wrote down his thoughts in his column, "As I Please," for the Labour weekly, *Tribune,* celebrating his commitment to an individual vision. He also started to compose those magnificent essays of his own special kind of sociological-anthropological observation that have been so influential on such topics as smutty comic postcards and boys' school stories. Although not paid much attention to nowadays in this context, he is a crucial figure in shaping our sense of the importance of non-canonical works of imagination.

To a lesser extent than had been true in Spain, he also saw during the Second World War itself that power could be maintained by its traditional leaders, with little more than lip service to changes in society, that ideology could be mere window dressing for the maintenance of power, that power in and of itself was the point. He had felt, in the early years, that a socialist revolution would be necessary to win the war, as argued in his splendid pamphlet with its characteristic patriotic title, *The Lion and the Unicorn.* But as the war progressed he recognized that the traditional power in England—which he was part of by birth and training—in fact could win the war without the revolutionary changes that he had thought essential and wanted.

As Orwell had been a premature anti-Fascist in his involvement with the Spanish Civil War, so too he was a premature anti-Communist in his involvement with the Cold War. There were, of course, many anti-Communists (but many of them, led by Churchill, had abandoned that position for the duration of the war) and some socialist anti-Communists. But, with the Soviet Union as an ally, their numbers dwindled. Orwell wrote *Animal Farm* from November 1943 to February 1944. He knew that it was "politically incorrect," and of course it was a great irony that it was turned down for that reason by the conservative T. S. Eliot, an editor at Faber & Faber, and by many other publishers. Orwell described *Animal Farm* as the first book in which he attempted "to fuse political purpose and artistic purpose into one whole."[2] Shortly thereafter he was also thinking about *Nineteen Eighty-Four.* Both books attest to the power of ideas and of myths but also demonstrate how they can be perverted. In that sense they continue to be extremely relevant. Both did play off the Soviet Union, and then became Cold War documents; now that the Cold War has ended, they have a new layer of history laid upon them.

*Nineteen Eighty-Four* was, in many ways, a variant of *Animal Farm* although its style was very different and it lacks, even if the Farm story is grim, that fabulist charm as well as an intense sense of sadness. The novel takes to extreme lengths real possibilities, as is implied by the dust jacket of the first English edition which had its spelled-out title superimposed on the year in numerals. In 1949, 1984 seemed a long way away. Through the literary title, he suggested a satire or fantasy or a warning of how existing tendencies might eventuate, not necessarily a prediction of what was likely to happen by 1984. His appreciation for technological discoveries in the future shaped part of what he put into the book; and at another level, so much of the political structure of the world as he imagined it—endless rivalry of superpowers justifying the state's actions— turned out to be correct up to the "fall" of the Soviet Union and the Communist regimes in Eastern Europe. Even so, it can be argued that this accuracy is almost coincidental to the main purposes of the book. By spelling out the title, Orwell was, in effect, telling us that we were not to take the novel too literally as a document; that we were to remember the ways in which it was a work of imagination. There is an unmistakable power (and violence) in the work that removes it from the literary genre to which it belongs—a novel of fantasy—and gives it an intensity that sears it into the minds of its readers.

Both *Animal Farm* and *Nineteen Eighty-Four* deal with the corruption of power, and how the corruption of ideas can support that. I think that the significance of *Nineteen Eighty-Four* itself, and how Orwell's life went into its making, was well summed up in a front page review in *The New York Times* on June 12, 1949, by the eminent critic Mark Schorer. He did make one statement that has proven wrong: "[The book's] greatness [may be] only immediate, its power for us alone, now, in this generation, this decade, this year." But Schorer followed that sentence with another that is absolutely correct: "Nevertheless it is probable that no other work of this generation has made us desire freedom more earnestly or loathe tyranny with such fullness." All of the *events* of Orwell's life, most importantly those during the Spanish Civil War, went into the making of *Nineteen Eighty-Four*. Ultimately, in the most literal way, the life of the man himself went into the writing of the book.

My title, "*Nineteen Eighty-Four* Ten Years Later," has been perhaps a little misleading. Of course, at this moment in 1994, it is correct: I am considering *Nineteen Eighty-Four* in 1994, ten years beyond its title. There can be little question that the existence of the Cold War during the first forty years since the book's publication was a cold fact about *Nineteen Eighty-Four*, and it has influenced our reading of it. Indeed the Cold War was a major reason why in 1984, the year itself, there would be so much fighting for possession of the text between right and left, most vehemently between such neo-conservatives as Norman Podhoretz and radicals as Christopher Hitchens. It is testimony to a great text that it can provide material for many differing and contradictory points of view. But has the end of the Cold War changed our reading of this particular text?

Orwell thought of himself as a democratic socialist. The adjective "democratic" represented, I believe, his commitment to the individual, his heritage from his English background, and his hatred of elitists such as the Fabians, prone to fall for dictators, who believed that ordinary persons needed things done to them for their own good. Socialist, as he used the word, stood for his commitment to egalitarianism, and his belief that a means must be found for redistributing the goods of the world. Individualism, with its commitment to privacy, was destroyed in Winston's world by the two-way tele-screen. (The technical aspects of the book are quite fascinating and seem far more believable now than they may have been when it was first published.) In Orwell's view, elitism led to a worship of power for its own sake, combined with—and this intensifies the nightmare quality of the book—the need to make others suffer as evidence of that power. Orwell did not believe in the possibility of an enlightened despotism. The crucial battle is between the rulers and "thoughtcrime," the attempts of Winston and Julia to rebel through private thoughts and through that most private of activities, the sexual. It is obviously significant that the Thought Police come crashing into their secret bedroom hideaway, chanting as Winston and Julia have just said themselves: "You are the dead." Those outside the system, the proles, might have some freedom as they are apolitical. For those within the system, the everlasting threat is of a boot crashing into one's face, one's worst horror being realized in Room 101: the reflective individual is destroyed.

Ten years ago the Western world went Orwell-mad, with conferences, books, articles, Peanuts, Walter Cronkite, the Today Show, art shows, an extraordinary demonstration of how the coincidence of choosing a title can have an effect. Perhaps many of the celebrants were simply grateful for having survived up to that point. But we should hardly be complacent, even though the Orwellian vision seems more firmly a warning now, rather than a prophecy, than it might have done in 1984. As Walter Cronkite, a benign Big Brother figure perhaps, wrote in his preface in the so-called "commemorative" edition, "It has been said . . . that Orwell's terrible vision has been averted. Well, that kind of self-congratulation is, to say the least, premature. 1984 may not arrive on time, but there is always 1985. Still, the warning has been effective; and every time we use one of those catch phrases, . . . recognize Big Brother in someone, see a 1984 in the future, . . . note something Orwellian [which is now a word in the dictionary], . . . we are listening to that warning again."[3]

Orwell was writing about what *might* happen, not what *would* happen. It is not, to my mind, a correct question that many asked, most notably at a grand conference I attended that year at Strasbourg, in the chamber of the European Parliament: "Was Orwell mistaken or had he correctly interpreted the history of his time?" To the degree that his book has proven to be "wrong," to that extent it has served one of its major purposes. What Orwell attempted to do was take to a logical conclusion the destructive elements inherent in Nazism and Stalinism, the two great totalitarian systems. Sometimes he was correct in crucial guesses, sometimes not. Was Orwell unusual in foreseeing two central developments of the post-war world? First, the extraordinary growth of technology that would permit a degree of mechanical manipulation of our lives and potential supervision of them not known in the 1940s. Though Orwell put more emphasis on television as a two-way system and less on computers, one has the impression that Winston must have done his work of rewriting the past with some sort of primitive computer. Second, a world divided into armed camps. Will the latter return or have we now achieved a permanent abandonment of that configuration?

To my mind one crucial question implicit in the book a half century after it was written is whether or not we have internalized a set of conformities to the needs of the state. Presumably it might be argued that if this *has* happened, we would not be aware of it. I suspect nonetheless, this has *not* happened: Orwell's direst warning of what the future might hold has not yet taken place. Most individuals are still free to think what they wish, although in many places there are severe restrictions on what they may say or do.

But what about the state? What has taken place in parts of the world where there are mini-totalitarian governments? Dictatorships of today do not appear to be threats to world peace. But obviously there is considerable death and destruction in the so-to-speak *small* wars that are still going on in the world. Perhaps, as with Oceania, wars are used as the way in which the state defines and justifies itself. But the situation is not the continual world-wide war envisioned in Orwell's book. It was the threatened universality of Orwell's picture that made it so terrifying; such a possibility now seems so much more unlikely than it might have been ten years ago.

It would be an intriguing but a difficult study to discover the degree and in what ways Orwell played a part in the changes in Eastern Europe. I suspect he should be given a decent amount of credit. The considerable number of readers of *Nineteen Eighty-Four* in the Soviet Union and Eastern Europe were helped by that book to see that, whatever their leaders might claim, they were not driven by a desire to create a better world but rather to maintain power for its own sake.

Despite the extraordinary developments in the computer world, the developments in hyperspace, and the information highway, and its quite scary potential for "Big Brother" and pretty much anyone who wants to know all about us, our present situation still hasn't reached the continual spying and the total ability to destroy the past that is present in the novel. On the other hand, even though its methods were more primitive, the range of activity of the Stasi in East Germany would seem to justify the novel's assumption that the state could run away with itself, and wish to supervise, know about, and control every aspect of an individual's existence. On a far less sweeping scale the FBI and the CIA have been guilty of invasions of our privacy and intrusion into legitimate activities. Through computer developments, the potential for such invasions have increased to an Orwellian degree.

Orwell had transformed his own nightmares and our half-conscious apprehensions into fiction; he asks us how we live and what are our primary political concerns. Are we free? Individual liberty and equality are, he believes, the cornerstones of our values, and his aim is to make untrue that powerful phrase in *Animal Farm*: "some are more equal than others." Orwell wrote *Animal Farm* before, and *Nineteen Eighty-Four* three years after, the Second World War ended, the war in which the Soviet Union was an ally of Britain and the United States. He built his vision of the particular dangers of totalitarianism on his experiences in the Spanish Civil War where he observed how the Communists were perfectly capable of rewriting the past to conform to their present needs and of executing those on the Left with whom they disagreed. Of course historians are always rewriting the past, and so they should, as they see it with different eyes. Presumably they try not do it in such a way that they are consciously forcing it to fit a particular agenda as was poor Winston's job. In an intriguing and perhaps disconcerting way the new ideas about the social construction of reality, increasingly important at the moment, not only in literary theory but also in historical thought, are connected with the idea of making us aware of how the present, and the past, may be constructed to conform to certain agendas. But these ideas run the danger of a post-modern nihilism that Orwell would not have shared.

The significance of the past, its shaping of the ideologies that are tearing some societies apart, has never been more critical than now when we no longer have a world divided into two armed camps. Stalin and his successors, and the lesser dictators, presumably for the sake of power, but also to ensure a certain degree of stability, suppressed the forces of nationalism and religion. They controlled the past in order to control the future. Although Orwell was deeply concerned with ideology, he might not have appreciated how explosive those feelings of nationalism and religion would prove to be in bringing about change.

*Nineteen Eighty-Four* is a rich text and it is a testimony to its strength that it provides material, as should all great texts, for multiple interpretations from varying points of view. Is it demonstrating that socialism can never work or is it demonstrating the dangers of the perversions of socialism? Now that we are in a different world than that of the Cold War for which it was in many ways a crucial document, it still talks to us of the dangers of the drive to power and the efforts made to crush individual thought and, indeed, love.

*Nineteen Eighty-Four* is about power, about words, about the past, about love, about the individual and the state. It is also a work of art and literature that is read for its ideas, for its skill as a novel, for the light that it sheds on the time it was written and on the time since. Will the text have different meanings in 2004 and beyond?

Fall Semester 1994

1. George Orwell, *Homage to Catalonia* (London, 1938), p. 314.

2. George Orwell, "Why I Write," in Sonia Orwell and Ian Angus (eds.), *Collected Essays, Journalism and Letters of George Orwell* (New York, 1968), I, p. 7.

3. Walter Cronkite, Preface, *1984* (New York, 1983), p. 3. Ellipses, except the first, in the original.

# 11

# Mountbatten Revisited

## PHILIP ZIEGLER

"The evil that men do lives after them, The good is oft interred with their bones." Mark Antony knew all too well that, after the briefest possible pause for mourning and polite obituaries, the death of a public hero is followed by mounting criticism designed to damage if not destroy his or her reputation. One of the few ways by which this process can be, if not prevented, then at least slowed up, is for the hero to perish suddenly and dramatically, preferably at the hands of an assassin. In the case of President Kennedy, to take a prominent example, this technique proved most efficacious. The trumpet blasts of Sorensen and Schlesinger had sounded in his honor long before the voices of hostile critics were seriously heard and a full-blooded assault on his reputation was thus deferred by several years. Such was also the good fortune of Admiral of the Fleet the Right Honourable Earl Mountbatten of Burma, Knight of the Garter, Knight Grand Cross of the Royal Victorian Order, Knight Grand Commander of the Most Eminent Order of the Indian Empire, and holder of enough other decorations from around the world to dress overall the battleship in which he would have felt so much at home.

Mountbatten was somewhat less fortunate than Kennedy. It took almost a year to appoint his official biographer, and that author then dallied over his task. It was six years after Mountbatten's death before my own trumpet blast—in any case, I hope, rather more muted than those of Sorensen and Schlesinger—was heard upon the biographical battlefield. By that time attacks upon Mountbatten's career and personality were already commonplace. He had the capacity to inspire unbridled animosity in those who criticized him. Mountbatten, wrote Nigel Hamilton, Field Marshal Montgomery's biographer, was "a master of intrigue, jealousy and ineptitude. Like a spoilt child he toyed with men's lives with an indifference to casualties that can only be explained by his insatiable, even psychopathic ambition."[1] But this onslaught was only the herald of worse to come. In the last decade Mountbatten has been attacked for his arrogance, his mendacity, his vanity, his impetuosity, his sexual proclivities, his snobbishness, his unscrupulousness, his indecision, his dishonesty, his exhibitionism—a brief flip through Roget's *Thesaurus* would yield a score of other charges. At the moment the field is led by Andrew Roberts's robustly intemperate essay in his *Eminent Churchillians,*[2] but even as I am speaking some new demolition job is probably on the way.

I must make my own position clear. I came to biographize Mountbatten, not to praise him. In no way do I consider myself to be the counsel for the defence. There is truth in nearly all the charges levelled against Mountbatten; most of them are illustrated in my own book, many of them are based on facts which I published there for the first time. Since my book has appeared, important new material has come to light which has caused me to rethink certain passages. If I were writing the book today, it would be in some ways still more critical of its subject. But I remain unshaken in my conclusion that he was a great man and that his considerable failings were more than outweighed by his far more important qualities. I concede the force of many of the attacks levelled against him; I protest only against the failure to give him credit where it is due.

In two fields in particular Mountbatten has been subjected to serious and, it must be admitted, damaging attacks: the raid on Dieppe in August 1942 and the partition of India in 1947. It is to these, especially the second, that I propose to devote myself. First, however, it might be of use if I were to put these two episodes into context by providing a brief summary of his career. Mountbatten sprang from the House of Hesse, a German principality closely linked with the British royal family. His father, Prince Louis, was the product of a morganatic marriage; a solecism of which Mountbatten was always conscious and which must partly have been responsible for the exaggerated importance he attached to his royal connections. Louis married his cousin, a grand-daughter of Queen Victoria, settled in England and joined the Royal Navy. By the outbreak of the First World War, he was its professional head, First Sea Lord. That Prince Louis of Battenberg should lead the British Navy in a war against Germany proved too much for the chauvinists. Battenberg, soon to be restyled Mountbatten, was hounded from office. For his son, by then a naval cadet, the blow was fearful. He always maintained that it was the determination to expunge his father's disgrace which fired his ambition to become First Sea Lord himself. Such protestations need not be taken too seriously. Mountbatten was intensely ambitious and would soon have found some other reason for wishing to get to the top. But the memory did lend an almost sacred significance to his quest. It also helped in another way. Winston Churchill always reproached himself with not having saved Prince Louis from dismissal; he felt a debt towards the son which he was to repay in full.

Mountbatten's naval career prospered; his success was helped, certainly, by his connections and the fact that he had married an immensely rich heiress, but owed far more to his energy, intelligence, charm, and capacity for grinding hard work. By 1939 he was a dashing destroyer captain—too dashing, indeed; he was a marvellous leader of men, but he was apt to lead them much too fast in the wrong direction, often to disaster. Churchill judged that his talents would be better employed in the fledgling service of Combined Operations, a force whose long-term function was to prepare the way for the invasion of Europe, but which, in the meantime, was responsible for raids on the continental mainland, by far the largest of which was, of course, aimed against Dieppe. Some argue that the resources pumped into Combined Operations could have been more usefully employed elsewhere; no one, I think, would deny that Mountbatten's energy, enthusiasm, and dedication produced astonishing results in building up a machine to undertake what was to all intents and purposes a new form of warfare.

Long before Combined Operations achieved its apotheosis on D-Day, Mountbatten had been translated to still higher things as Supreme Commander in South East Asia. He arrived when things seemed at their worst, though in hindsight it is now clear that the tide was already turning. How great his personal contribution was to victory in Burma is difficult to establish, in part because no one was ever quite sure what a Supreme Commander was supposed to do. At the least, however, he played a valuable role as a booster of morale and a man who could pull strings in the highest places in Washington and London. "We did it together," was the final verdict of General Slim, commander of the 14th Army. In fact, Mountbatten's abilities were tested most severely at the end of the war, when he found himself having to come to terms with the new nationalist movements that had sprung up in the vacuum left by the collapse of Japanese power.

It was his success in this role which, as much as anything, induced Clement Attlee to send Mountbatten to India as the last Viceroy. For Mountbatten, this was an enthralling but in many ways unwelcome diversion from the naval career to which he was still dedicated. He went back to the Navy in 1948, duly rose to the post of First Sea Lord and went on to become Chief of Defence Staff, supreme commander of all Britain's armed services. To him it fell to take the first, long step down the path towards the integration of army, navy, and air force. As with Combined Operations, there are those who claim that his efforts were misguided; as with Combined Operations, few would deny that he got more done in a shorter time than could have been achieved by any of his contemporaries. From there it was a long, energetic and on the whole enjoyable retirement, until the IRA saved him from the indignities of old age and restored briefly the heroic status which was already beginning to look a little frayed.

And so to Dieppe: probably the episode in his career which caused him the most acute embarrassment. The raid on—or mini-invasion of—Dieppe comprised two flank attacks, one of which achieved modest success, and a frontal attack on the port itself which was a bloody debacle. Of the 5,000 or so Canadian troops who made up the main striking force, 3,400 were killed, captured or wounded. Someone had blundered, as Lord Tennyson observed of an earlier, still more dramatic disaster, but who and why?

The operation must be put in the context of the war as a whole. The British desperately needed to mount some sort of operation against the mainland that would relieve pressure on the Russians and appease the Americans, who were calling urgently for a Second Front. At first the proposal was for a landing by ten or twelve divisions, who would remain ashore for a few weeks. Mercifully, it soon became obvious that the landing craft and air support were not available and the expedition was aborted. Dieppe was a stopgap, an operation made necessary—if indeed it *was* necessary—by political considerations. Its success, in military terms, was of secondary importance.

Nevertheless, Mountbatten and others sought to justify it on military grounds. It taught the invaders essential lessons, argued Mountbatten; it showed that the allies could not hope to storm and hold one of the major Channel ports; it proved the need for PLUTO, the pipeline under the ocean, and for Mulberry, the floating harbour. "I don't believe for a minute that Dieppe taught us anything about D-Day," retorted Ian Jacob, Assistant Military Secretary to the War Cabinet.[3] He was right, in that the lesson should not have been necessary; the lives of so many Canadians need not have been sacrificed to establish the impossibility of a direct attack on Dieppe or any other port. But the fact is that the commanders and Chiefs of Staff *did* need to learn the lesson; if the same mistake had been made on D-Day, the consequences would have been not painful but catastrophic.

Another lesson which should not have needed learning was that one person had to be in overall control. "As overall commander," wrote Andrew Roberts, it was Mountbatten's job to decide whether the attack should be frontal and preceded by a heavy bombardment.[4] But Mountbatten was not the overall commander. He thought he ought to have been, but Alan Brooke had emphasized that the powers of the Chief of Combined Operations ended when it came to the "actual execution of the raid."[5] The Dieppe plan, wrote the official historian of the Canadian Army, Colonel Stacey, "was the work of a large and somewhat indefinitely composed committee . . . There were a great many cooks and this probably had much to do with spoiling the broth."[6] Mountbatten himself had in fact favored powerful flank attacks to be followed by a pincer movement on the port; it was Montgomery who dismissed this idea on the not unreasonable ground that the raid would not last long enough to make the occupation of Dieppe a possibility. Mountbatten does bear the main responsibility for the decision to revive the operation after it had been postponed and, as it was thought at the time, abandoned. The original and revised operations were almost identical; to those who argued that it would be folly to relaunch an assault which had been so much advertised, Mountbatten retorted that Dieppe was the one place where the Germans would not expect a fresh attack to be directed. In fact no evidence has ever been found to suggest that the Germans thought a raid on Dieppe more or less likely than on any other Channel port.

Professor Brian Villa of the University of Ottawa has drawn a spectacular red herring across this issue with his contention that Mountbatten was solely responsible for remounting the Dieppe raid, without the authorization, explicit or implicit, of the Chiefs of Staff.[7] He bases this somewhat surprising charge on two contentions, to both of which the answer is "So what?" The minutes of the Chiefs of Staff Committee contain no reference to the operation—"So what?" It was by no means unheard-of for the Chiefs to keep no record of their most secret deliberations. One will, for instance, search in vain for any discussion of German progress towards the acquisition of an atom bomb, yet the subject was debated and important decisions taken as a result. No matter could have been more secret than the re-launching of the Dieppe raid. By an odd coincidence General Nye, Vice Chief of the Imperial General Staff, was staying with my parents on 19 August 1942. He was telephoned in the early morning and disappeared before breakfast after an explosion of most uncharacteristic bad language. Subsequently, he rang Alan Brooke to complain about having been kept in the dark. Brooke's answer was that information had been disseminated on the strictest possible basis of need-to-know. Nye had not needed to know, so he had not received the information.

But even if there had been no formal decision by the Chiefs of Staff—once again, "So what?" It is physically impossible that the Chiefs could have been unaware of such a matter—even Villa concedes this. Ismay also knew; he, in Villa's view, was the chief villain for keeping Churchill in the dark. So Churchill was Mountbatten's dupe? Yet, in his memoirs Churchill wrote: "After the Canadian authorities and the Chiefs of Staff had given their approval I personally went through the plans with the CIGS, Admiral Mountbatten and the Naval Force Commander." This formula, Villa suggests, was drafted by Mountbatten. So it may have been, but why on earth should Churchill have accepted it if he did not believe it to be true? He was not a man conspicuously ready to accept responsibility for the blunders of others. At the very least, he would have used a less categoric description of his role in the affair. The vision of Churchill meekly taking dictation from Mountbatten on a matter which he must have felt potentially damaging to his own reputation is so far fetched as to be laughable. The decision to relaunch the raid was taken collectively by the Prime Minister and the Chiefs of Staff.

Where Mountbatten can properly be blamed is over the provision of intelligence. He did not know, and should have known, that between the date of the aborted first raid and August 19, all the Channel ports had been reinforced, fortifications strengthened, superior troops brought in, new gun-emplacements built. The targets with which destroyers could possibly have coped in July were impregnable to such attack a month later. The need for the support of a battleship or aerial bombardment, strong even at the earlier date, was irresistible by the time the landings took place. The intelligence service most directly to blame was that of Combined Operations.

And so to India. It was inevitable that the man who was responsible for the dismemberment of the Indian Empire would incur criticism from many angles. Mountbatten concluded his task on 15 August 1947 to a paean of praise, but the euphoria soon dwindled. Over the last decade his record has been attacked by Muslims, Hindus, and Sikhs, left wing and right wing, Britons and Indians, soldiers and civil servants. Two lines of complaint have been sustained with especial ferocity: that he favored the Hindu cause over the Muslim, the future India over the future Pakistan, even to the extent of tampering with the partition line to the benefit of his preferred party; and that his whole policy was flawed, the breakneck speed at which he conducted the prelude to independence led directly to the collapse of law and order and the massacres in the Punjab.

Was Mountbatten prejudiced? I do not believe that he arrived in India with any predilection in favor of the Hindus. The British officer class to which he belonged traditionally preferred Muslims to Hindus. The Muslims, they felt, were straightforward, clean-limbed, good fighting men—pro-British too, if only because they felt themselves to be a minority who could best protect themselves against the majority Hindus with the help of the imperial power. The Hindus, on the other hand, were conceived as being cunning, devious, lawyers or would-be lawyers, rabidly anti-British and in favor of instant independence. This, of course, over-simplifies British attitudes. Most British officers working with native soldiers or sailors owed their loyalty to the unit to which they had been assigned, and this could have been predominantly Hindu, predominantly Muslim or, as often as not, a mixture of the two. They tried hard not to discriminate between the two elements and, for the most part, succeeded. Nevertheless, in so far as there was a predisposition to favor one against the other then, from the Commander-in-Chief, Field Marshal Auchinleck, downwards, the warmest affection was usually lavished on the Muslims.

Mountbatten began with no such preference. He was a man almost entirely free from racial prejudice. It is perhaps not too fanciful to attribute this in part to his family background. European royals for many generations have had scant regard for frontiers and the House of Hesse was among the most itinerant and cosmopolitan. In the generations before Mountbatten, his forbears married into the royal houses of Greece, Spain, Denmark, Russia, and Sweden as well as Great Britain; his brother married a Russian princess, his sisters respectively a Greek prince and the King of Sweden; his own wife was the grand-daughter of a German Jewish financier. To a degree remarkable among naval officers, Mountbatten took people for what they were, with little enquiry into their antecedents. On his tour of India with the Prince of Wales in 1921, he had grown to know and become friendly with some of the Indian princes, but he made no distinction between Muslim and Hindu. He had briefly met Jawaharlal Nehru in Singapore in 1946 and had found him attractive and sympathetic, but their acquaintanceship was no more than superficial; the only other Indian political leader whom he had met was Krishna Menon, and he too was far from being a friend. He knew that Mohammed Ali Jinnah, the Muslim leader, had the reputation of being cold and intractable, but he saw this more as a challenge than a deterrent. He had vast faith in what he felt to be his invincible charm and did not believe for a moment that Jinnah would be able to resist it. He arrived in Delhi genuinely resolved to be impartial and to establish the closest possible links with both his principal interlocutors.

His resolve did not last. Almost without his noticing it, Mountbatten found himself drawn into a closer and closer relationship with the Hindu leaders, inevitably to the detriment of his reputation among the Muslims. The pattern was set from his first meetings with the two leaders. Nehru was warm, responsive and apparently ready to be flexible—"Pandit Nehru struck me as most sincere," the Viceroy began his record of their first discussion.[8] Jinnah was remote, suspicious, patently intractable: "My God, he was cold!" Mountbatten exclaimed as his visitor left Viceroy's House.[9] The Viceroy's respect and affection for Mohandas Gandhi fortified this discrepancy: "An old poppet," Mountbatten described the Mahatma, hardly an adequate characterization but one which exemplified the warm, if slightly baffled incomprehension with which each viewed the other. In the eyes of the Muslims, however, it was not the fact that the Viceroy preferred Nehru to Jinnah which was most disturbing, but that the subtle and experienced V. P. Menon, the Reforms Commissioner, was admitted to the innermost councils of the Viceroy's House. Menon was a pragmatist and a moderate—his influence in the Viceroy's entourage was almost entirely beneficial—but he was an intimate of the toughest and most unscrupulous of the Hindu leaders, Sardar Patel, Tammany Hall-style boss of the Congress Party. The Muslims can hardly be blamed for deploring the fact that Patel's voice was thus heard in what should have been the rigidly neutral confines of the Viceroy's staff meetings, still less for their suspicion that all the secrets of the Viceroy's House were rapidly transmitted to the Congress leadership.

Such suspicions were not unjustified. It is impossible now to be sure who knew what, when, or how they found out, but such evidence as exists suggests that, through Menon and other Hindu officials, such as V. D. Ayer of the Boundary Commission,[10] Congress politicians knew more than was proper about Viceregal deliberations. The traffic was not entirely one way. In his strikingly frank diaries, Shahid Hamid, Auchinleck's private secretary, has recorded how he at once reported to Jinnah information which he had gleaned from his official position.[11] On the whole, however, Hindu officials were closer to the sources of power, and the Congress leadership had the better of the exchanges.

Nothing will persuade the Pakistanis today that the relationship between Nehru and Mountbatten's wife, Edwina, was not an important element in the links that bound Viceroy's House to the Congress leadership. That Nehru and Edwina were at one time very much in love is an open secret; whether the affair was consummated remains a matter of intense interest to even the most serious-minded of Indian historians. What, however, is certain is that there was nothing more than friendship between them until a certain weekend in May 1948 about which Nehru, in characteristically exalted vein, later wrote: "Suddenly I realized (and perhaps you did also) that there was a deeper attachment between us, that some uncontrollable force, of which I was only dimly aware, drew us to one another. I was overwhelmed and at the same time exhilarated by this new discovery."[12] When the negotiations leading up to the partition of India were under way, this "new discovery" was still nine months ahead.

Mountbatten believed that he was acting with impartiality. The nearest he came as Viceroy to an open admission of hostility to Pakistan occurred early in July 1947, when Jinnah told him that he proposed to reserve the Governor-Generalship of Pakistan for himself. Mountbatten had convinced himself that independent India and Pakistan could only evolve in harmony if the former Viceroy was appointed Governor-General of both countries and was thus enabled to see fair play. When Jinnah admitted that his decision to hold the post himself might lead to Pakistan losing out in the division of assets, Mountbatten exploded, "It may well cost you the whole of your assets and the future of Pakistan," and stormed from the room.[13] But though a combination of injured vanity and genuine distress at what seemed to him a disastrous decision led him to despair of the future of Pakistan, he on the whole remained commendably evenhanded when it came to the division of assets or the other problems arising from partition.

In no case have the Pakistanis found it so difficult to believe that this was true as over the future status of Kashmir. Mountbatten's public position was, and remained, that since the majority of the people of Kashmir were Muslim, the state should accede to Pakistan. The fact that the Maharajah himself was a Hindu did not affect the fundamental principle that every state should follow the wishes of the majority of its people. The most that could be contemplated was a partition of the province, with the predominantly Hindu Jammu acceding to India and the Muslim Vale of Kashmir to Pakistan. Few Muslims, however, believed that the Viceroy paid more than lip service to this doctrine. His great friend, Nehru, was a Kashmiri and determined to prevent the state from slipping into Pakistani hands. What could be more certain than that the Viceroy would secretly work to this end? But the evidence that shows Mountbatten as champion of an Indian Kashmir relates to the period when he was Governor-General and thus the servant of the Indian state. Even then his activities were confined to assisting military operations designed to check the advances of the Pathan

invaders. Much though Nehru would have liked him to do so, he
never changed his public stance that there should be a plebiscite in
Kashmir and that the state should then follow the wishes of the
people. When Mountbatten went to Srinagar in June 1947, he carried with him the assurance of Sardar Patel that the Indian government would not oppose Kashmir's accession to Pakistan if that was
clearly the wish of its people.[14] Even Nehru was induced to agree,
reluctantly and temporarily, that this might be an acceptable conclusion. The Maharajah, evasive and vacillating, contrived to avoid
serious discussions with his visitor, and Mountbatten returned to
Delhi empty-handed. The only point that has been adduced to suggest that Mountbatten as Viceroy was furthering Nehru's cause is
that the partition line in the Punjab was modified at the last minute
so as to transfer from Pakistan to India certain areas in the Gurdaspur
district that procured India direct road access to Kashmir. The question of Mountbatten's interference over the partition line needs
separate treatment, but so far as Gurdaspur is concerned there is
no reason to believe that he took up the matter with Lord Radcliffe
or that, if he did, it was the strategic significance of the district which
he had in mind. To have done so would have been at direct variance with everything that is known of his views at the time.[15]

   This point, however, does lead on to one of the most controversial issues of Mountbatten's time in India. Whether Gurdaspur was
or was not involved, did the Viceroy play any part in the drawing up
of the partition line? Mountbatten's public position has always been
that he had nothing whatsoever to do with the process. The lawyer,
Cyril Radcliffe, was imported specifically to perform this task. He
and the Viceroy kept each other at arm's length. When Radcliffe's
findings were delivered, they were placed in a sealed envelope and
locked away until the moment came for their publication. Whenever anybody urged on the Viceroy the inclusion of some area in
India or Pakistan, he would reply that it was no concern of his.

   When I published my biography in 1985, some circumstantial
evidence existed to suggest that changes to the partition line had
been made at the last minute, that the Viceroy might have been
aware of this, and that he might even have borne some degree of
responsibility for them. I stated that a nugget of doubt remained in
my mind but that, on the whole, I was inclined to accept
Mountbatten's story. In the light of new material which has become
available since 1985, my nugget of doubt has become a boulder;
indeed, I must now say that I am satisfied that the Viceroy did speak
to Radcliffe before the partition line was finalized and urged him to
bear certain considerations in mind when reaching his conclusions.
The questions for me are now what those considerations were, how

strongly and in what detail Mountbatten urged them, and how reprehensible his conduct therefore seems.

Two pieces of evidence in particular have led me to change my views. One is the testimony of the Secretary to the Boundary Commission, Christopher Beaumont.[16] Beaumont is convinced that, at lunch with Mountbatten and Ismay—a lunch from which Beaumont was most unusually excluded—Radcliffe was pressed to make modifications to the partition line in Ferozepur so that certain important headwaters were awarded to India rather than to Pakistan. Certainly, such a modification was made and, though *post hoc* is not necessarily *propter hoc*, certainly the change was made after the private lunch. Radcliffe never gave any explanation of the change or any other detail of the partition line and destroyed his working papers once the award was made, but Beaumont claims that he was "very sheepish" and shuffled off the matter when he was questioned some weeks later about what happened at the meeting.[17] Such evidence is only circumstantial but is nonetheless not to be ignored, particularly when taken in conjunction with the memoirs of Kanwar Sain, the Chief Engineer of Bikaner, who records a visit that he and his prime minister made to Mountbatten, in which they threatened that, unless the Ferozepur headwaters were assigned to India, Bikaner itself would have to accede to Pakistan.[18]

What I find conclusive, however, is a letter Ismay received from Mountbatten in April 1948.[19] The letter ended with an injunction to Ismay to burn it after reading—as usual a guarantee that the recipient will file it with particular care. In it Mountbatten referred to a meeting which they had had with Radcliffe, in which the lawyer had spoken of the difficulties he was encountering in sorting out certain irrigation issues, Ferozepur being a particularly knotty problem. Mountbatten had said that, if favors were to be done to Pakistan, he hoped it would be in Bengal rather than the Punjab, since there was no Sikh problem in Bengal. "Provided the overall east-west boundaries were scrupulously fair between the two dominions," he told Radcliffe, it seemed to him that it would be proper to "make any adjustments necessary for balancing out the boundaries in Bengal and the Punjab." If this version of the conversation is accepted, then Mountbatten hinted broadly that it would be in the best interests of both dominions, let alone the imperial power, if concessions were made to India in Ferozepur and a balancing advantage given to Pakistan in the east—as indeed was done in the case of the Chittagong Hill Tracts.

In an answer to a parliamentary question, redrafted by Radcliffe himself, the Minister stated that he had been assured by Radcliffe that his findings were "the result of his own unfettered judgment and that at no stage was any attempt made by the Governor-General to influence his decision."[20] Such a statement is compatible—just— with the scenario outlined in Mountbatten's letter to Ismay; Radcliffe was being no worse than economical with the truth. He was a man of monumental integrity and great strength of mind. "What is certain," wrote his biographer, Edmund Heward, himself a distinguished lawyer, "is that he could not have been persuaded against his better judgement. He found Mountbatten arrogant, did not care for him personally and had already shown his independence by refusing Mountbatten's request to delay the Award until after August 15."[21]

In my biography, I concluded that Mountbatten had not made any such demarche and went on to say that, though he might have been guilty of indiscretion, he was innocent of the "arrant folly as well as dishonesty of which his enemies accused him."[22] Now that I have changed my mind about the main issue, do I regret those words? I think they still seem pretty apposite. It was arrant folly on Mountbatten's part to jeopardize the position of neutrality which he had so painstakingly built up, on what was in fact a pretty trivial issue. It was dishonest to pretend that he had not done so and to keep up this lie until the day he died. In his defense, I would say that the Viceroy was physically exhausted and had been for months subject to the most gruelling psychological pressure. In such circumstances, it is not surprising that he should have attached exaggerated importance to this minor matter and have convinced himself that the entire settlement was at risk. But, in my biography, I have often found myself accusing my hero of folly and dishonesty; it causes me no particular embarrassment to add another charge.

Where I will still defend Mountbatten vigorously is on the wider issue, the charge that the massacres which followed partition were, in the crudest terms, his fault, that the intemperate haste with which he conducted the gallop towards independence led to a breakdown of law and order and caused untold misery and the deaths of hundreds of thousands, perhaps even millions of innocent victims.

At its most lurid, Mountbatten is accused not merely of bad judgment but of criminal irresponsibility. In his interesting and generally most judicious dissertation on the partition of India, Robert Osborn describes the Viceroy's decision to reduce drastically the time allotted for the lead-up to Independence and goes on: "The generally accepted reason for Mountbatten moving the date forward was that he wished to return to his naval career as quickly as possible."[23] I do not know where Colonel Osborn has found this implausible consensus. Even among Mountbatten's most bitter enemies—usually admirals over whose heads he was promoted—I cannot recall one who would have said as much. They knew that

Mountbatten had secured his line of retreat to the Royal Navy by obtaining a categoric assurance from the First Lord, endorsed personally by the Prime Minister, that his promotion prospects would not be jeopardized however long the task in India might keep him away from life at sea. They realized that, if Mountbatten had nevertheless been so desperately anxious to cut short his time in India, he would hardly have agreed to stay on after Independence as Governor-General, against the strong urging of his wife and most of his closest advisers. Above all, they accepted that, whatever Mountbatten's failings might have been, he was no fool. He knew that his work in India would be the most important that he would ever undertake, and that posterity would judge the failure or success of his career above all by his time as Viceroy. To imagine that he would have imperilled the outcome of this vital episode so as to return to the Navy a few months earlier would be to assume a lack of judgment so flagrant as to make its owner unfit to command a gunboat, let alone dissolve an empire.

If Mountbatten erred by so drastically accelerating the approach to Independence, then he did so because he honestly thought it to be in the best interests of India and Pakistan, not to mention Great Britain. No one in their senses would deny that the massacres which followed partition, costing at least two hundred thousand lives, were a tragic blemish on Mountbatten's achievement. The two questions which have to be answered are, first, could the Viceroy have foreseen and taken steps to prevent them, and, second, would they have been less disastrous if the move to Independence had been made at a more decorous pace?

Obviously, he was taken by surprise. He had always realized that the coming of self-government might be accompanied by major communal disturbances. What he had not foreseen was the massive and panic-stricken exodus from both sides of the new partition line. The stated policy of both the new governments was that racial minorities should stay where they were, in the villages that they had inhabited often for many hundreds of years. When asked at a press conference whether he believed that this would work out in practice, Mountbatten replied that he foresaw no mass movements of population "because of the physical difficulty involved . . . But I equally think that a measure of transfer of population will come about in a natural way, that is to say, people will just cross the boundary or the Government may take steps to transfer populations."[24] People did "just cross the boundary" but there was nothing "natural" about that monstrous pilgrimage. Yet if Mountbatten was taken by surprise, so were all the experts: Hindu and Muslim; civil servants, soldiers and politicians. No one had contemplated the immensity of the problem; no one therefore had proposed measures that might have mitigated the damage. "My country has gone mad!" exclaimed a distraught Nehru. He spoke of the bloody violence, but he could as well have been referring to the movement of population which fueled it. Panic is perhaps a form of madness; its consequences, anyway, will rarely be foreseen by rational men planning the future in the calm of their sequestered offices. In the words of that most rational of men, V. P. Menon: "It has been said that if a planned exchange of population had been arranged before the transfer of power, the communal holocaust could have been avoided. But could there be any question of an exchange of population between two sides which had agreed and publicly announced that they would retain their respective minorities? Indeed, the Congress was definitely against any exchange of population."[25] Even Evan Jenkins, the Governor of the Punjab, who was probably the most critical of Mountbatten's policies among those who were directly responsible for its execution, believed that if the partition line were accepted by both the new governments, relatively few people would see any need to move. Perhaps, over the next decade there might be a gradual migration, but though this would pose logistic problems it need not lead to serious disorder.

Supposing that an extra three or six months had been given to the process of drawing up the partition line and preparing for independence, would things have been any better? Mountbatten's critics argue that there would then have been time to prepare people for the idea of partition, to persuade them to stay put. If they still insisted on moving, then the migration would have been planned with deliberation, troops and police drafted to the danger spots, convoys of refugees organized and protected. But who would have managed such an operation? The British Army in India was rapidly running down, those who were left were for the most part due for demobilization and eager to be gone, to employ them in certainly protracted and probably dangerous policing operations would have been politically unacceptable in London. Mountbatten, rightly or wrongly, did not want to put British troops into the position of enforcing a settlement in the newly independent dominions, but even if he had advocated such a course his proposal would have been vetoed by Attlee's government.

There remained the Indian Army. But this, as a force drawn from and representing the whole sub-continent, was already disintegrating. It was tried. The Punjab Boundary Force, composed of Muslim, Sikh and Hindu soldiers, with officers drawn from every ethnic group including many British, and commanded by a British general, was set up specifically to safeguard the peace in the Punjab during partition. Though only 35,000 strong, far too small a body to maintain order in that vast and densely populated area, the Boundary Force was better than nothing. But its value was limited and even that value rapidly diminished. In Ismay's words: "the ingrained mutual trust of a lifetime—indeed many lifetimes—was dissipated."[26] Confronted by a situation in which they were required to enforce the law against representatives of their own race and faith, the different elements of the Force began to pull different ways. "This serious deterioration of morale," concludes Osborn in the dissertation from which I have already quoted, "combined with the desires of the two new Dominion Army Commanders, led to the disbandment of the Force after 32 days of service."[27]

The failure of the Boundary Force demonstrates vividly the pressures under which the Viceroy was operating and which impelled him into setting so hectic a pace. Mountbatten was playing from a weakening hand. The British elements in the Army, the police and the civil service were being rapidly run down, already reduced to a skeleton in certain critical sectors, and it was becoming every day more clear that in the rising swell of communal bitterness the Hindu and Muslim elements could not be relied on to administer the law with impartiality. Once the principle of partition had been accepted, it was inevitable that communalism would rage freely. The longer the period before the transfer of power, the worse the tension and the greater the threat that violence would spread. Today it was the Punjab, tomorrow Bengal, Hyderabad, any of the myriad societies in the sub-continent where Hindu and Muslim lived cheek by jowl. Two hundred thousand dead could have become two million, even twenty million.

Since the other approach was never tried, no one can state with certainty that it would have proved more or less successful. What is however evident is that those people who, from their position or their special knowledge, speak with authority on the subject agree that delay could only have provoked a far worse catastrophe. Ismay was an old India hand, as close as anyone to the center of the action, a man of determinedly independent mind. He was harrowed by the horror of the massacres and wrote to his wife of his mission's "grim and total failure." "The only consolation is that looking back over the last six months, I would not have changed, in essentials, a single decision that we took."[28] To Mountbatten he wrote of a conversation he had just had with a man who had insisted that the administration of India could have held the position for several more months at least. "You, and all of us who were with you, were not blind to the dangers of rushing things, but we were completely convinced that every day's delay was fraught with the utmost danger;

and we felt that the wisdom of your decision was completely vindicated by events."[29]

It would try your patience too far if I were to cite all those who have taken a similar line: Conrad Corfield, Mountbatten's most bitter critic; or Humphrey Trevelyan, his sometimes equivocal but generally whole-hearted defender; H. M. Patel and V. P. Menon; Nehru and Sardar Patel. The last word can perhaps be left to Rajagopalachari, who was in time to take Mountbatten's place as India's first Indian head of state. "If the Viceroy had not transferred power when he did," said Rajaji, "there could well have been no power to transfer."[30] That, in a sentence, is the case for Mountbatten.

Over the course of his whole career, not just during his time as Viceroy, Mountbatten made many serious mistakes and behaved with something less than perfect rectitude. All that I concede. I also believe that, if the scales of justice could ever be perfectly adjusted, he would be found to have done much more good than harm. In India, in particular, he performed an almost impossible task with courage, skill and distinction. That good, to revert to my opening quotation, should not be interred with his bones. To move from *Julius Caesar* to *Othello*, I would plead "nothing extenuate, nor set down aught in malice." There has been too much malice in recent attacks on Lord Mountbatten; let us avoid extenuation, but let him at least be treated fairly.

Fall Semester 1995

1. Nigel Hamilton, *Montgomery*, 2 vols. (London, 1981), I, p. 517.

2. Andrew Roberts, *Eminent Churchillians* (London, 1994), London, 1994, pp. 55–136.

3. Ibid., p. 69.

4. Ibid., p. 67.

5. 20 July 1942, COS (42)211, July 21, 1942, COS (42)213; and July 27, 1942 COS (42)218.

6. *Official History of the Canadian Army*, vol. I (Ottawa, 1966), p. 399.

7. Brian Loring Villa, *Unauthorized Action* (Toronto, 1990).

8. Viceroy's Intervi w, no. 3, March 24, 1947, *The Transfer of Power in India*, vol. X, p. 11.

9. Alan Campbell-Johnson, *Mission with Mountbatten* (London, 1951), p. 56.

10. For Ayer's putative role see Christopher Beaumont's privately distributed paper, "The Truth of the Partition of the Punjab in August 1947."

11. Shahid Hamid, *Disastrous Twilight* (London, 1986), p. 163.

12. Letter of Mar. 12, 1947, Broadlands Archive, uncatalogued.

13. Viceroy's Personal Report No. 11, July 4, 1947, *Transfer of Power*, vol. XI. Cf. W. H. Morris-Jones, "The Transfer of Power, 1947," *Modern Asian Studies*, 16, 1 (1982).

14. Lord Birdwood, "Kashmir," *International Affairs*, XXVIII, 3 (July 1952).

15. For a contrary view see Ian Stephens, *Horned Moon* (London, 1966), pp. 106–13.

16. "The Truth of the Partition of the Punjab."

17. Roberts, *Eminent Churchillians*, p. 97.

18. Kanwar Sain, *Reminiscences of an Engineer* (New Delhi, 1978), p. 90.

19. Apr. 2, 1948, Ismay MSS. (King's College, London), 111/7/13a.

20. India Office IOR L PJ/10/119.

21. Edward Heward, *The Great and the Good: A Life of Lord Radcliffe* (London, 1994), p. 51.

22. Philip Ziegler, *Mountbatten* (London, 1985), p. 422.

23. Robert Bruce Osborn, "Field Marshal Sir Claude Auchinleck, the Indian Army, and the Partition of India" (Ph.D. Dissertation, University of Texas at Austin, 1994).

24. *Time Only to Look Forward: Speeches of Rear-Admiral the Earl Mountbatten of Burma as Viceroy of India and Governor-General of the Dominion of India* (London, 1949), p. 30.

25. *The Transfer of Power in India*, vol. IX, p. 435.

26. Oct. 5, 1947, Ismay MSS, 111/7/66/3d.

27. Osborn, "Field Marshal Sir Claude Auchinleck."

28. *The Memoirs of Lord Ismay* (London, 1960), p. 167.

29. Mar. 6, 1962, cited in Ziegler, *Mountbatten* , p. 439.

30. V. B. Kulkarni, *British Dominion in India and After* (Bombay, 1964), p. 255.

# 12

# Myths about the Approach to
# Indian Independence

## JOHN GRIGG

T his lecture will be concerned with the political mythology
that developed during the last phase of British rule in India,
and has largely held the field since. Some of it is peculiar to
the British side, some to the Indian; but the most potent myth of all
has enthralled a great number of people on both sides, and throughout the world. According to this, the Indian national movement
under Gandhi's leadership undermined British power and weakened Britain's will to rule to the extent that the Raj ceased to be
viable. No single agency has done more to propagate and perpetuate this myth than Richard Attenborough's film *Gandhi*. The view
of history that it presents is flattering to both sides, since it shows
India as having produced a uniquely effective as well as uniquely
noble leader, and Britain as having been capable of responding creatively to his unprecedented form of national leadership.

A distinctively British belief is that Indian independence was, almost from the first, the goal of British rule in India, which would in
any case have been reached in the mid-twentieth century, give or
take a few years. A distinctively Indian belief is that the tragedy of
partition which accompanied independence was entirely due to
divide-and-rule policies practiced by the British, and in no degree
the result of inherent communal rivalry or of any failure by Indian
politicians to take adequate steps to overcome it. The cumulative
effect of these views about the approach to independence, jointly
or separately held, has been to generate on both sides an unwar-
rantable blandness and serious misunderstanding of many vital elements in the story.

My purpose is not to debunk any of the great personal reputations involved, though I shall be suggesting that some of them need
to be reinterpreted. Above all, I shall be trying to separate truth
from myth in a story of which, even when de-mythologized, both
sides have more reason to be proud than ashamed—though there
are considerable grounds for shame, and still more for regret, on
both sides. Moreover, since partition created a third side, I should
add that the genesis of Pakistan is rather more complicated than
most exponents of Indo-British mythology are prepared to admit.

Returning to the Gandhi film, one has to recognize its immense
significance in our audio-visual age. For millions it has provided
their first and only access to the subject, and for millions more a
version of events which is unlikely to be effaced. The film's superb
qualities as cinema, combined with Ben Kingsley's marvellous performance in the central role, must have given the message of the
film an impact and influence of vast proportions.

Up to a point the message is not false. Gandhi *was* a great man,
and in many ways an exceptionally good one. The leadership he
gave *was* different from that given by any previous national leader,
in India or anywhere else. He *did* make a big impression on many
British people and on the world at large, as well as on his own com-
patriots. His anti-communalism *was* perfectly sincere, and never
more heroically demonstrated than in the last months of his life,
ending with his death as a martyr to the cause. His personality *was*
singularly attractive and fascinating, its charm much enhanced by
the delightful humor that is well brought out in the film. In all these
respects the Attenborough spectacular does not mislead.

Yet, in other most important respects, the message conveyed by
it is gravely misleading. By concentrating so relentlessly on Gandhi
it suggests that other leaders of Indian nationalism were little more
than extras in the unfolding drama, a suggestion aggravated by the
bad casting of most of them; in particular, of Jawaharlal Nehru. Most
of the British figures in the film are grotesquely unconvincing, and
this is true above all of Lord Irwin (Viceroy 1926–31) played by
John Gielgud. Quite apart from the fact that Gielgud is always
Gielgud, with a voice and appearance so familiar that he can never
effectively impersonate anyone else, the nature of the Irwin-Gandhi
relationship is completely misrepresented. The film suggests that
Gandhi's salt march in 1930 was not just a public relations triumph
(which it was, making him *Time Magazine*'s "Man of the Year"), but a
substantive triumph (which it was not). Irwin is made to say to his
aides before the march begins, "Mr. Gandhi will find it needs a great
deal more than a pinch of salt to bring down the British Empire";
and then, after the march, to receive Gandhi stiffly at Viceregal

Lodge to tell him, as if conceding defeat, that he will be invited to London to discuss "independence for India." At about the same time Gandhi says (in the film), "They are not in control; we are."

Historical truth is far removed from this travesty. Irwin's Dominion Status declaration, which is the only conceivable basis for the "independence for India" remark, was made in 1929, the year *preceding* the salt march. Though it outraged Winston Churchill and others in Britain who regarded any idea of constitutional change in India with abhorrence, it committed the Imperial government (as Dr. Gopal has written) "merely in the sphere of ultimate purpose" and "from the British standpoint surrendered no ground."[1] There was no question of an early, let alone immediate, grant to India of the status enjoyed by Canada, Australia and the other self-governing Dominions. The declaration was no more than a statement of intent of a kind which, in slightly different terms, had been made before.

As for Irwin's direct dealings with Gandhi in the year following the salt march, these took the form not of a single brief, constrained encounter, but of eight meetings running to a total of nearly twenty-four hours. The two men got on extremely well, because they talked the same language, metaphorically as well as literally. Both were highly intelligent, and both were religious as well as worldly. But in Irwin's case worldliness was the stronger factor: if both were, in a sense, holy foxes, the British fox proved the foxier. Apart from the psychological advantage of seeming (as Churchill put it) to "parley on equal terms with the representative of the King-Emperor," Gandhi gained little from the talks.[2] Irwin's privately avowed aim was to drive a wedge between him and Congress radicals such as Nehru, and in this he largely succeeded. Whether or not he ever said that it would take more than "a pinch of salt" to bring down the British Empire, the comment was certainly correct.

It has to be understood that India's political independence was not won by Gandhi's leadership, any more than it was voluntarily conceded by enlightened British statesmanship. When it eventually occurred, after the Second World War, it was due to world forces and a fundamental change in the balance of power. Far from accelerating independence, in the sense of getting rid of the British, Gandhi probably delayed it by a quarter of a century. His unique characteristic as a national leader was that he was less concerned to make his people independent, in the commonly accepted sense, than to make them fit for independence. He wanted to purge Indian society of indigenous evils, such as Untouchability, more intensely than he desired the removal of foreign rule.

The nobility of Gandhi's distinctive form of nationalism cannot be doubted, and its long-term influence for good, not only in India but worldwide, has to be set against its short-term ineffectiveness. Not that it was altogether ineffective even in the short term. Gandhi did mobilize the Indian masses, inspiring them with a sense of national unity and dignity. He also achieved significant, though limited, results as a reformer. Yet the ambiguities that abounded in his character and thinking in many ways diminished his value as a leader, in the process damaging the national cause that he was so eager to serve.

For a start, Gandhi was ambiguous about his Indianness and his Britishness. Before he was twenty, but when he was already a husband and father, he left his family to spend two and a half years in London. He did so in defiance of caste taboos, showing early the moral courage and force of character that he never ceased to show. His time as a young man in England was unquestionably the vital formative period of his life. His training as a lawyer at the Inner Temple, which resulted in his being called to the bar in 1891, stood him in good stead during his fight for Indian rights in South Africa, the scene of the next phase of his career; and later, of course, in India. Much of his philosophy of life derived from what he heard and read in London, and when, soon after his arrival in South Africa, he founded a community dedicated to personal abstinence and manual labor, the immediate inspiration for it was his reading of Ruskin's *Unto This Last.*

Throughout his time in South Africa, and for some time after his return to India, he believed very firmly in the British Empire's beneficence. During the First World War he was convinced that Indian support for the British war effort would be rewarded by self-government for India within the empire. Though many other nationalists, including Mohammed Ali Jinnah, felt that cooperation should be given only in return for a guarantee of self-government after the war, Gandhi refused to take advantage of Britain's difficulties. More than that, he offered his services to the Viceroy as, in effect, a recruiting sergeant, regardless of his pacifist principles. His subsequent disillusionment may help to explain his very different attitude during the Second World War, when after a time he went too far the other way.

His attempt to identify himself with the Indian masses, by living among them and dressing like them, showed the flair for visual self-projection that great leaders have often shown. But it was all the more necessary in his case, granted the extent to which he was more British than Indian. His thoroughly un-British appearance disguised the profoundly anglicized Indian that he actually was.

This, surely, was one reason for the special bond that came to exist between him and Jawaharlal Nehru. Otherwise their differences of mentality and outlook might well have kept them apart. Whereas Gandhi was religious and, on many issues, deeply conservative, Nehru was agnostic, secularist, socialist, and orientated towards modern science. Whereas Gandhi believed that anything and everything could be achieved by non-violent methods, Nehru's instincts were by no means pacifist. Yet Nehru grew to revere Gandhi, and Gandhi to look upon Nehru as his favorite political disciple and the man best fitted to lead India in the future.

Nehru was the more anglicized of the two, having been brought up in a intensely anglophile home before being sent to England for education at Harrow (which he enjoyed, as he later enjoyed prison) and Trinity College, Cambridge. Gandhi said of him that he was "more English than Indian in thoughts and make-up."[3] Gandhi had spent his childhood and youth in India, in an undilutedly Indian atmosphere, before going, by his own choice, to England and thereafter spending twenty years in South Africa. So he merely had to *re*discover India in middle life, whereas Nehru, returning there as a young man, had to discover his native land more or less from scratch. Gandhi, being himself so anglicized, helped him to do so, providing a bridge from one culture to the other.

Though Nehru was the more radical nationalist of the two, he nevertheless shared, in large degree, Gandhi's ambivalence about Britain. Gandhi was aware of this, and appreciated his mixed feelings, knowing that, to Nehru, he did not have to use "British" or "English" as derogatory words. When, in 1934, Nehru was showing signs of restlessness at the failure of Congress to make sufficient headway, Gandhi wrote to reassure him of his own enduring commitment to the cause: "I want complete independence for the country in the full English sense of the term."[4] No greater compliment has ever been paid to the English political tradition than this remark, in a private letter, from such a man as Gandhi to such a man as Nehru.

If Gandhi's cultural ambiguity was a factor robbing him of the necessary single-mindedness as a fighter against alien rule, a more serious liability was his attempted conjunction of the roles of religious and political leader. Another Mr. G.—Gladstone—with whom he had quite a lot in common, brought religion into politics in such a way as, often, to perplex his supporters and infuriate his opponents. Politicians are not meant to be saintly, and often have to resort to maneuvers which, however idealistic in intent, may appear the reverse of saintly, at any rate to those who feel they have been outmaneuvered. In his activities as the formal or informal leader of Congress, Gandhi must often have caused people to react in the spirit of Labouchere's well-known comment on the other Mr. G., that he had no objection to Gladstone's habit of concealing the ace of trumps up his sleeve, but did object to the claim that God had put it there.

Yet Gandhi's vulnerability to such sentiments was not the worst consequence of his dual role. More damaging was his incapacity to give the sustained, unrelenting attention to politics that the leader of a huge and singularly complex national movement needed to give. And there was another, even more disastrous, consequence. Though his Hinduism did not preclude—indeed, most emphatically included—deep and genuine respect for other religions, in particular for Christianity and Islam, the mere fact that he was a Hindu revivalist as well as leader of Congress enabled sectarian fanatics or political enemies in other religious traditions to exploit the fear that Congress Raj would be Hindu Raj.

Nehru's secularism was, in this respect, more appropriate to the needs of Congress as a party which, in aspiration if not always in fact, was committed to the idea of a secular Indian state. But he, even more than Gandhi, made the capital error of underrating both the latent force of Muslim feeling and, above all, the formidable political qualities of the man who harnessed it to fatally divisive effect—Mohammed Ali Jinnah.

Jinnah was not always a wrecker. In his early career he was as good an Indian nationalist as anyone, dedicated not only to freeing India from foreign rule but to establishing its independence as a united country. He was a member of Congress before he joined the Muslim League, and between 1913 and 1920 was a member of both bodies, regarding their aims as perfectly compatible. In the Lucknow Pact between them (1916) they asserted together the demand for Indian self-government, while Congress accepted the principle of separate electorates and weightage for minorities which was to become such a bone of contention later.

The split that developed between Congress and the Muslim League was largely due to Jinnah's personal incompatibility with Gandhi, and later with Nehru. Like Gandhi, Jinnah was an anglicized lawyer (in his case, from Lincoln's Inn), and both were strongminded men. But there the resemblance ended. By temperament and conviction Jinnah was an elitist, whereas Gandhi, if not exactly a democrat, was an ecumenical populist with a mission to the masses. It was on that issue that Jinnah was estranged from Congress in 1920. Gandhi's determination to turn it into a mass organization was anathema to him, and he also regarded its claim to inclusiveness as a threat to his own position. He was no religious fanatic, no *ayatollah;* his commitment to Islam was cultural, not sectarian. But when it became apparent to him that Congress would not deal with him or his League on equal terms, he knew how to appeal to sectarian passion among his fellow-Muslims. Willy-nilly, the elitist then turned populist, with an effectiveness that few would have predicted.

Jinnah's essentially secular character might have made Nehru more congenial to him than Gandhi, and vice versa. Besides, the two men were even more Westernized than Gandhi. But the barriers between them were Nehru's socialism, his devotion to the democratic ideal, and his conviction that independent India, like Congress, must be unitary and all-embracing. The critical moment was in 1937, when the 1935 Government of India Act came into force. In the elections held that year Congress did extremely well and the Muslim League very badly, winning only 4.8 percent of the Muslim vote. Congress won 711 of the 1,161 seats contested, returning with a clear majority in five provinces and as the largest party in three others. Before the elections, when it did not expect to succeed on such a scale, it was glad to cooperate with the League, which campaigned on much the same program. The tacit understanding was that Congress-League coalition governments would be formed, wherever possible, to exercise the powers devolved under the Act. But in the flush of victory Congress treated the League with contempt, offering places in government only in return for virtual fusion with Congress.

Gandhi advised a more magnanimous attitude, but was in one of his periods of semi-detachment from the practical affairs of Congress, and so did not insist. Nehru's view at the time is summed up in his remark: "There are only two forces in India today, British imperialism and Indian nationalism as represented by the Congress."[5] Jinnah, who had been even more detached than Gandhi, spending four years in England in the early 1930s, but had returned to lead the League, took up Nehru's challenge: "No, there is a third party, the Mussulmans." Soon he was able to demonstrate, in a crucial by-election, that his appeal to Muslim fears of Congress was all too potent. His campaign gathered momentum, taking an increasingly separatist form. Three years later he proclaimed the concept of Pakistan.

Before considering the very last phase, from the Second World War to partition and independence, we must now turn to the British response to Indian nationalism, and to British mythology on the subject. Was the imperial government committed in practice to leading India to self-government at the earliest possible moment? Were the only obstacles to the attainment of this worthy goal the perversities and complexities of Indian life or were these, in effect, a convenient excuse for the perpetuation of British power?

A carefully selected anthology of statements by unrepresentative individuals might suggest that the British were, for at least a century, missionaries for Indian self-rule. But even those who might be termed enlightened on the issue had many reservations and viewed the end of the process as remote. John Morley, the Liberal secretary of state who put through an extremely modest measure of constitutional reform in 1909, wrote privately of his work, "We have to do our best to put a broken set of communities on a constructive road: to guide men over a long slow transition."[6] At about the same time Ramsay MacDonald, returning from his first visit to India, published a book on the subject in which he wrote that the country would not be ready for self-government in the foreseeable future. Britain, he said, was "the nurse of India," whose desertion of her charge would leave the country "the prey to disruptive elements within herself . . . to say nothing of what would happen to her from incursions from the outside."[7] Such was the opinion of one of the most radical politicians of the day, who was even more of a rarity in having taken the trouble to see India for himself. (When MacDonald formed the first Labour government in 1923, he was the first British prime minister to have had direct experience of India since the Duke of Wellington nearly a century earlier.)

One other important British politician visited India during the period immediately preceding the First World War. Edwin Montagu, as under-secretary for India in the Asquith government, went there in 1912–13. He went again in 1917–18, as secretary of state for India under Lloyd George. Meanwhile the First World War and India's contribution to it, together with strong, united demands for self-government from Hindus and Muslims, had elicited a pledge (August 1917) that the British government's policy was "the progressive realisation of responsible government in India as an integral part of the British Empire." The word "progressive" inevitably conveyed, and was intended to convey, the message that nothing dramatic was likely to happen for some time to come.[8] Even so, responsible government was the status enjoyed by Canada and other self-governing Dominions within the British Empire, soon to be renamed, so far as they were concerned, the British Commonwealth of Nations. It was the "Dominion status" later proclaimed—or rather re-proclaimed—as India's goal by Irwin.

The formula of responsible government under the Crown derived from Lord Durham's famous report on Canada in 1839, and it is worth recalling the circumstances in which that report came to be written and—more to the point—acted on. The loss of the American colonies was still a quite recent memory, so when, in the 1830s, disturbances broke out in Canada the imperial government was naturally alarmed. The need to make some concessions was recognized, if Britain's remaining large foothold in North America were not to be lost. The extent of the concessions proposed by Durham was neither anticipated nor, perhaps, fully appreciated at the time. But there was a general understanding that something had to be done to avert the threat of further trouble in Canada, and Durham was a major politician whose proposals could not be ignored. If there had been no fear of another North American rebellion, he would not have been sent and nothing would have been done.[9]

As well as the "responsible government" statement, India's role in the war was acknowledged by representation in the Imperial War Cabinet that Lloyd George set up. But whereas Canada and other Dominions were represented in it by their prime ministers, responsible to their own parliaments and electorates, India was merely represented by the secretary of state and three nominated "assessors," two of whom were Indian. Much the same pattern was followed at the peace conference, in which the Dominions participated as effectively independent states, while India remained all too obviously dependent.

In 1919 Montagu enacted the reform measure associated with his name and that of the Viceroy of the day, Lord Chelmsford. Again, it was a very modest affair. If he had been a free agent, he might well have gone the whole hog and introduced self-government on the Dominion model, but, unfortunately, he was anything but a free agent. The prime minister, Lloyd George, though a fellow Liberal, had never been to India and, whatever he might say, had no sense of urgency about far-reaching Indian reform. Had he visited India, as Montagu had, his vivid imagination might have grasped the country's political potential. But even then, he would have had immense difficulty in persuading his supporters in Parliament to vote for a more adventurous measure. Conservatives always predominated in his coalition, and after the 1918 election did so even more strongly. At all events, the Montagu-Chelmsford reforms left the central autocracy intact, while extending, to a very limited degree, both the franchise and the exercise of responsibility by Indians at the provincial level, in a system known as dyarchy. At the same time a tentative move was made towards involving princely India in the politics of India as a whole, by the creation of a Chamber of Princes.

In the 1924–29 Baldwin government, the secretary of state, Lord Birkenhead, was absolutely opposed to Dominion status for India, and an unashamed exponent of "divide and rule" on communal lines. "I have always," (he wrote to the viceroy, Lord Reading) "placed my highest and most permanent hopes upon the eternity of the Communal situation."[10] The rift between Jinnah and Congress was, of course, playing into the hands of those who shared his view on the British side. But most people were neither as reactionary as Birkenhead nor as progressive as Montagu would have liked to be. The inadequacy of constitutional reform in India between the wars was due, above all, to the instinctive reluctance of an established system of government to threaten its own existence, when not otherwise sufficiently threatened. The average British view of Indian self-government during the period was similar to St. Augustine's attitude to chastity—that it would come one day, but not yet.

The two chief developments on the British side between the Montagu-Chelmsford reforms and the Second World War were the Simon Commission and the 1935 Government of India Act. The Simon Commission outraged Indian opinion by consisting only of British members, including the future Labour prime minister under whom Indian independence—and partition—would come about, C. R. Attlee. While he was in India with the Commission, Attlee wrote to his brother Tom (echoing, and slightly misquoting, Danton) that what was needed in British policy towards the country was *"l'audace, toujours l'audace."*[11] But there was nothing audacious about the report that the Commission issued, and it is curious and rather piquant that Attlee signed it. In view of his later reputation one might have expected him to produce a one-man minority report arguing the case for immediate Dominion status. But the 1930s were not the 1940s, and even later he was, as we shall see, rather less audacious than mythology would have us believe.

The 1935 Act raised the franchise to about a quarter of the adult population, and made provincial autonomy almost complete. But the discredited concept of dyarchy was retained in the plan for a central government, which was to come into being as part of an all-Indian federal scheme. In fact, this scheme was never implemented (for reasons not wholly attributable to the British), but if it had been it would have fallen a long way short of Dominion status. Essential power at the center was not to be transferred. Nehru's description of the Act as a "charter of slavery" may have been somewhat over-polemical, but nobody could describe it as a charter of freedom.[12] Many of its provisions were useful and have survived in the constitution of independent India. But at the time it was bound to appear yet another measure to frustrate India's legitimate desire for full self-government.

At the outbreak of war in 1939 the British government had the chance to redress, by a single gesture, much of the harm done by inadequate constitutional reform. Despite the feelings stirred during the previous two decades, there was a massive willingness, even on the part of active nationalists, to support the British and democratic cause. In the circumstances it would have been overwhelmingly appropriate for representative Indian leaders to be consulted before India's participation in the war was proclaimed. Morally, if not legally, this was clearly what should have been done. Instead, the Viceroy, Lord Linlithgow, issued a proclamation without seeking, first, to associate Gandhi, Nehru, Jinnah or any other Indian leaders with it. And he did not respond positively when Nehru wrote to him, soon afterwards, offering cooperation.

Nehru of all people deserved to be taken seriously when he made such an offer. Nobody had a better record of principled opposition to the Nazi and Fascist dictators. While British politicians were visiting them and going to indecent lengths to appease them, he refused invitations to meet them. Even Churchill, so hostile to Nehru the nationalist, as to Nehru the socialist, appreciated his anti-appeasement record enough to send him, just before the war, a message of goodwill through an intermediary.

The result of the missed opportunity in September 1939 was that, far from cooperating, the Congress provincial ministries resigned, though Gandhi as yet would not embarrass the government by any resort to civil disobedience. One should add that the breach between the Congress and Jinnah was already, perhaps, too deep to bridge. If the two had stood together the Viceroy might have had to give way, but when Nehru proposed to Jinnah that they should make a joint approach, he was rebuffed.

The Second World War changed everything. The Japanese victories in 1941–42, culminating in the surrender of Singapore, fatally damaged Britain's imperial prestige, while showing how insecure were the foundations on which, for some time, it had been based. In 1942, when the Japanese were at the gates of India, a member of the War Cabinet, Sir Stafford Cripps, was sent to India with what amounted to a clear pledge of Dominion status after the war, and meanwhile an offer of close involvement for Indian leaders in many aspects of war direction, though not outright control of the armed forces and national defense. For Jinnah, there was no explicit assent to Pakistan, but provision that the provinces of British India, like the princely states, would be individually free to decide their own future.

The Cripps offer was not at first turned down by Jinnah, and among the Congress leadership several key figures, including Nehru and C. R. Rajagopolachari, were disposed to accept it, if only as a step in the right direction which would inevitably lead to others before long. But Gandhi intervened decisively against it. His experience after the First World War made him reluctant to accept a promissory note from the British government, and in any case he was more single-mindedly unwarlike than he had been during the First World War. While Nehru and others were acutely conscious of the need to defend India, by force of arms, against the Japanese, Gandhi favored opposing them by non-violent methods. So at length the offer was rejected by the Congress Working Committee, and also, for other reasons, by Jinnah.

The only hope of a breakthrough at that moment lay, probably, in a visit to India by Churchill himself. He had the idea of flying out, but was dissuaded from doing so by Linlithgow and the secretary of state, Leo Amery. His only experience of the country had been as a young cavalry officer in the 1890s, when he saw virtually nothing of its inhabitants beyond the barracks and the camp. But his mind was capable of big imaginative leaps, which could be disastrous but were quite often inspired. Direct contact with the Indian leaders might have resulted in inspiration, and if he had seen what needed to be done he, unlike Cripps, had the authority to do it. Moreover, he might have inspired the Indian leaders to work together. But he was headed off and another opportunity was missed. Worse still, his unreconstructed attitude ensured that further wrong decisions would be taken about India during the rest of the war.

During this episode the United States became, for the first time, seriously involved in the politics of India, though the involvement was short-lived. Since the end of 1941, President Roosevelt had been urging Churchill to do something fairly dramatic about Indian constitutional reform, and however unwelcome this pressure it undoubtedly had a lot to do with the decision to send Cripps on his mission with an offer of Dominion status after the war. While Cripps was in India, Roosevelt's personal emissary, Louis A. Johnson, though ostensibly concerned with other matters, took a hand in the negotiations, and Roosevelt also corresponded directly with Nehru. On April 12, 1942, just after the breakdown of the talks, the President sent Churchill a cable through Harry Hopkins (who was in London) begging him to postpone Cripps's departure and threatening a very adverse public reaction in America if the negotiations were allowed to collapse for the reasons stated. Churchill replied that Cripps had already left India, and since the cable was addressed to him on a personal rather than an official basis (as "Former Naval Person"), he declined to bring it to the attention of the Cabinet unless Roosevelt expressly asked him to do so. No such request was made.[13]

Surprisingly, on this issue Churchill's judgment of American public opinion seems to have been more accurate than the President's—if the President meant what he said, and was not merely trying to get his way by what he knew to be an empty threat. Though most Americans naturally looked with disfavor on the British Empire, and with favor on countries seeking emancipation from it, there was no Indian lobby in the United States remotely comparable with, say, the Irish lobby. Moreover, the attitude of Americans to the Indian national movement (and, for that matter, of Indians to America) was appreciably complicated by the racial problem in the United States. At all events Americans seem to have been largely satisfied by the Cripps offer, and to have felt that the British had done as much as could reasonably be expected of them in the circumstances. Roosevelt was, therefore, under no domestic pressure to pursue the theme of his cable to Churchill, and he made no further direct attempt to promote political change in India.

After the failure of the Cripps mission a grave mistake was made on the Indian side. This was the so-called "Quit India" campaign. The motivating force behind it was Gandhi, and the whole episode must be regarded as one of the least creditable of his career. Convinced that the British were on the run, and remembering, no doubt, his disappointment in the First World War, when he had backed their war effort at a time of crisis in the hope of postwar satisfaction, he persuaded Congress to issue an ultimatum. "Either they recognise India's independence or they don't . . . there is no question of one more chance . . . it is an open rebellion."[14] Nehru and a number of others were deeply unhappy about the policy, but felt obliged to go along with it. A few, however—and most notably Rajagopolachari, despite a close family tie with Gandhi—opposed it openly, arguing that, in the absence of agreement between Congress and the League, ending British rule would result in chaos which the Japanese would be able to exploit. Jinnah, for his part, denounced Gandhi's plan, saying that he was trying "to coerce the British government to surrender to a Congress Raj."[15]

But Gandhi was not to be deflected, and he carried the All-India Congress committee with him by an overwhelming majority. After the vote he uttered dangerously ambiguous words: "Here is a *mantra*. . . . 'Do or die'. We shall either free India or die in the attempt; we shall not live to see the perpetuation of slavery."[16] His intention was that the rebellion should be non-violent, but the words "Do or die" were clearly open to misinterpretation, and the disturbances that followed, though sporadic and in no sense a properly organized rebellion, involved a good deal of violence. He and other Congress leaders were arrested and imprisoned; in his case in the Aga Khan's palace at Poona (where the *Gandhi* film shows him, without any explanation of the reason for his being there). Early in 1943 he tested the nerve of the government with a fast which many thought he would not survive. But Linlithgow did not blink, and in the end Gandhi was not among the thousand or more Indians who died, to no avail, in the campaign.

"Quit India" succeeded only in weakening Congress and giving Jinnah every opportunity to build up the Muslim League's strength. The government was able to use its war emergency powers to telling effect, but only because the vastly expanded Indian armed forces, together with the police, remained firmly loyal to the government. Or rather, they remained loyal to India, at a time when the country was manifestly facing a deadly external threat. The British Raj did not collapse in 1942–43, because most Indians wisely felt that the top priority was to keep the Japanese out.

After his negative triumph against Gandhi, Linlithgow's long and, on the whole, unfruitful viceroyalty came to an end. Churchill tried to persuade Anthony Eden to take the post, but after much dithering Eden declined. The name of Lord Louis Mountbatten was mentioned, but he was appointed instead to the South-East Asia Command. Churchill's eventual choice was the commander-in-chief in India, Field-Marshal Wavell. Wavell was an intelligent, honest and scholarly man, with quite progressive instincts. But he did not have the instincts of a politician. Indeed, he had a strong distaste for politics, and was inclined to be taciturn in company. Such a man was unlikely to make much headway with the highly articulate leaders of a nation that revels in talk and argument, at a time of supreme political ferment. In appointing him, Churchill said "that it would probably be a war appointment, and that he would make a political appointment after the war." In other words, there was to be a moratorium on politics in India until the war was over.

We come now to the very last phase of the story, and one point has to be made at once, with emphasis: there was no way Britain's position in India could be maintained after the Second World War. Whichever party had been elected in 1945, the practical consequences in India would have been much the same. Until 1939 Britain was still—just—a superpower, but in 1945 the country was enfeebled and bankrupt. Its people were looking inwards to their own problems, and had lost whatever enthusiasm they may once have had (never, in fact, all that much) for imperial power. In the postwar world there were two superpowers, the United States and the Soviet Union, who were agreed at least in being opposed to all empires other than their own. The question was no longer whether the British would have to leave India, but when and in what circumstances.

The Labour government elected in 1945, and led by Clement Attlee, was committed to the principle of transferring power, but not to transferring it in the absence of agreement between the Indian parties. Yet the elections soon held in India showed how little chance there was of agreement, granted the polarization of opinion. The Muslim vote was overwhelmingly won by Jinnah, who therefore became all the more intransigent in his demands. For the rest, Congress maintained its strength. In March 1946 Attlee decided to send a three-man Cabinet mission, in which Cripps was the dominant figure. The Mission stayed in India for seven weeks, but its attempts to secure inter-party agreement came to nothing. Instead, it produced a plan of its own, which amounted to partition of the country under the guise of unity. There would be a central government, but responsible only for foreign policy, defense and communications. Jinnah accepted the plan, though probably only for tactical reasons. Nehru, as president of Congress, prevaricated, which gave Jinnah an excuse to withdraw his acceptance.

At the end of July 1946 the Muslim League, in its so-called Bombay Resolutions, reasserted its intention to settle for nothing less than an independent Pakistan, while also declaring that it would promote its cause by "direct action." An interim government was formed by the Viceroy, but this never functioned as a unified body, even when the League agreed to take up its quota of seats. Meanwhile, violence and unrest were growing throughout the country. The Viceroy—still Wavell—could see that the government's policy of seeking an agreed settlement before withdrawing was doomed, and in September he put forward a plan for a phased withdrawal to be completed by the end of March 1948.

Since this plan, known as "Breakdown," very largely foreshadowed the actual course of events, Attlee's reaction to it may surprise those who take too simple a view of his role. He rejected it outright. Though withdrawal from India "might eventually become a necessity," for the time being the plan was quite unacceptable. "World opinion," he said, "would regard it as a policy of scuttle unworthy of a great power."[17]

About three months later, he changed his mind, influenced by unmistakable evidence that the situation in India was getting out of hand. In early 1947 he sacked Wavell and appointed Mountbatten, essentially to give effect to Wavell's policy. He had offered Mountbatten the post (though without telling Wavell) the previous December, since when he had been discussing the practical implications. Though he had come round to the idea of a time-limit, he did not at first want this to be too precise; but Mountbatten insisted on precision, and eventually accepted the viceroyalty only when he had a clear instruction that power was to be transferred by June 1, 1948. He also obtained very wide, if not quite plenipotentiary, freedom to negotiate.

Mountbatten was the right choice, however unjust and ungracious the manner of Wavell's supersession. It was now definitely too late to save the unity of India, as Mountbatten soon discovered. But the situation called for resourcefulness, flair and panache, and with those qualities the last Viceroy was richly endowed.

Though he undoubtedly—and inevitably—made mistakes, his achievement as a whole is impressive. He may have given insufficient attention to warnings of trouble in the Punjab at the time of partition, and if so must share the blame for one of partition's most tragic consequences. But he cannot be blamed for partition itself, which was the supreme tragedy. Of all the major figures in the approach to independence he, surely, was the least responsible for what Gandhi called the "vivisection" of the country. Moreover, if he had not taken the decision he did to advance the date for transferring power to August 1947, the carnage would almost certainly have been on a vastly greater scale. Once it was recognized that partition had to happen, there was nothing to be said for delaying its implementation. The longer the delay, the more deadly the consequences were likely to be.

Some who condemn the speed with which he acted argue that partition might have been avoided if anyone other than Jinnah had been leading the Muslim League, and that in 1947 Jinnah was a dying man. But this was not known at the time, and he did not, in fact, die until September 1948, several months after the date originally fixed for the transfer of power. Even if Mountbatten had known that Jinnah was dying, he could only have played for time, and time was against him. While he waited for Jinnah's death millions of ordinary Indians would have died, and the country would have dissolved in chaos.

Yet to claim that Mountbatten came reasonably close to making the best of a bad job is not to pretend that what happened in India in 1947 was a resounding triumph for him or anybody else. Jinnah got only what he called a "moth-eaten Pakistan." Nehru's tryst with destiny was redeemed "not wholly or in full measure" (a considerable euphemism). Gandhi was heartbroken. The British, in leaving India, had to partake in destroying the proudest achievement of their period of rule, the country's unity.

Could the story have been different, or were all concerned in it the prisoners of an ineluctable fate? Is it entirely fanciful to picture an alternative scenario? I think not and will try, very briefly, to suggest what it might have been.

At the beginning of the present century India had a talented nationalist elite, which was still united; all the religious communities, if not all social cadres, were represented in it. If the British desire to work towards Indian self-government had been whole-hearted and unqualified, that was the time when, at the very least, the reforms enacted in 1935 should have been brought in. Dominion status might then have followed naturally after the First World War. Failing spontaneous action on the part of the British—which, for elementary human and political reasons, was hardly to be expected—the same result might well have been achieved if, in 1918, Indian nationalists had been more militant and had given the British government a serious fright, such as the Canadians had given ninety-odd years before. Instead, Gandhi's leadership in the immediate postwar period was irritating without posing any real threat to the British, while it divided the national movement—fatally, as events were to prove—through the alienation of Jinnah.

A fully self-governing and united India could have carried out its own internal reforms during the interwar years, establishing its own democratic structure. It could also have made its influence felt in the world. If, as I believe, it had decided of its own free will to enter the war in 1939, as Canada and the other Dominions did, it would have gained so much prestige, as well as power, by 1945 that its right to a seat at the world's top table could hardly have been denied. Indian leaders whose practical abilities were consumed, over twenty-five years, in largely futile campaigns of civil disobedience would, instead, have spent the best years of their lives governing their own country.

Alas, it did not happen. We have to deal with historical reality. History permits us to speculate about what might have happened. It does not permit us to perpetuate myths about what did.

Fall Semester 1995

1. Sarvepalli Gopal, Lecture on "All Souls and India," and "Drinking Tea with Treason: Halifax in India," in Wm. Roger Louis (ed.), *Adventures with Britannia* (London, 1995), p. 151.

2. Speech to West Essex Conservative Association, Feb. 23, 1931.

3. Michael Brecher, *Nehru: A Political Biography* (Oxford, 1959), p. 261.

4. Gandhi to Nehru, Aug. 17, 1934, quoted in B. R. Nanda, *Mahatma Gandhi: A Biography* (Boston, 1958), p. 369.

5. Mar. 1937. Both statements quoted in Brecher, *Nehru*, p. 231.

6. Morley to Andrew Carnegie, Jan. 15, 1909. Quoted in Stephen Koss, *John Morley at the India Office, 1905–10* (New Haven, 1969), p. 212.

7. R. MacDonald, *The Awakening of India* (London, 1910), p. 187.

8. Penderel Moon, *The British Conquest and Dominion of India* (London, 1990), pp. 977–78.

9. Durham, *Report on the Affairs of British North America* (submitted and signed January 31, 1839). The other major recommendation in the Report—that the language and culture of French Canada should be eliminated, and the French Canadians merged into a homogeneous English-speaking Canada—was, of course, never implemented.

10. Birkenhead to Reading, Mar. 1925. Quoted in H. Montgomery Hyde, *Lord Reading* (London, 1967), p. 387.

11. Kenneth Harris, *Attlee* (London, 1982), p. 79.

12. Presidential address to session of Congress at Lucknow, Apr. 14, 1936. Quoted in Brecher, *Nehru*, p. 222.

13. Martin Gilbert, *The Road to Victory* (London, 1986), pp. 88–9; Robert E. Sherwood, *The White House Papers of Harry L. Hopkins*, (London, 1948), pp. 515–17. Sherwood confuses the text, if not the spirit, of Roosevelt's message with that of one sent a month earlier.

14. Speaking to journalists 14 Jul. 1942. Quoted in Moon, *The British Conquest and Dominion of India*, p. 1114.

15. Quoted ibid., p. 1114.

16. Addressing All-India Congress Committee, Bombay, Aug. 8, 1942. Quoted ibid., p. 1115.

17. Harris, *Attlee*, pp. 370–72.

# 13

# "A Victorian Tory": Churchill, the Americans, and Self-Determination

## WARREN F. KIMBALL

*As any Englishman intuitively knows, pressure from the hypocritical Americans played a major role in causing the collapse of the British Empire during and immediately after the Second World War. Or did it?*

During World War II, the President of the United States, Franklin D. Roosevelt, and his close advisers routinely expressed concern that his British counterpart, Prime Minister Winston Churchill, held an outmoded and even dangerous worldview. At the root of FDR's distrust was the belief that Churchill, like most British leaders, represented and defended a class-structured society that militated against reform and fairness. British politics might have democratic forms, but class divisions made that democracy lack substance.

That conclusion on the part of the Roosevelt administration underlay its concern about two of Churchill's policies: his inclination to think in terms of "spheres of influence" or "power politics," and his outspoken defense of the British Empire—both policies that the Americans often labeled "Victorian."

Even before the two leaders held their first conference, the President expressed concern about the Englishman's antiquated, "Victorian" views and his excessive drinking. To be fair, Churchill expressed concern—horror might be a better word—about Roosevelt's drinking habits as well, though in this case it was the President's custom of concocting what he called martinis—a mixture of gin with both dry and sweet vermouth, stirred vigorously by FDR himself. Churchill loathed such mixed drinks, once going so far as to spit out a mouthful of what FDR's cousin, Polly Delano, labeled a Tom Collins.[1]

More substantive were Roosevelt's concerns about Churchill's old-fashioned, nineteenth-century views. The Prime Minister ruefully admitted that "in the White House, I'm taken for a Victorian Tory." Fittingly, when Churchill stayed in the White House, he slept in a room decorated with prints of the court of Queen Victoria. New Dealers and Roosevelt himself frequently spoke critically about Churchill's unsympathetic attitude towards the progressive reforms they felt were necessary in the United States—and throughout the world. According to Harry Hopkins, Roosevelt's closest adviser, the President "loves Winston as a man for the war, but is horrified at his reactionary attitude for after the war." Even though Roosevelt balanced that apprehension with the comment, "Isn't he a wonderful old Tory to have on our side," the unmistakable conclusion was that Churchill posed a barrier to the kind of postwar world sought by FDR. That certainly was the belief of Eleanor Roosevelt, who told their daughter, Anna, "I like Mr. Churchill, he's lovable and emotional and very human but I don't want him to write the peace or carry it out." But then, Eleanor Roosevelt also thought that Franklin was "much in the nineteenth century."[2]

That nineteenth-century image of Britain invariably began with colonialism. Americans opposed European colonialism for two connected but different reasons. One was the conviction that British trade policy, particularly the much-vilified Imperial Preference system, created dangerous and unfair restrictions on international commerce. Little matter that the Second World War had already demonstrated that Imperial Preference was dying if not dead, Roosevelt and the State Department assumed (in an inheritance from the French philosophes) that international economic interdependence would prevent war. Eliminating empires fit American desires to open all the world to commercial access—"free markets" in the political jargon of the 1990s. "Roosevelt did not confine his dislike of colonialism to the British Empire alone," wrote Anthony Eden, "for it was a principle with him, not the less cherished for its possible advantages."[3] Even in the midst of the Yalta Conference, Roosevelt prodded Churchill to open serious official talks on the matter. The Prime Minister responded with a vague statement about the usefulness of current informal talks and suggested that the entire question be postponed.[4] Economic liberalism promised tangible benefits for the United States, but Americans had pursued economic liberalism since their Revolution; the urge cannot be dismissed as merely two centuries of cynicism, whatever American domestic squabbles over tariffs.

Their second objection to colonialism was its denial of self-determination. The American image of Churchill's Victorianism received early confirmation shortly after the announcement of the Atlantic Charter in August 1941, with its call for territorial changes to have "the freely expressed wishes of the peoples concerned," and for "the right of all peoples to choose the[ir] form of government." In each instance, democratic choice was part of the process. For FDR, that included European colonies. Churchill, his attention focused on getting the Americans into the war, had initially assumed that self-determination referred to nations under Hitler's yoke. But he quickly exempted the British Empire, even if Clement Attlee said the Charter applied to "coloured peoples, as well as white." Stalin quickly recognized that self-determination posed a threat to more than just the colonial world. Whatever the extent of his territorial ambitions, the Baltic states and a westward shift in the Soviet-Polish boundary were his "minimum demands," and he excluded the Soviet Union from the self-determination provisions of the Charter.[5]

From the outset of the Grand Alliance, British policy makers understood that Soviet demands for frontiers as negotiated in the Nazi-Soviet Pact gave the USSR territory in violation of the Atlantic Charter—just as the Germans asserted.[6] In late 1941, Eden traveled to Moscow in an attempt to reach an accommodation with Stalin. At the start of the talks, the British Foreign Secretary tried to avoid recognition of Soviet territorial demands, but once Stalin explained that his nation's western frontier and the Baltic States "is really what the whole war is about," Eden decided to support recognition of Soviet claims to those lands—even though the British Cabinet had instructed otherwise.[7]

Churchill opposed Eden's proposals, and at once found the Atlantic Charter and self-determination a convenient way to avoid specific postwar commitments that might give the Soviets something they did not deserve and could not earn. Then, for reasons that must be inferred, in early March 1942 the Prime Minister told Roosevelt that the Atlantic Charter should not be interpreted to deny the Soviet Union the boundaries it had when Germany attacked, since that was the understanding when Stalin accepted the Charter. Perhaps the explanation for Churchill's reversal is found in the final paragraph of his cable to the President where, with seeming casualness, he raised the issue of India.[8]

The joining of the two themes was neither new nor accidental. A few months earlier one of Churchill's favorites, Lord Beaverbrook, had made a similar connection. After labeling the Baltic states "the Ireland of Russia"—an analogy pregnant with hints of disloyalty and vexations for Churchill—Beaverbrook argued that the "strict application" of the Atlantic Charter "would be a menace to our own safety as well as to that of Russia. It would involve us among other things in the surrender of Gibraltar to the Spaniards"—a reference designed to play on Churchill's contempt and anger towards Spain, just in case the Irish ploy failed to work.[9]

Whatever Roosevelt's preference for self-determination, he also had to deal with a wartime alliance and the hope of a postwar "family circle," as he later termed the Great Power relationship. At least briefly in the spring of 1942, FDR considered letting the Soviets get the Baltic States, eastern Poland, Bukovina, and Bessarabia, musing that he would not mind if that happened. Reminded that the Atlantic Charter might have something to say about that, he took the thought no further.[10]

Churchill, uncomfortable with anything that expanded Soviet influence, soon changed his mind again. In May 1942, he summarized his talks in London with Soviet Foreign Minister V. M. Molotov, assuring Roosevelt that Britain had avoided making any territorial concessions to the Russians. The proposals for an Anglo-Soviet treaty are, wrote Churchill, "entirely compatible with our Atlantic Charter."[11] But an issue that was "really what the whole war is about" would not go away that easily.

Ultimately, Roosevelt and Churchill themselves undermined the self-determination principle of the Atlantic Charter by agreeing that the Soviet Union retain the basic shape of its Nazi-Soviet Pact boundaries. That process began as soon as Stalin heard of the Charter, and continued throughout the war. It culminated in the Churchill-Stalin (TOLSTOY) talks of October 1944, the famous percentages deal whereby Churchill found a way to justify and arrange a spheres of influence settlement in Eastern Europe, from Greece to the Baltics—arrangements Roosevelt went along with. Yalta merely added some cosmetics to the agreement. Roosevelt's praise of plebiscites as "one of the few successful outcomes of the Versailles Treaty" may have been sincere in 1941, but by the end of the war, plebiscites had become a convenient means of providing the image of self-determination without having to confront the Soviets in Eastern Europe. Even Cordell Hull, disinclined to get involved in what he called the "piddling little things" of Eastern Europe, publicly stated in April 1944 that the major postwar goal was to provide security and prevent aggression, and "the Atlantic charter did not prevent any step including those relating to enemy States to achieve these goals."[12]

The other side of self-determination, decolonization, came up in Anglo-American relations even before the United States entered the war. In spring 1941, Hull suggested self-government for India, then the Atlantic Charter with its promise of self-determination in-directly raised the issue a few months later. The United States, with its own colonies, certainly practiced what one historian has called a "combination of populism and arrogance" about European empires, even if Roosevelt had scheduled independence for the Philippines as soon as the war ended (something FDR constantly threw at Churchill). But that did not stop Americans from believing that colonialism, with its closed economic systems and political repres-sion, would generate future wars.[13]

The intensity of American views prompted FDR to raise the issue with Churchill even while the U.S. Pacific Fleet still lay burning at Pearl Harbor. When Churchill visited Washington immediately af-ter the Japanese attack, Roosevelt directly confronted him about a timetable for Indian independence. We have only Churchill's brag on the substance of the remarks: "The President . . . discussed the Indian problem with me, on the usual American lines, . . . I reacted so strongly and at such length that he never raised it verbally again."[14] The Prime Minister claimed to have responded as he did whenever such proposals surfaced; with angry arguments that the Americans did not understand the bitter Muslim-Hindu feud, that only the Muslims (the minority) had proved effective as soldiers, and that he would resign before he would "yield an inch of the territory that was under the British flag."[15]

At times, Churchill played the British bulldog more as a terrier, substituting angry barking and bravado in an attempt to cover weak-ness. The President may not have raised Indian independence again with him face to face—FDR would later tell Stalin that discussing India with the Englishman was a waste of time. But Roosevelt, con-vinced that colonialism's day was over, never quit trying to push and persuade the British to beat the inevitable to the punch—to choose devolution over revolution. He insisted in January 1942 that India sign the wartime alliance pact, grandly titled the Declaration by the United Nations—a title that FDR took credit for, particularly once it became the name for the United Nations Organization.[16] Shortly thereafter, he unleashed Chinese leader Chiang Kai-shek, who vis-ited India and suggested that the Indians would fight more effec-tively against Japan if Britain promised independence. At the same time, the President opened a second front against colonialism by instructing his representatives in London, Averell Harriman and "Gil" Winant, to "get a slant" on Churchill's thinking about a changed relationship between India and Britain. All this in the wake of the humiliating British defeat at Singapore—to an army of "little yellow men." When later talks with Indian Congress leaders collapsed, Churchill "danced around the Cabinet room. No tea with treason [he said], no truck with American or British Labour sentimentality, but back to the solemn—and exciting—business of war."[17]

Of course Britain was not without sin. In Syria, a French protectorate since World War I, Britain encouraged the Free French to make commitments to independence so as to prevent popular uprisings and to promote Syrian opposition to German schemes. Free French leader Charles de Gaulle rejected British interference and accused them of having designs on the French Empire. When his officials arrested Syrian nationalists elected to office on an independence platform, the Prime Minister piously told FDR that "there is no doubt in my mind that this is a foretaste of what de Gaulle's leadership of France means. It is certainly contrary to the Atlantic Charter and much else that we have declared."[18] One French historian put the dispute in words that could have come from the general himself: "Even after Free French administrations were installed in French territories like Syria, Lebanon or North Africa, relations with the British were less than cordial. This was not only because local would-be Lawrences harboured secret designs of supplanting the French, or even because the British military . . . never quite understood de Gaulle's political importance. . . . It was above all because. . . . it could well be necessary to thwart the French in order to propitiate the natives."[19]

Neither then nor later in the war could Churchill or Roosevelt solve, or dismiss, the twin dilemmas of self-determination—Eastern Europe and colonial empires. Even postponement had its perils.

The problem of Soviet intentions crystallized around the issue of self-determination. Self-determination for European colonies was awkward and menacing to the British, but did not threaten the great power cooperation that FDR hoped for, since Britain's stake in postwar cooperation with the United States was too crucial to jeopardize. Moreover, colonial boundaries seemed clear (even if that proved deceptive). But by 1943, with the Germans stopped and the tide about to turn on the Russian front, European frontiers and self-determination became a major issue. As Woodrow Wilson had learned at Paris, Europe's boundary questions came burdened with irreconcilable pieces of historical baggage. At the same time, persuading Stalin to be a cooperative player in the postwar world required that he feel secure, satisfied, and sure of Anglo-American reliability. But self-determination for Lithuanians, Latvians, and Estonians—not to mention significant elements of Poles, Bulgarians, Finns, Hungarians, and Rumanians—was quite a different story, for Stalin had made clear from the outset that his territorial demands included large groups of those peoples.

If self-determination meant independence for the Balts and the establishment of an anti-Soviet government in Warsaw, then how to avoid the obvious? By February 1943, the Stalingrad battle had demonstrated the possibility, even likelihood, of Red Army occupation of the territory Stalin demanded. What recourse was left to London and Washington? Military confrontation was no option, at least not with Anglo-American forces still struggling in North Africa and an invasion of Western Europe fifteen months away. More to the point, British and American military leaders had long since concluded that the *defeat* of Germany, as opposed to merely halting Hitler's expansion, required the Soviet Army.[20] And what long-term hope for peace if the United States and Britain chose to confront the Russians? Perhaps the atomic bomb eventually changed that calculation, but that weapon was two years away. Then there was Japan waiting in the wings.

What the Americans and British agreed on, despite their significant differences about tactics, was to make the best of the situation. Rather than fruitlessly opposing any expansion of Soviet power in Eastern Europe, they opted to continue to promote long-term cooperation. As Roosevelt and Undersecretary of State Sumner Welles told Eden in 1943, "the real decisions should be made by the United States, Great Britain, Russia and China, who would be the powers for many years to come that would have to police the world." Self-determination would, quite obviously, be a gift from the Big Four, assuming they could agree on the details.[21]

FDR's four policemen would also act as trustees for colonial societies not ready for full independence (a category that Roosevelt seemed to apply to almost every colony). The Pacific islands held by the Japanese (the old League of Nations mandates), Korea (despite its being independent for centuries before the United States existed), and Indochina were his favorite examples. When he spoke to Eden of trusteeships for Japan's Pacific island empire, French Indochina, and Portuguese Timor, the Foreign Secretary knew the President meant all European empires. With Hong Kong in mind, Eden was dubious about Chinese intentions, commenting that "he did not much like the idea of the Chinese running up and down the Pacific," and he questioned whether Kuomintang leader Chiang Kai-shek would survive the civil war that would surely follow Japan's defeat.[22]

Nor was Churchill prepared to elevate China to world power status. Not only did that fly in the face of reality—China was far from a modern power and faced civil war—but that would provide "a faggot vote on the side of the United States in any attempt to liquidate the overseas British Empire."[23] The mirage of an Anglo-American world that had appeared briefly at the Churchill-Roosevelt talks in Casablanca was fading.

That is not to say, as some have, that Roosevelt's "hopes for his brave new world rested largely on the Soviets, not upon the fading and reactionary power of the British Empire."[24] Roosevelt did not dismiss Britain as some sort of minor player. If Britain was a "junior partner," it was still a partner in what was a very limited partnership. All of FDR's thinking about the postwar world required that the British exercise the responsibilities of a great power. In fact, Roosevelt and the Americans routinely exaggerated the wealth of Great Britain and its Empire. Britain's military image had suffered during the Second World War, but economic strength and political savvy would be the elements of power in the disarmed world Roosevelt imagined.

Churchill concluded, paradoxically, that the Americans would act too vigorously to defend self-determination in Asia, and too weakly to defend it in Eastern Europe. As he saw it, that was an old American pattern: activism in Asia, isolationism in Europe. Roosevelt's calls for Britain to grant independence to its Empire posed as great a threat to British interests as Soviet expansion into Eastern Europe. That conclusion brought Churchill to make not only the "percentages" deal at the TOLSTOY talks in Moscow in autumn 1944, but to raise with Stalin the issue of Britain's place in East Asia, specifically China.

The Prime Minister sought Stalin's support, or at least neutrality, in a region of intensifying nationalism, by suggesting concessions that should go to the Soviet Union in the Far East. The deal between Stalin and Churchill was implied, not the sort of explicit, spheres-of-influence arrangement they had made over Greece and Rumania, but the approach was the same. The Soviet Union should have "effective rights at Port Arthur," said Churchill. Why worry about Soviet naval power in the Far East, he told his Chiefs of Staff, the Soviet fleet was "vastly inferior" and would be "hostages to the stronger Naval Powers." More important, he said, "any claim by Russia for indemnity at the expense of China, would be favourable to our resolve about Hong Kong." The Hong Kong issue led Churchill quickly to instruct that no agreements be reached with the United States to oppose a "restoration of Russia's position in the Far East," and the Americans were, apparently, not apprised of the understanding.

Churchill's fears that the Americans would oppose such territorial deals proved groundless. Four months later at Yalta, Roosevelt worked out a Far Eastern settlement with Stalin that paralleled the quid pro quo Churchill floated at Moscow, but FDR's reasons were a bit different. First and foremost, the Soviet Union's entry into what all expected to be a long and bloody war against Japan had always been framed to include something for Russia. Roosevelt had no doubt Stalin would live up to his promise, so long as the United States and Britain lived up to theirs. Beyond that, FDR was, like Churchill, concerned about China. But it was the impending conflict between Mao and Chiang, not the decolonization of Hong Kong, that worried the President. He hoped to persuade Stalin not to throw in with the Chinese Communists, thereby giving the Kuomintang a chance to consolidate its rule.

The danger was that Chiang's chance would come at the expense of Chinese sovereignty and territory—elements of self-determination—running the risk of alienating the nationalism that Chiang had to harness in order to survive. It may be that Roosevelt sought to eliminate British influence from northern China when he suggested privately to Stalin that they exclude Britain from the occupation of Korea. But that latter proposal was more likely aimed at preventing Britain from being a "trustee" responsible for tutoring Korea (or any other nation) to be independent. Stalin, careful to follow his arrangements with Churchill, warned that "the Prime Minister might 'kill us,'" and suggested consulting him.[25] But whatever the differences in motives between Roosevelt and Churchill, and despite Churchill's later denials, they both gave positive endorsement to the commitments made to Stalin in return for Soviet entry into the war against Japan.[26]

But China was only part of the challenge raised by Asian nationalism. Roosevelt had steadily pursued his campaign against European colonial empires throughout the war, Churchill's braggadocio to the contrary notwithstanding. In countless ways, FDR kept the pressure on Churchill and the leaders of other European colonial powers to begin the process of decolonization. Roosevelt pushed one of his favorites, Dutch Queen Wilhelmina ("Minnie," he called her, with militant casualness), to begin the process of granting self-government to the Netherlands East Indies. But she would have none of it. She told FDR that Java could, perhaps, become independent in something between fifteen and fifty years, but anything for the backward areas was "sheer speculation." The president did not push the issue, leading the Dutch to believe that he agreed to a restoration of their control.[27]

But the Dutch confused politeness with agreement. Roosevelt was convinced that the pressure of self-determination in the European empires was a most serious threat to postwar peace. Yet he believed that the Europeans had time—perhaps as long as twenty-five or thirty years—to prepare for colonial independence, so long as they made public commitments to self-determination and established some sort of schedule for devolution. He more than once

offered the British a history lesson based on the American experience with their Articles of Confederation after the American Revolution. Churchill mocked the analogy, but missed the point (as have
so many historians). Decolonization was inevitable, Roosevelt believed. "India is not yet ready for home government," he told the
Pacific War Council. "That takes time. The training of thousands of
persons over a number of years is necessary for good government."
That, he explained, the United States had learned through trial
and error during the era of the Articles of Confederation.[28]

American policy did not create the desire for self-determination.
General de Gaulle gave the United States too much credit (or blame)
when he claimed it had forced the Dutch "to renounce their sovereignty over Java." Independence for India, Indonesia, and most of
the colonial world, came primarily from the demands of the native
peoples, not because of anything done or said by the United States.
By the end of the Second World War, the Asian colonies were neither Europe's to lose, nor America's to win—or to destabilize. Nationalism could not be denied—though it could be delayed.[29]

But Churchill remained adamant in his defense, arguing that
"the British alone had managed to combine Empire and Liberty."
In December 1944, he instructed Eden that "Hands off the British
Empire" is our maxim, and it must not be weakened or smirched to
please sob-stuff merchants at home or foreigners of any hue." Holding on to the Empire was part of why Britain had gone to war. Hitler
had challenged British interests in Europe, but Japan was a direct
rival for empire in Asia. Moreover, Japan's conquests had given Indian nationalists an opportunity to use the war as leverage for independence. Churchill's contempt for the Indians, heightened by what
he viewed as treasonous demands that Britain "quit India" as the
price of support for the war, only strengthened his resolve. India
was the very symbol of the Empire, and he would not negotiate that
symbol away. A number of other British leaders had begun to rethink the question of empire, but Churchill and Eden invariably
blocked American efforts to conduct direct Great Power discussions
about colonialism.[30]

With the instincts of a politician, Roosevelt had focused his attack against colonialism on two very visible examples—British India
and French Indochina. Churchill and the British Government had
rejected FDR's prompting about India ("pitiless publicity" was how
the President described his own tactic), although the ruthless suppression of Indian nationalists, which had required over 50 battalions in addition to police forces, had the effect Roosevelt
expected—heightened and angry nationalism.

That left Indochina, which, as early as May 1942, the President had held up as an example of colonial mismanagement. Exploitation and indifference had, he told the Pacific War Council, left the natives unprepared for self-government and in need of major reform. He and Stalin had agreed at Teheran that the colony should not be returned to French rule, and FDR made sure that Churchill learned of that conversation.[31]

But the Prime Minister and his Government would have no part of a piecemeal attack on colonial empires. If France could be kept out of Indochina, then India, Burma, and other parts of the British Empire were next. Moreover, the Foreign Office argued strenuously, Britain needed a strong and cooperative France in order to have a secure position in Europe—and General de Gaulle's conditions for cooperation began with retention of the French Empire. Churchill counseled against any discussions with Roosevelt about Indochina until after the presidential election of November 1944, but the British military had already that summer begun to integrate French military and political personnel into their Southeast Asian Command, headed by Admiral Louis Mountbatten. The President refused to recognize the French presence and rejected proposals to provide transport or supplies for the French in Indochina. But he could not force them out without British cooperation.[32]

Had empire been the only thing at stake, Roosevelt could have put near-irresistible pressure on the British to block the French in Indochina and to make specific commitments to the Indian nationalists—commitments that would have set a powerful precedent for other independence movements. But FDR's first prerequisite for avoiding another world war was Great Power cooperation—his Four Policemen—and Britain was to be one of those Policemen. Without the British playing that role, the system the President imagined could not work. He had managed to use agreements on postwar economics and international organization (Bretton Woods and Dumbarton Oaks) to keep cooperation as an option, but alienating the British over empire in Southeast Asia—particularly with Churchill openly emotional on the issue—might push them toward the narrow regionalism that FDR feared would only re-create the tensions that had led to two world wars.

Had China been ready and able to play the role of Great Power, Roosevelt would have had more options. But that society was about to plunge into civil war. Moreover, Roosevelt's designated policeman, Chiang Kai-shek, seemed all too inclined himself to expand into Southeast Asia at the expense of Britain and France. With FDR believing that "three generations of education and training would be required before China could be a serious [political] factor," he was left with little faith in the willingness or ability of either Chiang

or Mao to play a "responsible" role. With no American military force
scheduled to move onto the continent in East or Southeast Asia,
and with China needing "tutelage" before it could play the role of
responsible Policeman, Roosevelt's only option was to have the Europeans reclaim their empires. Self-determination in Eastern Europe had to be postponed in order to bring the Soviet Union into
the "family circle." Now expediency seemed to require a similar compromise in Southeast Asia.[33]

FDR was, in his own way, as stubborn as Churchill. For the President, decolonization had always been a process, not an immediate
act. His patience and belief in the superiority of American institutions brought him to conclude that most colonies would need long
periods of benevolent guidance (what he called trusteeships) before they could govern themselves. He agreed, for example, with
State Department arguments that Korea might require a forty-year
training period because the thirty-five-year Japanese occupation had
politically "emasculated" Koreans and left them without experience
in self-government. The idea of lengthy trusteeships tended to be
FDR's catch-all answer for any difficult territorial problem, as in the
case of the Croatians and Serbs.[34] That kind of paternalism did not
take into account the intensity of nationalism, but FDR's willingness to wait for the internal development of what Americans call
democracy distinguishes Roosevelt's foreign policy from the experiments in nation-building promoted by his Cold War successors.

All of which led Roosevelt to a tactic. He had long proposed that
the lengthy process of preparation for self-government be done
under the supervision of international "trustees." He could modify
that to allow the Europeans back into their Asian empires but only
if their actions as "trustees" would be monitored by the new international organization—the United Nations. FDR backed away from
any strenuous confrontation with Britain, or with France by proxy,
lest that jeopardize his plans for Great Power cooperation, but he
consistently argued for the colonial masters to become colonial trustees, accountable to an international community in which the United
States would be a dominant force. What Roosevelt feared, and with
good historical reasons, was that if the colonial powers were left to
decide when their colonies were "ready" for self-government, they
would act the way "Minnie" had spoken: the Europeans would drag
their feet, set one ethnic group against another, and do whatever
they could to spin a web of control around their colonies before
granting even the facade of self-determination.[35]

But Roosevelt never backed away from believing that a smooth,
non-violent transition from empire to independence for Europe's
colonies was a key to creating a peaceful world, even if he could not

prevent the Europeans from reclaiming their Asian empires. He spoke patronizingly of the Asians—"The Indochinese were people of small stature," he told Stalin, "and were not warlike." But that silly statement did not mean he abandoned them to colonialism. When the British Secretary of State for Colonies, Oliver Stanley, visited Washington late in the war, Roosevelt restated his conviction that European empires would disappear. Indochina would not be returned to France, he said, but would be "administered by a group of nations selected by the United Nations." The movement toward self-determination was irresistible, thought FDR, whether in Burma, the Netherlands East Indies, or even British Gambia and French Morocco. And the United States would support that movement.[36]

Asian nationalism—East European nationalism: two movements in the same symphony. Stalin had good reason to fear that the people of Eastern Europe "all wanted something of their own."[37] The Red Army may often have been greeted as liberators, but as Soviet political commissars moved in that welcome faded quickly—sometimes because they were Communists, but *always* because they were agents of a "foreign" government in Moscow.

The Pacific War, fought where colonial empires were at issue, complicated the European question—more for Roosevelt than Churchill. British concerns were defensive—hold on to India, "liberate" Singapore and Malaya, keep Hong Kong, and insulate Britain's Asian empire from any sort of international accountability. Over time, Stalin's crude behavior in Poland and eastern Europe would only have helped Churchill's campaign to persuade Roosevelt that British colonialism was far preferable to Soviet domination—which is what happened in the decade following the Second World War when the United States "gave priority to anti-communism over anti-colonialism," helping the Europeans to spin the very webs of control that FDR had tried to prevent.[38]

During the Yalta talks, the Soviets accepted the trusteeship principle and wanted it included in the Charter of the United Nations Organization. But when the President brought up the general concept, Churchill predictably exploded in protest:

> I absolutely disagree. . . . After we have done our best to fight in this war and have done no crime to anyone I will have no suggestion that the British Empire is to be put into the dock and examined by everybody to see whether it is up to their standard.[39]

The President had Stettinius explain to the Prime Minister that the whole system was "voluntary" except for the defeated Axis nations. But Roosevelt's notion of "voluntary" was different from Churchill's. When it came to trusteeships, he told a group of reporters, "Stalin liked the idea. China liked the idea. The British don't like it. It might bust up their empire, because if the Indo-Chinese were to work together and eventually get their independence, the Burmese might do the same thing to the King of England. . . ." But there was a bit of bluster in those comments, for he quickly added that "it would only make the British mad. Better to keep quiet just now." Britain was a Great Power, and the Great Powers had to get along.[40]

Nationalism frequently incorporated social reform as part of its appeal, often making it seem revolutionary to the Anglo-Americans. In Greece, republicanism and the "left" expropriated nationalism.[41] In France, it coalesced in the person of Charles de Gaulle, who, with single-minded intensity, rekindled French pride and self-respect after the debacle of 1940. In the colonial world, particularly South and Southeast Asia, Japanese and American propaganda reinforced long-repressed desires for self-determination. In China, while the civil war between Chiang and Mao remained in suspended animation, both protagonists worked to don the mantle of Chinese nationalism. In Eastern Europe, Polish self-determination became for many in the West the litmus test of Soviet intentions. Even in Italy, where British-sponsored and American-sponsored politicians vied for power, the maneuvering took on the cloak of republicanism and self-determination.

Republicanism, pride, independence, self-determination—all expressions of the nationalism that challenged Great Power cooperation and control. Power at the service of ideology, and vice-versa, would come to dominate the Soviet-Western relationship after World War II, but nationalism, particularly in its guise of self-determination, played a crucial role in preventing the extension of wartime cooperation into the postwar world. In Eastern Europe and, more briefly, in Asia, that self-determination was frustrated, in the process helping to create and solidify the Soviet-Western split.

Summer Semester 1996

1. Churchill's Victorianism is discussed in W. F. Kimball, *The Juggler* (Princeton, 1991), pp. 66–67, and seen as an asset by David Jablonsky in *Churchill, The Great Game and Total War* (London, 1991).

On FDR's fears of Churchill's drinking habits, see Michael Beschloss, *Kennedy and Roosevelt* (New York, 1980), p. 200. When Roosevelt and Canadian Prime Minister Mackenzie King met in April 1940, they spent much of the time gossiping about Churchill's drinking; J. L. Granatstein, *Canada's War* (Toronto, 1975), p. 117. When Churchill became Prime Minister, Roosevelt commented he "supposed Churchill was the best man that England had, even if he was drunk half of his time"; David Reynolds and David Dimbleby, *An Ocean Apart* (New York, 1988), p. 136. Wendell Willkie, asked by Roosevelt in 1941 if Churchill was a drunk, replied that he had as much to drink as Churchill did when they met, "and no one has ever called me a drunk." See Kimball, *The Juggler*, pp. 225–26, n. 6. The Roosevelt martini is described with distaste by Charles Bohlen, *Witness to History, 1929–1969* (New York, 1973), p. 143. See Robert Sherwood, *Roosevelt and Hopkins* (rev. edition; New York, 1950), p. 115, for some other "vile" concoctions, and G. Ward (ed.), *Closest Companion: The Unknown Story of the Intimate Friendship between Franklin Roosevelt and Margaret Suckley* (Boston and New York, 1995), p. 163, for a story of Churchill spitting out a mouthful of what FDR's cousin, Polly Delano, made with different kinds of rum and labelled a Tom Collins.

2. Lord Moran, *Churchill: Taken from the Diaries of Lord Moran* (Boston, 1966), entry for Feb. 5, 1945, p. 240. See also Ted Morgan, *FDR* (London, 1986), p. 759. Averell Harriman claimed that Roosevelt saw Churchill as "pretty much a nineteenth century colonialist"; Averell Harriman and Elie Abel, *Special Envoy to Churchill and Stalin, 1941–1946* (New York, 1975), p. 191. Sherwood describes Churchill's White House quarters; *Roosevelt & Hopkins*, p. 203. For the concerns of New Dealers see, for example, the diaries of Henry Morgenthau, Jr., at the Franklin D. Roosevelt Library (Hyde Park, NY) [FDRL], or the diaries of Assistant Secretary of State Adolf Berle, *Navigating the Rapids*, ed. Beatrice Bishop Berle and Travis Beal Jacobs (New York, 1973). See also Fraser Harbutt, *The Iron Curtain* (New York, 1986), esp. pp. 15–19. FDR's "wonderful old Tory" comment is from John Gunther, *Roosevelt in Retrospect* (New York, 1950), p. 16; Doris Goodwin, *No Ordinary Time* (New York, 1994), p. 312, quotes Mrs. Roosevelt's letter to Anna; Frank Freidel, *Franklin D. Roosevelt* (Boston, 1990), quotes Eleanor Roosevelt's quip about FDR in the 19th century; Oliver Harvey, *The War Diaries of Oliver Harvey*, ed. John Harvey (London, 1978), p. 228 (Mar. 11, 1943).

3. Anthony Eden, *The Reckoning* (Boston, 1965), p. 593.

4. See Randall Woods, *A Changing of the Guard* (Chapel Hill, 1989; and W. F. Kimball, "U.S. Economic Strategy in World War II," in W. F. Kimball (ed.), *American Unbound* (New York, 1992); W. F. Kimball (ed.), *Churchill & Roosevelt* (3 vols.; Princeton, 1984), III, R-707/1 (Feb. 10, 1945) and C-899/3 (Feb. 13, 1945).

5. The Charter began with the declaration that neither the U.S. nor Britain sought additional territory—a disavowal of the kind of secret treaties that had stimulated the territorial scramble following the First World War. But while that injunction against self-aggrandizement aimed at quieting the American anti-interventionists, it also fell under the broad rubric of self-determination. The Atlantic Charter is printed in U.S. Department of State, *Foreign Relations of the United States [FRUS]* (Washington, 1862–) 1941, I, 367–69. Attlee's comments are from the London *Daily Herald*, Aug. 16, 1941, as quoted in Wm. Roger Louis, *Imperialism at Bay* (New York, 1978), p. 125.

6. John J. Sbrega, *Anglo-American Relations and Colonialism in East Asia, 1941–1945* (New York, 1983), p. 29.

7. Lloyd C. Gardner puts the negotiations for an Anglo-Soviet Treaty in perspective in "A Tale of Three Cities: Tripartite Diplomacy and the Second Front, 1941–1942," in *Soviet-U.S. Relations, 1933–1942* [G. Sevost'ianov & W. F. Kimball, eds.] (Moscow, 1989), pp. 104–20. Some have suggested that Eden's policy of accommodation toward Stalin was what Cadogan, who had drafted portions of the Atlantic charter, sarcastically labelled the "Volga Charter." See Gabriel Gorodetsky, "Origins of the Cold War," *Russian Review*, 47 (1988), p. 166, for the "Volga Charter" as proposed by Eden. However, it may be that the phrase refers to Eden's initial plan to avoid discussions of frontiers and reparations in favor of British promises to aid in reconstructing the USSR after the war. Eden's notion of having the major powers all agree not to dominate the nations of central and eastern Europe—a "self-denying ordinance"—may also have been part of those early proposals. See Gardner, cited above, and references in Harvey, *War Diaries*, p. 63; and David Dilks (ed.), *The Diaries of Sir Alexander Cadogan* (New York, 1972) p. 414. See also G. Gorodetsky, *Stafford Cripps' Mission to Moscow, 1940–1942* (Cambridge, 1984), p. 271. The "self-denying ordinance" was part of Eden's diplomacy at the Moscow Foreign Ministers Conference in autumn 1943. See Kimball, *The Juggler*, pp. 94–95.

8. By January 1942, Eden had enlisted the British Ambassador in the United States, Edward Lord Halifax, into a campaign to convince Churchill to agree to letting the Soviets have the Baltic states. See Halifax to Churchill, Jan. 11, 1942; Halifax to Eden, Jan. 18, 1942; and Eden to Halifax, Jan. 22, 1942, all in FO 954/ 29/100818 [US/42/5–7], United Kingdom, Public Record Office (PRO), Kew, England. The story, called "A Dismal Tale," is told by Steven M. Miner, *Between Churchill and Stalin* (Chapel Hill, 1988), pp. 194–213. Stalin's comment about the importance of his frontiers is on p. 190. Miner argues that repossessing the Baltic states was one of Stalin's basic policy goals; see his "Stalin's 'Minimum Conditions' and the Military Balance, 1941–1942," in *Soviet-U.S. Relations*, pp. 72–87. Churchill's message is in Kimball, *Churchill & Roosevelt*, I, C-40, Mar. 7, 1942. Martin Gilbert, *Road to Victory* (Boston, 1986), p. 72, attributes the Prime Minister's shift on Soviet domination of the Baltic states to the pressure of British military defeats, particularly the abandonment of Rangoon, Burma on March 6. Those setbacks made the Prime Minister "fully aware" of the need to have good relations with the Soviet Union.

Alfred Duff Cooper, then a member of the Cabinet as Chancellor of the Duchy of Lancaster, warned that recognition of Soviet incorporation of the Baltics would "tear into ribbons the Atlantic Charter and brand us as the arch hypocrites of the world." Duff Cooper to Eden, April 22, 1942, FO 954/25A/100731 (PRO).

9. Memo to the War Cabinet, "Policy Towards Russia," Jan. 31, 1942, FO 954/ 25A/100731, PRO. Beaverbrook was British Minister of Supply at the time.

10. Berle and Jacobs (eds.), *Navigating the Rapids*, April 30, 1942, p. 412. This may be the source of the charge that FDR had been ready in early April to accede to Soviet territorial demands, but that Hull persuaded him to wait until war's end, as argued by Robert A. Divine, *Roosevelt and World War II* (New York, 1970), pp. 89–91: "Hull's insistence on adhering to the Atlantic Charter, laudable in principle, undermined Roosevelt's efforts to assuage Russian distrust of the West and strengthen the wartime alliance . . . In 1942, Roosevelt seemed to be indecisive and hesitant in his diplomacy, allowing others to impose their will on him. As a result, he failed to achieve a sound basis for wartime relations with the Soviet Union." Hugh Phillips, "Mission to America: Maksim M. Litvinov in the United States, 1941–43," *Diplomatic History*, 12:3 (Summer 1988), p. 269, quotes a message from Litvinov to Narkomindel Mar. 12, 1942 [published in Russian] to the effect that FDR would not object to an arrangement between USSR and UK, presumably

(according to Phillips) on the border issue regarding the Baltics, so long as the arrangement was informal and not public. Roosevelt's reference to the "family circle" is in *FRUS, Tehran*, p. 487.

11. Kimball, *Churchill & Roosevelt*, I, C-89, May 27, 1942.

12. See Kimball, *The Juggler*, quotes on pp. 95, 183; Lloyd C. Gardner, *Spheres of Influence* (Chicago, 1993); Sbrega, *Anglo-American Relations and Colonialism*, p. 30. During the British intervention in Greece in late 1944 early 1945, Churchill complained that Americans did not understand that British actions were, in fact, securing the ideals of the Atlantic Charter for the Greeks who were threatened by a Communist dictatorship; Gilbert, *Road to Victory*, p. 1147. The cosmetic value of plebiscites was recognized by Anthony Eden in December 1941, when he suggested "arranging the necessary vote" in the Baltic states to sanction Soviet control; Miner, *Between Churchill and Stalin*, pp. 194–97.

Soviet frontiers were not the only barrier to reconciling Atlantic-Charter practice and principle. Roosevelt recommended that his military Chiefs of Staff consider that Churchill's proposal for dealing with a collapse of the Italian regime failed to mention self-determination, and the basic American argument (often with Churchill in agreement) against de Gaulle was that the Frenchman had not secured public support in any formal way. But those were side issues, however illustrative of the dilemma.

13. D. C. Watt, "American Anti-Colonialist Policies and the End of the European Colonial Empires, 1941–1962," in *Contagious Conflict: The Impact of American Dissent on European Life*, ed. A. N. J. Den Hollander (Leiden, 1973), pp. 93–125, condemns American hypocrisy. John Charmley, *Churchill's Grand Alliance* (London, 1995), agrees, but is more concerned with condemning the Prime Minister for supposedly subordinating British interests to an alliance with the Americans. Robert Vitalis, "The 'New Deal' in Egypt: The Rise of Anglo-American Commercial Competition in World War II and the Fall of Neocolonialism," *Diplomatic History*, 20 (Spring 1996), pp. 211–39, offers Egypt as an exception where American anti-colonialism provided Egyptian commercial leaders an opportunity to throw off British economic control.

14. Winston S. Churchill, *The Hinge of Fate* (Boston, 1950), p. 209.

15. Churchill used those words when, talking to the American Ambassador to China in March 1945, the Prime Minister defended British control over Hong Kong; Louis, *Imperialism at Bay*, p. 548.

16. *FRUS, Teheran*, p. 486. Samuel Rosenman, *Working with Roosevelt* (New York, 1972), pp. 316–17; Ward (ed.), *Closest Companion*, pp. 384–85; Sherwood, *Roosevelt and Hopkins*, p. 453.

17. David Reynolds, *The Creation of the Anglo-American Alliance, 1937–1941* (Chapel Hill, 1982), p. 249; Christopher Andrew, *For the President's Eyes Only* (New York, 1995), pp. 121–22; John Dower, *War Without Mercy* (New York, 1986), pp. 100–02, 105. Churchill is quoted in Kimball, *The Juggler*, p. 134.

18. Kimball, *Churchill & Roosevelt*, II, C-504, Nov. 13, 1943.

19. François Kersaudy, "Churchill and de Gaulle," in *Winston Churchill: Studies in Statesmanship*, R. A. C. Parker, ed. (London and Washington, 1995), "Churchill and de Gaulle," p. 127.

20. See W. F. Kimball, "Stalingrad: A Chance for Choices," *The Journal of Military History*, 60 (Jan. 1996), pp. 89–114.

21. *FRUS*, 1943, III, p. 39.

22. Eden, *The Reckoning*, p. 437; Sherwood, *Roosevelt & Hopkins*, p. 716; Llewellyn Woodward, *British Foreign Policy in the Second World War* (5 vols.; London: HMSO, 1970–76) V, p. 36. For additional discussions of China see *FRUS*, 1943, III, pp. 36–38; Eden, *The Reckoning*, p. 440.

23. Churchill, *The Hinge of Fate*, p. 562.

24. Charmley, *Churchill's Grand Alliance*, p. 74.

25. Diane Clemens, *Yalta* (New York, 1970), pp. 244–52; *FRUS, Yalta Conf.*, p. 770; Soviet troops entered Korea before Japan surrendered. The United States agreed to dividing occupation duties (thus dividing the country), although Truman thought about trying to exclude the Russians; William Stueck, *The Road to Confrontation* (Chapel Hill, 1981), p. 21; Bruce Cumings, *The Origins of the Korean War,* (Princeton, 1981).

26. Churchill minute to Eden and the COS Committee, Oct. 23, 1944, M.1024/4, Churchill papers; Gilbert, *Road to Victory*, pp. 1038–39; WSC, VI, pp. 389–90; FRUS, *Yalta Conf.*, p. 984. Churchill makes no mention of this quid pro quo in his war memoirs, though he discusses Stalin's commitment to join the war against Japan; WSC, VI, pp. 236–37. I have found no evidence of Churchill-Roosevelt agreement (or disagreement) prior to the Yalta talks regarding Far Eastern concessions to the USSR. For a fuller discussion see Warren F. Kimball, *Forged in War: Roosevelt, Churchill, and the Second World War* (New York, 1997), pp. 286–88.

27. Albert E. Kersten, "Wilhelmina and Franklin D. Roosevelt: A Wartime Relationship," *FDR and His Contemporaries: Foreign Perceptions of an American President*, ed. Cornelis A. van Minnen and John F. Sears (New York, 1992), pp. 85–96.

28. Minutes, 17th Pacific War Council meeting, Aug. 12, 1942, Map Room papers, Franklin D. Roosevelt Library (FDRL); Kimball, *Churchill & Roosevelt*, I, R-116, R-132, C-68, draft A (not sent); *FRUS*, 1945, I, p. 210; Louis, *Imperialism at Bay*, p. 492, and chaps. 30 and 32. For full details on Roosevelt's thinking about colonialism see Fred Pollock and Warren F. Kimball, "'In Search of Monsters to Destroy': Roosevelt and Colonialism," in Kimball, *The Juggler*, pp. 127–57. FDR's reference to the Articles of Confederation may well have come from a 1939 best-selling book, *Union Now* (New York, 1939), by Clarence Streit, in which he called for a world federation dominated by the Anglo-Saxons and referred to the League of Nations as a learning experience, just as the Articles of Confederation had been for the United States. Now, Streit concluded, the time had come to write a Constitution for the world, as the United States had done for itself in the 1780s (courtesy of Douglas Brinkley).

29. Charles de Gaulle, *The Complete War Memoirs of Charles de Gaulle* (New York, 1972), p. 530.

30. Churchill to Eden, Dec. 31, 1944, FO 371/50807 (PRO); Randolph Churchill as quoted by Colville in John Wheeler-Bennett (ed.), *Action This Day* (London, 1968), p. 74; Kimball, *The Juggler*, pp. 140–41; Louis, *Imperialism at Bay* and Christopher Thorne, *Allies of a Kind* (New York, 1978), both discuss growing British awareness that decolonization was necessary.

31. *FRUS, Tehran Conf.*, pp. 485–86; 8th PWC meeting, May 23, 1942, MR (FDRL); Moran, *Churchill*, pp. 144–45; Kimball, *The Juggler*, pp. 144–46.

32. Stein Tønnesson, *The Vietnamese Revolution of 1945: Roosevelt, Ho Chi Minh and de Gaulle in a World at War* (London, 1991), pp. 34–72; Kimball, *The Juggler*, pp. 147–48.

33. Ronald Spector, *Eagle Against the Sun* (London, 1987), p. 494; Tønnesson, *The Vietnamese Revolution*, pp. 167–69, 274; *FRUS, Yalta Conf.*, pp. 544–45; Kimball, *The Juggler.*

34. Kathryn Weathersby, "Soviet Aims in Korea and the Origins of the Korean War, 1945–1950: New Evidence from Russian Archives," Working Paper No. 8 (Nov. 1993), Cold War International History Project, Woodrow Wilson International Center (Washington, DC) p. 6, n. 16; U.S. Department of State, *Post World War II Foreign Policy Planning: State Department Records of Harley A. Notter* [microform] (Bethesda, 1987) pp. 548–51, summary dated March 18, 1943 of a White House meeting on Feb. 22, 1943.

35. Louis, *Imperialism at Bay*, pp. 436–40. The American military pushed hard for the United States to imitate the very nation they were fighting in the Pacific and to acquire a series of islands that seemed essential to American military security (if it was to fight World War II once again). Roosevelt agreed on the need for overseas bases, but insisted that those territories maintain sovereignty rather than being incorporated into the United States. A few days before he died he set up a meeting just with delegates headed for the United Nations Conference in San Francisco to reinforce his insistence on international trusteeships for the colonial world, including the Pacific islands; Kimball, *The Juggler*, p. 155.

36. *FRUS, Yalta Conf.*, p. 770. Not all historians agree. The debate is very well summarized in Tønnesson, *The Vietnamese Revolution*, pp. 13–19.

37. Minutes of the TOLSTOY Conference as quoted in Gilbert, *Road to Victory*, p. 1026.

38. See Wm. Roger Louis and Ronald Robinson, "The Imperialism of Decolonization," *The Journal of Imperial and Commonwealth History*, 22:3 (Sept. 1994), pp. 462–511.

39. James F. Byrnes, *Speaking Frankly* (New York, 1947), p. x. Even the understated official conference record caught Churchill's anger and outrage:

> The Prime Minister interrupted with great vigor to say that he did not agree with one single word of this report on trusteeships. He said that he had not been consulted nor had he heard of this subject up to now. He said that under no circumstances would he ever consent to forty or fifty nations thrusting interfering fingers into the life's existence of the British Empire. As long as he was minister, he would never yield one scrap of their heritage. . . .

That less inflammatory State Department phrasing is in *FRUS, Yalta*, p. 844.

40. Franklin D. Roosevelt, *Complete Presidential Press Conferences of Franklin D. Roosevelt* (25 vols.; New York, 1972), 25:70–73 (Feb. 23, 1945); Lloyd C. Gardner, *Approaching Vietnam* (New York, 1988), pp. 51–52.

41. The "left" is an inclusive term that defies precise definition. It always encompassed the extreme—Communism—and thus was a powerful political pejorative that often blurred significant distinctions, often driving moderates and extremists together. For example, many in the United States, including a few members of Roosevelt's cabinet, viewed the British Labour Party as part of the "left," yet Party leaders like Attlee and Ernest Bevin were adamant anti-Communists. In Greece, the British used the term to describe any element opposed to a restoration of the monarchy or a some sort of British-sponsored regency.

# 14

# "That Will Depend on Who Writes the History": Winston Churchill as His Own Historian

JOHN RAMSDEN

When President Harry Truman introduced Churchill at Westminster College in Fulton, Missouri, in March 1946, he described him merely as "one of the great men of the age." This was graceful without actually saying much, especially since Truman went on to bracket Churchill with Stalin as the type of leader that the world then so needed. At home, Churchill had already been forced into opposition by the 1945 general election, and, while this did not indicate ingratitude for his war services, it nevertheless cast a shadow on his standing. His admirers were in 1945 gloomy about his prospects; Harold Nicolson recorded in his diaries during the first year after the War complaints by several younger backbenchers that Churchill was now "too old" or "too embarrassing." Having heard even Churchill's great friend Jan Smuts voice similar opinions in May 1946, Nicolson concluded sadly that "they all feel that Winston must go." When a journalist consulted sixty political and military leaders in the United States in 1946, only two of them thought that Churchill had any political future.

The "iron curtain" speech provided Churchill with an international success on a grand scale early in his period out of office. By calling for strong resistance to Russian expansion, Churchill took a big gamble at Fulton before almost anyone else had publicly voiced that argument. This was subsequently confirmed by criticism both in Congress and in Parliament. There were all too many who thought in 1946 that Churchill was "conjuring up a savage dragon" simply so that he could appear as St. George (as a contemporary press report put it). As Churchill's own deputy, Anthony Eden, confided to a friend, Winston "almost wants a war, in order to stage a comeback." Senator Claude Pepper argued that Churchill had now thrown in his lot with the old Chamberlainite Tories, "who strengthened the Nazis as part of their anti-Soviet crusade." This was just about as damning a comment on Churchill as you could make.

Such a mood did not last long. By 1948 what Churchill had claimed at Fulton seemed vindicated by Russian activities in Iran, Germany, and Czechoslovakia. By then, the United States had adopted the Truman Doctrine and Marshall Aid and was moving towards the creation of NATO, the alliance that Churchill had demanded at Fulton. As the American journalist Quentin Reynolds summarized the general view, "Many people criticized Churchill for being so harsh with Russia in that [Fulton] speech, but time proved him to be right."

In 1963, in striking contrast to 1946, President Kennedy concluded that Churchill was *the* man of the century and "a legend in his own lifetime." By then, Kennedy was not even saying anything unusual. When Churchill died in 1965, *Life* magazine's cover bore just his picture together with the words "Giant of the Century." There was apparently no way to review Churchill's career either in 1955 when he retired or in 1965 when he died without invoking the word "great" with reference to his unique status. His old rival Clement Attlee declared in 1965 that he thought Churchill to have been "the greatest citizen of the world of our time."

And so it remained. In 1968, when the Overseas Press Club of New York polled 3,500 international pressmen, Churchill was voted "the one individual who has made the greatest mark for good upon our times." President Franklin Roosevelt came second, Harry Truman tenth, and Dwight Eisenhower twelfth. Three years later, after interviewing seventy current heads of states—surely the most sophisticated of all electorates—a Gallup poll found that Abraham Lincoln beat Churchill for the title of "most admired person in history," but that Churchill came second. Gandhi ran third, followed closely by Shakespeare and Socrates. This was by any standard the world series in celebrity status.

How did Churchill become, in the two catch-phrases much used both in 1955 and in 1965, "the greatest living Englishman" and "the man of the century"; and how far did Churchill personally shape his own mythic image? Back in the 1930s, he famously concluded a Commons exchange with Stanley Baldwin with the words: "History will say that the Right Honourable Gentleman is wrong in this matter," and then added after a pause, with a broad grin on his face, "I know it will, for I shall write that history." Likewise, when Dorothy

Thompson told the postwar Churchill that history would place him among the world's great men, he replied, "That will depend on who writes the history."

Much of the fixing of Churchill's elevated reputation came through the reception of his own *War Memoirs*. The key review was that of the second volume of the memoirs by Isaiah Berlin, which had the rare privilege for an academic reviewer of republication in book form as *Mr. Churchill in 1940*, and influenced virtually all later accounts, not least because of the formidable intellectual standing that Sir Isaiah himself acquired in post-war Britain. When Arnold Toynbee and George Steiner were asked to write on Churchill in 1964, each of them quoted and explicitly endorsed Berlin's explanation of Churchill's wartime role. Without discounting either British patriotism or ordinary people's courage, Isaiah Berlin declared of Churchill: "He had the lion's share in creating Britain's mood in 1940 as well as the right to voice it." This was a neat reversal of Churchill's own words about providing only "the lion's roar," and a reversal that sticks in the mind.

It was generally recognized that Churchill's Second World War writings, like all his books, were to an extent autobiographical. As his wartime ministerial colleague Malcolm MacDonald put it, Churchill "acted as his own Boswell to his own Dr. Johnson—and no more zealous Boswell ever scribbled about a grander Johnson." But these memoirs could not just be discounted as egotism, as most had dismissed *The World Crisis*, Churchill's books on the First World War. Stephen Graubard reminded his readers of the popular 1920s gibe that Churchill had written his autobiography and called it the world crisis, but he added that: "In 1948 such witticism would have been meaningless and impossible. Churchill's position in the Second World War made his personal history and that of the nation indivisible; the presentation of one was the representation of the other." Writing about the similar case of Abraham Lincoln's role in the American Civil War, Ralph Waldo Emerson claimed that "there is properly no history, only biography," for Lincoln "is the true history of the American people in his time." Even Lincoln, however, did not also go on to write the standard six-volume history of his own presidency.

As his historian-collaborators William Deakin and Maurice Ashley have pointed out, in Churchill's *War Memoirs* the autobiographical aspect was deliberately reinforced, by printing far more of Churchill's own dispatches, letters and Cabinet papers than the replies that they produced or the in-letters that provoked them. The impression that Churchill's leadership was always about "action this day" owes much to this simple literary stratagem. As John Connell once put it,

> there was no indication [in the memoirs] of the way in which . . .
> subordinates *reacted* to the endless series of questions, vigorous
> prods and stern summonses to "action this day." Their explana-
> tions, their protests, their occasional outraged and absolute nega-
> tives were not given. The memoirs, therefore, give a one-sided
> picture of the war's conduct and administration, but as [Churchill]
> himself would have said, *some side.*[1]

Churchill alone among historians was given access to those public
records, well over a decade before any program was adopted for
their release for scholarly use. He used some papers in the 1940s
that still seem not to have been released for anyone else to consult
half a century later.

Churchill's own attitude toward the publication of recent documents was highly opportunistic. Early in the process of his memoirs,
Churchill appealed to Harry Truman when the US State Department refused his request to publish his wartime correspondence
with Roosevelt. Churchill stressed that this eight-year-old material
was merely "past history," but he rather contradicted this view by
immediately volunteering to keep the documents out of view until
after the forthcoming United States Presidential elections. Truman
concluded that he could hardly prevent Churchill from quoting his
own cables, but the President insisted that Churchill only paraphrase
Roosevelt's replies. Churchill adopted a similarly "open-government"
tone when he asked the Americans in 1951 for permission to publish the 1943 Quebec Agreement on nuclear policy. The request
was motivated entirely by his recent discovery that his wartime agreement had been abrogated by the Attlee Government and by his wish
to embarrass the Labour Party with the information. This eight-year-
old story, he argued, "belongs to the past and to history." Though
he failed on that occasion to convince the American Government,
he blurted the secret out anyway in a Commons debate in 1954. In
1952, again to embarrass Labour he was all prepared to publicize
Anglo-American discussions on Korea in a Commons debate, only
to be headed off by the Americans. In this case, the information,
only two years old, was so secret that even the State Department in
Washington was not thought secure enough to have a copy of the
document.

Conversely, Churchill consistently opposed publication in
America of documents from his premierships that could not be read
in Britain. In 1955, he strongly opposed the publication of papers
relating to the Yalta Conference. When the general principle had
been lost, he sought to exclude from view at least interpreters'
records of his private meetings with Stalin. In 1962, he refused to
allow Eisenhower to reprint in his presidential memoirs a letter that

Churchill had written in 1954 in support of American policy in Indo-China on the grounds that the letter dealt with issues "of quite recent date and still alive." Such reasoning would have outlawed nearly all of Churchill's own memoirs if it had been systematically applied.

At times, Churchill's selection of documents went so far as to amend the story that the documents were supposed only to illustrate. When Eisenhower became President in 1953, and Churchill looked forward to the renewal of their wartime partnership, he was uncomfortably aware that the imminent publication of *Triumph and Tragedy*, his final volume of war memoirs, would describe Anglo-American disagreements in 1945 in which they had been on opposite sides. Churchill not only went over the book again and took out any reference "which might imply that there was in those days any controversy or lack of confidence between us," but he then also invited Ike to read the manuscript himself and make further revisions if he wished. This consorted badly with Churchill's statement only a week earlier that "I prefer to be judged by what I wrote at the time, rather than rely on present narrative and argument which is liable to be influenced by after-events." Truman's literary adviser, after checking out the texts involved, noted various ways in which, given past performance, Churchill was likely to distort the record, and concluded sadly that, "Mr. Churchill is an honorable man—but a British statesman with typical British retrospective flexibility, no matter what he says in his letter to the contrary."

Nevertheless, the publication of so many documents in Churchill's *War Memoirs* did give them a distinctive air of authenticity and impressed even the well-informed. General Eisenhower told Churchill in 1949 that his reading of "the historic memorandum you wrote to General Ismay on the 4th of June 1940" had deeply impressed him when published in *Their Finest Hour.*

> I never before saw it in verbatim form, although I knew of its existence from the very day that I first met the British planners in January 1942. To see it in print brings home to me again, and with emphasis, the virtue and farsightedness of your leadership in those dark days.[2]

Ordinary reviewers invariably referred to the authenticity of Churchill's documentary account, as for example when Hanson Baldwin, headlining his review of *Triumph and Tragedy* "Churchill Was Right," explicitly rejected earlier American accounts that had sought to vindicate US policy in 1944–45; he credited Churchill with unique farsightedness, credit that depended almost entirely on the selection of 1944–45 documents that Churchill had reprinted. In all this self-quotation, Churchill had the quite inestimable advantage that the documents of his official life, unlike for example Anthony Eden's when printed in his memoirs, were such a good read. The texts of his books could be larded with quotations from telegrams and military instructions without any danger of boring the reader. As John Kenneth Galbraith once pointed out, "It is hard to think of any misfortune for any politician [being considered for the Nobel Prize for Literature] that would be as devastating as the release of his official prose. Churchill survives."

Churchill clearly knew that in writing about world-shattering events in the epic tone of voice he was elevating the stature of the major participants in the War, including himself. Conversely, he disparaged the rather mundane discourse published by Ike's former naval aide, Harry Butcher:

> The articles are, in my opinion, altogether below the level upon which such matters should be treated. Great events and personalities are all made small when passed through the medium of this small mind. Few people have played around with so much dynamite and made so little of it.[3]

Eisenhower, who correctly divined that Churchill placed him among the great minds in this summary division of mankind, took much the same view when General Montgomery cheekily wrote to him to ask for a copy of Kay Summersby's book that described her wartime romance with Ike. The President replied that he had not read the book and would not know how to find a copy. He dismissed as pointless all "inquiries arising from inconsequential, personal accounts of anything that was as *big* as the war was." Nobody would ever accuse Churchill of penning "inconsequential accounts" of the War. Indeed, reviewers of his *War Memoirs* wrote again and again about the perfect match between the epic scale of his prose and his topic: "When before," asked the *Spectator*, "through all the centuries of this island's history, has such a theme matched such a pen?"

Churchill's answer to critics who felt that Churchill's *War Memoirs* magnified his own role was that his books offered only "a contribution to history" and that it would be for others to decide how much they contributed. The same view was held privately by his friends. Although General Sir Hastings Ismay agreed with Eisenhower that Churchill—both in the War and in his memoirs—had placed "a wholly disproportionate emphasis . . . on the importance of the islands in the Eastern Mediterranean," he reported that earlier drafts of the books had been so obsessed by the Mediterranean as to be "downright boring." Ismay lamented that although "we got him to cut a good deal of it . . . on the main issue he was, and still is, as obstinate as a mule." Ismay confided that he agreed with Ike's view that Churchill's talents lay in grand strategy rather than the logistics and mechanics of modern warfare, on which "he was, and still is, completely ignorant." But he felt that none of this really mattered:

> [for] the great thing to remember is that his book does not pro-
> fess to be history; it is merely the story of the Second World War
> as it struck him personally. And I have no doubt that when the
> full history comes to be written, many of his contentions will not
> hold water.[4]

Since Churchill wrote about his time as war leader, this in itself gave his work an authority and weight that tended to obscure the fact that he still presented only one man's view—*some* man.

Churchill was well aware of what he was doing. A former Conservative Party researcher recently recalled how during a visit to Chartwell in the late 1940s on Conservative Party business he had been kept waiting for hours while Churchill labored on the war memoirs. Eventually, the great man returned to the present and apologized profusely and charmingly for the delay. "I must justify myself before history," he explained. It might well be said that for Churchill justification came before history in every sense.

In any case, the problem with the argument that Churchill's was just a personal view was that such people as Ismay and Eisenhower, who could have offered modifications of Churchill's version, resolutely refused to do so. Ike did permit himself criticisms of British military subordinates that greatly ruffled British feathers, but he expressed not a syllable of doubt about the military wisdom of Churchill. When Lord Alanbrooke had the temerity to publish his wartime diaries, an incensed Ike wrote, "I could not imagine myself as being guilty of writing anything, ten years after the war was over, that could be construed as disparaging the accomplishments of the wartime Prime Minister." Adopting the same view, Ismay was gratified to find that his own memoirs were well received in 1960, for, "my purposes in writing the book were to show . . . that so far as the U.K. was concerned, Winston Churchill was head and shoulders above anybody else."

If such key witnesses recognized that Churchill had written autobiography and not history—but then only wrote in support of his version without offering correctives, it is difficult to see how historians are supposed to reach a more balanced verdict. Ismay wrote in his own memoirs:

> if I could have found any more superlatives to apply to Winston I
> would gladly have used them. And I hope that when his full-scale

biography comes to be written some fifty years hence, the pen picture that I have drawn of him will be taken as accurate.[5]

And Ike, having collaborated in the doctoring of *Triumph and Tragedy* so that it would say nothing to embarrass Anglo-American relations in the 1950s, then congratulated Churchill—without apparent irony—on "this final volume of your masterful *history* of World War II."

One must bear in mind that Ismay and Eisenhower, and all the inner group of Churchillians, knew exactly how cavalier Churchill could be in his manipulation of documents. When asked to comment on the military direction of the War, Ismay reminded Ike:

> I was not present at many of the talks that you had with Winston, and he was often rather naughty about not telling me what had transpired. Nor did he invariably show me your written communications, unless they were in exact accord with his own arguments.[6]

If Churchill's instruction to Maurice Ashley when Ashley came to work on the *History of the English-Speaking Peoples*—"Give me the facts, Ashley, and I will twist them the way I want to suit my argument"— was clearly a joke, then like many good jokes it diverted attention away from at least part of the truth.

Just as significant as the content of the *War Memoirs*, was the impact that they made on the worldwide market. The United States serial rights alone brought in a million dollars and prompted Churchill himself to jest that "I'm not writing a book. I'm developing a property." A comparison with Churchill's First World War memoirs is instructive here: the initial edition of *The Second World War* sold about twenty-five times as many copies (and much more quickly) as had *The World Crisis*, and then also went into reprinting for much longer. They remain in print nearly fifty years after the event, and still command a fair second-hand price, which is quite extraordinary for books that so flooded the market. Between 1948 and 1954, the *War Memoirs* were serialized in eighty magazines and newspapers worldwide, and then appeared in book form in fifty countries in eighteen languages. Churchill was, therefore, able to produce at exhaustive length and for a colossal audience of international readers a coherent narrative of the 1930s and the War years that would have a long head start over any competitor.

As Robert Blake reminded us, while Churchill's *The World Crisis*, published in 1923–24, was already being debunked by military historians like Sir Charles Oman in 1928, "no one has [yet] tried to do a similar *critique* of the six volumes on the Second World War." The

Book of the Month Club all too plausibly claimed of Churchill in 1955, "He retires, but never from history!"

Beyond the books themselves came dramatizations and films, generally less balanced even than the books had been. When ABC set out to serialize the war memoirs as *The Valiant Years* in 1960, the producer's concept of the Second World War was that it had been a duel between Hitler and Churchill: "It will be like a Western: Winston Churchill hiding behind rocks as a sharpshooter or leading the charge down the valley. We have a good leading man and a good heavy." When Jack le Vien condensed the million-and-a-quarter-word war memoirs into a single feature film, *The Finest Hours*, still greater compression led to an even less balanced account. The London *Times* was moved to point out that even Churchill had admitted to making some mistakes during the war that the film did not, though it left it to the *Daily Worker* to remind moviegoers that the Red Army had actually taken part in the Second World War, as well.

Because of the advantages that surrounded its initial publication, Churchill's general view of the Second World War and its origins was not seriously contested for twenty years. An example that makes this point squarely is the extent to which Churchill's highly partisan account of his campaigning against appeasement in the 1930s remained the received truth for so long. There was little in *The Gathering Storm*, for example, to acknowledge the economic problems within which Baldwin and Chamberlain had to make foreign policy; little recognition that the ruination of Churchill's reputation through anti-Bolshevism, India and the abdication made even the most sensible people reluctant to listen to him; no reference at all to the fact that Churchill had been utterly and consistently wrong about Japan. Indeed, if anyone still thinks of Churchill as infallibly prophetic on military matters, he might like to consider Churchill's prediction, just a week before the Japanese bombed Pearl Harbor, that in the event of war the Japanese would "fold up like the Italians." "The Japs," said Winston, "are the wops of the Far East." Even as a whistling-in-the-dark-to-keep-cheerful remark, this was extraordinarily unperceptive.

Nor did Churchill ever substantiate in *The Gathering Storm* his core argument that Hitler could have been painlessly stopped by early action by the democracies. Writing of the Rhineland Crisis of 1936, Churchill thundered that if the French had only mobilized "there is no doubt that Hitler would have been compelled by his own General Staff to withdraw; and a check would have been given to his pretensions which might well have been fatal to his rule." Note how that sentence slides imperceptibly from a confident "there is no doubt," through two "would have been"[s] to a hopeful "might well have been." This syntax was the frail thread on which was based Churchill's oft-repeated claim that (as he put it at Fulton) "there never was a war in all history easier to prevent." But there was as a matter of fact considerable doubt about it. Current historiography would probably agree that the Second World War could indeed have been prevented from breaking out in 1939—but only by starting it in 1936 or in 1938. It might well have been a lesser war with far fewer people killed (a matter of no small importance, even if this was not what Churchill was claiming). But it would have been war nonetheless, with all the risks and uncertainties that any war brings. It was surely a fallacy to suppose that Adolf Hitler could have been stopped in his tracks for good by bluff rather than actual war. And it does not even require the wisdom of hindsight to achieve this verdict, for, as Neville Chamberlain put it at the time, the expectation of Hitler accepting humiliation without fighting was "not a reliable estimate of a mad dictator's reactions."

Equally, it is difficult to match Churchill's autobiographical picture of his six-year crusade against Nazism before 1939 with the fact that he did not cast a single vote against British foreign policy until September 1938, while he cast rebel votes regularly over India, and denounced Gandhi with even stronger language than he used against Hitler, even as he refused ever to attack Franco at all. The Spanish Civil War, for most contemporaries the acid test of anti-fascism, is notable mainly by its absence from *The Gathering Storm*, simply because over Spain Winston's record was much like Baldwin's and Chamberlain's. And more broadly, as Richard Powers long ago showed from an analysis of his Commons speeches, Churchill did not quickly denounce the Naval Treaty with Hitler in 1935, he hoped for a deal with Mussolini to split the Fascist dictators, he did not support effective action to stop Mussolini in Abyssinia, and he was initially relieved when Britain and France did not act to kick Hitler out of the Rhineland in 1936. Late in 1937, Churchill was still advocating the return to Hitler of former German colonies, a policy more usually associated with Chamberlain. And when Anthony Eden resigned as Foreign Secretary in February 1938, Churchill was the fourth quickest of four hundred Tory backbenchers to sign a round-robin expressing undiminished support for Neville Chamberlain. Again, none of this is to be found in *The Gathering Storm*, which in the last case at least gives exactly the opposite impression of what Churchill said and did at the time.

But throughout the 1950s, such truths were just not spoken, and not until the 1970s did any official papers appear that would provide evidential support for revisionist accounts of the war years either. As Sir John Plumb put it in 1969, "Churchill the historian lies at the very heart of all historiography of the Second World War, and will always remain there."

In this context, it is important to remind ourselves that Churchill's reputation did not necessarily have to soar in the post-war period. After all, Field Marshall Montgomery, whose popularity as a war hero with the British people stood second only to Churchill's own in 1945, then went steadily downhill, so that he ended his life generally regarded as self-centered, foolish, and eccentric. This decline was caused to a large extent by memoirs that backfired and a post-retirement career that was seen to be a desperate and demeaning search for publicity. Churchill managed both maneuvers far more skillfully. Nigel Hamilton has argued as Montgomery's biographer that Monty's fall from favor was due to his character defects: lack of subtlety, grace, flexibility of mind, cunning, charm, and the ability to see and exploit other people's weak points. But these were all qualities that Winston Churchill also possessed in abundance.

Where therefore does the Fulton speech of 1946 fit into the picture of Churchillian recovery, coming as it did precisely at another "hinge of fate" between the aftermath of War, when election defeat had suggested that he was on the way out, and the full-blown Churchill as superhero media industry that got going by 1950? Churchill was a regular revisiter of his own successful predictions: his Commons speeches of 1939, for example, carefully but selectively referred to earlier speeches, and so gave the impression that he had an exemplary record both on rearmament (which he certainly did have) and on foreign policy (where the record was far more mixed).

After Fulton, Churchill was quick to show how others had caught up with views he had already expressed. He was saying so by the summer of 1946, and it soon became a feature of almost every Churchill speech on foreign policy. At M.I.T. in March 1949, he argued:

> three years ago I made a speech at Fulton . . . Many people here and in my own country were startled and even shocked by what I said. But events have vindicated in much detail the warnings which I deemed it my duty to give at that time. Today there is a very different climate of opinion.[7]

Where Churchill led, his admirers were quick to follow. This time, the key interpreter was not Isaiah Berlin or A .L. Rowse but the Dutch writer J. H. Huizinga, whose 1948 article on the Fulton speech was quoted by Randolph Churchill when editing Winston's collected speeches and then regularly quoted or plagiarized by others. For Huizinga, the prize for moral leadership went to Churchill, for, who dared to call a spade a spade and a Russian an enemy of democracy? Who turned the "cards on the table" face upwards and showed the public what sort of cards they were more than a year before this salutary revelation received its official blessing? In other words, who led and who followed?[8]

These remarks ignored the fact that it was Harry Truman who actually ensured that Churchill went to Fulton, well knowing what he would say, and went with him to ensure the attendance of the world's press, and that the British Foreign Office helped make the arrangements for the whole trip.

When summarizing recent writing on Fulton in 1954, A. L. Rowse mused:

> we wonder now what all the fuss was about, for Churchill was only, as so often before, pointing out what was in front of people's noses. To do that in politics is the prerogative of genius . . . At Fulton he merely pointed out the obvious.

From there it passed into the orthodoxy of history: Martin Gilbert reached much the same conclusion in the official biography in 1988. In other words, like Churchill himself, Gilbert still ignored the alternative historiographical school that has argued that the Fulton speech, by alarming Stalin, actually helped to start the Cold War. Rather than merely announcing its arrival, Churchill's warning was in effect self-fulfilling. This is not to argue that historians who believe that the West caused the Cold War have won the historiographical argument—far from it. They have contributed, however, to the more balanced view that now prevails, and only writers on Churchill still seem so summarily to ignore them.

The popular memory of the 1930s, substantially shaped by Churchill's own speeches and writings, was a powerful tool with which he could shape perceptions of the postwar world. In 1951, Churchill's early biographer J. G. Lockhart wrote of Fulton:

> As had happened so often before, his warnings were decried by many, and he himself was denounced as a mischievous, even a warmongering man. And as had happened so often before, events were soon to show who was right . . . His opponents might sometimes deprecate his counsel, but could not ignore it, for graven in the memories of all were the thirties, the years the locust had eaten, when a prophet, without honour in his own land, had told the truth and been rejected.[9]

If these thoughts were indeed graven in popular memory, then Churchill himself had done much of the chiselling. Lockhart's use of Churchill's own biblical phrase about the locusts rather demonstrates that fact. There is then a great deal to be said for the view that Diana Coolidge expressed in 1960, that the post-Fulton "outcry" against "that old Russian-hater, that warmonger Churchill" merely preceded a time in which "it was seen that Churchill's position in his country and the world was subtly altered. Instead of becoming the obstinate old man who would not retire he had come forward once again as a leader and a statesman." All the other positive developments in Churchill's postwar reputation would be contingent on this "subtle transformation" that took place in the aftermath of Fulton and of the first volumes of his *War Memoirs.*

The *New York Times* acknowledged this transformation by 1953, when it wrote that Churchill had already become "a part of world history for half a century. His great decisions—to fight on in 1940, to oppose Stalinism in 1946, altered its course . . ." "The first rough draft of history," as Peter Hennessy has called the serious, political press, was setting the tone for all that would follow, and the mass of uncritical biographies of Churchill published in the 1950s and 1960s duly did follow, regularly quoting such press eulogies as independent confirmation of their authors' views. But the pressmen were not left to their own devices, for Churchill never abandoned his lifelong habit of cultivating newspaper proprietors, and he never visited Washington after 1941 without lunching at the National Press Club for discussions which, he assured the British Ambassador, were always scrupulously confidential. The Ambassador assumed that this must be a little joke on Winston's part, since what he said there was always quoted in full in the next day's newspapers. Much of that first rough draft of history was therefore, more or less, in Churchill's handwriting.

As Churchill himself told the National Press Club in Washington in 1954, referring back to Fulton, "I got into trouble being in front of the weather that time. But it's all come out since—I won't say all right, but it's all come out." This was almost exactly the phrase that Churchill had long ago applied in *Great Contemporaries* to Joseph Chamberlain; "Joe," he wrote, was the man who "made the weather," and wrote the political agenda with which others then had to deal. No wonder Winston so admired Joe. For the "iron curtain speech" at Fulton and the writing and reception of his Second World War memoirs demonstrated that—on a global scale—Churchill could not only "make the weather" but that he could to a large extent write the weather reports too.

Spring Semester 1996

1. John Connell, *Winston Churchill* (London, 1956), p. 37.
2. General Eisenhower to Winston Churchill, Feb. 16, 1949, Dwight D. Eisenhower Presidential Papers, Name Series Box 22, File Churchill, 2, Eisenhower Library.
3. Churchill to Eisenhower, Jan. 22, 1946, Box 22, File Churchill, 2.
4. Lord Ismay to General Eisenhower, Oct. 11, 1951, Box 60, File Ismay, 1.
5. Ismay to Eisenhower, Dec. 30, 1960, "Presidential Papers," Box 19, File Ismay, 3.
6. Ismay to President Eisenhower, Dec. 2, 1960, Box 19, File Ismay, 3.
7. Randolph Churchill (ed.), *In the Balance: Winston Churchill Speeches, 1949 and 1950* (Boston, 1951), p. 49.
8. Randolph Churchill (ed.), *The Sinews of Peace: Winston Churchill Speeches, 1945 and 1946* (London, 1948), p. v.
9. J. G. Lockhart, *Winston Churchill* (London, 1951), p. 156.

*Biographical Note*

In the academic year 1995–1996, the author was Robertson Visiting Professor of British History at Westminster College, Fulton. Thanks are here expressed to Westminster College and the Winston Churchill Memorial at Fulton, and to the Fulbright Commission, for making possible the research on which this paper is based. The author is grateful to colleagues at Queen Mary and Westfield College and at many U.S. universities who commented on earlier drafts, and to the staffs of the Dwight D. Eisenhower Presidential Library (Abilene), the John F. Kennedy Presidential Library (Boston), the Lyndon B. Johnson Presidential Library (Austin), the Minnesota Historical Association (St. Paul), and the Harry S. Truman Presidential Library (Independence), for assistance with research and permissions to make quotations. A fuller version of this lecture, including full footnote references, is available as an offprint, from the author, Professor J. A. Ramsden, Department of History, Queen Mary and Westfield College, London E1 4NS.

# 15

# British Historians and the Debate over the "Postwar Consensus"

## PAUL ADDISON

One of the most widespread concepts in the analysis of post-war Britain is that of "the postwar consensus." By this is meant a period from the 1940s to the 1970s during which party differences were transcended by a broad agreement over certain fundamentals of government policy: Britain's world role, the welfare state, the mixed economy, and the goal of full employment are the most frequently cited. But, in recent years the validity of the concept has been hotly contested. A debate has been in progress between a "consensus" school of historians and an "anti-consensus" school who contend that consensus is a retrospective myth invented by historians.

The aim of this lecture is to review the current state of controversy and the direction in which it appears to be going. As yet, it will be argued, there is no sign that the anti-consensus historians have achieved the knock-out blow they are seeking. They have, indeed, failed to take the true measure of the "consensus thesis," which is more complex and supple than they suppose. But, in putting that thesis under pressure, they have contributed much to the development of a more sophisticated analysis of conflict and consensus in postwar Britain.

To understand the debate, it is necessary to trace the consensus theory back to its origins. It is not known who coined the phrase "postwar consensus" or when it first entered into general use. The idea that the Second World War generated a "consensus" was first articulated by Angus Calder in his book *The People's War*, published in 1969. By the time I made use of the phrase in *The Road to 1945,* published in 1975, it was a fairly commonplace term.[1] In this book I argued that the Second World War and the Coalition government of 1940–1945 gave rise to a new consensus at the top in British politics—a consensus in favor of an expansion in the role of the state in order to prevent a return to the social and economic conditions of the 1930s. The consensus was to be found in the proposals drawn up by the Coalition government between 1942 and 1945 for social reform in the fields of education, health, social security, land use, and employment policy. The Labour and Conservative parties were still divided over the nationalization of industry. Otherwise the Labour and Conservative election manifestos ran on parallel lines, and the incoming Labour government inherited a program much of which had been agreed in advance by the civil service and the leadership of the Conservative party.

This thesis seemed to be underlined by the polarization of politics in the mid-1970s. It was the declared intent of Mrs. Thatcher, who had been elected leader of the Conservative party six months before the publication of the book, to break with the policies of the "progressive consensus." Indeed, she strongly attacked consensus politics, which she equated with cowardly compromises and a lack of conviction. Any suspicion that she herself would relapse into consensus was dispelled by the record of the Thatcher governments of 1979 to 1990. Meanwhile, the rise of a new right-wing historiography gave some support to the consensus thesis. In his book *The Audit of War* (1986), Correlli Barnett attacked the postwar plans of the wartime Coalition as a mistaken exercise in the building of a New Jerusalem at a time when priority ought to have been given to the re-equipment of British industry and the expansion of scientific and technical education. "That the Conservatives too offered a version of New Jerusalem, based on the Coalition's 'four-year plan,'" he wrote, "demonstrated that New Jerusalem had indeed become the political consensus."[2]

*The Road to 1945* is sometimes alleged to have established a new orthodoxy, but in my experience this was not so. A procession of historians contested the view that a consensus had been established by the time of the General Election of 1945. Among them were David Howell, J. M. Lee, José Harris, and Jonathan Schneer.[3] Yet few historians doubted that a consensus of some kind did come into existence *at some later date*—the late 1940s, perhaps, or the early 1950s. Historians such as Kenneth Morgan or Peter Clarke dated the consensus from the acceptance by the Conservatives after 1945 of much of the work of the Attlee governments.[4]

In 1986 two enterprising historians, Peter Hennessy and Anthony Seldon, founded the Institute of Contemporary British History, with the aim of stimulating research into British history since 1945. With some qualifications, both Hennessy and Seldon were subscribers to the idea of a postwar consensus. When they commissioned a series of texts on postwar history, they invited two political scientists, Dennis Kavanagh and Peter Morris, to contribute a study entitled *Consensus Politics from Attlee to Thatcher.*

Kavanagh and Morris argued that the postwar consensus could be defined in terms of five main areas:

1. The mixed economy
2. Full employment
3. Conciliation of the trade unions
4. The welfare state
5. Retreat from empire, Britain's role as a nuclear power, and membership in the Atlantic Alliance.[5]

The concept of a postwar consensus figured increasingly in text-books on contemporary Britain by historians and political scientists: to such an extent, in fact, that it came close to being an orthodoxy.[6]

A vigorous counter-attack began in 1988 when Ben Pimlott, the biographer of Hugh Dalton, published an article entitled "The Myth of Consensus." He argued that fundamental conflicts between the Conservative and Labour parties were unresolved by the Second World War, which culminated in one of the most bitterly contested general elections of the twentieth century. But he also maintained that no consensus had existed at any time in postwar Britain: it was time to consign the idea to the waste-paper basket.[7]

Where Pimlott led, younger historians followed. Their first target was *The Road to 1945*, to which they gave an altogether new lease on life by the force of their attacks. Both Kevin Jefferys and Stephen Brooke wrote books whose main purpose was to refute itz But this was only the preliminary to the opening up of an intensive bombardment across the whole front of postwar British history. This was intended to demolish every last vestige of the concept of consensus by replacing it with a vision of a nation so torn by strife that it resembled Northern Ireland without the violence. Among the historians who were most prominent in carrying the critique of consensus into the postwar era were Harriet Jones, Neil Rollings, and Ina Zwarziger-Bargielowska.

Much therefore has been written about the alleged flaws in the "consensus thesis." But now the critical spotlight has begun to fall on the claims of the revisionists, which have been examined and, for the most part, rejected in articles by Anthony Seldon and Dennis Kavanagh.[9] Here it must be said that it is impossible to lump together all the anti-consensus historians as though their assumptions are identical and that the same is true of the consensus historians as well. Judgments therefore have to be qualified. But, in broad terms the claims of the revisionists are open to question on two main grounds.

The first can be dealt with briefly. Most definitions of the postwar consensus include Britain's foreign and imperial policy: the commitment to NATO and the Anglo-American special relationship, the maintenance of a British nuclear deterrent, the retreat from Empire, and the conversion to membership of the European Common Market. These are all major areas of postwar British politics in which, as yet, the consensus thesis has scarcely been challenged at all. Here it is worth noting that, a year after the publication of *The Road to 1945*, a parallel study of the politics of wartime foreign policy was published by Trevor Burridge. Burridge demonstrated that Labour ministers, especially Attlee and Bevin, were important participants in the planning of the peace settlement. Furthermore, they led the Labour Party—with much dissent from the Left—away from the ideological positions it had occupied in the 1930s towards a traditional British foreign policy based on the balance of power. This brought them into close harmony with Churchill and Eden, and set the scene for the bipartisan foreign policy of the Attlee governments. "The Coalition government," wrote Burridge, "was nowhere more a political partnership than in the field of foreign affairs."[10] These findings have yet to be seriously questioned. Perhaps in time the debate over consensus will spread to foreign policy and defence, but for the present it seems that an important part of the consensus thesis still commands support.

The second flaw in the revisionist case arises from the ambiguity of the term "consensus." Like the concept of class, it means different things to different people, but everyone appears to insist that his or her definition is the only "correct" one. As a result, the revisionists often miss the point by attacking positions that most consensus historians have never held. According to Ben Pimlott, the word consensus derives from the Latin for agreement, and was first used by physiologists to describe the harmony between organs of the body. As applied to British politics, it refers to consensus between the political parties. Such a consensus, furthermore, "is said to exist not when people merely agree, but when they are happy agreeing, are not constrained to agree, and leave few of their number outside the broad parameters of agreement."[11]

Much of the critique of the consensus school has been grounded on this narrow definition of the "correct" meaning of the word. But there are two reasons why the critique is misplaced. First of all the consensus historians do not define consensus in terms of agreement *between the parties*. They define it as a measure of agreement *between civil servants and ministerialists of both parties:* an elite consensus, reflected in a high level of continuity between the policies of Labour and Conservative governments. The concept of an elite consensus is perfectly compatible with the existence of a conflict of interests and philosophies between the parties. It is indeed a theory of containment in which conflicts are resolved by a political process that impels governments of both parties away from ideological goals and towards the middle ground.

In spite of this, the revisionists claim that the consensus historians have left the conflicts out of contemporary British history. I have often come across the assertion that there is no recognition of party conflict, or differences within the wartime Coalition, in *The Road to 1945*. No doubt I understated some of these points: but they are almost all documented and discussed. This is true of divisions of opinion over the Beveridge Report, town and country planning, the future of industry, and the National Health Service. It is even true of the General Election campaign of 1945. The main difference between my understanding of wartime politics and that of later historians is that I regarded the degree of consensus established as more important than the conflicts that remained.

Yet critics still take me to task for opinions I never expressed. Writing of the origins of the National Health Service, for example, Charles Webster attributes to me the view that "Labour merely gave legislative effect to an already agreed programme."[12] I was in fact careful not to say this. I pointed out the differences between the parties over the 1944 White Paper, the antagonism it aroused among the British Medical Association, and the subsequent concessions made by the Conservative Minister of Health, Henry Willink, to the doctors. Of the role of the Labour government I wrote:

> To some extent they exercised the right to go beyond the Coalition framework and implement specifically Labour party ideas. But this was often because the Left of the party, which had strongly opposed many of the Coalition policies, managed to exert itself successfully. Aneurin Bevan, the new Minister of Health, refused to start from the point where the wartime White Paper on the National Health Service had left off, and devised his own approach. After an heroic struggle against the BMA, the Conservative press, and Churchill (who dubbed him "the minister of disease"), Bevan was able to introduce a fully fledged National Health Service on 5 July 1948.[13]

Another fertile source of misunderstanding on the part of the critics is to be found in Pimlott's claim that consensus necessarily implies cheerful and unconstrained agreement. In the view of the consensus historians, consensus arises as much from the structure and process of politics as from agency and intention. This is what Anthony Seldon has in mind when he lists the factors that led to a convergence of policies between governments of different parties. These include the continuity provided by the civil service, the preference of the mass of the electorate for moderate policies, constraints of time, constraints of money, and the climate of ideas.[14] Similarly, Kavanagh and Morris accept that constraints were built into the making of consensus, which they define as "a set of parameters which bounded the set of policy options regarded by senior politicians as administratively practical, economically affordable and politically acceptable."[15]

Critics of the consensus school would no doubt argue that such definitions of consensus are incorrect. But words are living things, the meaning of which is defined by the way in which they are used from day to day. The terms "consensus" and "postwar consensus" are frequently used in the broad, Whiggish sense favored by the consensus historians. Hence, the Conservative politician, Sir Ian Gilmour, can write that—

> consensus implies a desire to keep party controversy within limits and a willingness to consider the convictions of opponents. And in Britain, at least, consensus politicians have recognised that, under our unusual system which normally gives the whole of the executive and the control of the legislature to one party even if it has only a minority of the votes, the winning party does not have *carte blanche* to do whatever its extremists may happen to want. However much it was despised by some in the seventies and eighties, consensus has usually been considered one of the marks that distinguish liberal democracies from less civilized states.[16]

Much of the debate over consensus arises from the inability of the revisionists to engage with the thesis they claim to be revising. It is when they turn to the behavior of politicians in office that the critique begins to bite. The consensus thesis places a great deal of emphasis on continuities of policy between the wartime Coalition government and its Labour successor. The implication is that a Conservative government after 1945 would also have introduced something like the Labour welfare state. Similarly, it has been argued that the scrapping of economic controls by the Churchill government after 1951 was merely an extension of the Labour policy of pruning them back. Here, for once, is solid ground where the two sides can agree what it is they are arguing about. The attempts of Kevin Jefferys and Stephen Brooke to demonstrate that the Coalition government was deeply divided over social reform may or may not be convincing: but they are very much to the point. Neill Rollings has argued that the return of the Conservatives to office in 1951 marked a watershed in economic policy.[17]

The revisionists claim that the "myth of consensus" can be disproved by research. But, like a punchball, the idea of consensus is so flexible and accommodating that it can take plenty of punishment without being damaged. Historians may therefore be up to date with the latest literature, and well acquainted with the revisionist case, but still convinced that consensus is a valid and useful term.[18]

By campaigning to proscribe the phrase "postwar consensus," the revisionists are in danger of maneuvering themselves into a cul-de-sac. If it continues to be used, this is not because historians are incapable of telling the difference between Labour and Tory, or because they suppose that Labour and Conservative Cabinets pursued identical policies. It is because the phrase is a useful if imperfect measure of the difference between two contrasting periods of postwar British history. For thirty years after the war, British politics were dominated by the achievements of the Attlee governments and the continuing industrial and political power of Labour. Throughout that period, the Conservative party retained its distinctive values. But, Conservative leaders, and Conservative governments, attached a high priority to the maintenance of the postwar settlement. Lady Thatcher describes the situation as follows:

> [The Labour Party] gloried in planning, regulation, controls and subsidies. It had a vision of the future: Britain as a democratic socialist society, third way between east European collecticism and American capitalism . . . The Tory Party was more ambivalent. At the level of principle, rhetorically and in Opposition, it opposed these doctrines and preached the gospel of free enterprise with very little qualification. Almost every postwar Tory victory had been won on slogans such as "Britain Strong and Free" or "Set the People Free." But in the fine print of policy, and especially in government, the Tory Party merely pitched camp in the long march to the left. It never tried seriously to reverse it.[19]

There may be some exaggeration here, but in my opinion this is the essential truth, "the big picture." Nor would it be difficult to document with a long list of quotations from Conservative leaders in their more consensual moments.

The anti-consensus historians may not succeed in eliminating the "c" word from the vocabulary of historians. But they have already achieved something that may be more important in the long run. By ensuring that the concept of consensus is now used in a more sceptical and discriminating fashion, they have sharpened its analytical force. There could be no better demonstration of this effect than Rodney Lowe's article, "The Second World War, Consensus, and the Foundations of the Welfare State," published in 1990. Lowe subjected the concept of consensus to a rigorous analysis in which he first defined the meaning of the term as "a historically unusual degree of agreement," and then went on to distinguish between short-term and long-term consensus, consensus at different levels of the political system, and the different degrees of consensus at different periods. Lowe concluded that the war did produce a consensus in favor of a short-term program of welfare reforms. But, he maintained, this only turned into a long-term consensus in support of the framework of the welfare state in the late 1940s, when "a retreat to consensus" was forced on both major parties by the pressure of events.[20]

The debate over consensus has given us a more extensive vocabulary with which to describe the harmonies and discords of British politics. But why have historians devoted so much time and energy to such arguments? Why has the debate over consensus become (alongside the debate over economic decline) one of the defining debates in the field of postwar British history? The key, perhaps, is to be found in the fact that the majority of the consensus historians are over the age of 40, and the majority of the anti-consensus historians under 40. Historians over the age of 40 grew up in the shadow of the Second World War and the belief that whatever the differences between classes and parties, they were offset by an underlying national unity that made compromise and agreement both possible and desirable. But historians under the age of 40 grew up in a society polarized by ideology and industrial strife in a nation that seemed to be losing its identity. Each generation, therefore, interprets the past in the light of its own experience. The younger generation believes that the national unity of Britain was always a myth. The older generation maintains that, even if it was a myth, it was a myth that led the rulers of postwar Britain to seek a truce in the class war and a government founded on a broad basis of consent. The existence of a consensus thus defined has indeed been corroborated by a witness of impeccable authority. Queen Elizabeth II has presided over every Conservative and Labour government since 1952. Her latest biographer confirms that she was critical of the policies of Mrs. Thatcher's government because they threatened to undermine "the consensus in British politics which she thinks has served the country well since the Second World War."[21]

1. *The People's War* (London, 1969); Paul Addison, *The Road to 1945: British Politics and the Second World War* (London, 1975). According to Ronald Butt, the term "consensus politics" was "much used around 1964" and was "a natural development of *Butskellism* . . ." See *The Fontana Dictionary of Modern Thought* (London, 1977), p. 131.

2. Correlli Barnett, *The Audit of War: The Illusion and Reality of Britain as a Great Nation* (London, 1986), p. 37.

3. David Howell, "Revisionist History in Britain" in *Government and Opposition*, 12, 1 (London, 1977), pp. 110–114; J. M. Lee, *The Churchill Coalition 1940–1945* (London, 1980); José Harris, "Political Ideas and the Debate on State Welfare 1940–1945" in Harold L. Smith (ed.), *War and Social Change: British Society in the Second World War* (London, 1986), pp. 233–63; Jonathan Schneer, *Labour's Conscience: The Labour Left 1945–1951* (Boston, 1988).

4. Kenneth Morgan, *Labour in Power 1945–1951* (Oxford, 1984), pp. 490–91; Peter Clarke, "Attlee: The Making of the Postwar Consensus" in Peter Clarke, *A Question of Leadership: Gladstone to Thatcher* (Harmondsworth, 1992), pp. 193–210.

5. Dennis Kavanagh and Peter Morris, *Consensus Politics from Attlee to Thatcher* (Oxford, 1989).

6. See for example Bill Coxall and Linton Robins, *British Politics since the War* (London, 1994 edition), p. 19.

7. Ben Pimlott, "The Myth of Consensus" in Lesley M. Smith (ed.), *The Making of Britain: Echoes of Greatness* (London, 1988); later reprinted in Ben Pimlott, *Frustrate Their Knavish Tricks* (London, 1994), pp. 229–39.

8. Kevin Jefferys, *The Churchill Coalition and Wartime Politics 1940–1945* (Manchester, 1991); Stephen Brooke, *Labour's War: The Labour Party during the Second World War* (Oxford, 1992).

9. Anthony Seldon, "Consensus: A Debate Too Long?" *Parliamentary Affairs*, 41, 4 (1944), pp. 501–513; Dennis Kavanagh, "The Postwar Consensus," *20th Century British History*, 3, 2 (1992), pp. 175–89.

10. T. D. Burridge, *British Labour and Hitler's War* (London, 1976), p. 13.

11. Pimlott, *Frustrate Their Knavish Tricks*, p. 230.

12. Charles Webster, "The Making of the National Health Service," *Modern History Review*, 6, 4, pp. 11–13.

13. Addison, *The Road to 1945*, pp. 240–2, 273.

14. Seldon, "Consensus", pp. 509–11.

15. Kavanagh and Morris, *Consensus Politics*, p. 13.

16. Ian Gilmour, *Dancing with Dogma: Britain under Thatcherism* (London, 1992), p. 9.

17. Neil Rollings, "'The Reichstag Method of Governing': The Attlee Governments and Permanent Economic Controls" in Helen Mercer, Neil Rollings, and Jim Tomlinson (eds.), *Labour Governments and Private Industry: The Experience of 1945–1951* (Edinburgh, 1992), pp. 15–36.

18. See for example, Alec Cairncross, *The British Economy since 1945* (Oxford, 1992); Geoffrey Searle, *Coalitions in British Politics* (London, 1995); Daniel Ritschel, "The Making of Consensus: The Nuffield College Conferences during the Second World War," *20th Century British History*, 6, 3 (1995), pp. 267–301; Jim Phillips, "The Postwar Political Consensus and Industrial Unrest in the Docks 1945–1955," *20th Century British History*, 6, 3 (1995), pp. 302–19. For a selective and critical use of the phrase, see Nicholas Timmins, *The Five Giants: A Biography of the Welfare State* (London, 1995).

19. Margaret Thatcher, *The Downing Street Years* (London, 1995 edition), pp. 6–7.

20. Rodney Lowe, "The Second World War, Consensus, and the Foundations of the Welfare State," *20th Century British History*, 1, 2 (1990), pp. 152–82.

21. Ben Pimlott, "A Queen Who Found Herself Left of the Tories," *The Independent*, 3 Oct. 1996, p. 19.

# 16

## *Our Age* Revisited

### NOEL ANNAN

Some years ago I made an audit of the contribution my generation made to British life. I was astonished, delighted, and
alarmed when Roger Louis suggested that I should reconsider
what I wrote in *Our Age*. Delighted because I could once again visit
the University of Texas and express my admiration for its achievements and my gratitude for its generosity. Astonished because I could
not believe that the book was well enough known there to sustain
such a talk. Alarmed because although I was heartened by those
who enjoyed the book, at least two of those who carved me up make
cogent and justifiable criticisms; and therefore the judgments of
professional historians at Austin who have spent years of study on
post-war Britain are likely to be even more trenchant.

They will be right to be so because I write as a historian, not as a
journalist. I do not use the term journalist as a mark of contempt.
The brilliant columnists who comment each week or month on current events have the ability to see through the propaganda of ministers and political parties or pressure groups. They take a line and
they dish it out to the men and women in public life.

But a historian, I judge, should go further and treat ideas dispas-
sionately. Indeed the more he is repelled by a personality or an ideology the more determined he should be to describe him and his
ideas as sympathetically as possible. Or, if not sympathetically, the
historian should at least make it comprehensible why the man or
woman in question held such ideas and acted as he or she did. He
should do so because there are likely to exist among those ideas
some serious and deadly criticisms of his own vision of life. The
trouble was that my critics sometimes imagined that, when I was
describing with all the force that I could muster what exactly someone stood for or said, I was endorsing those views myself.

This particularly applied to the account I gave of Margaret Thatcher. I wanted to put as vividly as possible her criticism and contempt for the *mentalités* of my generation. I did so, apparently effectively enough that several commentators imagined that I had suffered a Pauline conversion and endorsed her policies and culture. In fact, I detest her narrow vision, her vindictive, bullying manner. She shared Lloyd George's genuine contempt for the upper classes, but she had none of his sympathy for the unprotected poor. Nor was she guided by Churchill's magnanimous view of history. But her mastery of business and understanding of the root causes of British discontents in 1979—namely, shoddy self-indulgent management; authoritarian trade union rapacity that ham-strung management; and the syndicalism that spread to the professional classes—this understanding made her the only Prime Minister this century who can be mentioned in the same breath as Lloyd George and Churchill. The bare four pages in which I questioned whether Margaret Thatcher had turned the country round, as she said she had, were ignored.

Then again I spoke of the folly of the House of Commons in opposing the agreement that Foreign Office ministers had made with Argentina. The agreement was to transfer sovereignty and lease back the Falkland Islands. But I spoke apparently so eloquently that one critic imagined that I opposed the expedition of the task force sent to reconquer the islands. This was a view that a number of intellectuals took. But I put—though clearly with insufficient vigor—the opposite case. Namely, that however maladroit and irrational the government's policy had been before Galtieri invaded the islands, to have let him get away with it would have had a devastating effect upon the morale of the country, already shaken by the surge of unemployment as monetarism shattered uncompetitive industry.

But let me say at once that authors have only themselves to blame if reviewers misunderstand what they have written. What is clear to them, they must make crystal clear to their readers. What then did I not make crystal clear and what did I leave unsaid that I ought to have said? And where was I palpably wrong?

I think I was wrong to give way to temptation and use Bowra's arresting phrase "Our Age." I extended Oxbridge to include the LSE as the cradle of the intelligentsia of my generation, and I had to admit that there were certainly marked temperamental differences between such sound level-headed men such as the former chairman of the University Grants Committee, Fred Dainton, or Alan Bullock, or sagacious top civil servants. Certainly they could not be accused of putting a high premium on cleverness and irreverence or wanting to be amused and amusing. But even so, they shared with their more colorful colleagues a belief in moderate collectivism—the corporate state and full employment, high taxation and a fairer share of the country's resources for the poorer classes. They went along with appeasement of the trade unions in the hope of obtaining industrial peace.

But the concept of *Our Age* could not encompass the foot-soldiers of my generation—the staff in colleges of education, school-teachers, the National Council of Labour Colleges, and the Workers Educational Association. Many of them contributed to the discourse of the times in articles in magazines and less well-known academic publications.

There was, I think, one group among our age to whom I did not do justice. Frank Kermode thought I made a knee-jerk reaction whenever they were mentioned. They were the Progressives. Progressives are not the analogs of American liberals though they have something in common with them. In a previous generation Bernard Shaw and H.G. Wells were notable progressives, as was the popular philosopher of wartime brains-trust fame, C. E. M. Joad. Progressives are by nature suspicious of government. They deplore its insensitivity, its inadequacy, its cowardice. Progressives champion causes: nuclear disarmament, feminism, racial equality, causes designed to protect the environment and so on. In the days before the war they were the natural readers of the *New Statesman* and today of the two daily newspapers the *Guardian* and the *Independent*. Turgenev knew them well:

> Marianna belonged to a special class of unhappy persons . . . Justice satisfies them but does not rejoice them, while injustice, which they are terribly keen in detecting, revolts them to the very depths of their being.

Some are hard-working lobbyists, others the leaders of demos and protests. Progressives often hold views which appear to be contradictory—like Dickens, who castigated government for doing nothing to mitigate terrible social evils yet pilloried the civil servants and reformers, the charitable ladies and church-going moralists who believed they knew how to mend matters.

And yet, the sense of injustice in the world and the determination to awaken one's contemporaries to it is often noble. Who can forget the passage in *Bleak House* where Alan gets the dying boy Jo, the crossing-sweeper, to recite the Lord's Prayer as he dies? David Cecil used to say that it is a passage reeking with sentimentality, but it is moving, because Dickens is so enraged that any child like Jo should have lived and died in such misery that he bursts out,

> Dead your Majesty. Dead my Lords and gentlemen. Dead right
> Reverends and wrong Reverends of every order. Dead, men and
> women, born with heavenly compassion in your hearts. And dy-
> ing thus around us every day.

Inevitably, some progressives become convinced that there is an
explanation why government is so indolent, complacent and disinclined to rid society of its ills. Is it not that the state needs to be
transformed? Certainly that was the answer many of my contemporaries felt on finding the explanation in Marxism. Later when they
were older and the Soviet Union had been discredited, they still
retained their faith in Marxism and formed splinter groups to the
left of the Labour Party. They were astonished to be outflanked by
the young of the Sixties and their ideal of participatory democracy
in which meetings were called at any hour of day or night and were
never concluded.

Among these students of the sixties was my most merciless critic,
who asked why I was so ready to air-brush the fellow-travelers of the
Axis powers when I had been so hostile to the Communists and
fellow-travelers of my generation. Why later did I virtually ignore
the Vietnam War, totally ignore Rhodesia and apartheid in South
Africa, and make no analysis of Northern Ireland and its divided
population? Why did I not explore my generation's reaction to immigration from the Caribbean and the Indian subcontinent? Future generations may well judge the emergence of sizable brown
and black communities to be the most distinctive change in Britain
in the second half of the twentieth century. Why did I not admit
that time and again the commissions and committees that my contemporaries set up to sort out, for instance the problems of Northern Ireland and Rhodesia, were futile? Why did I not denounce the
betrayal by Wilson of the Seaman's Union strike? Why did I praise
the clichés of my generation, which assimilated with the establishment and said hardly a word of praise for those who rejected the
despicable compromises of government between 1950 and 1980?

The critic was the brilliant journalist Christopher Hitchens who,
as you know, now lives in America. He delights me by his command
of the vernacular. He is an exponent of the New Left that rejected
Soviet Union communism no less than capitalism and denounced
all forms of compromise with either system. To Hitchens and many
like him, it was self-evident that American generals and admirals
were itching to nuke the Soviet Union, and that the CIA was working to destabilize any government of the left and support the vilest
of dictatorships if they judged it was in the interests of America.
This theory of politics assumed that, even where government appeared to be innocent of wrongdoing, such actions were probably

part of a cover-plan to disguise a conspiracy to commit yet greater evil. Secret intelligence services such as the CIA or SIS were agents of the devil, and the Official Secrets Act in Britain should be flouted or evaded since the aim of politics should be to operate open government. Above all, never compromise. Whatever the cost, whatever the excuses politicians offer for dubious actions, stick to the principle of comforting the afflicted and afflicting the comfortable.

This is a well-known vision of politics, although, as I shall finish by saying, it ignores in my view the nature of politics itself. It was practiced in London by Ken Livingstone, the last leader of the Greater London Council until Margaret Thatcher abolished it. For instance Livingstone used the money designated for the arts, not to support opera and high art, but to finance street theatre groups, gay and lesbian clubs and a raft of other activities that made life less dreary and hopeless for the black communities of south London. It was less successfully practiced in Liverpool. There Derek Hatton, a member of the extreme left splinter group Militant Tendency, captured control of the City Council, as Livingstone had done by the usual methods of infiltration and disruption. True to the radical ideology, he spent the city revenues on projects he considered essential until Liverpool was on the verge of bankruptcy. His rule ended when he was forced for lack of funds to send out a fleet of taxis to deliver letters firing a large number of the council's employees. Certainly this was a dramatic way of breaking the news to those who were fired though not perhaps the most economical. Hitchens is the Derek Hatton of political commentators.

But he scored several points. Vietnam plagued my generation. Ever since the humiliation of Suez, British governments had been determined to march with America on foreign policy. Macmillan had been willing to alienate de Gaulle when he did his deal with President Kennedy to preserve Britain's independent nuclear deterrent. As a result de Gaulle vetoed Britain's entry to the European Community. Moreover, Britain had not forgotten that she was a client state of America. And when the Labour government was in the end forced to devalue and looked to America to support the pound, Harold Wilson considered he was bound to lick President Johnson's boots—though he refused to send troops to Vietnam. Vietnam opened the rift between left and right in the Labour Party. The Foreign Secretary, Michael Stewart, became a much hated figure, and we in the universities soon learned that Vietnam was the perfect issue for student radicals in those days of student unrest—not that our students, like yours, stood in danger of the draft. But there was one good reason why I glided over Vietnam. There was nothing that

Britain could have done to stop that war—a fact that Hitchens ignores.

But was there not something Britain could have done to force the issue of African rule in Rhodesia, or to end apartheid in South Africa? The Left demanded that British troops should be sent to cow the white minority into surrender. Anyone with military experience would doubt whether a British expeditionary force would have fared well against a white Rhodesian Army with an open frontier to South Africa.

Consider what happened when British troops were despatched to Northern Ireland to defend the Catholic minority against the Ulster loyalists. Within a few weeks British troops were defending themselves against the IRA and the Catholic population they had come to protect.

Terrorism in the form of guerrilla warfare was something that defeated my generation. What do you do when an organization, which has no difficulty in laying hands on Semtex, small arms and mortars, what do you do when they refuse to negotiate on any terms other than total surrender to their wishes? It could be argued—indeed was argued by myself in the House of Lords in 1971—that the British should give Ulster total independence and remove not only the Army but the Queen's sovereignty and all the benefits of the welfare state. What would happen? We would see ethnic cleansing on a Serbian scale by the Protestant majority, which would provoke Dublin to intervene. Dublin would probably implore the United States to mediate. But if anyone thinks a United Ireland under some guarantees to the Protestant minority would be acceptable to them, he or she is under an illusion. The loyalist thugs would simply take the place of the IRA and Britain would be pilloried for running away from a problem that is inescapably hers.

One of the errors of my generation, it may be said, was to believe that consensus can always be bought without coercion. I myself believe that coercion can and should be brought against the Orange Order and the loyalist paramilitaries. Yet you cannot get agreement in Britain to do anything which will give victory to the IRA.

Certainly, I was wrong not to consider immigration. Allowing for the fact that America finds difficulty in controlling illegal immigrants across the Mexican border, I have always thought that your policies were coherent. In Britain my generation did not have a policy at all. At first we simply accepted anyone from the former British Empire and then anyone who could claim kinship with them. Our successors do not seem to me to be doing much better, particularly since they are allowing only a fraction of Hong Kong citizens to claim British citizenship and ignoring the benefit America is getting from such people. Nevertheless, Europe faces a more severe problem than America. All states are besieged by thousands seeking asylum from regimes that torture and imprison any dissident and hundreds of thousands more who believe correctly that life in a European state with a welfare system will be paradise, however low down they are in the social scale, compared to the poverty they face in their own country.

The central theme of my book was that my generation had nothing to be ashamed of concerning their contribution to scholarship and science—the list of Nobel prizes alone was the glory of a golden age in the universities. Our contribution to the arts may have been more problematical but not despicable. Yet in the management of our political affairs, whether at home or abroad, we failed; and I thought we would be judged harshly by future generations. I still believe that this emphasis on decline was right. The seventeenth century is marked by the decline of Spain, the eighteenth by the decline of the Austrian Hungarian Empire, the nineteenth by the decline of France and the twentieth by the decline of Britain. Both Acheson and David Bruce, stout anglophiles, regarded the upper-class Tory rulers as inadequate as the middle-class-managers and trade-union labour leaders were. What part, I asked, did my contemporaries play in the decline? And how do they compare—the comparison is suggestive—with American statesmen of the post-war years—with Stimson, Marshall, Kennan, Acheson, Harriman, Rusk, Bohlen, McCloy and Bruce? Why was America blessed with such an incomparable wealth of talent? They were not self-seekers but devoted to furthering their country's cause. Yet they also concerned themselves with civilization. To them Europe owes an unpayable debt.

My critics pressed a graver charge. How could I be so ignorant, as a historian, to ignore the verities of Braudel and the French Annales school, and not admit that the impersonal forces of history were responsible for our decline? I wince. The criticism has force. Paul Addison hinted that the permissive society owes less to Roy Jenkins than to market forces—the prosperity that created a teenage spending public. It is true that I spent some pages analyzing what economic historians had said about the decline of the British economy; and I added that one of the reasons was the absurd attempt by British governments that continue to this day to buy ultra-modern armaments and play the role of a Great Power. But in my defense I plead that to have gone back to the 1880s and covered the ground that Eric Hobsbawm has done, marshaling all the forces, the movements of capital and goods that affected the British economy, would have added another 100 pages to the book. No doubt some would argue better do that and delete the material on the sexual revolution. But in this book I was interested in what men and women actually do rather than in the forces that limit their choices. I was not writing a history of post-war Britain—quite a number have already been written. My book was a sketch of what a generation of intellectuals and politicians had thought and done.

What topics would I now include if I were writing *Our Age* today? The monarchy is one. A Conservative, my friend John Grigg, as a young man inherited a peerage, but he disclaimed it as soon as he legally could. He became plain Mr. John Grigg. He had already outraged public opinion by an article he wrote in the 1950s criticizing the Queen's tone of voice, and the courtiers who surrounded her in Buckingham Palace, not one of whom was brown or black. Then, there was the socialist Michael Young who wrote an article with Edward Shils predicting that the Royal Family was fast becoming a soap-opera family, enabling the elderly to identify with the Queen Mother and so on. John Osborne called the Royal Family "the gold-filling in a mouth of decay." But my generation thought it a waste of time to debate the future of the monarchy. It was too popular.

Today there is brisk discussion about its future. Who wants to identify with a family three of whose children have made unsuccessful marriages and divorced? Indeed the gossip is that the monarch herself is calling for a change. The gossips declare that the Queen has raised several issues on which she wants to be advised. For instance, if the eldest child of a sovereign is a girl, should she not automatically succeed? Discount this gossip. The Queen will not be raising the issue as to whether a Roman Catholic should be debarred from becoming sovereign. That is a matter on which she would wait for her Prime Minister to raise. But the finances of the Royal Family may well be raised. When a few years ago a fire burnt down part of Windsor Castle and the Minister was asked on television who would pay for the rebuilding, he replied that the state would pay; unlike Sandringham or Balmoral, Windsor Castle is not a private residence but belongs to the State. There was an outcry in the press. As a result the Queen accepted that she would pay for the damage, opened Buckingham Palace to tourists, and later agreed to pay tax on her private income. The Royal Yacht was finally declared obsolete and Conservative back-benchers urged it should be replaced. It is said that when the Minister told the Queen of this proposal she asked, "Who pays?" "Oh the State will pay, Ma'am." "I see," came the reply. "You pay. I get the blame."

Recently, Channel 4 on British TV held a "Deliberative Poll" of 261 people on the monarchy. It was conducted by Professor James Fishkin of this university and two British colleagues. The panel were asked their views on a number of questions before they met. They then discussed these questions over a week-end and were polled for the second time. This time round the number of those who favored abolition did not change appreciably. It remained steady at only nine to ten percent. After the debate 20 percent *more*, i.e. 68 percent, wanted *more* not less public funds to be spent on the monarchy. There was a shift from 55 to 68 percent among those who wanted the monarch to resign if he "could not win popular support." Just over half after the discussion wanted a referendum held on the issue and just over a half wanted the public to have a say on which member of the Royal Family should be the next King or Queen. Yet the debate increased support for the view that the monarch united the country.

Did anyone during the discussion point out that the election of a monarch is a contradiction in terms? If you want to *elect* a Head of State, you elect a President who holds office for a term of years. The whole point of a monarchy is that the head succeeds to the headship automatically by virtue of an ancient Act of Parliament. The nation is not formally divided, whatever individuals may think. Nor does this contradict the findings of the panel who thought that a monarch who lost support should abdicate. That is what happened to Edward VIII—but the loss of support was formalized through Parliament.

If anything can bring down the monarchy, it is the press. Within a few years the press will be moralizing or chortling over every adolescent mishap or misdeed of Prince William and Prince Harry. Horrifying as the question will appear to Americans with virtually limitless free speech built into the Constitution, how long can a monarchy sustain the invasion of privacy that the Royals suffer daily? The office of President remained unscarred when Nixon resigned. Presidents come and go. But the monarchy and the heirs apparent and presumptive depend upon the unspoken mystique that Bagehot alluded to.

Between the wars France had a press that poisoned national morale. After the war a law of privacy was passed to prevent the private lives of public figures being traduced—some would say that is far too protective. But in Britain any minister or member of Parliament who is exposed as an adulterer is forced to resign. The Prime Minister, John Major, called for "a return to basics" first as one minister was caught in bed with an adventuress, another was pilloried for having two illegitimate children, another was accused of having five mistresses, another's wife committed suicide and another was shown to have shared a bed with a man—though if you looked at him you could be sure he was totally innocent. At each resignation the tabloids chortled and gloried in their power to force the resignations of ministers. As President Mitterrand said, if that were so in France he would be left with a Cabinet of homosexuals.

Another topic on which today I have to enlarge is Thatcherism.

Shares in Thatcherism after a shaky start in 1980 dived in the recession of 1981. But bears who had sold short were caught by the success of the Falklands War, when shares went through the roof. They firmed in the mid-Eighties and remained buoyant until the end of the decade, particularly after the managing director showed such courage and resolution when the IRA narrowly failed to kill her by exploding a bomb in her hotel in Brighton during the Conservative Party conference. Then suddenly the bull market burst and she lost, first her Chancellor of the Exchequer, and then the Deputy Prime Minister. She was compelled to resign. But she remained an unofficial President of the corporation and so plagued her successor that today the corporation looks as if it might downsize and split over the issue of Britain's role in the European Union.

What else did she achieve? The answer is so paradoxical as to be incredible. She reformed the Labour Party so that it could again challenge the Conservatives on equal terms. With an unerring penchant for error, that incorrigible progressive of my generation, Michael Foot, chose Kinnock a kindly, young, Welsh windbag, to succeed him as leader because he reminded him of his hero Aneurin Bevan. Kinnock was unelectable but he hoed the grass roots of the Labour Party in order to destroy the weeds of militant Marxists whom Foot had allowed to infiltrate. Blair has gone further and cut down the power of the trade unions within the Labour movement besides overthrowing all the old dogmas of the past such as nationalization. In other words, he has done what Thatcher did on a national scale. He has cut back trade-union power—her greatest achievement in my opinion.

Did she turn the country round? The jury is still out on that issue. At the time when she fell from power Britain had moved into recession, and unemployment and interest rates rose; inflation was higher in 1990 than in 1987. Some observers say that Britain still lacks the will and the infrastructure to perform well in the new world market where the East Asian offensive gets more critical every year. Britain, they say, lacks social discipline, will not spend sufficiently on research and development, lacks entrepreneurial aggression and does not coordinate the power of the state with private investment. But other observers argue that today inflation continues to fall, unemployment is the lowest among the major European states, and the economy is in relatively good shape even on balance of payments. The Conservative government continued to privatize as many state-owned enterprises as possible from water, electricity and gas concerns to the railways and even the agency which selects candidates for the Civil Service.

I should have to add today that the division of opinion about the European Union has deepened. The Labour Party stays quiet about the issue and would probably at once sign the clauses in the Maastricht treaty about social benefits. Yet, what will it do if it wins the general election next year? Britain is one of the net contributors to the Union. It is in the interests of the Mediterranean countries to force an increase in those contributions. So, Britain has few natural allies to withstand what the Franco-German Axis decides. The Axis can always count on Benelux support. Britain is still resentful of the way the Brussels bureaucracy works. The British cherish the ability to challenge and overturn the decisions of Whitehall and local government. They have also, as I said, been cutting the size of the bureaucracy by privatization. By contrast the French bureaucracy, on which Brussels is modeled, is all-powerful, and it is enormous.

Someone may well comment that one of the most sinister developments under Margaret Thatcher was the drive towards centralization, the drive to emasculate local government and to politicize the Civil Service. Margaret Thatcher was determined to make civil servants cost-conscious and to force them to introduce modern management techniques. Civil servants who could respond to this demand were promoted: numbers of others were sidelined. She used her Press Secretary in an outrageous manner. Although he was a civil servant, he was employed to leak and undermine any Minister or individual who opposed her will. In revenge, civil servants themselves began to leak sensitive documents.

My generation used to boast that it had perfected a device called in short the quango, or quasi non-governmental organization. The one you will know well was the University Grants Committee. Quangos were composed of people rightly mocked as the Great and the Good. There would be among them a trade unionist, someone who could speak for Scotland, someone for Wales, representatives of interested parties and some neutrals, dons, lawyers and businessmen presumed to be dispassionate under a neutral chairman. Margaret Thatcher packed such quangos with her own personal appointees. No more Royal Commissions or Committees of Inquiry. No neutral, let alone liberal, chairman was ever appointed.

But this ruthlessness has evoked a response—from the British judiciary. When the government is believed to have exceeded its powers, it can be challenged by calling for a judicial review of the government's decision. In 1976 there were 500 applications for judicial review. In 1993 there were 3,000 applications and 236 were allowed to proceed. The Conservative Home Secretary was slapped down five times within a year by the judges. After the rules of the courts were changed in 1976 the judges were left to develop the substance of the law without Parliamentary admonition or control. As all people do when a new power is put in their hands, the judges used it at once. And since both political parties fear the press and will not bring in a bill to ensure privacy for the individual, it may well be that this will be the next area where judicial review may operate.

Of course every civilized country has a substantial system of control of administrative acts and over the executive. In France, which has a highly developed system, it is to some extent muffled by the fact that judges are appointed by the Minister of Justice. French judges are much more a part of that tight-knit bureaucracy which is dominated by the products of the Polytechnique, Science Po, and ENA. In Britain, more people want a written constitution and therefore inevitably a body resembling the Supreme Court of the United States. Indeed, this may come in the form of two Supreme Courts of the European Union and the European Court of Civil Rights. But if Britain does not yet have a rigid division of powers, it has a balance of powers; and judicial review is something which the judges of the generation succeeding mine have exploited.

Only now are the nations of the European Union beginning to face the problem of sustaining expensive welfare systems with an ageing population and a longer expectation of life. How can they sustain the cost of pensions, housing, and child benefits, compensation for the handicapped, and a hundred other special provisions? Medical costs under National Health schemes grow ever more expensive as people live longer and medical science progresses. Yet at the same time political parties grow more terrified of raising taxes.

Many people believed that defense costs would fall after the death of the Soviet Union. But they keep on escalating as the demand for peace-keeping forces grows. Not only peace-keeping. As in America, the British military-industrial complex prevents numbers of swords being beaten into ploughshares. Britain's balance of payments is sustained by the sale of armaments abroad.

My generation still agonizes over the future of the welfare state. We accepted that every citizen ought to have the vote, be able to get justice in the courts, get a decent job, get free medical treatment and not suffer want in old age. To lack these offends against justice. Worse still it humiliates the poor. Many of us still fear that a market-led economy, and the lifting of state controls, will do nothing to alleviate the lot of the under-class in our cities, the resentful unemployed.

When I wrote, the movement for devolution had receded. To-day, the tide is coming in fast. Scotland returns only a handful of Conservative MPs (there are far more Scottish MPs, I should add, than the population of Scotland warrants); the Labour Party does not want to be outflanked by the Scottish Nationalist Party (who want to dissolve the union). So Labour is proposing—if elected—to set up a Scottish Parliament. If it is to have any meaning it will have to be given limited powers to impose taxes or raise money. If that occurs there will be demands by Wales and perhaps by English regions to do the same. Local government, many of its powers broken by Thatcherism, may revive. I say nothing of long-overdue plans by Labour to reform the House of Lords. But once that is on the agenda, not only the composition but the powers of the second chamber will come into question.

Let me end by quoting my most satirical critic. He was a historian of ideas at Cambridge, Stefan Collini. Collini declared that my book had been written by two people. There was the lively iconoclast of the 1940s and 1950s Noel Annan, on the one hand, and on the other the inevitable chairman Lord Annan who had sold out to the Establishment and betrayed the life of the mind—a man who had lost touch, as he put it, with—

> that constitutive experience of the intellectual life, the sustained, disciplined, effortful attempt to get beneath the surface appearance of things, to challenge the terms of the agenda. The combination of complacency and tendentiousness evident in the closing pages of *Our Age* suggested that the chairman's summing-up at a meeting had gone on too long.

I agree that the life of committees and administration takes the edge off the intellect and makes one less able to see through the platitudes of discourse. Old age takes its toll as well. But only a few months ago I found a parallel to the two Annans which put new heart in me. Last year, Quentin Bell wrote a book of reminiscences about those he called his elders and betters, in Bloomsbury, and he used the same trope as Collini to account for the shock that he and old Bloomsbury felt when in 1938 Keynes read to them his memoir *My Early Beliefs*. In it, Keynes analyzed what as a young man he had believed to be true. He praised G. E. Moore's religion as a very good religion to grow up under "and it is still my religion under the surface." But, he said, he and his Bloomsbury friends forgot the importance of what he called "the elaborate framework of society"—i.e. the social controls and traditions that bind human beings together. They also dismissed the reverence that one should show towards the past and towards institutions. Finally they neglected the irrationality of nations and the dark forces that possessed people and released them from the constraints of decent behavior.

Quentin Bell admitted there were signs of the young Keynes when he said, "I remain and always will remain an immoralist." But it was an elderly Keynes, later to be Lord Keynes, the Squire of Tilton who spoke of reverence and dark forces. Reverence for a church and state that falsified evidence to prove Dreyfus's guilt? Respect for "an elaborate framework" that sent homosexuals to prison? And what did he mean by saying that "some spontaneous outbursts of human nature can have a sort of value"? Hitler's outbursts? Bell remembered slinking out of the Memoir Club that evening convinced that Keynes had become a reactionary—and he held that view to his dying day.

Like Keynes I still believe in the principles that inspired me when I was young. I still wish to diminish divisions between the social classes and diminish unemployment even if the policies of my generation adopted to do so are obsolete. I still think the reforms of the Sixties in personal morality were sound and that respect for the arts and life of the mind is the best of all creeds.

But to this I add a corollary. At the end of the first chapter in my book, I recorded how I formed the opinion as an undergraduate that Machiavelli was right, to the despair of my tutor, a liberal and a pacifist. Not the Machiavelli of *The Prince* but the Machiavelli of *The Discourses on the First Ten Books of Titus Livy*. In that book, he argued that there was a conflict between on the one hand the life of personal relations and the life of the mind; and on the other the life of politics, of getting and gaining, and of using power to attain civil ends. Only a few people, he said, want to go into politics. The vast majority want security to live as they please within the laws. He once added that his own plan of life was to spend the hours of the day in talking to people at their work; in the evening he would put on fine clothes and read noble books.

Machiavelli was no advocate of participatory democracy. Nor was he a theorist of citizenship. Statesmanship was his subject and he painted an alarming picture of what you have to face if you choose the life of politics. Politics is a noble calling, but it is not morally attractive because a prince has to face the fact that the minority who also want to go in for politics are his political enemies even when some of them are his allies. Politics is often a choice between evils. A statesman has to pursue virtue, he has to be flexible, be ready to pursue any course including assassination and massacres. *Oderint dum metuant*—let them hate so long as they fear. It sounds like a justification of Stalin. But not quite. Machiavelli distinguished between tyrants. He praised Cesare Borgia but Agathocles was beyond the pale. The line between a successful ruler and an odious tyrant is so fine that it defies precise analysis. The British philosopher, Bernard Williams, attempted to draw it when he said "only those who are reluctant or disinclined to do the morally disagreeable when it is really necessary have much chance of not doing it when it is not necessary."

My book was about my generation and each generation has to learn the bitter truth that its end has come and another is taking its place. No one put this more poignantly than Homer in the Iliad when the Trojan Glaucus meets Diomede the Greek on the plains of Troy. Diomede asks, "What is your name?" Glaucus replies:

> Great son of Tydeus, why do you ask who I am? As the generation leaves, so is the generation of men. The wind scatters the leaves on the earth but the living wood brings other leaves to bud as the season of spring comes round. So one generation of men springs to birth, and another passes away.

My generation is passing away. Our leaves are falling one by one. Perhaps the greatest benefit I got was good teaching and being treated by my teachers as their equal, though not quite as far along the road of life. I owe everything to my teachers. They made me want to learn, and if I got above myself, they told me how much more I had to learn. Not just about books but about how to live. *Sit anima mea cum magistris meis.* Blessed be those who taught me to think more clearly, to feel more deeply, to hope, and to put my trust in life.

Fall Semester 1996

# 17

# The Rise and Fall of Party Government in Britain and the United States, 1945–1996

## SAMUEL H. BEER

I n the early postwar years, when I first took up the study of British politics, many Americans—including politicians as well as professors—looked to Britain as the exemplar of how democracy could cope with the problems of modern capitalism. From the end of the war until the late 1960s, the Westminster model compiled a record of solid social, economic, and political success. Building on prewar foundations, successive governments created a welfare state and a managed economy that provided proximate solutions to some of the worst problems of industrial society. Although marred by miscalculation and misfortune, the overall economic record was, in the words of Professor James E. Meade, "an outstanding success story for a quarter of a century."[1]

The political success was that this radical program of the Attlee Government, although initially enacted by a partisan majority, was to a great extent accepted by the Opposition, signifying that it had won the general assent of the British nation. Majoritarianism had been converted into consensus.

In admiring American eyes, the key to this political success was party government: that is, a stable, competitive two-party system based on mass party memberships that, by providing governments with cohesive legislative majorities supporting distinctive programs, gave voters an effective choice. In this system, the prime minister and his cabinet enjoyed that combination of executive and legislative power that had been passed on to them from the old monarchy as it gave way to popular government. Thanks to this constitutional fusion of powers, the British legislature could decide who governs, though it could not itself govern, since, if it turned out one monopolist of executive and legislative power, the only option was to put in another. Policy would presumably be changed but the ministerial monopoly of power would not. Quite a few American reformers did propose the adoption of some features of Britain's constitutional system, such as allowing heads of departments to be members of Congress, or giving the President the power of dissolution. Most advocates of party government in the United States, however, thought that changes in party organization, requiring no constitutional amendment, could sufficiently bridge the separation of power established by the Constitution to approximate the British fusion.

In 1950 in a celebrated report, entitled *Toward a More Responsible Two Party System* and sponsored by the American Political Science Association, a committee of eminent authorities showed how such a concentration of political power could be achieved by reforms of party organization in the legislature and in the country.[2] Among political scientists and generally among people who took a professional interest in the study of American politics, this idea of a more responsible party system was soon widely accepted.

This American attraction to party government had a considerable history going back at least to Woodrow Wilson's *Congressional Government* in 1885. Inspired by contrast with the glowing portrait of the British system in Walter Bagehot's *English Constitution* (1867), Wilson gave a depressing report of the disorderly regime of a weak Presidency and a fragmented Congress, which he saw in the years after the Civil War. In the 1940s, the same logic informed the impassioned pleas of the leading advocate of party government and the principal author of the APSA Report of 1950, Prof. E. E. Schattschneider of Wesleyan University. Starting from his study of the self-destructive political process that brought the Smoot-Hawley Tariff into existence in 1930, Schattschneider enlarged his analysis to demonstrate the need for more orderly and responsible government, which emerged from the growing interventionism in the years of the Great Depression.[3]

The history that gave urgency to the topic in the 1940s spoke to these weightier concerns. As the Great Depression devastated the capitalist economies of the Western world, their governments often found themselves distracted to the point of paralysis by the chaos of conflicting interests and pressures. Their consequent inability to muster the central power to control events weakened their hold on their citizenry and heightened the appeal of dictatorship. The most compelling illustration was the bitter group conflict in German politics which opened the way for the fall of the Weimar Republic and Hitler's surge to power.

This wider relevance gave rise to the topic of "stable democracy," a bland denomination for a deep affliction of modern politics. The 1950 report was fully aware of this context, as one can see from its sober concluding passages. They echoed the ancient wisdom of the West, from Plato to St. Thomas Aquinas to Machiavelli and Montesqieu, warning against the self-destructive pluralism of popular government. In my generation's quest for "the secrets of stable democracy," students of politics looked to Britain.[4]

Understanding the British phenomenon, however, required more than a study of organizational design and constitutional principle. Underlying these was the "civic culture." This term comes from the title of that magisterial work by Almond and Verba published in 1963, in which they sought by comparative analysis to get at the basic attitudes and values that best support a regime of both governmental order and democratic responsiveness.[5] Britain and the United States led the field, but Britain clearly had the edge, thanks to its unique integration of traditional and modern values, which provided the cultural foundation for what the book called its "strong and effective government" and "efficient and independent administration."

On the one hand, there was Toryism, a tradition which still managed to show recognizable traces of the social and political deference and the *noblesse oblige* dating from the premodern sense of hierarchy. On the other hand, there was the solidarity among Socialists which also drew on the values of an older organic community. In both Tory and Socialist conceptions, class, that premodern graft onto modern capitalism, was an essential force for integration, for the Tory acting vertically and for the Socialist acting horizontally. A third tradition, weaker than the other two and entertained by Britain's center party, the Liberals, embraced the values of radical democracy, more egalitarian than the Tory and more individualist than the Socialist. As all readers of Louis Hartz will know, American politics is dominated by this liberal tradition to the virtual exclusion of Toryism and Socialism.[6]

In Britain itself, as the 1960s dawned, the mood was euphoric. In 1959, Macmillan won reelection on slogans that have not inaccurately been summarized as "You never had it so good!" and, at the same time, the cheerful data for the civic culture study were being gathered, showing British trust in their government and politics at a peak among nations. In these same years, the United States discovered its affluence, reported its high pride in its government and, despite the menace of the Cold War and the trauma of Kennedy's assassination, acclaimed the reforms of Johnson's Great Society. "For," as our foremost journalistic authority on the Presidency, Theodore White, proclaimed in 1965, "Americans live today on the threshold of the greatest hope in the whole history of the human race . . ."[7] Was it only incidental that, as one political scientist revealed, during the period 1948–1964, the voting of Democrats in Congress—setting aside the Southern dissidents—had moved "quite closely to the model of responsible party government"?[8]

In both countries, this happy continuum was disrupted by a series of government failures, which began in the 1960s and stretched on into the following decades. Their essence was a loss of control: a loss of control by governments over the economy, displayed in soaring inflation, and a loss of control of governments over themselves, displayed in an explosion of public spending. Nor were these afflictions confined to Britain and America.

Students of the period, attempting to explain the collapse of control in Britain, often claim that the cause was at bottom economic, specifically the long-run decline in the British economy. But this view does not fit the facts. As Peter Jenkins, who favored this hypothesis, granted: how can one speak of economic decline when output is growing and standards of living are rising?[9] Although, in comparison with other countries, Britain was falling behind, in comparison with its own past, it was growing faster in the postwar years than ever before. As for its one-time economic leadership, we must recognize that Britain had never been a fast-growing economy; it simply got started on capitalism and industrialization before the rest of the world.

My explanation of the loss of control is more political, namely an upheaval in culture which transformed the political process and the character of the party system. This cultural revolution attacked authority and order in every sphere: in dress, music, manners, education, sex, marriage, work, religion, race relations, and perhaps most harshly in politics and government. It struck not only Britain and America, but raged through all Western nations. Nor was the Roman Catholic church spared: recall Vatican II and the rise of Liberation Theology. And similarly the secular church of Marxism lost its old discipline, succumbing to the romantic anarchism of student protest in American, British, and other Western universities.

Moreover, the sentiments of alienation generated in the 1960s have persisted, being expressed today in a pervasive distrust of and cynical dissatisfaction with government. Opinion surveys continually and abundantly confirm that finding for both countries. They show that in the United States trust in government has fallen steadily, with only brief recoveries under President Reagan and during the Gulf War. In Britain likewise, the decline of the civic culture has continued steadily. From the high level of the 1959 data, which reported that 83 percent of respondents said that they expected to get equal treatment in dealings with government officials, trust in government had fallen off sharply by the early 1970s, well before the economic deprivations of the decade had set in. By 1993, a Gallup Poll could find that 90 percent of respondents believed that politicians could not be trusted.[10]

It helps to understand the causes and effects of this upheaval in political culture to look at it as another stage in modernization. Its rationale was "the will to equality" which Nietzsche identified as the very root of modernity. Constituting a major force guiding the development of the modern state, this value has been embodied in a politics of inclusion that extended the various rights of citizenship, legal, political, and social, to ever wider circles of the polity. This egalitarian norm has also had a sharply negative thrust towards dissolving the old bonds of subjection and obligation. The resulting erosion of community has haunted Western thought since the eighteenth century.

In the United States and Britain during the 1960s and 1970s, this pressure for equalization was expressed in a demand for greater participation, such that "participatory democracy" became a catch word in agitation and a principle of reform. It was also expressed in a demand for greater equalization in policy outcomes, often taking the form of a claim on new legal rights and new government benefits.

Given the relative absence of feudal and communal targets in this country, the effect on Americans was less radical. Since we had long since experienced Jacksonian democracy, the renewed assertion of participatory values was simply more of the same. But it did make a difference as forms of direct democracy were imposed on established structures of representative democracy. The most significant change was the disintegration of the process of Presidential nomination. In my recollection, it is also the most vivid, since I attended and took part in nearly all Democratic conventions from the 1950s to the 1970s.

One measure of the change was the substitution in many states of the direct primary for the caucus-convention system in the choice of the delegates to the nominating convention. The important fact, however, was not the change in formal organization, but the use made of the structure, whether based on primary or on caucus. Judging by my experience in Massachusetts, even if a state had a primary system, as Massachusetts did, the active partisan became a delegate thanks to the influence of a party leader who put him on an official slate, which would then be elected in a modest turnout of registered party members.

The changing function of the convention began to show as early as the 1960 meeting, when Kennedy's use of television and primaries pretty well clinched the nomination before the delegates assembled in Los Angeles. But the turning point was the tumultuous meeting in Chicago in 1968. That was the last occasion when party leaders did make the choice. Thereafter in each party the convention became a body that ratified the outcome of an intense and vastly expensive competition in the state-by-state contests and otherwise served as a public relations event to launch the nominee's election campaign.

As experience with the direct primary in other elections to legislative and executive office had shown, the rapidly expanding mass participation in the nominating process tended to shift the focus of the general election toward the candidate and away from the party. Organized interest groups gained increasing leverage as aspirants pieced together support in the intraparty contest.

The party bond was further weakened and the power of groups increased by reforms in delegate selection introduced by the McGovern-Fraser Commission of 1969–1972, of which I happen to have been a member. In an attempt to offset the very real discrimination against blacks, especially in the South, the Commission mandated reforms in delegate selection that were couched in such broad formulations that other groups could call on them to legitimate their demands for similar advantages.[11] As a result, in many contests quotas were recognized, in effect extending proportional representation to women, homosexuals, young people and in due course various ethnic groups.

At the same time, there was a falling off of partisanship among voters and legislators. The proportion of voters identifying with a party, especially the strong identifiers, declined and the proportion of self-declared independents rose. Ticket splitting increased as more and more voters broke from their habit of supporting the candidates of the same party for President and Congress.[12] The long period of unified government, whether Republican or Democratic, came to an end, and American politics reverted to an earlier pattern of divided government with the Presidency going to one party, usually the Republicans, while Congress went to the other, usually the Democrats. The outcome of these shifts toward a candidate-centered, group-empowered, unpartisan politics was to weaken the President as a party leader and to cause him to rely more on his constitutional powers and his personal political skills. The promise of party government was giving way to the strong bias of the American system toward Presidential leadership.


The pluralism of American politics was enhanced not only by the decline of parties, but also by the rise of a new group politics, which, ironically, had been brought into existence thanks in no small degree to party government.

Pressure groups are active in all democratic polities. The programs of the New Deal had been a response to the grievances of farmers, workers, homeowners, bankers, depositors, businessmen, and other groups suffering from the effects of the depression. In the governmental response to those grievances, spending was important. It was regarded as an emergency measure, however, and in fact as prosperity returned, it did taper off, except in some programs such as social security. The other great permanent programs of New Deal liberalism depended less on spending and more on the exercise of the regulatory powers of the federal government, especially the commerce power.

The civil-rights reforms of the Great Society widened still further the politics of inclusion of the New Deal. Moreover, the legal rights established by these measures, primarily intended to remedy discrimination against blacks, were also claimed by other groups suffering similar disabilities. Often related to the same groups, the main Great Society programs, however, originating from government, not the private sector, and involving massive public expenditure, gave a new meaning to liberalism.[13]

Brought into existence during a period of marked party vitality among the Democrats, the new group politics led the way in an enormous expansion of the public sector. While spending was not the only medium of government action, it provided the handiest measure of this outcome of the new liberalism. In the decade 1954–1964, leaving out defense and looking only at domestic expenditure, the ratio of government expenditure at all levels, federal, state and local to national income, rose from 12.9 percent to 17.5 percent. In the decade 1964–1974, after the advent of the Great Society, that same ratio of expenditure to income reached 25.4 percent, almost twice the rate of increase per year. It was not Vietnam but the Great Society that inaugurated the sharp surge in public expenditure in the mid-sixties.

Reflecting the continuing power of the new group politics, the rising ratio of expenditure to income was not reversed by the conservative shift of opinion that ushered in the period of divided government in the 1970s and 1980s. Far from producing gridlock, this political change led to an even more incoherent process of "growth without purpose." While President Nixon sought to decentralize the burgeoning welfare state, he also encouraged more spending by both federal and state governments. In 1981 Ronald Reagan took office pledged to reduce big government, especially at the federal level. Instead, with no inconsiderable help from Democrats, he sent the deficit into orbit.

The government's loss of control of itself was reflected in its loss of control of the economy, as inflation, likewise dating from the late 1960s, soared.

Such profligacy was no doubt what one would expect from the easy-going, populistic Americans with their fragmented political and constitutional system. The surprise for admirers of the Westminster model was that Britain's centralized, top-down system produced the same results in its reaction to the collapse of the civic culture. Deprived of the guidance of that invisible hand, party government faltered and failed. As surveys of opinion and the darkening mood of political discourse show, the 1960s was the period when the attitudes supporting the old civic culture faded. This was also the hinge of time on which the door swung shut on the successful politics of the postwar era and opened on the self-defeating pluralism of the 1970s and later years.[14]

In Britain, the very success of party government contributed to its failure, as the pluralism engendered by the welfare state and the managed economy rose up and defeated the agent of their creation. In a sense, party government suffered from the weakness of its strength. Like parties in any democratic system, British parties bid against one another in their campaign promises. The distinction of the British system was that, thanks to the constitutional and organizational strength of a victorious party, it could actually deliver on its promises. So situated and motivated, the two evenly matched parties in their competition for the votes of the beneficiaries of the new social programs raised public expenditure to inflationary heights. At the same time, efforts to manage the economy failed, as groups of producers in business and labor frustrated government attempts to make them serve the ends of public policy. Strategies of coordination and control that had worked in the heyday of the civic culture failed in the context of the self-defeating pluralism of the new group politics.

Reflecting the culture change, class decomposition weakened the class-party tie which had sustained party government in its days of strength. From the late 1960s there was a two-way switching of party supporters. Skilled workers moved toward the Conservatives, while higher occupational groups suffered losses to Labour. This growing convergence in the social foundations of the parties coincided with a decline in strong party identification expressed in a pronounced fall in the aggregate two-party vote. Class decomposition therefore weakened governments by the decline in not only the solidarity, but also the relative size of their electoral support. The same processes of decline in class solidarity and party identification led to a huge decline in the mass memberships and the corresponding organizational strength of the two parties.

In Parliament, a similar break from the norms of party government appeared fairly suddenly in the late 1960s. Institutional recognition of the less deferential and more participant attitudes of backbenchers was embodied in a new system of select committees, dealing with special fields and exercising wide powers of review and criticism of policy, although still without authority in law-making.

In this weakened condition in the electorate and in Parliament, party government was confronted in Britain as in the United States by the rising strength of a new group politics. It had been party government itself which in its prime had brought forth this new pluralism. In this development, Labour like the Democrats in the United States had played the leading role. When it came to power in 1945, Labour was still, as it had been at its inception, a coalition of pressure groups. The members of these groups were, however, also a body of partisans who in their millions were united in varying degrees by faith in the Socialist commonwealth. This commitment gave momentum and direction to the furious whirl of legislation and reform generated by the Attlee government. By the time it left office in 1951, Labour had created a welfare state, a managed economy, and an extensive array of nationalized industries, which were socially, economically, and politically a remarkable success but which, however, flourished within what was still a distinctly capitalist order.

The failure of the old orthodoxies of nationalization and planning in the midst of this success caused a severe crisis in the early 1950s, especially among the intellectual elite of the party. The solution was a radical and rapid transformation of the meaning of socialism, set forth preeminently in the writing of Tony Crosland and exemplified politically in the leadership of Hugh Gaitskell.[15] In this new conception, the traditional socialist goal of equality of condition would be achieved not by the old methods, but by the redistributive spending of the welfare state and the corporatism of the managed economy in a capitalist system now admittedly moved by self-interest. Although much more radical than the ideas of the

Kennedy-Johnson liberals, the new methodology of government action brought the British much closer to the American left—also unintentionally inviting similar difficulties in the future.

Rejecting the egalitarianism of Labour for the paternalism of One Nation Toryism, the Conservatives, inspired by Rab Butler and led by Harold Macmillan, adopted, however, a similar methodology when making their contribution to the developing convergence on policy. As program and method converged, the party battle subsided into intense bidding for the support of interest groups. As in the United States, new programs created new lobbies. From the late 1950s a spectacular increase in the number of pressure groups accompanied an unprecedented surge in social spending, which contributed substantially to the price inflation that plagued the British economy for the next twenty years.

How far party government was failing, however, appeared only in the 1970s when Conservative and Labour party leaders successively sought to break with the consensus in order to impose a sharply partisan alternative, which would restore fiscal discipline and economic control. First Edward Heath's move toward a free market economy and then Harold Wilson's effort in the opposite direction toward more state control was defeated by the pressures of the new group politics, each Government being forced to execute a painful U-turn back to the consensus.

For the sake of more concrete illustration of this analysis, I will follow the fortunes of the Labour party. They had taken the initiative in the postwar reforms, and the failure of their attempts to cope with the problems of the sixties revealed the failure of the collectivist polity that they had fathered. The crux was the inability of the Wilson government to persuade the trade unions to accept a wage policy in 1968. The immediate background of that crucial nondecision was the spending explosion which Macmillan had ignited by his generous social policies and which Wilson more than matched, even though, contrary to his promise, no "white-hot technological revolution" had produced the growth in the economy necessary to finance the expenditure.

While, after some delay, Roy Jenkins's austerity at the Treasury did cope with the fiscal excesses, it did not reestablish control over the economy. Rather, it shifted the lack of control from the clamant consumer groups of the spending explosion to the resistant producer groups of the wage-price explosion. Specifically, if the fruits of Jenkins's regime were to be gathered, wage demands had to be moderated. For this purpose the Government offered the unions a fabulous deal. The government paper entitled *In Place of Strife* would have given the unions real power in making policy, if they had been willing in return to agree not to resist government sanctions against unofficial strikes. The unions refused—and thereby, as Tommy Balogh said in despair, "smashed the most hopeful social experiment of our time."[16] The ensuing wage scramble, which set off the wage-price explosion of the late 1960s, continued to foil government efforts to control inflation. The bogus social contracts of the 1970s arranged by Labour and the unions culminated in the winter of discontent of 1978–79, which put Thatcher in power.

Various conditions contributed to the failure of 1968. Most important was the maintenance of full employment by all governments, Conservative as well as Labour, which enormously strengthened the bargaining power of individual groups of workers and local leaders. Another contributing cause was the loose structure of British unions in contrast, say, with German or Swedish centralization. Yet these conditions were not new; they had prevailed for a quarter of a century, indeed, since the recovery brought on by war production.

The novel force was the new political situation, the increasing fragmentation of the Labour movement. The old sense of working-class identification was in sharp decline, eroding the class basis of the Labour party and weakening the solidarity of trade unions and their deference towards their leaders. What has been called the "new unionism" of the 1960s had sharpened interunion and interoccupational rivalry. The growing independence of local groups and the greater sectional competition among categories of workers fomented these "self-destructive bonanzas," to use Robert Taylor's apt characterization, of the unfettered wage bargaining in the following years.[17]

The long-run political effect of the inability of British Governments to negotiate an effective wages policy can hardly be exaggerated. For any fully employed economy, socialist or capitalist or in between, some such instrument of wage restraint is indispensable. Students of the problem had expected that trade unions under a favorable (i.e. Labour) government would be able to deliver this essential outcome. When such a government proved unable to do so, when union leaders found that they could not mobilize support among their members for wage restraint, neither in 1968 nor under the bogus social contracts agreed by later Labour Governments and the unions, the unions became useless to the Labour party and indeed a burden as partners of a party which aspired to become a Government.

In 1981, therefore, it made eminently good sense for the Gang of Four to secede from the Labour party, and as the Social

Democratic Party, to try to lead the British Left to a new posture, breaking with the unions and shedding socialism. Quite apart from other things, the failure of the unions had shown the impossibility of a democratic socialism in Britain. Such good sense did the SPD make that the Labour party itself, painfully instructed by repeated defeats, gradually came to the same conclusion under the leadership of Neil Kinnock, John Smith and above all Tony Blair.

The creation of the SPD, however, was premature. Speaking of their secession, Denis Healey has commented: "Its most important effect was to delay the Labour Party's recovery by 10 years and to guarantee Mrs. Thatcher two more terms in office."[18] For whatever reason, the prolonged unpopularity of Labour struck a deep and damaging blow to party government by removing that crucial balancing force of the two-party Westminster model, the credible Opposition. It thereby opened the way for a full-scale assault by Thatcher upon the postwar settlement.

The fate of the Heath Government of 1970–74 illustrates this function and power. Although as seen today in retrospect, Heath, in contrast with Thatcher, looks like a One-Nation Tory, he actually sought to follow a not dissimilar neo-conservative policy, explicitly rejecting the paternalistic interventionism of Butler-Macmillan Conservatism. To be sure, one reason for his U-turn was that at the time the miners were a far more formidable economic power than they were later on when Thatcher fought out her momentous battle with Arthur Scargill. The main cause, however, was political—the still vital presence of a very credible Opposition. With unemployment rising much higher than he had expected, Heath faced an Opposition that he had defeated by only the narrowest margin in 1970. In those circumstances, he felt obliged to switch to a policy of expansion, swinging back to the consensus. In Thatcher's time, by contrast, after Labour had been diminished by its internal split and its own leftward swing, she could carry on with her deflationary policy, despite an unemployment rate unheard of since pre-war days, and yet win handily in 1983 and 1987. In the light of those results and the unexpected victory of 1992, it was no exaggeration for Anthony King to see the arrival of "one-Party Government."[19]

What did Thatcher make of the exceptional opportunity presented by this breakdown of party government? As a party, the Conservatives suffered from the partisan dealignment and other forms of political deterioration of recent years, their electoral strength remaining well below what Labour had enjoyed under Attlee and what the conservatives themselves had maintained under Macmillan.

Thatcher's personal appeal did nothing to strengthen the standing of the party with the voters, the Gallup poll showing her to be the second least popular prime minister since the war, surpassed in that negative respect only slightly by Edward Heath. Yet the formidable constitutional authority of the British executive was still available, now being driven by the ideological single-mindedness of the prime minister.

Thatcher's most striking success was her demolition of that pillar of the managed economy, nationalization. Her adventure with monetarism, on the other hand, was such a failure as to inspire a corrosively critical report from a Select Committee chaired by a prominent member of her own party.[20] Subsequently under John Major, Conservative chancellors of the exchequer were obliged to revert to the usual stratagems of taxing and spending and even to devaluation in their attempts to "steer" the economy.

The attack on corporatism was a complicated but instructive mixture of success and failure. In Britain, war production had been organized and directed in great part by government-industry combinations comprising representatives of business, labor, and government. After the war these arrangements were used not only by Labour but also by Conservative Governments, as in Macmillan's grandiose scheme for tripartite planning on the French model. In the 1960s and 1970s a vast array of such representative bodies arose, administering a massive program of subsidies intended to boost investment and heighten productivity. The self-defeating scramble among the multitude of firms represented on these bodies frustrated their efforts to discriminate rationally among the claims for assistance. Looking back over some twenty years of public assistance to industry, one economic historian concluded: "Industrial policy in the United Kingdom since the 1960s can only be characterized as incoherent."[21]

Needless to say, these bodies, which had been jokingly christened "quangos," short for "quasi-autonomous non-governmental organizations," were immediately attacked by Thatcher.[22] She abolished the system of subsidies for industry and set about dismantling the structure of public-private cooperation by which they had been administered. Despite her pledge to reduce the size and cost of government, the quangos actually increased in number and in expenditure. By 1993 their number at the national, regional and local levels had risen to 5,521. Between 1978 and 1993, their expenditure (in constant prices) increased from £35.2 billion to £46.7 billion, the latter figure amounting to about one-third of total central government spending.

Quangos have been much criticized in recent years. Patronage is

one charge, since many of their members have substantial ties with
the Conservative Party. More to the point, the new structure has
been criticized as one-sided, in effect a "selective corporatism," in
which the businessmen who predominate in their membership cannot help being biased in favor of the interests of employers. The
most serious fault, however, has been a loss of control, made de-
pressingly evident in the enormous increase, unintended and indeed contrary to declared policy, in the number and expenditure
of the quangos. The lack of coordination which defeated the earlier attempt to carry out an industrial policy through a system of
subsidies has not been remedied. As a recent study of public policy
has concluded, the dispersion of administrative power has been
accompanied by a diminution of both party and parliamentary
government.[23]

From the financial point of view, the welfare state in Britain has
survived more than a decade of Conservative dominance virtually
intact.[24] The privatization of council housing was popular and successful, adding to revenue and reducing subsidies. Pension reform
also brought some budgetary savings, although the Government
was obliged to retreat from its more radical proposals. Repeatedly,
it also backed off from fundamental reforms of the health service
and by the end of the decade was continually assuring voters that
"the NHS is safe with us." As a whole, apart from housing and pensions, social spending remained almost unchanged. As a percent of
gross domestic product, total outlays on social programs for merit
goods and income transfers, which stood at 27.5 percent in 1979,
remained at 27.4 percent in 1990. Total government spending, including defense, likewise was stable, falling slightly from 44.9 percent to 43.2 percent of GDP.

For the sake of comparison we may look at the American figures.
While these measurements are smaller as totals, they show the same
relative stability. For the decade 1979–1989 our social spending rose
slightly from 20 to 21.4 percent of GDP, while our total government
outlays rose from 33.2 percent to 36.9 percent. In both countries
the size of the bureaucracy has been reduced hardly at all. In Britain from 1980 to 1990 government employment as a percent of
total employment fell from 21.1 percent to 19.2 percent. In the
United States for the same period the reduction was from 15.4 percent to 14.4 percent. In both countries, as elsewhere in the West,
over the past two decades of acclaimed austerity, Big Government
has not been reduced, but consolidated.

The political forces that sustained the British welfare state were
not those that brought it into existence. The Labour party, which
had been the prime initiating and driving force in the early postwar

years, could not—even as a credible Opposition—make a contribution to its maintenance. When one looks for explanations, it appears that the new group politics had struck again. Elicited by the programs of the welfare state and the managed economy, these offsprings of collectivism had assisted at the convergence of party policies in the 1960s and had turned back the ideological attempts to escape from the consensus in the 1970s. Now through the 1980s and into the 1990s, in the teeth of the Thatcherite revolution, they had successfully preserved the great bulk of social spending.

The failure of the Conservatives' attack, despite their exceptional political opportunity, vividly illustrates the power of pluralism in the modern democratic state. Big Government has come to stay. But coordination of this massive and complex force is no less needed today than it was half a century ago when the prospects of party government were much brighter.

The model of party government requires that each party will not only assemble the preferences of a set of private interests, but will also assimilate them to some overall view of the common good expressed as a public philosophy or in what is currently called "vision." Not much of the Tory paternalism, which traditionally lent this sort of coherence to British conservatism, has survived Thatcher. The rationale that ordered most of her policies was to move social choice from public choice to market choice.

As put into effect by Thatcher and her successor, John Major, that public philosophy, however incomplete its achievement, has had such disastrous effects upon British society that, at the time of this writing, support for the Conservatives has fallen precipitously to the lowest point since the war. Low in public esteem, weak as an organization, neither greatly diminishing the welfare state nor fully imposing order on government intervention in the economy, Conservatism in recent years has also suffered such bitter division over the European Union that it is far from unreasonable to foresee a split as definitive as that which followed on the repeal of the Corn Laws in the nineteenth century. No one should underestimate the capacity of the Tory phoenix for rebirth. Under the spell-binding leadership of Tony Blair, however, New Labour has become so credible an Opposition that it will almost certainly form the next Government. Do these developments signify a revival of party government? Specifically, has Blair given Labour a conception of the common good sufficiently coherent and relevant to control and guide the welfare state of the future?

Blair's ferocious attack on Thatcherism at the 1994 party

conference was superb as oratory and as criticism. His attempt to accentuate the positive has been less successful. He has clearly broken not only with the Webbian socialism of fellowship and planning, but also with the Gaitskellite socialism of what he has called the "tax and benefit regime." Marking a third phase in the adaptation of the concept, Blair, while accepting the free market, has picked up the One Nation rhetoric, which the Thatcherites had so ostentatiously discarded, to justify far-reaching intervention for social purposes. Historically, nationalism has been a powerful force offsetting the fragmenting effects of modernization. The communitarian pledge to restore social cohesion—"to bring us together"—can stir the heart. But if it is to satisfy the mind, it must be embodied in programs that convincingly promise movement toward that goal. So judged, Blair's substantive proposals are few, cautious and disconnected.

When Blair, however, turns from substance to procedure, from social and economic reform to constitutional and institutional reform, he draws on a wide array of weighty and specific proposals, informed by a coherent outlook and backed by a powerful movement. Rising out of the explosion of the 1960s, the movement for constitutional reform has expressed the demand of the politics of inclusion for more responsive government. Massive public support has been won for a program of radical reforms including such items as a written constitution, a bill of rights, devolution for Scotland and Wales, an elected second chamber, proportional representation, and a fixed term for Parliament.[25] According to its advocates, constitutional reform would do much to cure the cynicism and distrust of recent years. Blair himself regards constitutional reform as a remedy for that "disaffection with politics," which he says citizens feel under "THE most centralized government of any large state in the western world."[26] Yet this program of institutional reform, if enacted, would fatally weaken that very monopoly of power that enables British Governments to carry out radical reform. It is implausible to suggest that Tony Blair, who within the Labour Party has so sharply centralized power in the leadership, indeed in the Leader, would dissipate the energies of his Government on institutional reform at the expense of the far more vital concerns in economic and social fields.

Can anything helpful be learned from American experience? Our present condition, surely, cries out with the lesson that the American system has all the institutions (except proportional representation) proposed by constitutional reformers in Britain, yet distrust of politics and dissatisfaction with government run as deeply here as there. Like the British, we stand in need of a vision that will coordinate public needs with a huge public sector. That linkage cannot be accomplished without the mediation of a party system.

In the 1970s and 1980s in the United States as in Britain, a conservative realignment of public opinion took place. A party realignment comparable to the dominance of the Conservatives in Britain did not, thanks in no small part to the rapid Democratic shift to the right. In 1994–95, however, the long-awaited transformation threatened to materialize, and the American party system appeared to be taking a giant step toward the Westminster model. In the Congressional elections of 1994, the Republicans took over not only the Senate, but also, for the first time in 50 years, the House of Representatives. For a year and more thereafter, the new Speaker, Newt Gingrich, in a performance as theatrical and unfamiliar as his name, launched and led a massive legislative program, mandated by an election manifesto, titled *Contract with America,* and supported by a firmly united party in the Congress. Through months of furious battle with President Clinton and the Democrats, Gingrich, despite intense and continual strains of group pressure, held his majority together and prevented the breaches of party unity that are usual in American legislative behavior. For a time it looked as if 1996 would see a Presidential race in which the Republican candidate, presumably Senator Dole, would lead the battle on behalf of the Gingrich program against the Democratic President in harmony with the campaigns of Republican candidates for Congress—all much in the style of a British general election.

But that was not to be. Aided by the hostility of voters to Gingrich conservatism, the structural pressures and opportunities of the separation of powers disrupted this brief dalliance with party government. Protected by his constitutional position, which he trailed before critical Democrats in Congress in the phrase "but this is a different house," Clinton, following familiar precedents of Presidential leadership, blunted the Gingrich thrust by compromises that won support from Republicans in Congress, sometimes at the price of greatly annoying his own fellow partisans. In structure and process, American parties remained as distant as ever from the British model.

Yet there were striking similarities between the policy—and the predicament—of the two party leaders, Blair and Clinton. Clinton like Blair appealed to a New Nationalism. For example, when proclaiming his tripartite slogan of "opportunity, responsibility, and community," he was careful to specify that his reference was to our national community. But how should he give body to this appeal of national communitarianism in specific proposals of government action? Unlike Blair, Clinton has eschewed institutional reform.

Reminding one of Blair's fiscal caution, he has reined in the deficits resulting from the spending spree initiated by Reagan. His preoccupation, however, has been to manage a tactical retreat in defense of certain core programs of the American welfare state: Medicare, Medicaid, and basic measures relating to poverty, education, and the environment.

But can he change that strategy from defense to offense? The challenge is to give body to the New Nationalism in specific programs that are consistent with one another and relevant to the circumstances of the time. Tony Blair's advice would be to avoid what he disparagingly calls "the tax and benefit regime," that major policy misadventure of both countries in the 1960s and 1970s. Such schemes of distributive politics dispense benefits to particular constituencies at the cost of dividing a coalition that must recognize its interdependence if it is to be effective. The premise of a program should be not the presumed "right" of the beneficiary, but rather the contribution which the program enables the beneficiary to make to the common good. Benefits are provided, whether as money, services, tax relief or legal remedies, but they function as instrumentalities of a national purpose. In this way, rights and responsibilities are reciprocal. Most important of all, this interdependence is not a static exchange, but a function of movement toward a goal. Parties, like nations, thrive on a sense of motion. Hence political leaders in moments of hyperbole boast of "growth" and "progress" and offer the eternal promise "to get this country moving again," summoning their followers to a "crusade" or proclaiming a "revolution." Liberal or conservative, they must promise "change." Rightly so, since collective action necessarily entails order and coherence.

These are the not impossible prescriptions, if party politics is to thrive and a civic culture of trust is to be restored in Britain and in the United States. The similarities in the politics of the two countries have brought to their famed special relationship a new and different, but even closer, bond. Brought together by foreign policy during the struggle against Hitler, they remained differentiated in their domestic politics by British exceptionalism, specifically, the Toryism of their conservatives, and the socialism of their progressives. In recent years that gap also has been closed, as British parties have become more like American parties, Blair's purge of socialism from the Labour Party nicely complementing Thatcher's demotion of paternalism among the Conservatives. This special relationship in domestic politics, first personified by the mutual admiration of Thatcher and Reagan, has now been strengthened by the close personal contacts and the similarity of views and rhetoric of Blair and Clinton. Sharing a communitarian outlook that is liberal and national, each faces the challenge of forging the programmatic instruments that will control the unruly pluralism and direct the huge public sector of the modern democratic state. Their task, in short, is to fit Big Democracy to Big Government.

Fall Semester 1995

1. Wayland Kennet (ed.), *The Rebirth of Britain* (London, 1982), p. 172.
2. Supplement, *American Political Science Review*, XLIV (Sept. 1950).
3. See esp. his *Party Government* (New York, 1942).
4. Richard Rose, *Politics in England* (London, 1965) provides an epitome of the argument.
5. Gabriel A. Almond and Sidney Verba, *The Civic Culture: Political Attitudes and Democracy in Five Nations* (Princeton, 1963).
6. Louis Hartz, *The Liberal Tradition in America* (New York, 1955).
7. Theodore H. White, *The Making of the President 1964* (New York, 1965), pp. 391–92.
8. Julius Turner, *Party and Constituency: Pressures on Congress*. Rev. ed. by Edward V. Schneier, Jr. (Baltimore, 1970), p. 245.
9. Peter Jenkins, *Mrs. Thatcher's Revolution: The Ending of The Socialist Era* (Cambridge, Mass., 1988) p. *xv*.
10. Alan Marsh, *Protest and Political Consciousness* (Beverly Hills and London, 1977), Table 5.5, p. 118. Gallup Poll cited in Trevor Smith, "Post-modern Politics and the Case for Constitutional Reform," *Political Quarterly* 6, 2 (April–June 1994), p. 134.
11. At the meeting of the Commission on Oct. 3, 1969, after a discussion of the need for black delegates from the South, a rule was proposed which would require state delegations to include members of "minority groups" in numbers "bearing a reasonable relationship to the group's presence in the population of the State." This rule, which in my pencilled marginalia I termed "the fatal amendment" and "the bomb," was then also applied to women and young people, over my strenuous objections. Troubled by the generality of this rule and its restriction of the voters' power to choose, I expressed my fear to Chairman McGovern during the lunch hour that we had mandated quotas. Surprised by that reading, but sharing my concern, McGovern with the Commission's approval added a footnote to the rules categorically rejecting "the mandatory imposition of quotas." In the later battles over quotas, however, this footnote fell by the wayside.
12. I will not attempt even to sample the immense literature on the subject of party decline. A good, brief, general account with copious references to other works is the enlarged and updated edition of Martin P. Wattenberg, *The Decline of American Political Parties 1952–1994* (Cambridge, Mass. and London, 1994).
13. I have discussed this change in program structure in "In Search of a New Public Philosophy," in Anthony King (ed.), *The New American Political System* (Washington, 1978), pp. 20–22.
14. *Britain against Itself: The Political Contradictions of Collectivism* (New York and London, 1982) elaborates this analysis, summarized in the introductory chapter.
15. The confusion and distress arising from the failure of the old Webbian socialism is expressed in *The New Fabian Essays* (1952), edited by R. H. S. Crossman; the new approach is set out in C. A. R. Crosland, *The Future of British Socialism* (London, 1957).
16. *New Statesman and Nation*, Dec. 11, 1970, pp. 789–90.
17. Robert Taylor, *The Fifth Estate: Britain's Unions in the Seventies* (London, 1978), pp. 337–38, 353.
18. Denis Healey, *The Time of My Life* (London, 1989), p. 480. For a contrary view, see Ivor Crewe and Anthony King, *SDP: The Birth, Life and Death of the Social Democratic Party* (Oxford, 1995), pp. 467–68. For the opinions of Alliance voters (Social Democrats plus Liberals), see Table 16.7 of Appendix 5, in Crewe and King, *SDP*.
19. Anthony King, and others, *Britain at the Polls 1992* (Chatham, N.J., 1993), ch. 7.

20. Treasury and Civil Service Committee, Session 1980–81, Third Report, *Monetary Policy*, chapters 8 and 9. Edward duCann (C., Taunton) was chairman.

21. Geoffrey Denton, "Financial Assistance to British Industry," in W. M. Corden and Gerhard Fels (eds.), *Public Assistance to Industry: Protection and Subsidies in Britian and Germany* (London, 1976), p. 161.

22. Stuart Weir and Wendy Hall (eds.), *EGO Trip: Extra-governmental Organizations in the United Kingdom and their Accountability* (London, 1994), p. 6. This work is the principal source for the following discussion of quangos.

23. Stephen P. Savage, Rob Atkinson, and Lynton Robbins (eds.), *Public Policy in Britain* (New York, 1994).

24. The principal sources of the following discussion of the financial aspects of the welfare state in Britain and the United States are Paul Pierson, *Dismantling the Welfare State? Reagan, Thatcher and the Politics of Retrenchment* (Cambridge, 1994) and Pierson, "The New Poltics of the Welfare State" in *World Politics* 48 (Jan. 1996), pp. 143–79.

25. Market and Organizational Research Institute, Ltd., *State of the Nation 1995*. Survey for the Rowntree Reform Trust (London, 1995).

26. John Smith Memorial Lecture (London, Feb. 7, 1996).

# 18

# Who Ran the British Empire?

## JOHN W. CELL

H ardly anybody, really! On the eve of World War II the Indian Civil Service had a maximum of 1,250 covenanted members—"holding" a population of 353 million. Britain's African colonies had about the same number of elite administrators, and the Sudan (twice as large as Texas) had 125. Kenya averaged 19,000 per administrator, Nigeria 54,000.[1] Although the services had different modes of selection—India, Hong Kong and Ceylon by competitive exams, the African and Sudan services by interview—they were very much alike. They were overwhelmingly upper-middle class: sons of civil servants, corporation executives, doctors, or clergy. And they mostly attended public schools, factories for gentlemen, where they were given a generalist education: classics and mathematics, games, teamwork, exaggerated masculinity, cold showers, stiff upper lips. The fagging system taught how to obey, punish, and rule. Although less rigidly, universities were dedicated to the same ideals.[2]

Although the British educational system is often regarded as authoritarian and militaristic, it also produced the elite classes at home, people likely to support the appeasement policies of Neville Chamberlain in the late 1930s. The men who went overseas may have been a little more inclined toward autocratic personalities than those who stayed home. But on-the-job experience was a good deal more significant.

The British imperial services were remarkable for assigning young men to lonely positions of great responsibility—and then backing them up. "I've been four months alone now," the future novelist Joyce Cary wrote to his wife from Northern Nigeria in 1917, "but I haven't been unhappy." He had found out a lot about himself: "One does in solitude. I often wondered how I should stand being alone."

Owing to his position and lack of linguistic fluency he hadn't "exchanged a word of rational conversation since May, and this is getting on to the end of September." Leonard Woolf, who later wrote books denouncing economic imperialism, seems not to have regretted his youthful service in Ceylon, not that he had done anything to repent. He recalled being assigned to a religious festival that drew pilgrims from all over South India, the assumption being that because a single white man and a token police force were on hand order would prevail—and somehow it did. Sir Frank Swettenham said the same about the Residency System in Malaya: a British officer or two would "be sent into a country where white men were unknown; where everything that could be wrong was wrong"—lawless, undeveloped, unpoliced, anarchic, tyrannical. "It was apparently conceived that . . . the single white man would reduce everything to order by the exercise of tactful advice."[3]

What has been called the dominance-dependency complex was hard to avoid. In India caste and client networks produced henchmen, always at your elbow, ready to do whatever you wanted.[4] In Africa the racial hierarchy had much the same effect. The usual result was an authoritarian personality, a man accustomed to giving orders and having them obeyed. To some degree checking the authoritarian motif, the concentrated, overpowering force behind colonial rule was usually remote. Officials had to learn to make concessions, not to give orders unless confident they would be obeyed. With so few officials spread so thinly, even experienced officers had wide latitude; ordinarily they could expect to be backed up.

At 29, to take one example, Malcolm Hailey (the future Indian governor and director of the *African Survey*) was sent to develop a new canal colony on the Jhelem river in Shahpur District in the western Punjab. He was responsible for everything: surveying, choosing town sites, collecting taxes, planting a seed farm, overseeing anti-plague measures. Exercising enormous power, alone and virtually autonomous, speaking English only with his wife, this was his formative experience. While at school, he later recalled, he had been inspired by Kipling; in the secretariat at Lahore he had been indoctrinated into the paternalistic Punjab School. But it was founding a new society on the Lower Jhelum that shaped the last great imperial pro-consul, Lord Hailey of Shahpur.[5]

In two ways the imperial services differed markedly. The first was the number of indigenous members. Although admission into the ICS had supposedly been color-blind ever since Queen Victoria's proclamation of 1858, holding exams in England and lowering age limits had kept non-British entrants to a trickle. In 1919, however, the Government of India committed itself to gradually Indianize both the ICS and the officer corps of the Indian Army. Although to nationalists the timetable sounded ludicrous, by 1939 a quarter of the ICS were Indian. In Ceylon the pattern was similar. In Malaya, although there were few non-European members of the elite civil service before the Japanese conquest in 1942, there was a separate Malayan Administrative Service which, despite the large number of Chinese residents, was restricted to Malays.[6] The situation in Africa was entirely different. Until after World War II, British colonies in East and Central Africa had no Africans whatever above the level of minor clerk. Although education and other specialist departments in West Africa and Sudan did contain a few, their presence in important slots had actually decreased since the 1890s. Even there, despite the recommendation of the Hailey Report of 1941 that Africans be appointed to all layers and sectors of the colonial government, very little happened until the 1950s.[7]

The second important variable was the size of the supporting bureaucracies. If police and specialist departments were added to the 1,200 elite administrators in Britain's African colonies, the total number of European civil servants by the late 1930s still came to slightly below 8,000. Although no figures are available on the number of Africans in subordinate clerical or other positions, they would still not have brought the total much above 25,000. According to the 1931 census India had a million government employees, making the covenanted ICS .001% of the total, more like a spider's web than Lloyd George's famous metaphor of a steel frame. That discrepancy, made possible by the existence in India of a large educated class, was the difference between direct and indirect rule.

The non-European or dependent portions of the British Empire in the twentieth century contained the following types of what was called native administration:

(1) Direct rule: British India had a huge bureaucracy, somewhat resembling those of the Russian or Chinese empires, with central, provincial, district, and local services linked from top to bottom, and incorporating village headmen and record-keepers. Although the British reform program did not fundamentally alter this centralized chain of authority, it did add representative and democratic features, including central and provincial Legislative Councils with elected non-official members. After 1919 the provinces had Dyarchy, with ministers responsible to the legislature in charge of some of the less powerful departments. At the center, although the Viceroy's

Council remained entirely official, it faced an elected majority in the National Assembly. After 1937 provinces had responsible government, with governors taking advice of ministers able to command the legislatures' confidence, though subject to being suspended by the Governor-General in Council during emergency (as in 1939)—and President's Rule is still a feature of the Indian constitution. Ceylon had comparable features—a hierarchical structure incorporating headmen and other local officials; an increasingly elective legislative council; gradual evolution toward responsible government—but without the huge bureaucracy.

(2) Indian Princely States: These ranged from large important states such as Kashmir or Hyderabad to postage stamps with populations under 100,000. Although they were outside British India's revenue base, neither did they have to be administered; their autocratic nature insulated most of them from nationalist agitation; and they contributed substantially to the Indian Army. Depending on personalities, the period, and circumstances, relationships between individual residents and native rulers varied enormously. Although the tale is complicated, the British used the princes as obstructions in the river up which the Indian National Congress had to swim. Under the constitution of 1935, which left princely states free to remain outside the eventual Dominion, their representation was weighted so heavily that Congress would *never* have obtained a majority in the central legislature. In the end, however, despite the maneuvers of British members of the Political Department right up to the eve of independence, Mountbatten polished off the issue in a few sentences at a press conference—though the former princely states, especially Kashmir, remain an explosive issue.[8]

(3) The third type were coastal enclaves, such as Cape Coast Colony in the Gold Coast or the island of Lagos off what became Nigeria. Products of the early or mid-nineteenth century, before the so-called New Imperialism, they had Legislative Councils with nominated and then elected unofficial members who regarded themselves as a loyal opposition, newspapers critical of government, and (though their numbers declined in the early twentieth century with the rise of racism and improvement in tropical medicine) Africans in important administrative positions.

(4) Virtually everywhere else the pattern was some variety of indirect rule, governing through traditional authorities and

institutions. Malaya had a Residency System, modeled after the Indian princely states, with British advisers at the Sultans' courts. As in India, relationships varied enormously. If Residents behaved as rulers rather than advisers, warned the Colonial Office, they would be charged with responsibility for the consequences. That was all very well, one Resident reflected, except that "we must first create the government to be advised." In practice, explained another, except for religious issues, it was the Resident who conducted the government, referring to the Sultan for advice when *he* thought necessary.[9] The closest African approximations were the kingdoms of Buganda and Bunyoro in Uganda, classed as Protectorates, with whom the British had negotiated treaties. These states were not incorporated into the British bureaucratic structure. Instead, there was direct rule by the chiefs, subject to British overrule (including removal).[10]

The best-known form of indirect rule was associated with the regime of Sir Frederick Lugard in Northern Nigeria, comparable versions being found in the Gold Coast's Northern Territory, Barotseland in Northern Rhodesia, Matabeleland in Southern Rhodesia, as well as Zululand and Transkei in South Africa itself. In this category strong native authorities were incorporated into the British (or South African) governing structures, running on what were said to be authentic African lines. Although the grouping of Nigeria with the Transkei would have horrified Lugard, they actually had much in common.[11]

A third variation of indirect rule was found in Ashanti in the Gold Coast and parts of Nigeria: government by negotiation with African rulers, such as the Asentehene of Ashanti, whose positions were guaranteed by treaty. This was the type that prevailed in the Southern and Western regions of Nigeria under Sir William MacGregor and Sir Walter Egerton in the early twentieth century, while Lugard was creating his much more authoritarian version in the North. Still another version developed with respect to the so-called stateless peoples of Southern Nigeria, Kenya, or Tanganyika, whose political institutions had either remained rudimentary or been destroyed by European military action. Here "foreigners," such as the Akidas under German rule in Tanganyika, or relatively minor native leaders, such as the Warrant Chiefs in Southern Nigeria, were imported or raised above their stations. Finally, provided the emphasis is on "indirect" rather than on "administration," provided it is defined in terms of power rather than some sort of civilizing mission, then the British practiced indirect rule very widely indeed throughout the Middle East, Persian Gulf, and other regions especially in the Muslim world.

It is easy to take this categorization much too seriously: not only structures but genealogies. The historiography of indirect rule has been preoccupied by a hunt for precedents, ranging to the Indian princely states, Malaya, Fiji, nineteenth-century Natal—and the book of Deuteronomy.[12] But the main point is not whether governance was direct or indirect. It was the adoption right across the Dependent Empire of some version of the bureaucratic structure common to all empires, whether land-based (Mughal, Ottoman, Chinese, or Russian) or sea-borne. "It was a prefectural administration," Bruce Berman has written, "staffed by an elite cadre of political officers acting as direct agents of the central government and exercising diffuse and wide-ranging powers within the territorial subdivisions."[13]

The prefectural system works like a military chain of command. Although British colonial officials were ultimately subject to a democratically elected Parliament, their education and especially their early job experiences bent them in an authoritarian direction. They did not necessarily represent social forces or classes dominant at home. Although some of them did fit the model of an atavistic military class, they were more likely to be middle class: aspiring rather than what in India would have been called "pukkha" gentry. Their main loyalty was to the largely self-defined missions of their services, to the entities they helped to imagine called "India," "Nigeria," or "Palestine." It has recently been argued that the dominant class behind British imperialism were "gentlemanly capitalists." These prefects were elite administrators. Although their brothers or cousins might be bankers or corporations executives, they themselves were apt to see economic development as disruptive. Some of them were gentlemen. Few were capitalists.[14]

In India the decision to retain princely states was a political choice. In Africa, except for Little Indias such as Egypt and the northern Sudan with their large educated classes, or South Africa, with its white population, the option of using local people as manpower for a direct, centralized administration was not available. Some sort of indirect approach, using native authorities that were or were thought to be authentic, was ubiquitous, not only for the British who made a virtue of it, but for the French and Portuguese who did not.

Until recently credit for developing what was widely regarded as Britain's distinctive contribution to the science of governing subject peoples went to Lugard. According to his biographer, Dame Margery Perham, Lugard created in Northern Nigeria "the most comprehensive, coherent, and renowned system of administration" in British colonial history.[15] Although he was less successful in exporting that system to the Southern and Western regions, she admitted, his great achievement could not be denied. In Tanganyika his former lieutenant Sir Donald Cameron developed indirect rule as a counter-force to Kenya's white settlers. In the late 1920s Sir John Maffey, who had worked with princely states in India, imported it into the Sudan. Meanwhile, Lugard's classic *Dual Mandate* (1922), consolidated his reputation. For nearly two decades, until he was replaced by Lord Hailey in the late 1930s, he was the leading figurehead of Britain's Africanist establishment. Indirect rule became *the* hallmark of British tropical Africa, hailed as a humane and far-sighted alternative to either the French policy of assimilation or the tradition of segregation in southern Africa.

After a quarter-century of revisionism, not much of that is left. Lugard was neither a great nor even a very competent administrator, his detractors contend, but a skillful propagandist. Above all he was a obsessive autocrat. He found the Muslim emirs of the North attractive because they too were authoritarian and because as recent invaders they depended on the British to maintain them. By every normal test of colonial government—finance, trade, education, public health—Northern Nigeria was a failure, especially compared to the more prosperous, less militaristic administrators in the West and South, where indirect rule meant not folding a ruling class into a chain of command, but rather the humbler task of getting along with Africans in power. The *Dual Mandate* has also been demolished: a strange book, often referred to but seldom read, full of old feuds with the Colonial Office, strong prejudice against educated Africans, and racist views that read strangely even for the 1920s.[16]

The earlier version of the spread of indirect rule has also been revised. In Northern Nigeria, at least, Lugard had no alternative. That was not the case in the Sudan, where Egyptians and educated northern Sudanese had been employed since the 1890s. When Sir John Maffey instituted the system formally in the 1920s, however, his intention was to seal off the backward South from the advanced North, and the whole territory from the still more rebellious Egyptians. Indirect rule would split the South into "nicely balanced compartments, protective glands against the septic germs" that would "inevitably be passed on from the Khartoum of the future."[17] As an administrative system indirect rule amounted to an inefficient, unprogressive, but relatively inexpensive form of local government. But it had no role for educated Africans, little connection to the center, and thus no relevance whatever to the political future of independent states. The fact that indirect rule became known as the antithesis of segregation was more the achievement of Margery Perham than of the governors she wrote about. The primary importance of indirect rule was not as a system of administration but as an ideology, a rationale of British colonialism in tropical Africa.


Like other bureaucracies, Britain's imperial services needed ideologies to reinforce morale and justify to outsiders what it meant to be "something in India" or Africa.[18] Such justifications needed to be not only morally defensible but intellectually fashionable, compatible with existing scientific and especially anthropological knowledge. During the century before World War II, at which point colonial nationalism threw imperialism in all its guises on the defensive, two doctrines were outstanding. The first, which had its heyday in nineteenth-century India, was the social-evolutionary theory centering on the village community. The second, prevailing in British West Africa and other colonies where white settlers did not gain power, was indirect rule, in alliance with the functional school of anthropology. Into these ideologies imperial civil servants were indoctrinated: in examinations (and cramming courses), in probationary years at university, in Margery Perham's Oxford summer school sessions for officials on leave.

The village-community concept had a long run. It first gained prominence among early nineteenth-century Orientalists such as Sir Charles Metcalfe and Sir Thomas Munro, who made it one of the cornerstones of their conception of Indian civilization.[19] Marx used it in developing his model of an Asiatic Mode of Production. In India itself, the doctrine gained strength during the recoil after the rebellion of 1857–58 against the Westernizing program of the Utilitarians, which was widely regarded as its principle cause. It was closely associated with Sir Henry Maine, author of *Ancient Law*, who was Law Member of the Viceroy's Council and an instructor to a generation of aspiring ICS probationers at Oxford and Cambridge. In Maine's work the village was the primordial unit of all Indo-European (or Aryan) societies, still in working order in India though long since superseded in Europe. Originally, villages had been miniature republics: self-contained, self-sufficient, self-regulating. But they might have been taken over by outsiders, who owned the means of production and governed despotically, in which case they became Little Kingdoms. The Indian village was thought to be much like the German-Scandinavian *mark*, the revered forest seedbed of Western constitutional liberty.[20]

Like Marx's scheme of historical epochs, based on dominant modes of production, Maine's village-community was a simple but powerful comparative model. Since societies in different parts of the world were supposed to have gone through the same stages of evolution, contemporary India held the keys to Europe's past. In the historical laboratory of India the same forces could be observed that had determined the great medieval transitions: from mark to manor, from lordship to kinship, from communal to private property, from custom to law, from status to contract. The village model enabled district officers to work with small, tangible units that could be seen, smelled, surveyed, and counted, all within the boundaries of their own jurisdictions. The village was the pulse of India, and what could be felt could be controlled. Breaking a civilization down into components made it easier to reify or construct other essences, such as caste, ethnic or religious communities: cards that could be played in the game of divide and rule.

In twentieth-century Africa the successor to Maine's village-community doctrine was indirect rule, supported by the functional school of anthropology associated with Bronislaw Malinowski of the London School of Economics. The organizational base was the Institute of African Languages and Cultures, founded in the 1920s by the missionary leader Joseph Oldham, in partnership with the ubiquitous Lugard. Malinowski gave the enterprise academic connections and prestige. African societies could accept some changes, he argued, provided they did not disrupt the fragile whole of primitive society—and anthropologists could tell you just which ones. In 1927, skimming the *Dual Mandate* before talking with Lugard, Malinowski noted that if the author "had wanted to control Scientific Anthrop[ology], so as to fit into his Imp[erial] idea . . . , he couldn't have done anything but to create Functional School." Indirect rule was "a Complete Surrender to the Functional Point of View." Or was it the other way around?[21] Although later anthropologists have naturally been troubled by the close connection between their discipline and colonialism, the influence of their predecessors on colonial administration was mixed and limited. They were much more significant at the level of ideology.[22]

Indirect rule thrived in the Tropical Dependencies of West Africa, possessing climates unattractive to Europeans and cash-crop economies centered on peasant production. It spread to the Sudan, Tanganyika, and Uganda. It did not take root in colonies of settlement: the White Man's Countries of South Africa, Southern Rhodesia, or even Kenya. In this second, very different part of Africa, where Cecil Rhodes, Leo Amery, or Jan Smuts conceptualized great White Dominions, the prevailing doctrine was segregation. During the 1930s, and especially after World War II, when the British colonial reform movement confronted an insurgent Afrikaner nationalism, indirect rule and segregation did come to represent increasingly hostile camps. The earlier relationship between the two ideologies

had been much less antagonistic. They employed a common vocabulary, shared assumptions about race and culture, and wrote
checks on the same anthropological bank. Segregation was British
(and of course American) as well as Afrikaner.[23] Native Authorities,
as the young Margery Perham wrote, before she learned to express
her views more correctly, looked a lot like Bantustans.[24]

Where, Malcolm MacDonald asked Lord Hailey in 1940, before
sending him on a tour of Africa, was indirect rule going? Hailey's
answer was "nowhere." Why then did a generation of colonial officials, as well as thoughtful, well-meaning academics like Margery
Perham, paint such an optimistic picture? One reason is that interwar Europeans were disillusioned with their own civilization: better
retain African customs and institutions, modifying slowly rather than
discarding altogether. Indirect rule was like scaffolding around a
building, Perham put it, the temporary plans European, the permanent core African. One day the scaffolding would be removed. Africans should not be turned into pseudo-Europeans, Lugard and
General Smuts alike insisted. Instead they should evolve on "their
own lines."

Like the village-community doctrine in India, indirect rule gave
officials a sense of mission, a belief that they were doing something
important, instead of simply holding power for its own sake until
Africans became sufficiently advanced in the technique of political
agitation to make clear that the time had come to leave. It gave
district officers "a fascinating practical job to do." Like the village,
the model of the tribe reduced the huge, complex, baffling continent of Africa to a scale "well within their compass"; they could "see
results inside the sphere of [their] own activity."[25] As Lord Hailey's
wartime report warned, however, nationalism in Africa would surge
forward as it had in India. Any form of governance with no place
for educated Africans would very soon become obsolete. Once the
British began to take African self-government seriously, indirect rule
went on the rubbish heap.[26]

Although indirect rule had limited importance as a working system of administration, in other ways its impact was considerable.
First, it severely curbed the political experience of future African or
Asian leaders. When members of the educated, Westernized elite
took control, as they did nearly everywhere, they knew how to organize political parties but not how to govern, and certainly not how
to tolerate a loyal opposition. Second, indirect rule built up some
groups or factions at the expense of others. Examples abound. In
Malaya the Residency system enhanced the power of the Sultans
against the chiefs in the second tier.[27] But for their alliance with the

British, the Muslim emirs of Northern Nigeria might have been forced to retreat.

Third, indirect rule oversimplified and stereotyped groups and institutions. Historians now agree that African identities and allegiances were much less permanent than used to be supposed. Colonialism in general, and indirect rule in particular, lumped Africans into at least partly fabricated units called "tribes," a word implying something too large and formal for some political systems, too small and informal for others.[28]

Fourth, the ideologies of imperialism produced uncanny echoes. In India, long after investigators had raised doubts about the village-community, Gandhi made the partly mythical village decision-making body called the Panchayat an important feature of his program. In Africa the language of indirect rule bore a striking resemblance to that of African Socialism. The skepticism of a Lugard or a Hailey about whether Africans could manage a Westminster-style political system was repeated by politicians justifying *de jure* one-party rule as the authentic African way.

Except in true White Man's Countries like Australia or the United States, where native peoples were decimated to a degree approaching extinction, colonial domination required collaboration, which in turn shaped the character and operation of the regime.[29] Although collaborators might be inevitable, their identity was often a matter of choice. They might come from the comprador class, a modernizing Western-educated elite much like Europeans themselves, such as the *Bhadralok* in Bengal or educated Africans along the West African coast. At least until experience taught them otherwise, such people were likely to favor British expansion. Hoping the colonial state would cut down reactionary leaders and institutions, thereby providing a shortcut toward their goal of modern, progressive nations, they saw themselves as natural allies and successors of the colonizers.[30] Many from this class did find roles within the colonial regime. Moreover, Western-educated leaders proved adept at leading agitation, developing political parties and other means of mobilizing the masses, and gaining control of the state after independence.

During the colonial era itself, however, Westernized elites were usually bitterly disappointed. Instead of removing reactionaries the British tended to form alliances with them. How ironic, observed Jawaharlal Nehru, the product of Harrow and Cambridge, to see representatives of the dynamic, progressive West allying themselves with the princely and landlord classes, the most conservative elements of the static, backwards East.[31] However it might be disguised by anthropological jargon, indirect rule in all its forms—the princely states in India, the sultanates in Malaya, the kingdoms of Buganda or Bunyoro in Uganda, the emirates in Lugard's Northern Nigeria—was an attempt to freeze colonial societies, to control and slow down the pace of change. Lord Hailey described it as a cushion, softening the impact of Western influence.

The final rationale of the British imperial service emerged in the 1950s in West Africa and the Sudan: active preparation for self-government, with the end clearly in sight. In India, although the objective of Dominion Status after the war was declared in 1942, until 1947 the ICS was preoccupied with the Quit India movement and then the nasty communal conflicts of the partition era. Although independence came in East and Central Africa only a few years later than in the West, there the decision to leave was a snap one, prompted by the long and never quite completed suppression of the Mau Mau insurrection in Kenya. In West Africa, with landfall in sight and no intervening tailwinds, British officials had no choice but to work at development, train their successors, and prepare the ship to sail without them into turbulent, uncharted waters. They have been accused of setting the compass in a neocolonialist direction. But the administrators had been largely unconcerned with economic matters outside their own districts. Their often passionate professional commitment to the success of the independent countries they had helped to imagine, which came to the surface for example during the Nigerian civil war of the 1970s, was apparent to all who know them.[32]

                                        Summer Semester 1996

1. Anthony H. Kirk-Greene, "The Thin White Line," *African Affairs, 79* (1980), pp. 24–44, and "The Sudan Political Service: A Profile in the Sociology of Imperialism," *International Journal of African Historical Studies, 15* (1982), pp. 21–48; David C. Potter, *India's Political Administrators* (Oxford, 1986); J. de Vere Allen, "Malayan Civil Service, 1874–1941: Colonial Bureacracy/Malayan Elite," *Comparative Studies in Society and History, 12* (1970), pp. 149–78; Robert Heussler, *Yesterday's Rulers: The Making of the British Colonial Service* (Syracuse, 1963); Ralph Furse, *Aucuparius: Recollections of a Recruiting Officer* (London, 1962). The relatively well-manned Malayan Civil Service had some 220 elite officials for a mere 3.2 million people.

2. On public schools see Philip Mason, *The English Gentleman: The Rise and Fall of an Ideal* (New York, 1982), p. 170; Rupert Wilkinson, *Gentlemanly Power: British Leadership and the Public School Tradition: A Comparative Study in the Making of Rulers* (London, 1964); Simon Raven, *The Decline of the Gentleman* (New York, 1962). On universities, Sheldon Rothblatt, *The Revolution of the Dons: Cambridge and Society in Victorian England* (London, 1968); Richard Symonds, *Oxford and Empire: The Last Lost Cause?* (London, 1986).

3. Molly Mahood, *Joyce Cary's Africa* (Boston, 1965), pp. 39–40; Leonard Woolf, *Growing: An Autobiography of the Years 1904–1911* (New York, 1962); Frank Swettenham, *British Malaya* (London, 1948), pp. 213–14.

4. Philip Mason, *A Shaft of Sunlight: Memoirs of a Varied Life* (London, 1978), p. 97.

5. John W. Cell, *Hailey: A Study in British Imperialism, 1872–1969* (New York, 1992), ch. 2.

6. Sir Charles Collins, "Ceylon: The Imperial Heritage," and Robert O. Tilman, "Bureaucratic Development in Malaya," in Ralph Braibanti (ed.), *Asian Bureaucratic Systems Emergent from the British Imperial Tradition* (Durham, 1966), pp. 444–84, 550–604; Allen, "Malayan Civil Service"; Rupert Emerson, *Malaysia: A Study in Direct and Indirect Rule* (New York, 1937).

7. William Malcom Hailey, *Native Administration in British Tropical Africa*, ed. Anthony H. Kirk-Greene (Nendein, 1979). Two Africans did become district officers in the Gold Coast during WWII.

8. Press conference of June 19, 1947, Nicholas Mansergh, et al. (eds.), *The Transfer of Power* (12 vols.; London, 1970–1983), *11*, pp. 114–22. On the princely states see Robin Jeffrey (ed.), *People, Princes and Paramount Power* (Delhi, 1978), especially Jeffrey's introduction and Ian Copland, "The Other Guardians: Ideology and Performance in the Indian Political Service," pp. 275–304; Copland, *The British Raj and the Indian Princes: Paramountcy in Western India, 1857–1930* (Bombay, 1982); Barbara N. Ramusack, *The Princes of India in the Twilight of Empire: Dissolution of a Patron-Client System, 1914–1939* (Columbus, 1978); Terence Creagh Coen, *The Indian Political Service: A Study in Indirect Rule* (London, 1971); Jeffrey, "The Politics of 'Indirect Rule': Types of Relationship among Rulers, Ministers and Residents in a 'Native' State," *Journal of Commonwealth and Comparative Politics, 13* (1975), pp. 261–81; Michael Fisher, *Indirect Rule in India: Residents and the Residency System, 1764–1858* (Delhi, 1991).

9. Simon C. Smith, *British Relations with the Malay Rulers from Decentralization to Malayan Independence, 1930–1957* (Kuala Lampur, 1995), p. 4.

10. Donald Anthony Low and R. Cranford Pratt, *Buganda and British Overrule, 1900–1955* (London, 1960); Low, *Buganda in Modern History* (Berkeley, 1971); Low, *The Mind of Buganda: Documents of the Modern History of an African Kingdom* (Berkeley, 1971); Michael Twaddle, *Kakunzulu and the Creation of Uganda, 1868–1928* (London, 1993).

11. As Margery Perham perceived when she first visited southern Africa—before she learned the Lugard party line. *African Apprenticeship: An Autobiographical Journey in Southern Africa 1929* (London, 1974).

12. See Peter France, *The Charter of the Land: Custom and Colonization in Fiji* (Melbourne, 1969); David Welsh, *The Roots of Segregation: Native Policy in Colonial Natal, 1845–1910* (Cape Town, 1971). The reference to Deuteronomy was tongue-in-cheek by Sir Donald Cameron.

13. Bruce Berman, *Control and Crisis in Colonial Kenya: The Dialectic of Domination* (London, 1990), p. 73.

14. Peter Cain and Anthony Hopkins, *British Imperialism* (2 vols.; London, 1993). See Joseph A. Schumpeter, *Imperialism and Social Classes* (New York, 1951).

15. Margery Perham, *Lugard* (2 vols.; London, 1956–60), 2, p. 138.

16. See especially I. F. Nicolson, *The Administration of Nigeria: Men, Methods and Myths* (Oxford, 1969); John E. Flint, "Nigeria, The Colonial Experience from 1880 to 1914," in Lewis Gann and Peter Duignan (eds.), *Colonialism in Africa, 1870–1960* (5 vols.; Cambridge, 1969–1975), *1*, pp. 220–60; Flint, "Frederick Lugard: The Making of an Autocrat, 1858–1943," in Gann and Duignan (eds.), *African Proconsuls: European Governors in Africa* (New York, 1978), pp. 290–312; A. Afigbo, *The Warrant Chiefs: Indirect Rule in Southeastern Nigeria, 1891–1929* (New York, 1972); J. Atanda, *The New Oyo Empire: Indirect Rule and Change in Western Nigeria, 1894–1934* (New York, 1973).

17. Martin W. Daly, *Empire on the Nile: The Anglo-Egyptian Sudan, 1898–1934* (Cambridge, 1986), p. 366.

18. See Max Weber, *From Max Weber,* ed. H. Gerth and C. Wright Mills (New York, 1958).

19. Ronald Inden, *Imagining India* (Oxford, 1990); Thomas R. Metcalf, *Ideologies of the Raj, New Cambridge History of India,* Pt. 3, vol. 4 (Cambridge, 1994).

20. Henry S. Maine, *Ancient Law: Its Connection with the Early History of Society and Its Relation to Modern Ideas* (1861; Boston, 1963) and *Village-Communities in the East and West* (7th ed.; London, 1895). See Clive Dewey, "The Influence of Sir Henry Maine on Agrarian Society in India," in Alan Diamond (ed.), *The Victorian Achievement of Sir Henry Maine* (Cambridge, 1991), pp. 353–75, and *The Settlement Literature of the Greater Punjab: A Handbook* (New Delhi, 1991); J. W. Burrow, *Evolution and Society: A Study in Victorian Social Theory* (Cambridge, 1966). On the Utilitarians see Eric Stokes, *The English Utilitarians and India* (Oxford, 1959) and Javed Majeed, *Ungoverned Imaginings: James Mill's "The History of British India" and Orientalism* (Oxford, 1992).

21. Bronislaw Malinowski, "Practical Anthropology," *Africa,* 2 (1929), pp. 22–38; George W. Stocking, Jr. (ed.), *Functionalism Historicized: Essays on British Social Anthropology* (Madison, 1984); Stocking (ed.), *Colonial Situations: Essays on the Contextualization of Ethnographic Knowledge* (Madison, 1991); Henrika Kuklick, *The Savage Within: The Social History of British Anthropology, 1885–1945* (Cambridge, 1991); Adam Kuper, *Anthropologists and Anthropology: The British School, 1922–1972* (New York, 1975).

22. Talal Asad (ed.), *Anthropology & the Colonial Encounter* (Atlantic Highlands, 1975).

23. Welsh, *Roots of Segregation;* Martin Legassick, "The Making of South African 'Native Policy,'" and "The Rise of Modern South African Liberalism," seminar papers, Institute of Commonwealth Studies, University of London (1972–73); John W. Cell, *The Highest Stage of White Supremacy: The Origins of Segregation in South Africa and the American South* (Cambridge, 1982).

24. John E. Flint, "Planned Decolonization and Its Failure in British Africa," *African Affairs, 82* (1983), pp. 389–412.

25. Note of Frederick Pedler, Mar. 11, 1946, CO 847/25/4724.

26. Circular No. 41, Feb. 25, 1947, CO 847/35/47234/1.

27. J. M. Gullick, *Rulers and Residents: Influence and Power in the Malay States, 1870–1920* (Singapore, 1992).

28. Elizabeth Colson, "African Society at the Time of the Scramble," *Colonialism in Africa, 1,* pp. 27–65.

29. Ronald Robinson, "Non-European Foundations: Sketch for a Theory of Collaboration," in Roger Owen and Bob Sutcliffe (eds.), *Studies in the Theory of Imperialism* (London, 1972).

30. Flint, "Nigeria, the Colonial Experience."

31. Jawaharlal Nehru, *The Discovery of India* (New York, 1946).

32. See John Smith, *Colonial Cadet in Nigeria* (Durham, 1968); Anthony H. Kirk-Greene (ed.), *Crisis and Conflict in Nigeria: A Documentary Sourcebook* (Oxford, 1971).

# 19

# From Africa to Empire

ANTONY HOPKINS

H ow should historians position themselves with respect to the external influences that beckon (and threaten) them? Should they move with the times or should they hold their ground—gaining either a reputation for flexibility (or is it inconstancy), or for steadfastness (or is it conservatism)? Our practice indicates that most of us stick to what we think we can do best, but by initiative, osmosis, or lethargy adopt a few innovations once they have proved themselves and if they seem to increase our productivity. Nevertheless, the fact that we typically achieve a compromise, often without conscious effort or public proclamation, does not alter the principle that choices have to be made. It is this issue that I propose to address today, inevitably superficially, with reference to imperial history and what has become known, generically, as Area Studies (specifically African history) during the past thirty years.

That these fields have been favored by fashion and have also experienced neglect is well-known and accepted. The interesting question is why such changes of fortune have occurred. A large part of the explanation, it seems to me, lies in seeing how the external world has impinged on scholarship, particularly in the United States, which, in assuming the virtual direction of Area Studies, has also influenced the view taken of imperial history. The quest for liberation, development and democracy that has inspired so much of the best (and worst) of scholarship in the field expresses a well-intentioned concern for the welfare of other people; it is also the projection abroad of an implicit concern with the American soul and the American destiny.

The knowledge revolution that was the central feature of the boom in Area Studies from the 1960s onwards is too familiar to require elaboration. It is sufficient here to confirm that this was the time when the subject, in all its diversity, was put on a modern professional basis, and the panoply of centers, programs, journals and monograph series which are, for the most part, still around, was established.

This development was linked with the coming of political independence in the British and French empires and with the Cold War in its final phase of competitive co-existence. Among academics there was an outpouring of goodwill associated with anti-colonialism and with the prospect of assisting newly independent countries to achieve their aspirations. At the policy level there was a determination to ensure that the Free World prevailed in the post-colonial struggle for the hearts and minds of men—women at that stage did not count, even on the Left.

The new history of Africa written in the 1960s was concerned mainly with great states and great leaders, showing how Africans had run their own affairs in the past and were therefore fitted to do so again. The achievements were considerable, but we can now see that they were also limited, both by the selection of topics and by the way they were treated. A Nigerian scholar has recently castigated the early nationalist school of historians for their "wanton optimism"—a comment that could not have been made at the time—such were the pressures to promote a sanguine view of the past in order to support unrealistic hopes for the future.

My small contribution to this new field of study was to try to mark out an unexplored sub-specialism: economic history. My motive was not political, unlike many of my contemporaries, who were attracted to the liberation movements: it was academic. My interest in economic development came through studying Tudor and Stuart economic history as an undergraduate; after graduating, I decided to look at issues relating to the rise of capitalism in another part of the world. Since the economic history of Africa is now a well-established area of study, and is marked by standards that have risen greatly since I first put my toe in the water, it is perhaps worth recording that, when I started, it was regarded as mission impossible: there were no specialized studies and, so I was told, no source materials. Consequently, my doctoral thesis, when first registered in 1960, proposed to cover the whole of southern Nigeria throughout the greater part of recorded time. There were other problems too: in studying economic history I became aware of inequalities of wealth and power in precolonial Africa. This was not a popular finding at the time, however conventional it has since become. In fact, the first time I was called a racist was by a white man in Nigeria who interpreted my greenhorn comments about inequalities of wealth as being anti-Nigerian. He refused to drive me further into Lagos, saying that Nigeria was now independent and that whites had to decide if they were for or against the country and its people. I entered the capital for my first visit on foot—not something I would be happy to do today.

After completing my Ph.D. in 1964, I produced some articles in the 1960s that sought to put various topics—from labor history to monetary history—on the research agenda. One essay, the first specialized article on Africa published by *Past & Present* (in 1966), was discussed by the editorial board, so my distinguished colleague, Rodney Hilton, informed me at the time. Was it that good, I wondered? Alas no: the piece was discussed because the managers of even that enlightened journal were concerned about whether they should give space to detailed articles on obscure parts of the world. Times have changed in that respect—and much for the better. In the 1960s, however, my specialization produced unknowing smiles at conferences, where nearly all the participants were wading in the warm and friendly waters of the industrial revolution. I was in the tropics, but I was also out in the cold.

After a typically long gestation, my *Economic History of West Africa* was published in 1973. The book presented a long-run argument, using the concept of the market as a viewpoint and organizing principle, explaining the particular constraints on economic development in West Africa. It attempted to show that many of the assumed limits to growth rested on notions of primitive economic behavior that would not pass the test of the historical record. Behavior was more rational and profit-maximizing than had been thought. The constraints lay elsewhere—in underpopulation and in associated technological limits, notably high transport costs.

The wider inference of the argument was that modernization theory, the prevailing approach of the day, was vulnerable to the criticism that it had produced a false stereotype of "traditional" societies by inferring that these were, indeed had to be, the opposite of the ideal we had of ourselves. This ideal was then taken to be supreme and supremely desirable. In the aftermath of World War II the combination of the atomic bomb, bakerlite, sliced bread and Hollywood was so powerful that no one doubted that, suitably adapted, it could win the peace just as it had, in a manner of speaking, won the war.

The publication of my book coincided, approximately, with a major sea-change in academic thinking in the United States. In the aftermath of the great political and intellectual crisis of 1968, a new generation of historians abandoned the post-war version of the American Dream and instead sought a cure for what was seen to be, instead, the American Predicament—inequality, racial tension, urban squalor, violence. As they did so, their counterparts, historians of the Third World, abandoned modernization theory and what suddenly became known, derisively, as the "bourgeois" nationalist historiography of the 1960s, and began to place their bets elsewhere, not with the fat cats, the "Wabenze" and the "Been Tos" who had let them down, but with those social groups who had still to do so.

In the 1970s American academics working on the Third World converted to radical analysis, *en masse*, for the first time. The conversion took two forms. One caused the congregation to embrace the dependency thesis (first popularized by André Gunder Frank and then—and still, though now wavering—Immanuel Wallerstein, himself a convert from modernization theory). Overnight we had answers to problems that had long baffled lesser minds: Africa was poor because it had been underdeveloped by capitalism. If repetition was truth, this message would have been imprinted for all time, and history would indeed have come to an end. Repetitive books and articles, many unreadable and most now long unread, comforted by simple verifying procedures and welcomed by like-minded reviewers and commentators, proclaimed both diagnosis and remedy with a stunning uniformity that appeared to have achieved a monopoly of truth.

The second form of conversion issued in a more specifically Marxist concern with the search for an African proletariat, which began in the 1970s. My unread essay in *Past & Present* was discovered and reprinted several times during the decade. When the proletariat failed either to emerge in sufficient force or to behave as predicted, historians of Africa—of necessity an inventive tribe—discovered, or rather constructed, a "peasantry" instead, taking inspiration this time from Mao in China and Nyerere in Tanzania. Younger scholars present may not be aware that, before AS (Arrighi and Saul), historians did not apply the term "peasants" to tropical Africa as a matter of routine, as they do now. By re-labeling cultivators, small-holders, and farmers, however, it was possible to alter the historical record almost overnight—a task made easier by the fact that Arrighi and Saul's definition was so generous (peasants were people who did not live in towns) that no potentially worrying exceptions were left outside the analysis.

My *Economic History of West Africa* thus found itself in choppy waters. On the one hand, I was fortunate that its publication anticipated the new interest in the economic history of Africa and of the Third World generally that developed as the 1970s progressed. On the other hand, the book was roundly criticized by keen converts for lacking class analysis, for not having workers and peasants in sufficient abundance, and for failing to see that all foreign trade was exploitative. On the whole, I think it benefited from being in place at the right moment: people had become interested in the subject. As all scholars know, their greatest misfortune is not be criticized but to be ignored. I was fortunate in being criticized.

Looking back, I am glad that I did not rush to improve my work in the light of the revelations produced by dependency theorists and Marxists, as I was tempted to do. I sensed then that many of the new landmarks in the literature would become tombstones, and so it has turned out. Very little of this work has survived its short time. All the same, the limitations of my own book are as clear to me now as they were obscure at the time of publication. In my concern to establish the territory of economic history, I distanced the subject too far from political history; I would now try to integrate the two. In my eagerness to establish the rationality of African economic behavior and to destroy the myth of what I termed Merrie Africa, I paid insufficient regard to the complexity of cultural values and their relationship to economic behavior. Of course I can easily explain away these weaknesses in public by referring to the paucity of relevant literature at the time. In the end, however, and in the ultimate confrontation—with the shaving mirror—I must accept that these were significant imbalances that reduced the quality of my work.

There were undoubtedly some gains from applying both the dependency thesis and Marxist analysis to the African past: the former made the study of external relations and the colonial era permissible once more; the latter pushed back the frontiers of African history by authorizing the wider study of what, in the language of the day, were called relations of production (known generically as "history from below"). It was possible, finally, to venture criticisms of African leaders and societies without being called a racist, though you might be called a fascist, because radical thinking had identified the bourgeoisie of all colors and stripes as the enemy.

A price was paid for these advances: many redwood trees were felled to aid the fruitless discussion of what a mode of production was, and what you would do if you found it—especially on a dark night without a torch; the search for proletarians ran into the ground tilled by newly discovered peasants; and the whole enterprise was fatally compromised by the adoption of a simple verifying procedure, whereby authors knew exactly what they were looking for and, not surprisingly, found it with impressive speed. Most of this literature is now interred in the bunkers librarians keep for unwanted but indisposable books, and constitutes a veritable cemetery for the hopes of the post-Vietnam generation, who were using Africa to illustrate the validity of ideas that seemed to make good sense of their own world and to offer a route towards future progress for everyone. The heart was in the right place; the mind, however, was often elsewhere.

The obverse of these developments in the 1960s and 1970s was the decline of imperial history. This point has to be made with care—especially here! It was not that imperial history suffered an absolute decline: the historical profession as a whole was expanding during this period; and notable studies, such as Gallagher and Robinson's celebrated *Africa and the Victorians* (1961), held out the prospect of blending the new history with the old. It was rather that imperial history became relatively less significant. It was no longer in sole command of the history of the world beyond Europe and the United States; it seemed (or it was made to seem by the Young Turks in Area Studies) dated and apologetic—except that it did not apologize enough.

This development is easily explained and so is not worth dwelling on, except to make the obvious point that the end of empire brought down with it the old style of imperial history. The center could not hold. A process of continental drift carried the segments farther from what had once been their center. Just as the former subjects of empire wanted to run their own states, so too they aspired to write their own histories—and this applied as much to New Zealand as to Nigeria. The outcome, increasingly, was national histories or at least nation-based histories loosely joined, where joined at all, by broader themes, such as international trade. Topics of this kind were still capable of floating as the ship of empire sank because they were linked to issues, such as economic development, that continued to claim attention. Speaking generally, however, imperial history simply became less visible. The new frontiers lay elsewhere.

It was at about this point, in the late 1970s, that I decided that the old, established theme of the causes of imperialism needed to be looked at afresh. This decision stemmed from two considerations. The first was that African economic history was becoming established and was now in the hands of fresh and capable scholars, even if some of them had, in my prejudiced view, applied more snake oil than was good for them. The second consideration arose from a course on imperialism that I was teaching with Peter Cain at the University of Birmingham. Although we were hugely impressed by our ability to see the flaws in every explanation of British imperialism that had ever been offered, we had also reached the point where the students were, rather unfairly we thought, demanding some constructive answers. So, we began the painful task of civilizing ourselves: instead of destroying the work of others we tried to become architects and builders.

As our work progressed and frequently regressed during the 1980s, we were helped by developments on three fronts: new research on British history, especially economic and social history, was beginning to suggest new ways of looking at the process of modernization; the expansion of Area Studies had produced a host of specialized studies that had simply not been available to imperial historians of a previous generation; and the continuing interest in imperial policy had thrown up clusters of revisionist work, notably on decolonization, that needed to be incorporated. Taken together, all three suggested that it might be time to represent imperial history in a general form that was not hopelessly compromised at its inception either by being an apologia for the civilizing mission or by demonizing the whole colonial experience.

Our final formulation appeared in two volumes, entitled *British Imperialism*, in 1993. In essence, we tried to relocate the causes of imperial expansion in the *metropole*, thus reeling them in from the periphery, to where "excentrically" (in Robinson's delightful phrase), they had been exiled, while also avoiding the alternative fate of being caught in the tired embrace of heavily painted and surgically improved Marxist and marxisant theories of empire-building. This we did, to the extent that we did it at all, by redefining the nature of modernization since the late seventeenth century, emphasizing the longevity and enduring nature of the role of finance (but not of what, technically, is known as finance-capitalism) and commercial services, linking these activities to a particular social group, and joining this group, in turn, to political authority. The whole complex we termed "gentlemanly capitalism," perhaps not the most felicitous phrase but one that served to underline the connection between "tradition" and "modernity"—a theme I had already explored in the very different circumstances of pre-colonial Africa.

The books set this theme in motion in two ways: they first traced the evolution of gentlemanly capitalism on the domestic front; they then sought to show how the general argument applied to particular cases across the world and over several centuries, culminating in the process of decolonization itself. Leaving aside for the moment the question of the robustness of the argument itself, I would hope that our work will contribute to two processes: the reintegration of domestic and imperial history and the reintegration of centuries that specialists have divided among themselves.

The reception of our work is still in its early stages; there is rather a lot to digest on several fronts. However, diverse reactions are already apparent. The books stirred some deep waters in Britain (though scarcely rippling a pond in the USA) because they were thought to contribute to the latest version of the Condition of England Question. On the Right (*The Spectator* and *Daily Telegraph*) our argument was seen as providing definitive historical support for the view that Britain's strength lies in her finance and services, which should be given priority in the future. On the Left (*New Statesman* and *Guardian*) our books were seen as providing the definitive historical case against the City, the final proof of the true cause of Britain's decay as a manufacturing power.

In the slightly more real world of academia, the books have aroused critical comments from two main directions, both of which we anticipated. First, there has been a predictable, though restrained, reaction from the guardians of the industrial revolution, who have claimed that we exaggerated the role of finance and services and failed to accord proper weight to manufacturing. The second reaction has come from historians who feel that our predominantly metropolitan standpoint has diminished the significance of the constituent parts of the empire. Some area specialists have gone on to suggest that, in writing imperial history, we are trying to turn the clock back and efface the advances made by a generation of scholars. These criticisms are certainly worth discussing, though this is not the occasion to do so.

In the light of these developments, it seems reasonable to suppose that imperial history has a future and not just a past; the shape of the future, however, is not entirely clear. There are, as usual, contradictory signals. The following examples illustrate some of the positive omens suggesting that the subject may well move closer to the center of the discipline.

The growing importance of international issues (from debt to the environment) and transnational organizations (from business corporations to Amnesty International) has increased the interest of social scientists in the historical dimensions of supranational institutions. Environmental history, for instance, has already produced studies that cross conventional boundaries in pursuit of subjects such as forestry, famine, game and conservation. The rising status of the Commonwealth is also indicative of these trends, and particularly of the development of English as the supranational language of communication.

A further significant development is the unforeseen resurgence of ethnicity as a force in world, as well as in local, politics. Between the transnational at the global level and the local *communitas* or *patria* stands our current uncertainty about the future of the nation state and the nature of the political institutions that will influence the world order (or disorder as it has been called) in the next century. Such concerns are likely to direct renewed attention to the nature of the competing empires that shaped the world system down to the middle of the twentieth century, and to the types of unity that imperial governments laid thinly over their diverse subject peoples.

To these developments in the outside world can be added the ongoing expansion of research within the academic community. As I mentioned earlier, imperial history became less visible as a result of the rise of Area Studies but it did not, of course, disappear. A sizeable number of scholars—witness the long list of contributors to the *Oxford History of the British Empire*—continue to work in the field, and new entrants have joined it. The reaction against the subject that accompanied decolonization has diminished with the passage of time. New possibilities—such as the opening of archives covering the period of decolonization—have stimulated fresh research, and there is a greater awareness that the subject, conceived as a branch of international history and shorn of ideology, is simply too important to be relegated to the byways of history.

However, the revival of the subject, real and prospective, faces difficulties, one coming from within the subject itself, and the other (as in the past) coming from the world outside the ivory tower.

The internal difficulty arises from the fragmentation of the subject, which in turn is a consequence of the expansion of the knowledge we have ourselves produced both about the center and about what we call, with diminishing confidence, the periphery. How can the massive literature now available be comprehended and so organized as to produce a coherent story? And, if a coherent story can be told, is it one that inevitably produces an unacceptable degree of injustice in dealing with the constituent parts? Any answer to this question will have to take account of what, I suspect, is the growing separation of research and teaching. The specialized research output is impressive, but how will the next generation of historians acquire the breadth of knowledge needed to draw the voluminous literature together?

Perhaps the biggest challenge at present, however, comes from postmodernism, known in the age of the soundbite as Pomo. Although this influence has now been internalized, it is also, and to a significant degree, a reaction to events in the outside world. As this is a large, topical and much-discussed subject, I shall proceed on the assumption that everyone here is familiar with the main teachings of postmodernism, and that, consequently, I am free to move directly to a consideration of its influence on the study of imperial history.

In general terms, postmodernism takes a hostile view of imperial history because it sees the imperial "master narrative" as part of the Enlightenment "project," propagating false universals that in turn perpetuate misleading, derogatory stereotypes of what is now known as The Other. Given this position, the only kind of imperial history approved by postmodernism is one that studies the way in which stereotypes have been produced and authority exerted via "print capitalism" and its associates. The most obvious illustrations of this trend are to be found in the avalanche of studies exposing the racism of nineteenth-century European travel writers and explorers, in the rediscovery of agencies of domination, such as Christian missions, education and the spread of scientific knowledge, and in the values symbolized by imperial exhibitions, museums, and ceremonies. This emphasis, reinforced by the rise of cultural history generally in recent years, has undoubtedly added vitality to the subject and enlarged the range of topics conventionally treated by imperial historians, and to this extent is to be welcomed. However, the Pomo "project" also has costs, both trivial and fundamental, which ought to be noted as a warning to the innocent and the unwary.

Among the trivial costs are claims to novelty from newcomers to the subject who are reinventing the wheel without knowing it. Do we really need any more books informing us, with barely contained excitement, that Livingstone, Burton and most of the other explorers of the time held racist views of the peoples they reported on? And do we need to be told this again in the impenetrable and pretentious language in which terms such as "discourse," "totalizing," "essentialism," "alterity," and the capitalized "Other" are used as clubs to bludgeon the reader into submission?

The more serious costs are either unobserved or rarely mentioned. I offer two for consideration. First, although the advocates of Pomo see themselves as a liberating advance guard, they are in fact responsible for perpetuating some very conservative scholarly qualities. A focus on "the text" rather than on a proliferation of texts amounts to a reversion to an old-style, stepping-stone version of the history of intellectual thought that a generation of scholars has labored to replace. Moreover, the rapid application of "lit crit" to history often produces a semi-informed and timeless version of the past, and can resurrect stereotypes that some of us had hoped were long since dead and buried. Even more important, the very notion of "The Other" is itself a gigantic stereotype, a gross oversimplification of nineteenth-century opinion and one that fails to do justice to the heterogeneity of the research completed by area specialists in the course of the last thirty years. The corollary (and irony) is that "The West" is now being presented in a compressed and stereotyped form, thus producing a new type of Eurocentrism, which fails to recognize either the diversity of Western "discourse" or the range of motives behind Europe's interest in the wider world.

The second objection to the Pomo agenda is that it seeks to eliminate a huge range of important issues either because they are deemed to be part of a mistaken totalizing endeavor, or because it is held that there is no reality beyond the text itself. The only exception of consequence is the astonishing discovery and promotion of Subaltern Studies by non-historians like Gayatri Spivak, who have projected the Indianist school on to the world stage. But the admirable work of the subaltern studies group is not new. It is an Indian version of history from below that seeks to avoid clamping Eurocentric theories on to the rest of the world; as such, the approach has long been a familiar part of the research scene.

The appeal of postmodernism is easily understood. In filling the vacuum left by the demise of Marxism, Pomo provides a program for a new generation of commentators whose radical instincts would otherwise be deprived of plausible intellectual backing. But the influence of postmodernism, which is especially marked in the United States, is also driven by powerful political and ideological forces. In particular, Pomo claims to express the aspirations of minority groups, whose position in the United States has led to a major, and still developing, debate on issues of multiculturalism and pluralism, as well as on civil rights generally. These matters have come to the fore because of the changing demographic structure of the United States, but they are prominent, too, in the post-colonial world generally— from Bosnia to Rwanda and beyond to French Canada and to the aspirations of the Maoris in New Zealand. Not surprisingly, these contemporary problems have directed scholarly attention towards representations in general and racial stereotypes in particular.

There is nothing exceptional or particularly worrying about this— in principle. On the contrary, a concern with current issues is a legitimate and stimulating source of historical inquiry. Problems arise with Pomo, as with its predecessors on the Right as well as on the Left, first when the claims become exclusive (as they invariably do), and then when the political imperative is fed into a friendly hypothesis and is applied to the evidence with a degree of selectivity that ensures that the desired result will be forthcoming without undue delay. The results are hailed by other members of the club and may even enjoy a bubble reputation, but all too often they lack the qualities of self-awareness and self-criticism that are necessary if a degree of individuality and independence is to inform a work of scholarship. Consequently, they burst and vanish once the mood of the moment changes.

If imperial history is to experience a renaissance in the twenty-first century, it needs to be both reinvented and rediscovered to deal with the challenges I have outlined and to find acceptable ways of attaching emphasis to themes that have yet to be given their full prominence or that have been consigned to obscurity by post-modernists. Given the time available, I shall list just three (admittedly large) connected themes for consideration.

First, and surely long overdue, is a reconsideration of the imperial state and how it found expression in the empire and was also reinforced by the imperial connection. Peter Cain and I have suggested one set of connections, but we did not have the space to pursue the many sub-sets. Selective examples include: a review of the composition of the political elite (and the professions) to reinvigorate the stereotyped debate about relations between the aristocracy and the bourgeoisie; a reassessment of the composition and role of the armed forces, drawing on the new and broader form of military history that has come to the fore in recent years; a fresh look at the function of Christian beliefs and their connection with state authority, following the lead given by Boyd Hilton and others; and the need to re-examine the role of commercial pressure groups, which, generally speaking, have been neglected for many years.

A refurbished history of the imperial center implies—and the weight of Area Studies compels—the production of a new colonial history that goes well beyond the limits set by representations of The Other or even of the subalterns. Can the character of the "colonial state" be defined more closely? How far were colonial rulers, by social background and training, agents of the metropolitan elite, and how far did they have wills of their own or wills that were shaped by the societies they were supposed to be dominating? How, in creating new states, did policy interact with local realities to codify property rights, and colonial law generally, and to put in place that vital keystone of the state: taxation—a subject that has long been bypassed by virtually everyone? Such work would join that already under way on military history, which is giving us a clearer view of the coercive aspects of the liberal empire. New histories of Christian missions are needed to recast their activities in the field to reflect the approaches to the history of religious ideology in the metropole referred to earlier. There is considerable room for progress, too, in studies of business interests, these having been conducted, to the extent that they have been conducted at all, with motives of praise or blame too frequently at the fore. Finally—though for reasons of time only—it is important to join colonial and precolonial history more subtly than many recent converts to the subject have done. Instead of producing a superfluity of studies of how ethnicity was "invented" by colonial rulers, we need to inquire more closely into the degrees of identification and differentiation that already existed, and to see how resistance to and accommodation with colonial rule caused indigenous spokesmen to seek to manipulate identities of themselves in order to influence (and thereby to control) their new masters.

The third theme concerns the international links that connected the center to its satellites. Of the many possibilities, I shall list just a few in the field of economic history. As far as the empire is concerned, this is now an unfashionable subject; it is, therefore, exactly the right time to enter it. Consider, for example, the movement of peoples so excellently studied by Bernard Bailyn for the eighteenth century, but with much scope for further work in later periods; the emergence of commodity markets in the nineteenth century; the transmission of prices via the submarine cable telegraph; the standardization of time—a much underestimated force for integration between and within continents and colonies. Think, too, of the possibilities for comparing the results of settlement in different parts of the world. Among recent writers, Donald Denoon has made a start; others have begun to compare settlement patterns in Canada, Australia and Argentina, linking them, via recent versions of staple theory and the frontier thesis, to issues of long-run economic development.

The aim of my talk has been to draw attention to the fact that knowledge is indeed socially constructed, though in ways that, if recognized, would usually be unpalatable to those of us who are more comfortable unmasking the self-deceptions of others than facing up to our own frailties.

In particular, I have tried to show how successive phases in the evolution of Area Studies and imperial history during the past thirty years have been driven by a concern to harness the study of the past to current preoccupations at home and abroad, and how these priorities have either responded to, or called into prominence, the theoretical apparatus thought most relevant to the task in hand. In situating my own work on this bumpy road, I tried to suggest how it fitted into and departed from the conventional wisdom of the day and how its limitations were related to its starting point, which in my case can be understood, as far as I can understand it, rather more by looking at academic failings than by a bias stemming from a political program—though I am not claiming that this is the lesser evil. As for the future, which now mostly lies behind me, I am returning to Africa, but without forsaking imperial history, in order to produce a study of partition that integrates indigenous history with that of the expanding foreign powers. The direction is clear; the terminus less so, but I am already confident that my text will be distinctive, if only because I have resolved nowhere to use the terms "project," "discourse," "interrogation," or "The Other."

The moral of my story is that we must somehow try to keep our heads while others are losing theirs. Novel elixirs are to be sipped not quaffed. Each of the phases I have described has brought something of value to the study of the subject, but there has also been a price to pay. It is in the nature of enthusiasms that the merits of the wares are extolled while the drawbacks are minimized. Indeed, at the peak of their influence each of the phases I have described appears to have had a providential, certainly an exclusive, route to truth. It has been hard to think of any other way of looking at the problem until suddenly—for it usually is quite sudden—the lens cracks. Yet, once deprived of our rose-tinted spectacles, we can see quite clearly that the Emperor had no clothes.

Criticizing current fashions is in some ways difficult because it casts the critic in a conservative role in a field of study that rightly respects innovation and also associates it with progressive thinking. Exorcism and exclusion are among the sanctions used. But the risk, such as it is, has to be taken if some of the adverse consequences of applying simple theories to a complex world are to be avoided. It is in this spirit that I have welcomed some of the new emphases that have been given to imperial history while drawing attention to the real opportunities that lie, in my opinion, neither in doing what everyone else is doing nor in being willfully perverse, but in identifying major neglected or understudied themes and realizing that they are important enough to survive and eventually to demand attention.

Fortunately, the body of historians working on imperial history is as large, as varied, and as scattered as the empires they study. Disunity has its drawbacks: wheels are reinvented more often than they should be. On the other hand, heterogeneity is a crucial safeguard against intellectual tyranny. No one viewpoint, however influential, can assert itself either completely or for very long. And, of course, it is from diversity that alternative perspectives emerge. When they do, we should be informed and stimulated by them, but we should bear in mind, too, that novelty inspires imitation more readily than it guarantees truth.

Fall Semester 1996

# 20

# British and North American University Presses

## JOANNA HITCHCOCK

T he concept of a university press in North America is clear
enough for it to receive an entry in the Columbia Encyclopedia. In the United Kingdom, however, the differences between all the publishers with "university press" in their titles are too
great for the term to convey anything like so precise a meaning.
Comparing university presses in North America with those in Britain therefore means comparing an entity that clearly exists with something a great deal more amorphous. The term "university press" is
used frequently in the United States to refer to a type of publisher,
whereas in Britain university presses are rarely considered to be a
special category. Most major universities in the United States and
Canada have presses: there are over one hundred of them altogether.
Through the Association of American University Presses, they work
closely together on common problems and initiatives and present
one face to the public on important issues. Britain is the home of
the two largest university presses, Oxford and Cambridge, which
are both international publishers with branches throughout the
world, most notably in the United States; but they have little in common with the scattering of smaller university presses that operate
independently not only of the giants but of each other. The British
university presses have not found enough in common to form an
association of their own comparable to the American one.

While Oxford University Press now publishes over 3,000 new titles
a year (from all its offices combined) and Cambridge University
Press over 1,500, the other British presses, with the exception of
Manchester and the Open University Press, all publish fewer than
80 new books a year. But Oxford and Cambridge had a 400-year
start on most of the others. Those two trace their origins back to the

mid sixteenth century; of the "provincial" university presses, only three came into existence before the Second World War.

In the United States, university presses have existed for a little over a century. None are as big as Oxford University Press and Cambridge University Press and few are as small as the provincial presses in Britain. The five largest U.S. presses (excluding Oxford and Cambridge) published between 220 and 300 new titles each in 1995. At the other extreme, eleven presses published fewer than ten new titles. The majority, though, are medium-sized, with output ranging from 35 to 150 new books a year.

Many of the smaller university presses in Britain have more in common with commercial scholarly publishers—still a flourishing breed there—than with OUP or CUP or with university presses in North America. Some of them are university presses in name only, failing to meet the criteria that are normally used to qualify a press for that status. What is meant by a university press is best understood in its historical context.

Daniel Coit Gilman, the first president of Johns Hopkins, believed that a great university had three functions: teaching, research, and the dissemination of the results of that research. "It is one of the noblest duties of a university to advance knowledge, and to diffuse it not merely among those who can attend the daily lectures—but far and wide." Jaroslav Pelikan recently wrote, in *The Idea of the University*, "The diffusion of knowledge through publishing is fundamental to the vocation of the university, but the university cannot fulfill that vocation without the university press." University presses were founded primarily to serve their universities, and later the world of learning generally, by publishing the results of advanced scholarship, books that would not be taken on by other publishers because they were too specialized to be commercially viable.

Whereas a commercial publisher must turn a profit, a university press exists primarily to serve scholars and scholarship, not to make money. Two defining characteristics follow logically from this mission and from the press's relationship to the university. The first is editorial: every book published must have been approved by representatives of the parent university, whose name appears on the title page. Anyone who sees a university-press imprint in a book knows that certain procedures have in principle been followed before publication to make sure that it meets high standards of scholarship—in other words, that the university has judged it to be worthy of that imprint. The director and staff may reject a manuscript but they may not, on their own, decide to publish one. Typically, the final decision is made by an editorial board or faculty committee appointed by the president of the university, but before a manuscript reaches the committee it will have been evaluated by the sponsoring editor and usually read by two specialists in the field. The second characteristic is a financial one: university presses are tax-exempt, nonprofit institutions, deriving this status from the fact that they share the educational function of their universities.

Constitutionally, the typical press is an integral part of its parent institution. Many university presses report to the dean of graduate studies, some to the provost, and a few directly to the president—or, if they are unlucky, as Harvard was years ago, to the official in charge of buildings and grounds. Some, like Harvard, Yale, Princeton, and Columbia, have governing boards that include faculty, university officials, and outsiders—often commercial publishers. Some are separately incorporated but with ultimate editorial control nonetheless remaining with their universities.

Oxford and Cambridge provided the model for the North American university press. They are both integral parts of their universities. Their imprints are guarded by the "delegates" (Oxford) and the "syndics" (Cambridge), both rather larger bodies than the typical North American university press faculty committee but with a similar function—to make sure all books published meet high standards. These committees must approve books that originate overseas as well as in the United Kingdom. For its New York office, OUP has a special system of what used to be called "surrogate delegates" (now called "American delegates"). There is one or more surrogate (an academic resident in the U.S.) for each subject, and this person's approval is needed before a project originating in New York can go forward. All such decisions must be reported to the U.K. delegates, who have to retain confidence in their surrogates.

Editorially, then, there is little difference between the procedures at OUP and CUP and those in North America. The main difference lies in their financial structure. Scholarly publishing in the U.S. has always been subsidized publishing. Most university presses depend on operating subsidies from their parent institutions in order to break even and are provided with rent-free premises. Some of the smaller presses require and receive subsidies as high as 50 percent of net sales. In recent years some universities have withdrawn their financial support, but, even when university presses receive no operating subsidies from their parent institutions, they still need to raise funds to support the publication of particular individual books. A few of the largest presses have endowments, the interest from which is used to support specific projects. Others, like Chicago with its *Manual of Style* and Columbia with its *Encyclopedia*, are helped by perennial moneymakers on their backlists. But financing remains a problem for most presses. In the last decade several presses, following the leads of Washington and California, have begun to organize formal development programs, and, with the help of challenge grants from the National Endowment for the Humanities, have succeeded in building endowments to support books in specified fields; others are now following suit.

So far from being subsidized by its university, OUP generates a surplus and pays back to the university a certain proportion of that surplus, after putting some of it into a reserve fund. And Cambridge has long been expected to be more than self-sufficient financially and to make a contribution to the university's exchequer. This healthy financial situation is secured partly through economies of scale and partly because both presses have large backlists, developed over many years, that include such profitable items as the Bible and Episcopalian prayer books, schoolbooks, books for English-language teaching, professional books, and reference works. It does not affect their nonprofit status.

Beyond the two giants in Britain, there are about a dozen other publishers, all much smaller, that call themselves university presses or have at one time been associated with a university. Only a few of them now meet both the editorial and financial criteria outlined above. In most of these presses, some form of editorial supervision is exercised by the university, but that form varies, and in some it is distinctly distant. At the University of Wales Press, for instance, the decision to publish is made by the director after he has obtained one or more academic reports on a manuscript and made a sales projection; he then simply reports that decision to a university management committee. At Exeter, the faculty committee does not actually meet, but reports are circulated and members' written comments are sent to the committee chair, who makes the final decision. Manchester University Press has a board made up of senior academics, but, once the proposals have been reviewed by outside referees, they require approval only by "the relevant member" of that board. The Athlone Press, originally part of the University of London but now privately owned, retains an academic advisory board consisting of senior members of the university, whose approval is "sought but not required," and which exists to "see that Athlone is conducting itself properly as an academic university press, i.e., publishing books of substance and quality."

Financially, the British university presses that operate as nonprofit organizations within the university structure are now in the minority. At least two of these, Wales and Exeter, also receive small subsidies from their universities, but at Wales the basis for this subsidy is now changing so that it is targeted toward Welsh-language and Welsh-studies books only, and at Exeter the subsidy only covers the rent. At

Liverpool, the small direct subsidy has recently been phased out. The majority of so-called university presses in Britain not only receive no subsidy but have ceased to be nonprofit institutions altogether. They are now incorporated as limited companies. Some, like Edinburgh, are still owned by their universities, while others, like the Open University Press (the Open University is a university-level correspondence college), which was bought by its management team in 1988, reinvest part of their profits and distribute the rest to shareholders. Leicester University licensed the right to publish under the Leicester University Press imprint to Frances Pinter in 1988, and it is now an imprint within the academic division of Cassell. The UCL Press (University College, London) is a profit-oriented company founded in 1991 by two former Allen & Unwin publishers with the College as one of two institutional shareholders. It is clear, then, that some of these presses conform more closely than others to the university-press model first developed by CUP and OUP and followed by the North American presses. I leave it to the reader to determine exactly how to classify each one! The point is that in Britain, as in Europe generally, the fruits of scholarly research are often distributed by for-profit publishers. In the U.K. there is not the same distinction, either in reality or in the public's mind, between university presses and commercial houses. There is virtually no difference in their publishing programs and procedures between these university presses and a publisher like Berg, founded in Oxford in 1981, which publishes some sixty new titles a year in history, social science, sociology, economics, philosophy, and literary criticism; or Duckworth, famous for its line in classics; or Christopher Hurst, whose monographs in area studies would be too specialized for most American university presses to have the courage to take on nowadays; or Polity Press, which is run by academics, publishes scholarly books, and seeks outside specialist evaluations.

One of the reasons for the paucity of university presses in the U.K. may be that there is little advantage in the relationship either for the university or for the publisher. The universities do not want or cannot afford to subsidize the presses. The publishers need more freedom if they are to operate successfully as businesses. They may need to publish some profitable books that fall outside the mission of a university press and they cannot always afford to be hamstrung by the necessity of following procedures that slow down the editorial process. There is one advantage to the university connection, though, and that is the name; clearly, the prestige is still perceived to be valuable even if it no longer means as much as it once did. So a workable system has emerged, in the true British spirit of compromise. As a result, though, while university presses in North America form a distinct and influential body of publishing, no such clear distinction between university presses and trade publishers is visible in Britain.

To understand both the peculiarities of university presses and the differences between them it helps to know a little about their history.

Cambridge University Press was founded in 1534, Oxford in 1632. (At least, those seem to be the dates currently accepted, after years of wrangling over an issue that brought out varsity loyalties almost as intense as those generated by the annual boat race.) Then comes a gap of 267 years before the first provincial university press was founded at Liverpool in 1899, followed by Manchester (1912) and Wales (1922). The other British university presses, as mentioned earlier, were all founded after the Second World War: Edinburgh, the Athlone Press, Leicester, and Exeter were founded in the 1940s and 1950s; the Open University Press and Hull in the 1970s and 1980s; and UCL, Keele, and Nottingham in the early 1990s. Some of the older provincial presses have come and gone like Alice's Cheshire cat (a phenomenon not unique to Britain): it is encouraging that several have sprung back to life, and that university presses are still being founded.

CUP and OUP had their origins in the information revolution that followed the invention of printing in the mid fifteenth century. Cambridge University Press, founded by a royal charter granted to the university by Henry VIII, can boast of being the oldest surviving printing and publishing house in the world, although the Press did not actually publish its first book until fifty years thereafter. Oxford's interest in printing and publishing was intermittent in the century after Gutenberg, but in 1586 it obtained a decree from the Star Chamber (England's highest judicial body at that time) confirming its privilege to print books. The university first appointed delegates to oversee this privilege in 1633, minute-books recording their deliberations were started in 1668, and from that time on OUP began to develop into its present form. By the early eighteenth century, the Press had become sufficiently successful to erect its magnificent Clarendon Building, which was partly financed out of profits from the publication of Lord Clarendon's history of the English Civil War, and the name of Clarendon has been associated with the Press (and in particular with its scholarly imprint) ever since.

In the seventeenth century, London and Cambridge publishers competed over the printing of Bibles. Bibles printed in London were as full of errors as other books printed at that time—"girded their lions," "he who hath ears to ear," and, most famously, "Thou shalt commit adultery." The typographical errors moved Charles I to grant the almost exclusive—and very lucrative—right to print Bibles to Oxford and Cambridge. With the Bible as their "cash cow," these university presses became two of the largest and most important publishers in the world. And the Bible warehouse that OUP set up in London was the starting point for that press's growth into a major publisher of educational books intended for the general reader, as well as of school and children's books. The distribution of Bibles spurred the Press on to found offices in other parts of the English-speaking world, beginning with the United States in 1896, extending to outposts of the British Empire, and culminating in a network of offices extending round the world today. (Those colonial outposts were where fresh male graduates used typically to be sent after learning the ropes at the home base, and where, unless they were careful, they might spend the rest of their lives. If they succeeded in achieving repatriation, they would return to the head office sporting a tan, dressed in white, looking as though they came straight out of a Merchant-Ivory movie, and expect to continue their progress upwards.) Cambridge has expanded in recent years into an international operation comparable to Oxford's, with its U.S. and Australian branches publishing their own books as well as representing the list originating from the home office. Crossing the Atlantic in the other direction, Yale University Press has a London-based office that is a full-scale publishing enterprise.

A century after the founding of CUP, the Reverend Josiah Glover sailed for Massachusetts, bringing his wife and his printing press with him. Glover died before the ship reached port, but his wife completed the journey and went on to marry the president of Harvard, who thus acquired the press for the college in 1643. It was used to print psalm-books and almanacs, as well as a Bible in the language of the local Indians. But more than two centuries elapsed before any formal program of scholarly publishing was established in the New World.

The oldest continuously operating university publishing house on the American continent, Johns Hopkins University Press, was founded in 1878, 344 years after Cambridge, and, in fact, exactly 400 years after the first book was *printed* in Oxford. A few others followed quickly—Chicago, Cornell, and Columbia among them—and by the First World War many of the major American universities had set up presses, including California, Princeton, Yale, and Harvard. But the greatest expansion of university presses in the United States took place in the 1930s and 1940s.

The term "press" is an anachronism that may now be confusing because almost no university presses are still printers as well as publishers. In the early days of printing—and indeed for most of the history of book-printing—editing, printing, and distributing a text were all part of the same trade. As "publishing" as a distinct business arose out of and gradually became separate from printing, many commercial publishers on both sides of the Atlantic still had their own printing plants in the last century, and some until well into this one. This was true of university publishing houses as well—not only of Oxford and Cambridge but of some of the older and larger U.S. presses. With their specialized experience in technical typesetting, the Oxford and Cambridge printers—and, in the U.S., the Princeton University Press printing plant, among others—were, moreover, able to sell printing services to other publishers. On the other hand, OUP's trade list had long outgrown its own plant's capacity, and most of the books bearing an OUP imprint in this century were printed by companies outside Oxford, even before OUP closed down its printing works in 1989. Stanford's had gone a decade before, Princeton's was to go shortly afterwards, and now Cambridge is the only university press with a real "press" to its name.

Every campus needs its printing shop for campus printing jobs, however, and some of these even now cooperate to help out their publishing houses. The University of California's printing office for a while printed its university press's monographs, though not without tension between the two; for a time before and during the Second World War, in a remarkable reversal of the historical trend, its press and its printing office were merged under a manager with a reputation as a fine printer, and the books they turned out were certainly elegant, if otherwise undistinguished. At Texas, "University of Texas Press" meant (reasonably enough) the printing department until the University Press itself was founded in 1950: before that the imprint simply indicated that a faculty member who obtained a grant for publishing a piece of research had taken his manuscript to the printing shop and directed all other aspects of its publication himself.

Historically, university presses began by publishing books by members of their own faculties and only gradually evolved into publishers of works by scholars from all over the country for the world of learning at large. In the course of this evolution, university presses came to concentrate their programs on particular areas of knowledge.

While some of the larger presses now publish in many different academic areas, not even OUP and CUP attempt to cover the waterfront, and for some of the smaller presses niche publishing has become a tactic for survival. While university presses were founded with the common purpose of publishing works of scholarship, individual historical and geographical circumstances account for some of the variations between their programs both in subject area and in type of book published.

OUP began chiefly as a Bible publisher, and as late as the 1890s there were still those who were prepared to censure the university for allowing its press to publish the secular and profane literature of Spenser, Marlowe, and Shakespeare. But this phase passed, and the reputation of the Clarendon Press in Oxford came to depend on the publication of scholarly monographs. The London office, on the other hand, became known for books intended rather for the general reader. Some of them were also intended to be profitable, so that together with the Bible they could help subsidize the publication in Oxford of learned books that would not cover their costs. This philosophy of balancing specialized books with ones that reached out to a broader public also permeated the North American university presses, which were concerned both to fulfill their primary purpose of advancing knowledge and to balance the ledger. University presses came to regard it as their mission not only to serve the scholarly community but, by means of what Arthur Rosenthal, former director of Harvard University Press, called "extension books," to bridge the gap between the academic community and society as a whole by making the research and ideas of scholars accessible to a wider world of intelligent men and women generally and not merely to the small circle of their academic peers. Some of these "trade" books, sold largely through general bookstores, might equally well have been found on the lists of commercial publishers. In recent years, university presses have increasingly come to aim a significant portion of their lists at the trade, stepping into the gap created by commercial publishers' near-total abandonment of the book that is likely to sell fewer than four or five thousand copies. North American university presses are now also publishing in increasing numbers, and in paperback, books for use by students in courses, a type of publishing in which OUP and CUP preceded them.

The scholarly monograph, which used to form the backbone of scholarly publishing, proliferated partly as a result of the need for scholars to publish in order to achieve tenure and advance their careers. For young scholars, the choice was to "publish or perish," and the publication of revised dissertations became an industry in itself. Two or three books of Shakespeare criticism and a couple on Spenser or Milton might emerge from one large press in a single year. One wonders how anyone attempting to keep up with all this scholarship ever found the time to study the texts themselves. But sales of the scholarly monograph have dropped significantly over the last decade and in some fields this kind of specialized study is becoming an endangered species. While most North American university presses still publish a few monographs each season and some are determinedly seeking ways to keep the form alive, OUP and CUP are now taking the lead in ensuring its survival. Traditionally, though, the emphasis placed on monograph publishing as a condition for academic advancement was not as great in Britain, and in the past authors of the specialized books coming from OUP and CUP were not motivated as much by this particular concern. It was considered as important to publish texts and editions as books of criticism and interpretation, if not more so.

The British presses, like their universities, have tended to adhere to the subjects of the traditional curriculum, while some of the North American presses were among the first in such developing fields as women's studies, the environment, and media studies. Some presses in the United States have not just been quick to follow these trends but have helped to set them. Though some of the smaller presses in Britain are now listing environmental studies, cultural studies, and women's studies among their offerings, these are more recent developments. Some of the small U.K. presses, though, publish books that would be more likely to be found on the lists of professional publishers in North America—books in fields like medicine, dentistry, nursing, management, and agriculture.

Regional publishing, which is a recognized task of the presses at U.S. state universities and at some Canadian ones and a good source of income, is also performed by some of the provincial university presses in Britain. Wales, for example, publishes Welsh studies, "intelligent tourism, etc.," and Exeter's regional list includes a hardy perennial on the geology of Devon and Cornwall. In the U.S., cookbooks are also common fare nowadays, especially at state university presses.

A few North American university presses publish poetry, and, in recent years, some have begun cautiously to publish fiction, stepping into the breach as New York publishers have tended to focus more and more exclusively on bestsellers. British university presses, too, have idiosyncratic lines of their own, some of which go back for centuries. The Waldock Committee, appointed by Oxford University in the late 1960s to investigate the press and its relations with the university, noted that OUP's music department was the second largest in the country and found it "too late to ask how or why"; the committee also found the publishing of children's books a little questionable, not the most obviously appropriate way of engaging the energies of a university press. But today these programs are regarded as a vital part of OUP's list, which also includes contemporary poetry. OUP and CUP took the lead in publishing reference books, followed by Columbia in 1935, and later Chicago, Harvard, Yale, and other U.S. presses. And both British presses have journals programs, as do about a quarter of the university presses in North America.

Unlike the British university presses, their North American counterparts have worked together from their early days to solve common problems. At first it was an old boys' club of colleagues getting together informally to swap stories. Then in 1937 the Association of American University Presses was created as a formal organization; and in 1959 its central office was established in New York. The member presses furnish its president, treasurer, board of directors, and committee members. The Association, with the help of its executive director and central-office staff, cultivates relationships with foundations and the government and with the library, trade publishing, and academic communities. It offers a host of useful services and tools to the membership, including workshops, publications, and common representation at scholarly meetings. Recently, for example, it created a joint online catalog available on the Internet through the World Wide Web, articulated a position on intellectual property rights in the electronic environment, expressed staunch support for the National Endowment for the Humanities, and began monitoring and encouraging the many experiments in electronic publishing now under way at member presses. Presses cooperate outside the association, too. The MIT Press and Harvard operate joint warehouse facilities; and Johns Hopkins provides an order-fulfillment and shipping service for a number of presses. British publishers cooperate too, of course, but their Publishers Association serves trade publishers and university presses alike and—as might be expected from the account of the British publishing scene presented earlier—there is no separate association devoted exclusively to the special needs of scholarly publishers.

OUP and CUP have more in common, then, with some of the U.K. commercial publishers and with the larger North American presses than with the other British university presses. These small presses, in turn, are more similar in their operation to commercial scholarly publishers in size, programs, and structure. This does not mean that the books they publish are any less worthy as works of scholarship, only that the imprint does not guarantee that a certain procedure has been followed in evaluating the books before publication. And although commercial scholarly presses must turn a profit overall while university presses "merely" break even, neither kind of publisher is likely nowadays to take on a book that is actually expected to lose money. The difference is that, if the university press believes that a book will make an important contribution to scholarship, it is more likely to seek a subsidy to make publication feasible than to turn it away.

Despite some basic distinctions, publishers who call themselves university presses on both sides of the Atlantic have on balance more to join than to divide them. They have all found ways to survive the succession of crises that have beset scholarly publishing over the years—though for some of the British presses this has meant becoming commercial, while university presses proper have had to broaden the appeal and marketability of their books in order to strengthen their ability to fulfill their primary mission to scholars. It is this resilience, a willingness to adapt while retaining their sense of purpose, that has served university presses well in the past and will enable them to continue to make a major contribution to intellectual life on both sides of the Atlantic in the coming century.

Fall Semester 1995

For providing information about their presses, I gratefully acknowledge the help of Simon Baker (University of Exeter Press), Robin Bloxsidge (Liverpool University Press), Vivian Bone (Edinburgh University Press), the late Francis Brooke (Manchester University Press), Roger Jones (UCL Press), Janet Joyce (Cassell-Leicester University Press), Nicola A. Pike (Keele University Press), John Skelton (Open University Press), and Ned Thomas (University of Wales Press); for their comments and suggestions, Ivon Asquith (OUP), Martyn J. Hitchcock, Donald Lamm (W. W. Norton), and Wm. Roger Louis (The University of Texas at Austin). I alone am responsible for any errors of fact or interpretation.

# 21

# British Studies at
# The University of Texas, 1975–1998

*Fall Semester 1975*

Paul Scott (Novelist, London), 'The Raj Quartet'

Ian Donaldson (Director, Humanities Research Centre, Australian National University), 'Humanistic Studies in Australia'

Fritz Fellner (Professor of History, Salzburg University), 'Britain and the Origins of the First World War'

Roger Louis (Professor of History and Curator of Historical Collections, Humanities Research Center), 'Churchill, Roosevelt and the Future of Dependent Peoples during the Second World War'

Michael Holroyd (Biographer, Dublin), 'Two Biographies: Lytton Strachey and Augustus John'

Max Beloff (former Gladstone Professor of Government, Oxford University, present Principal of Buckingham College), 'Imperial Sunset'

Robin Winks (Professor of History, Yale University), 'British Empire-Commonwealth Studies'

Warren Roberts (Director, Humanities Research Center), and David Farmer (Assistant Director, Humanities Research Center), 'The D. H. Lawrence Editorial Project'

Harvey C. Webster (Professor of English, University of Louisville), 'C. P. Snow as Novelist and Philosopher'

Anthony Kirk-Greene (Fellow of St. Antony's College, Oxford), 'The Origins and Aftermath of the Nigerian Civil War'

*Spring Semester 1976*

Joseph Jones (Professor of English), 'World English'

William S. Livingston (Professor of Government), 'The British Legacy in Contemporary Indian Politics'

John Higley (Associate Professor of Sociology), 'The Recent Political Crisis in Australia'

Elspeth Rostow (Dean of General and Comparative Studies), Standish Meacham (Professor of History), and Alain Blayac (Professor of English, University of Paris), 'Reassessments of Evelyn Waugh'

Jo Grimond (former Leader of the Liberal Party), 'Liberal Democracy in Britain'

Gaines Post (Associate Professor of History), Malcolm Macdonald (Professor of Government), and Roger Louis, 'The Impact of Hitler on British Politics'

Robert Hardgrave (Professor of Government), Gail Minault (Assistant Professor of History), and Chihiro Hosoya (Professor of History, University of Tokyo), 'Kipling and India'

Kenneth Kirkwood (Rhodes Professor of Race Relations, Oxford University), 'The Future of Southern Africa'

Lord [C. P.] Snow, 'Elite Education in England'

Hans-Peter Schwarz (Director of the Political Science Institute, Cologne University, and Visiting Fellow, Woodrow Wilson International Center for Scholars), 'The Impact of Britain on German Politics and Society since the Second World War'

B. K. Nehru (Indian High Commissioner, London, and former Ambassador to the United States), 'The Political Crisis in India'

Robert A. Divine (Professor of History), Harry J. Middleton (Director, Lyndon Baines Johnson Library), and Roger Louis, 'Declassification of Secret Documents: The British and American Experiences Compared'

*Fall Semester 1976*

John Farrell (Associate Professor of English), 'Revolution and Tragedy in Victorian England'

Anthony Honoré (Regius Professor of Civil Law, Oxford University), 'British Attitudes to Legal Regulation of Sex'

Alan Hill (Professor of English), 'Wordsworth and America'

Ian Nish (Professor of Japanese History, London School of Economics), 'Anglo-American Naval Rivalry and the End of the Anglo-Japanese Alliance'

Norman Sherry (Professor of English, University of Lancaster), 'Joseph Conrad and the British Empire'

Peter Edwards (Lecturer, Australian National University), 'Australia through American Eyes: The Second World War and the Rise of Australia as a Regional Power'

David Edwards (Professor of Government), Steven Baker (Assistant Professor of Government), Malcolm Macdonald, Bill Livingston, and Roger Louis, 'Britain and the Future of Europe'

Michael Hurst (Fellow of St. John's College, Oxford), 'The British Empire in Historical Perspective: The Case of Joseph Chamberlain'

Ronald Grierson (English Banker and former Public Official), 'The Evolution of the British Economy since 1945'

Marian Kent (Lecturer in History, University of New South Wales), 'British Oil Policy between the World Wars'

Constance Babington-Smith (Fellow of Churchill College, Cambridge), 'The World of Rose Macaulay'

William Todd (Kerr Professor of English History and Culture), Walt Rostow (Professor of History and Economics), and James McKie (Dean of Social and Behavioral Sciences), 'Adam Smith after 200 Years'

*Spring Semester 1977*

Carin Green (Novelist) and Elspeth Rostow, 'The Achievement of Virginia Woolf'

Samuel H. Beer (Professor of Government, Harvard University), 'Reflections on British Politics'

David Fieldhouse (Fellow of Nuffield College, Oxford), 'Decolonization and the Multinational Corporations'

Gordon Craig (Wallace Professor of Humanities, Stanford University), 'England and Europe on the Eve of the Second World War'

John Lehmann (British Publisher and Writer), 'Publishing under the Bombs—The Hogarth Press during World War II'

Philip Jones (Director, University of Texas Press), William S. Livingston (Christian Professor of British Studies), Michael Mewshaw (Assistant Professor of English), David Farmer,

Roger Louis, and William Todd, 'The Author, his Editor and Publisher'

Dick Taverne (former Member of Parliament), 'The Mood of Britain: Misplaced Gloom or Blind Complacency?'

James B. Crowley (Professor of History, Yale University), Lloyd C. Gardner (Professor of History, Rutgers University), Akira Iriye (Professor of History, University of Chicago), and Roger Louis, 'The Origins of World War II in the Pacific'

Rosemary Murray (Vice-Chancellor of Cambridge University), 'Higher Education in England'

Burke Judd (Professor of Zoology) and Robert Wagner (Professor of Zoology), 'Sir Cyril Burt and the Controversy over the Heritability of I.Q.'

Sandy Lippucci (Government), Roger Louis (History), Bill Livingston (Government), Walt Rostow (Economics), 'The Wartime Reputations of Churchill and Roosevelt: Overrated or Underrated?'

### Fall Semester 1977

Donald L. Weismann (University Professor in the Arts), 'British Art in the Nineteenth Century: Turner and Constable—Precursors of French Impressionism'

Standish Meacham, 'Social Reform in England'

Joseph Jones, 'Recent Commonwealth Literature'

Lewis Hoffacker (former United States Ambassador), 'The Katanga Crisis: British and other Connections'

James M. Treece (Professor of Law), Roger Louis, Warren Roberts, and Bill Todd, 'The Copyright Law of 1976'

Charles Heimsath (Visiting Professor of Indian History), Bob Hardgrave, Thomasson Jannuzi, (Director, Center for Asian Studies), C. P. Andrade (Professor of Comparative Studies), and Bill Livingston, 'Freedom at Midnight: A Reassessment of Britain and the Partition of India Thirty Years After'

Lord Fraser of Kilmorack (Chairman of the Conservative Party Organization), 'The Tory Tradition of British Politics'

Bernth Lindfors (Professor of English), 'Charles Dickens and the Hottentots and Zulus'

Albert Hourani (Director, Middle East Centre, Oxford University), 'The Myth of T. E. Lawrence'

Mark Kinkead-Weekes (Professor of English, University of Kent) and
  Mara Kalnins (British writer), 'D. H. Lawrence: Censorship
  and the Expression of Ideas'
J. D. B. Miller (Professor of International Relations, Australian National University), 'The Collapse of the British Empire'
Peter Green (Professor of Classics), Robert King (Dean of Social
  and Behavioral Sciences), Bill Livingston, Bob Hardgrave,
  Roger Louis, and Warren Roberts, 'The Best and Worst Books
  of 1977'

## Spring Semester 1978

Peter Green, Malcolm Macdonald, and Robert Crunden (Professor
  of American Studies), 'British Decadence in the Interwar
  Years'
Terry Quist (University of Texas Undergraduate), Steve Baker, and
  Roger Louis, 'R. Emmet Tyrrell's *Social Democracy's Failure in
  Britain*'
Stephen Koss (Professor of History, Columbia University), 'The
  British Press: Press Lords, Politicians, and Principles'
John House (Professor of Geography, Oxford University), 'The
  Rhodesian Crisis'
T. S. Dorsch (Professor of English, Durham University), 'Oxford in
  the 1930s'
Stephen Spender (English Poet and Writer), 'Britain and the Span-
  ish Civil War'
Okot p'Bitek (Ugandan Poet), 'Idi Amin's Uganda'
David C. Goss (Australian Consul General), 'Wombats and
  Wivveroos'
Leon Epstein (Professor of Political Science, University of Wiscon-
  sin), 'Britain and the Suez Crisis of 1956'
David Schoonover (School of Library Science), 'British and Ameri-
  can Expatriates in Paris in the 1920s'
Peter Stansky (Professor of History, Stanford University), 'George
  Orwell and the Spanish Civil War'
Alexander Parker (Professor of Spanish), 'Reflections on the Span-
  ish Civil War'
Norman Sherry (Professor of English, Lancaster University), 'Gra-
  ham Greene and Latin America'
Martin Blumenson (Office of the Chief of Military History, Depart-
  ment of the Army), 'The Ultra Secret'

*Fall Semester 1978*

W. H. Morris-Jones (Director, Commonwealth Studies Institute, University of London), 'Power and Inequality in Southeast Asia'

Hartley Grattan (Emeritus Professor of History), Gilbert Chase (Professor of American Studies), Bob Crunden, and Roger Louis, 'The British and the Shaping of the American Critical Mind: A Discussion of *Edmund Wilson's Letters on Literature and Politics*'

James Roach (Professor of Government), 'The Indian Emergency and its Aftermath'

Bill Todd, 'The Lives of Samuel Johnson'

Lord Hatch (British Labour Politician), 'The Labour Party and Africa'

John Kirkpatrick (HRC Bibliographer), 'Max Beerbohm'

Brian Levack (Associate Professor of History), 'Witchcraft in England and Scotland'

M. R. Masani (Indian Writer), 'Gandhi and Gandhism'

A. W. Coates (Visiting Professor of Economics), 'The Professionalization of the British Civil Service'

John Clive (Professor of History and Literature, Harvard University), 'Great Historians of the Nineteenth Century'

Geoffrey Best (University of Sussex), 'Flightpath to Dresden: British Strategic Bombing in the Second World War'

Kurth Sprague (Instructor of English), 'T. H. White's *Once and Future King*'

Gilbert Chase, 'The British Musical Invasion of America'

*Spring Semester 1979*

Peter Green (Professor of Classics), Sandy Lippucci (Instructor in Government), and Elspeth Rostow (Dean of the LBJ School of Public Affairs), 'P. N. Furbanks's Biography of *E. M. Forster*'

Roger Louis, Bob Hardgrave, Gail Minault (History), Peter Gran (History), and Bob King, 'E. M. Forster and India'

Paul M. Kennedy (East Anglia University, Visiting Professor of History, Institute of Advanced Study, Princeton), 'The Contradiction between British Strategic Policy and Economic Policy in the Twentieth Century'

Richard Rive (Visiting Fulbright Research Fellow from South Africa), 'Olive Schreiner and the South African Nation'

Charles P. Kindleberger (Professor of Economics, Massachusetts Institute of Technology), 'Lord Zuckerman and the Second World War'
John Press (English Poet), 'English Poets and Postwar Society'
Richard Ellmann (Goldsmiths' Professor of English Literature, Oxford University), 'Writing a Biography of Joyce'
Michael Finlayson (Scottish Dramatist), 'Contemporary British Theater'
Lawrence Stone (Professor of History, Institute of Advanced Study, Princeton), 'Family, Sex, and Marriage in England'
C. P. Snow, 'Reflections on the Two Cultures'
Theodore Zeldin (Oxford University), 'Are the British More or Less European than the French?'
David Edwards (Professor of Government), 'How United the Kingdom: Greater or Lesser Britain?'
Michael Holroyd (British Biographer), 'George Bernard Shaw'
John Wickman (Director, Eisenhower Library), 'Eisenhower and the British'

*Fall Semester 1979*

Robert Palter (Professor of Philosophy), 'Reflections on British Philosophers: Locke, Hume, and the Utilitarians'
Alfred Gollin (Professor of History, University of California at Santa Barbara), 'Political Biography as Political History: Garvin, Milner, and Balfour'
Edward Steinhart (Assistant Professor of History), 'The Consequences of British Rule in Uganda'
Paul Sturges (Loughborough University), and Dolores Donnelly (Toronto University), 'History of the National Library of Canada'
Sir Michael Tippett (British Composer), 'Moving into Aquarius'
Steven Baker (Assistant Professor of Government), 'Britain and United Nations Emergency Operations'
Maria Okila Dias (Professor of History, University of São Paulo), 'Intellectual Roots of Informal Imperialism: Britain and Brazil'
Alexander Parker (Professor of Portuguese), 'Reflections on *Brideshead Revisited*'
Barry C. Higman (Professor of History, University of the West Indies), 'West Indian Emigrés and the British Empire'
Gaines Post (Associate Professor of History), 'Britain and the Outbreak of the Second World War'

Karen Gould (Lecturer in Art) 'Medieval Manuscript Fragments and English 17th Century Collections: New Perspectives from *Fragmenta Manuscripta*'

John Farrell (English), Eric Poole (HRC) and James Bieri (English): Round Table Discussion of Jeanne MacKenzie's new biography of *Dickens: A Life*

Joseph O. Baylen, (Regents Professor of History, Georgia State University), 'British Journalism in the Late Victorian and Edwardian Eras'

Peter T. Flawn (President of UT), 'An Appreciation of Charles Dickens'

*Spring Semester 1980*

Annette Weiner (Assistant Professor of Anthropology), 'Anthropologists in New Guinea: British Interpretations and Cultural Relativism'

Bernard Richards (Lecturer in English, Oxford University), 'Conservation in the Nineteenth Century'

Thomas McGann (Professor of History), 'Britain and Argentina: An Informal Dominion?'

Mohammad Ali Jazayery (Director, Center for Middle Eastern Studies), 'The Persian Tradition in English Literature'

C. Hartley Grattan (Professor of History), 'Twentieth-Century British Novels and the American Critical Mind'

Katherine Whitehorn (London *Observer*), 'An Insider's View of the *Observer*'

Guy Lytle (Assistant Professor of History), 'The Oxford University Press' *History of Oxford*'

C. P. Snow, 'Reflections on *The Masters*'

Harvey Webster, '*The Masters* and the Two Cultures'

Brian Blakeley (Associate Professor of History, Texas Tech University), 'Women and the British Empire'

Stephen Koss (Professor of History, Columbia University), 'Asquith, Balfour, Milner, and the First World War'

Tony Smith (Associate Professor of Political Science, Tufts University), 'The Expansion of England: New Ideas on Controversial Themes in British Imperialism'

Stanley Ross (Professor of History), 'Britain and the Mexican Revolution'

Rowland Smith (Chairman, Department of English, Dalhousie University), 'The British Intellectual Left and the War 1939–1945'
Richard Ellmann (Goldsmiths' Professor of English, Oxford University), 'Oscar Wilde: a Reconsideration and Problems of the Literary Biographer'
James Bill (Professor of Government), 'The United States, Britain, and the Iranian Crisis of 1953'

*Fall Semester 1980*

Decherd Turner (Director, Harry Ransom Humanities Research Center), 'The First 1000 Days'
Roger Louis, 'Britain and Egypt after the Second World War'
Alistair Horne (Visiting Fellow, Woodrow Wilson Center, Washington, D.C.), 'Britain and the Fall of France'
Edward Rhodes (Associate Professor), 'Roper and the Hermit of Peking'
Mark Kinkead-Weeks (Professor of English, Kent University), 'D. H. Lawrence's *Rainbow*. Its Sense of History'
Sir John Crawford (Vice-Chancellor, Australian National University), 'Hartley Grattan: In Memoriam'
John Stubbs (Assistant Professor of History, University of Waterloo), 'The Tory View of Politics and Journalism in the Interwar Years'
Donald L. Weismann (University Professor in the Arts), 'British Art in the Nineteenth Century'
Fran Hill (Assistant Professor of Government), 'The Legacy of British Colonialism in Tanzania'
R. W. B. Lewis (Professor of English, Yale University), 'What's Wrong with the Teaching of English?'
Charlene Gerry (British Publisher), 'The Revival of Fine Printing in Britain'
Peter Gran (Assistant Professor of History), 'The Islamic Response to British Capitalism'
Tina Poole (Humanities Research Center) 'Gilbert and Sullivan's Christmas'

*Spring Semester 1981*

Bernard N. Darbyshire (Visiting Professor of Government and Economics), 'North Sea Oil and the British Future'

Christopher Hill (Master of Balliol College, Oxford), 'The English Civil War'

Elizabeth Heine (Assistant Professor of English, University of Texas at San Antonio), and Roger Louis, 'A Reassessment of Leonard Woolf'

Bernard Richards (Brasenose College, Oxford), 'D. H. Lawrence and Painting'

Miguel Gonzalez-Gerth (Professor of Spanish), 'Poetry Once Removed: The Resonance of English as a Second Language'

John Putnam Chalmers (Librarian, Harry Ransom Humanities Research Center), 'English Bookbinding from Caedmon to Le Carré'

Peter Coltman (Professor of Architecture), 'The Cultural Landscapes of Britain: 2,000 Years of Blood, Sweat, Toil & Tears to Wrest a Living from this Bloody Mud'

Thomas H. Law (former Regent, University of Texas), 'The Gold Coins of the English Sovereigns'

Sidney Weintraub (Rusk Professor of International Affairs, LBJ School), James W. McKie (Professor of Economics), and Mary Williams (Canadian Consulate, Dallas), 'Canadian-American Economic Relations'

Amedée Turner (Conservative Member of the European Parliament), 'Integrating Britain into the European Community'

Muriel C. Bradbrook (Fellow of Girton College, Cambridge), 'Two Poets: Kathleen Raine and Seamus Heaney'

Ronald Sampson (Chief of the Industrial Development Department, Aberdeen), 'Scotland—Somewhat of a British Texas?'

*Fall Semester 1981*

Jerome Bump (Professor of English), 'From Texas to England: The Ancestry of Our Victorian Architecture'

Lord Fraser of Kilmorack, 'Leadership Styles of Tory Prime Ministers since the Second World War'

William Carr (Professor of History, University of Sheffield), 'A British Interpretation of American, German, and Japanese Foreign Policy 1936–1941'

Iqbal Narain, (Professor of Political Science and former Vice-Chancellor, Rajasthan University, Jaipur), 'The Ups and Downs of Indian Academic Life'
Don Etherington (Assistant Director, Humanities Research Center), 'The Florence Flood, 1966: The British Effort—or: Up to our Necks in Mud and Books'
E. V. K. Fitzgerald (Visiting Professor of Economics), 'The British University: Crisis, Confusion, and Stagnation'
Robert Crunden (Professor of American Studies), 'A Joshua for Historians: Mordecai Richter and Canadian Cultural Identity'
Bernth Lindfors (Professor of English), 'The Hottentot Venus and Other African Attractions in Nineteenth-Century England'
Chris Brookeman (Professor of American Studies, London Polytechnic), 'The British Arts and Society'
Nicholas Pickwoad (Free-lance Book Conservator), 'The Libraries of the National Trust'
Kurth Sprague, 'John Steinbeck, Chase Horton, and the Matter of Britain'
Martin J. Wiener (Professor of History, Rice University), 'Cultural Values and Socio-Economic Behavior in Britain'
Werner Habicht (Professor of English, University of Würzburg), 'Shakespeare in Nineteenth-Century Germany'

*Spring Semester 1982*

Stevie Bezencenet (Lecturer in Photography, London College of Printing), 'Contemporary Photography in Britain'
Jane Marcus (Assistant Professor of English), 'Shakespeare's Sister, Beethoven's Brother: Dame Ethel Smyth and Virginia Woolf'
Wilson Harris (Professor of English) and Raja Rao (Professor of Philosophy), 'The Quest for Form: Britain and Commonwealth Perspectives'
Al Crosby (Professor of American Studies), 'The British Empire as a Product of Continental Drift'
Lord St. Brides (Visiting Scholar, University of Texas), 'The White House and Whitehall: Washington and Westminster'
Elizabeth Fernea (Senior Lecturer in English and President of the Middle East Studies Association), 'British Colonial Literature of the Middle East'
Maurice Evans (Actor and Producer), 'My Early Years in the Theater'

Joan Bassin (Kansas City Art Institute) 'Art and Industry in Nine-
teenth-Century England'
Eugene N. Borza (Professor of Ancient History, Pennsylvania State
University), 'Sentimental British Philhellenism: Images of
Greece'
Ralph Willett (American Studies Department, University of Hull),
'The Style and Structure of British Television News'
Roger Louis, 'Britain and the Creation of the State of Israel'
Peter Russell (Professor of Spanish, Oxford University), 'A British
Historian Looks at Portuguese Historiography of the Fif-
teenth Century'
Rory Coker (Physics), 'Frauds, Hoaxes and Blunders in Science—a
British Tradition?'
Ellen DuBois (Professor of History, SUNY Buffalo), 'Anglo-Ameri-
can Perspectives on the Suffragette Movement'
Donald G. Davis, Jr. (Professor of Library Science), 'Great Expecta-
tions—and a Few Illusions: Reflections on an Exchange
Teaching Year in England'
Anthony Rota (Managing Director, Bertram Rota Ltd.), 'The Chang-
ing World of the Bookdealer'
Eisig Silberschlag (former President, Hebrew College, Visiting Gale
Professor of Judaic Studies), 'The Bible as the Most Popular
Book in English'

*Fall Semester 1982*

Woodruff Smith (Professor of History, University of Texas at San
Antonio), 'British Overseas Expansion'
The Rt. Hon. George Thomas (Speaker of the House of Commons),
'Parliamentary Democracy'
Nigel Nicolson (English Historian and Biographer), 'The English
Country House as an Historical Document'
Lord Saint Brides, 'A Late Leaf of Laurel for Evelyn Waugh'
Lt. Col. Jack McNamara, USMC (Ret.), 'The Libel of Evelyn Waugh
by the *Daily Express*'
James Wimsatt (Professor of English), 'Chaucer and Medieval French
Manuscripts'
Christopher Whelan (Visiting Professor, UT Law School), 'Recent
Developments in British Labour Law'
Brian Wearing (Senior Lecturer in American Studies, Christchurch,
New Zealand), 'New Zealand: In the Pacific, but of It?'

Robert Hardgrave (Professor of Government), 'The United States and India'

James McBath (Professor of Communications, University of Southern California), 'The Evolution of *Hansard*'

Paul Fromm (Professor of Economics, University of Toronto), 'Canadian-United States Relations: Two Solitudes'

John Velz (Professor of English), 'When in Disgrace: Ganzel's Attempt to Exculpate John Payne Collier'

Roger Louis, 'British Origins of the Iranian Revolution'

### Spring Semester 1983

Sir Ellis Waterhouse (Slade Professor of Fine Arts, Oxford University), 'A Comparison of British and French Painting in the late Eighteenth Century'

E. J. L. Ride (Australian Consul-General), 'Australia's Place in the World and Her Relationship with the United States'

Edward Bell (Director of the Royal Botanic Gardens, Kew), 'Kew Gardens in World History'

The Very Rev. Oliver Fiennes (Dean of Lincoln), 'The Care and Feeding of Magna Carta'

C. V. Narasimhan (former Under-Secretary of the United Nations), 'Last Days of the British Raj: A Civil Servant's View'

Warren G. Osmond, 'Sir Frederic Eggleston and the Development of Pacific Consciousness'

Richard Ellmann (Goldsmiths' Professor, Oxford University), 'Henry James among the Aesthetes'

Janet Caulkins (Professor of French, University of Wisconsin at Madison), 'The Poor Reputation of Cornish Knights in Medieval Literature'

Werner Habicht (Professor of English, University of Würzburg), 'Shakespeare and the Third Reich'

Gillian Peele (Fellow of Lady Margaret Hall, Oxford), 'The Changing British Party System'

John Farrell (Professor of English), 'Scarlet Ribbons: Memories of Youth and Childhood in Victorian Authors'

Peter Russell (Professor of Spanish, Oxford University), 'A Not So Bashful Stranger: *Don Quixote* in England, 1612–1781'

Sir Zelman Cowen (Provost of Oriel College, Oxford), 'Contemporary Problems in Medicine, Law, and Ethics'

Dennis V. Lindley (Visiting Professor of Mathematics), 'Scientific Thinking in an Unscientific World'

Martin Blumenson (Office of the Chief of Military History, Department of the Army), 'General Mark Clark and the British in the Italian Campaign of World War II'

## Fall Semester 1983

Anthony King (Professor of Politics, University of Essex), 'Margaret Thatcher and the Future of British Politics'

Alistair Gillespie (Canadian Minister of Energy, Mines, and Resources), 'Canadian-British Relations: Best and Worst'

Charles A. Owen, Jr. (Professor of English, University of Connecticut), 'The Pre-1400 Manuscripts of the *Canterbury Tales*'

Major-General (Ret.) Richard Clutterbuck (Reader in Political Conflict, University of Exeter), 'Terrorism in Malaya'

Wayne A. Wiegand (Associate Professor of English, University of Kentucky), 'British Propaganda in American Public Libraries during World War I'

Stuart Macintyre (Australian National University, Canberra), 'Australian Trade Unionism between the Wars'

Ram Joshi (Visiting Professor of History, former Vice-Chancellor, University of Bombay), 'Is Gandhi Relevant Today?'

Sir Denis Wright (former British Ambassador in Iran), 'Britain and the Iranian Revolution'

Andrew Horn (Head of the English Department, University of Lesotho), 'Theater and Politics in South Africa'

Philip Davies (Professor of American Government, University of Manchester), 'British Reaction to American Politics: Overt Rejection, Covert Assimilation'

H. K. Singh (Political Secretary, Embassy of India), 'United States–Indian Relations'

Roger Louis, Ram Joshi, J. S. Mehta (LBJ School), 'Two Cheers for Mountbatten: A Reassessment of Lord and Lady Mountbatten and the Partition of India'

## Spring Semester 1984

M. S. Venkataramani (Director of International Studies, Jawaharlal Nehru University), 'Winston Churchill and Indian Freedom'

Sir John Thompson (British Ambassador to the United Nations), 'The Falklands and Grenada in the United Nations'

Robert Farrell (Professor of English, Cornell University), 'Medieval Archaelogy'

Allon White (Lecturer in English, University of Sussex), 'The Fiction of Early Modernism'

Peter Green (Classics), Roger Louis (History), Miguel Gonzalez-Gerth (Spanish-Portuguese), Standish Meacham (History), and Sid Monas (Slavic): 'Orwell's *1984*'

Uriel Dann (Professor of English History, University of Tel Aviv), 'Hanover and Britain in the Time of George II'

José Ferrater-Mora (Fairbank Professor of Humanities, Bryn Mawr), 'A. M. Turing and his "Universal Turing Machine"'

Rüdiger Ahrens, (University of Würzburg), 'Teaching Shakespeare in German Universities'

Herbert Spiro (Professor of Political Science, Free University of Berlin), 'What Makes the British and Americans Different from Everybody Else: The Adversary Process of the Common Law'

Nigel Bowles (Lecturer in American Government and Politics, University of Edinburgh), 'Reflections on Recent Developments in British Politics'

Harold Perkin (Mellon Distinguished Visiting Professor, Rice University), 'The Evolution of Citizenship in Modern Britain'

Christopher Heywood (Senior Lecturer, Sheffield University), '*Jane Eyre* and *Wuthering Heights*'

Dave Powers (Curator, Kennedy Library), 'JFK's Trip to Ireland, 1963'

R. W. Coats (Visiting Professor of Economics), 'John Maynard Keynes: the Man and the Economist'

David Evans (Professor of Astronomy), 'Astronomy as a British Cultural Export'

### Fall Semester 1984

John Henry Faulk, 'Reflections on My Sojourns in the British Middle East'

Lord Fraser of Kilmorack, 'The Thatcher Years—and Beyond'

Michael Phillips (Lecturer in English Literature, University of Edinburgh), 'William Blake and the Rise of the Hot Air Balloon'

Erik Stocker (Humanities Research Center), 'A Bibliographical Detective Story: Reconstructing James Joyce's Library'

Amedée Turner (Member of the European Parliament), 'Recent Developments in the European Parliament'

Michael Hurst (Fellow of St. John's College, Oxford), 'Scholars versus Journalists on the English Social Classes'
Charles Alan Wright (William B. Bates Professor of Law), 'Reflections on Cambridge'
J. M. Winter (Fellow of Pembroke College, Cambridge), 'Fear of Decline in Population in Britain after World War I'
Henk Wesseling (Director of the Centre for the History of European Expansion, University of Leiden), 'Dutch Colonialism and the Impact on British Imperialism'
Celia Morris Eckhardt (Biographer and author of *Fannie Wright*), 'Frances Wright and *England as the Civilizer*'
Sir Oliver Wright (British Ambassador to the United States), 'British Foreign Policy—1984'
Leonard Thompson (Professor of African History, Yale University), 'Political Mythology and the Racial Order in South Africa'
Flora Nwapa (Nigerian Novelist), 'Women in Civilian and Military Rule in Nigeria'
Richard Rose (Professor of Political Science, University of Strathclyde), 'The Capacity of the Presidency in Comparative Perspective'

*Spring Semester 1985*

Bernard Hickey (University of Venice), 'Australian Literary Culture: Short Stories, Novels, and "Literary Journalism"'
Kenneth Hafertepe (American Studies), 'The British Foundations of the Smithsonian Castle: The Gothic Revival in Britain and America'
Rajeev Dhavan (Visiting Professor, LBJ School and Center for Asian Studies), 'Race Relations in England: Trapped Minorities and their Future'
Sir John Thompson (British Ambassador to the United Nations), 'British Techniques of Statecraft'
Philip Bobbitt (Professor of Law), 'Britain, the United States, and Reduction in Strategic Arms'
David Bevington (Drama Critic and Theater Historian), 'Maimed Rites: Interrupted Ceremony in *Hamlet*'
Standish Meacham (History), 'The Impact of the New Left History on British and American Historiography'
Iris Murdoch (Novelist and Philospher) and John O. Bayley (Thomas Warton Professor of English, Oxford University), 'Themes in English Literature and Philosophy'

John P. Chalmers (Librarian, Humanities Research Center), 'Malory Illustrated'
Thomas Metcalf (Professor of History, University of California at Berkeley), 'The Architecture of Empire: The British Raj in India'
Robert H. Wilson (Emeritus Professor of English), 'Malory and His Readers'
Lord St. Brides, '*Passage to India:* Better Film than Novel?'
Derek Pearsall (Medievalist at York University), 'Fire, Flood, and Slaughter: the Tribulations of the Medieval City of York'
E. S. Atieno Odhiambo (University of Nairobi, Visiting Professor, Johns Hopkins University), 'Britain and Kenya: The Mau Mau, the "Colonial State," and Dependency'
Francis Robinson (Reader in History, University of London), 'Indian Muslim Religious Leadership and Colonial Rule'
Charles B. MacDonald (Deputy Chief Historian, U.S. Army), 'The British in the Battle of the Bulge'
Brian Levack (Associate Professor of History), 'The Battle of Bosworth Field'
Kurth Sprague (Senior Lecturer in English), 'The Mirrors of Malory'

*Fall Semester 1985*

A. P. Thornton (Distinguished University Professor, University of Toronto), 'Whatever Happened to the British Commonwealth?'
Michael Garibaldi Hall (Professor of History) and Elizabeth Hall (LBJ School), 'Views of Pakistan'
Ronald Steel (Visiting Professor of History), 'Walter Lippmann and the British'
Douglas H. M. Branion (Canadian Consul General), 'Political Controversy and Economic Development in Canada'
Decherd Turner and Dave Oliphant (Harry Ransom Humanities Research Center), 'The History of the Publications of the Harry Ransom Humanities Research Center'
Robert Fernea (Professor of Anthropology), 'The Controversy Over Sex and Orientalism: Charles Doughty's *Arabia Deserta*'
Desley Deacon (Lecturer, Department of Government), 'Her Brilliant Career: The Context of Nineteenth-Century Australian Feminism'
John Lamphear (Associate Professor of History), 'The British Colonial "Pacification" of Kenya: A View from the Other Side'

Kingsley de Silva (Foundation Professor of Ceylon History at the
    University of Peradeniya, Sri Lanka), 'British Colonialism
    and Sri Lankan Independence'
Thomas Hatfield (Dean of Continuing Education), 'Colorado on
    the Cam 1986: From "Ultra" to Archaeology, from Mr.
    Micawber to Mrs. Thatcher'
Carol Hanbery MacKay (Assistant Professor of English), 'The
    Dickens Theater'
Ronald Brown, Jo Anne Christian, Roger Louis, Harry Middleton,
    and Ronald Steel—Panel Discussion: 'The Art of Biography:
    Philip Ziegler's *Mountbatten*'

*Spring Semester 1986*

B. J. Fernea (English and Middle Eastern Studies), Bernth Lindfors
    (English), and Roger Louis (History), '*Out of Africa:* The
    Book, the Biography, and the Movie'
Robert Litwak (Woodrow Wilson International Center for Scholars,
    Washington, D.C.), 'The Great Game: Russian, British, and
    American Strategies in Asia'
Gillian Adams Barnes (English) and Jane Manaster (Geography),
    'Humphrey Carpenter's *Secret Gardens* and the Golden Age
    of Children's Literature'
Laurie Hergenhan (Professor of English, University of Queensland),
    'A Yankee in Australia: the Literary and Historical Adven-
    tures of C. Hartley Grattan'
Brian Matthews (Flinders University of South Australia), 'Austra-
    lian Utopianism of the 1880s'
Richard Langhorne (Fellow of St. John's College, Cambridge),
    'Apostles and Spies: The Generation of Treason at Cam-
    bridge between the Wars'
Ronald Robinson (Beit Professor of the History of the British Em-
    pire, Oxford University), 'The Decline and Fall of the Brit-
    ish Empire"
William Rodgers (Vice-President, Social Democratic Party), 'Britain's
    New Three-Party System: A Permanent or Passing Phenomenon?'
John Coetzee (Professor of Literature, University of Cape Town),
    'The Farm Novel in South Africa'
Ayesha Jalal, (Fellow, Trinity College, Cambridge), 'Jinnah and the
    Partition of India'
Andrew Blane (Professor of History, City College of New York), 'Am-
    nesty International: from a British to an International Movement'

Anthony Rota (Antiquarian Bookdealer and Publisher), 'London Pride: 1986'
Elspeth Rostow (Dean, LBJ School), 'The Withering Away of Whose State? Colonel Qaddafi's? Reflections on Nationalism at Home and Abroad, in Britain and in the Middle East'
Ray Daum (Curator, Humanities Research Center), 'Broadway— Piccadilly!'

*Fall Semester 1986*

Dean Robert King and Members of the '"Unrequired Reading List" Committee—The British Component': Round Table Discussion
Paul Sturges (Loughborough University), 'Popular Libraries in Eighteenth-Century Britain'
Ian Bickerton (Professor of History, University of Missouri), 'Eisenhower's Middle East Policy and the End of the British Empire'
Marc Ferro (Visiting Professor of History), 'Churchill and Pétain'
David Fitzpatrick (Visiting Professor of History, Queen's University, Kingston, Ontario), 'Religion and Politics in Ireland'
Adam Watson (Center for Advanced Studies, University of Virginia, former British Ambassador to Castro's Cuba), 'Our Man in Havana—or: Britain, Cuba, and the Caribbean'
Norman Rose (Chaim Weizmann Professor of History, Hebrew University), 'Chaim Weizmann, the British, and the Creation of the State of Israel'
Elaine Thompson (Senior Fulbright Scholar, American University), 'Legislatures in Canberra and Washington'
Roger Louis (Kerr Professor of English History and Culture), 'Suez Thirty Years After'
Antonia Gransden (Reader in Medieval History, University of Nottingham), 'The Writing of Chronicles in Medieval England'
Hilary Spurling (British Biographer and Critic), 'Paul Scott's *Raj Quartet*: The Novelist as Historian'
J. D. B. Miller (Professor of International Relations, Australian National University), 'A Special and Puzzling Relationship: Australia and the United States'
Janet Meisel (Associate Professor of History), 'The Domesday Book'

*Spring Semester 1987*

Miguel Gonzalez-Gerth (Liberal Arts), Robert Fernea (Anthropol-
    ogy), Joe Horn (Psychology), Bruce Hunt (History), and
    Delbert Thiessen (Psychology): 'Contemporary Perspectives
    on Evolution'
Alistair Campbell-Dick (Chief Executive Officer, Research and De-
    velopment Strategic Technology), 'Scottish Nationalism'
Anthony Mockler (British Freelance Historian, and Biographer),
    'Graham Greene: the Interweaving of His Life and Fiction'
Michael Crowder (Visiting Professor of African History, Amherst
    College), 'The Legacy of British Colonialism in Africa'
Carin Green (Lecturer in Classics), 'Lovers and Defectors: Autobi-
    ography and *The Perfect Spy*'
Lord Saint Brides, 'The Modern British Monarchy'
Victor Szebehely (Richard B. Curran Professor of Engineering), 'Sir
    Isaac Newton'
Patrick McCaughey (Visiting Professor of Australian Studies, Harvard
    University; Director, National Gallery of Victoria, Mel-
    bourne), 'The Persistence of Landscape in Australian Art'
Adolf Wood (Deputy-Editor of *The Times Literary Supplement*), 'An
    Informal History of the *TLS*'
Nissan Oren (Visiting Professor of Political Science, Johns Hopkins
    University; Kaplan Professor, Hebrew University, Jerusalem),
    'Churchill, Truman, and Stalin: The End of the Second
    World War'
Sir Michael Howard (Regius Professor of History, Oxford Univer-
    sity), 'Britain and the First World War'
Sir John Graham (former British Ambassador to NATO), 'NATO:
    British Origins, American Security, and the Future Outlook'
Daniel Mosser (Virginia Polytechnic Institute and State University),
    'The Chaucer Cardigan Manuscript'
Sir Raymond Carr (Warden of St. Antony's College, Oxford), 'Brit-
    ish Intellectuals and the Spanish Civil War'
Michael Wilding (Reader in English, University of Sydney), 'The
    Fatal Shore? The Convict Period in Australian Literature'

*Fall Semester 1987*

Peter Green (Dougherty Professor of Classics), Winfred Lehmann
    (Temple Professor of the Humanities), Roger Louis (Kerr
    Professor of English History and Culture), and Paul Wood-

ruff (Professor of Philosophy), 'Anthony Burgess: The Autobiography'

Robert Crunden (Professor of History and American Studies), 'Ezra Pound in London'

Carol MacKay (Associate Professor of English) and John Henry Faulk, 'J. Frank Dobie and Thackeray's Great-Granddaughter: Another Side of *A Texan in England*'

Sarvepalli Gopal (Professor of Contemporary History, Jawaharlal Nehru University, and Fellow of St. Antony's College, Oxford), 'Nehru and the British'

Robert D. King (Dean of Liberal Arts), 'T. S. Eliot'

Lord Blake (Visiting Cline Professor of English History and Literature, former Provost of Queen's College, Oxford), 'Disraeli: Problems of the Biographer'

Alain Blayac (Professor of Comparative Literature, University of Montpellier), 'Art as Revelation: Gerard Manley Hopkins's Poetry and James Joyce's *Portrait of the Artist*'

Mary Bull (Oxford University), 'Margery Perham and Africa'

R. J. Moore (Professor of History, Flinders University), 'Paul Scott: The Novelist as Historian, and *The Raj Quartet* as History'

Ian Willison (Head of the Rare Books Division of the British Library), 'New Trends in Humanities Research: the History of the Book in Britain Project'

The Duke of Norfolk, 'The Lion and the Unicorn: Ceremonial and the Crown'

Hans Mark (Chancellor, The University of Texas System), 'The Royal Society, the Royal Observatory, and the Development of Modern Research Laboratories'

Henry Dietz (Professor of Government), 'Sherlock Holmes: A Centennial Celebration'


*Spring Semester 1988*

Lord Jenkins (Chancellor of Oxford University), 'Changing Patterns of British Government from Asquith via Baldwin and Attlee to Mrs. Thatcher'

Lord Thomas (author of *The Spanish Civil War* and *Cuba, or the Pursuit of Freedom*), 'Britain, Spain, and Latin America'

Barbara Harlow (English), Bernth Lindfors (English), Wahneema Lubiano (English), and Robert Wren (University of Houston), 'Chinua Achebe: The Man and His Works'

Charles Townshend (Professor of History, Keele University), 'Britain, Ireland, and Palestine, 1918–1947'
Richard Morse (Program Secretary for Latin America, Woodrow Wilson Center), 'T. S. Eliot and Latin America'
Chinua Achebe (Nigerian Novelist), 'Anthills of the Savannah'
Tapan Raychaudhuri (Reader in Indian History, Oxford University), 'The English in Bengali Eyes in the Nineteenth Century'
Lord Chitnis (Chief Executive of the Rowntree Trust and Chairman of the British Refugee Council), 'British Perceptions of U.S. Policy in Central America'
Kurth Sprague (Senior Lecturer in English), 'Constance White: Sex, Womanhood, and Marriage in British India'
George McGhee (former U.S. Ambassador to Turkey and Germany), 'The Turning Point in the Cold War: Britain, the United States, and Turkey's Entry into NATO'
Robert Palter (Professor of the History of Science, Trinity College), 'New Light on Newton's Natural Philosophy'
J. Kenneth McDonald (Chief Historian, Central Intelligence Agency), 'The Decline of British Naval Power 1918–1922'
Yvonne Cripps (Visiting Professor of Law), '"Peter and the Boys Who Cry Wolf": *Spycatcher*'
Emmanuel Ngara (Professor of English, University of Zimbabwe), 'African Poetry: Nationalism and Cultural Domination'
Kate Frost (Assistant Professor of English), 'Frat Rats of the Invisible College: The Wizard Earl of Northumberland and His Pre-Rosicrucian Pals'
B. Ramesh Babu (Visiting Professor of Government), 'American Foreign Policy: An Indian Dissent'
Sir Antony Ackland (British Ambassador to the United States), 'From Dubai to Madrid: Adventures in the British Foreign Service'

In the Spring Semester 1988 British Studies also helped to sponsor four lectures by Sir Brian Urquhart (former Under-Secretary of the United Nations) on 'World Order in the Era of Decolonization.'

*Fall Semester 1988*

Round Table Discussion on Richard Ellman's *Oscar Wilde:* Peter Green (Dougherty Professor of Classics); Diana Hobby (Rice University, Editor of the *Yeats Papers*); Roger Louis (Kerr

Professor of English History and Culture); and Elspeth
Rostow (Stiles Professor of American Studies)

Hugh Cecil (University of Leeds), 'The British First World War Novel
of Experience'

Alan Knight (Worsham Professor of Mexican History), 'Britain and
the Mexican Revolution'

Prosser Gifford (Former Deputy-Director, Woodrow Wilson Center,
Washington, D.C.) and Robert Frykenberg, (Professor of Indian History, University of Wisconsin at Madison), 'Stability
in Post-Colonial British Africa: the Indian Perspective'

Joseph Dobrinski (Université Paul-Valéry), 'The Symbolism of the
Artist Theme in *Lord Jim*'

Martin Stannard (University of Leicester), 'Evelyn Waugh and North
America'

Lawrence Cranberg (Consulting Physicist and Fellow of the American Physical Society), 'The Engels-Marx Relationship and
the Origins of Marxism'

N. G. L. Hammond (Professor of Greek, Bristol University), 'The
British Military Mission to Greece, 1943–1944'

Barbara Harlow (Associate Professor of English), 'A Legacy of the
British Era in Egypt: Women, Writing, and Political Detention'

Sidney Monas (Professor of Slavic Languages and History), 'Thanks
for the Mummery: *Finnegans Wake*, Rabelais, Bakhtin, and
Verbal Carnival'

Robert Bowie (Former Director, Harvard Center of International
Affairs and Deputy Director, Central Intelligence Agency),
'Britain's Decision to Join the European Community'

Shirley Williams (Co-Founder, Social Democratic Party), 'Labour
Weakness and Tory Strength—or, The Strange Death of
Labour England'

Bernard Richards (Fellow of Brasenose College, Oxford), 'Ruskin's
View of Turner'

John R. Clarke (Professor of Art History), 'Australian Art of the
1960s'

Round Table Discussion on Paul Kennedy's *The Rise and Fall of the
Great Powers*: Sandy Lipucci (Government), Roger Louis
(History), Jagat Mehta (LBJ School), Sidney Monas (Slavic
Languages and History), and Walt Rostow (Economics and
History)

*Spring Semester 1989*

Brian Levack (Professor of History), 'The English Bill of Rights, 1689'

Hilary Spurling (Critic and Biographer), 'Paul Scott as Novelist: His Sense of History and the British Era in India'

Larry Carver (Director of the Humanities Program), 'Lord Rochester: The Profane Wit and the Restoration's Major Minor Poet'

Atieno Odhiambo (Professor of History, Rice University), 'Re-Interpreting Mau Mau'

Trevor Hartley (Reader in Law, London School of Economics, and Visiting Professor, UT Law School), 'The British Constitution and the European Community'

Archie Brown (Fellow of St. Antony's College, Oxford), 'Political Leadership in Britain, the Soviet Union, and the United States'

Lord Blake ( Former Provost of Queen's College, Oxford, and Editor of the *Dictionary of National Biography*), 'Churchill as Historian'

Weirui Hou (Professor of English Literature, Shanghai University), 'British Literature in China'

Norman Daniel (British Council), 'Britain and the Iraqi Revolution of 1958'

Alistair Horne (Fellow of St. Antony's College, Oxford), 'The Writing of the Biography of Harold Macmillan'

M. R. D. Foot (former Professor of History, Manchester University, and Editor of the *Gladstone Diaries*), 'The Open and Secret War, 1939–1945'

Ian Willison (former Head of Rare Books Division of the British Library), 'Editorial Theory and Practice in the History of the Book'

Neville Meaney (Professor of History, University of Sydney), 'The "Yellow Peril": Invasion, Scare Novels, and Australian Political Culture'

Round Table Discussion on *The Satanic Verses:* Kurth Sprague (Associate Professor of American Studies); Peter Green (Dougherty Professor of Classics); Robert A. Fernea (Professor of Anthropology); Roger Louis (Kerr Professor of English History and Culture); and Gail Minault (Associate Professor of History and Asian Studies)

Kate Frost (Associate Professor of English), 'John Donne, Sunspots, and the British Empire'

Lee Patterson (Professor of English, Duke University), 'Chaucerian Commerce'

Edmund Weiner and John Simpson (Editors of the new *Oxford English Dictionary*), 'Return to the Web of Words'
Ray Daum (Curator, Humanities Research Center), 'Noel Coward and Cole Porter'
William B. Todd (Kerr Professor Emeritus in English History and Culture), 'Edmund Burke on the French Revolution'

## Fall Semester 1989

D. Cameron Watt (Stevenson Professor of International History, London School of Economics), 'Britain and the Origins of the Second World War: Personalities and Politics of Appeasement'
Gary Freeman (Associate Professor of Government), 'On the Awfulness of the English: The View from Comparative Studies'
Hans Mark (Chancellor, University of Texas System), 'British Naval Tactics in the Second World War: The Japanese Lessons'
T. B. Millar (Director, Menzies Centre for Australian Studies, London), 'Australia, Britain and the United States in Historical Perspective'
Dudley Fishburn (Member of Parliament and former Editor of *The Economist*), '*The Economist*'
Lord Franks (former Ambassador in Washington), 'The "Special Relationship"'
Herbert L. Jacobson (Drama Critic and friend of Orson Wells), 'Three Score Years of Transatlantic Acting and Staging of Shakespeare'
Roy Macleod (Professor of History, University of Sydney) 'The "Practical Man": Myth and Metaphor in Anglo-Australian Science'
David Murray (Professor of Government, the Open University), 'Hong Kong: The Historical Context for the Transfer of Power'
Susan Napier (Assistant Professor of Japanese Language and Literature), 'Japanese Intellectuals Discover the British'
Dr. Karan Singh (Ambassador of India to the United States), 'Four Decades of Indian Democracy'
Paul Woodruff (Professor of Philosophy), 'George Grote and the Radical Tradition in British Scholarship'
Herbert J. Spiro (Professor of Government), 'Britain, the United States, and the Future of Germany'
Robert Lowe (Wine Columnist for the *Austin American-Statesman*), '"God Rest you Merry, Gentlemen": The Curious British Cult of Sherry'

*Spring Semester 1990*

Thomas F. Staley (Director, Harry Ransom Humanities Research Center), 'Harry Ransom, the HRC, and the Development of Twentieth Century Literary Research Collections'

Thomas Cable (Blumberg Professor of English), 'The Rise and Decline of the English Language'

D. J. Wenden (Fellow of All Souls College, Oxford), 'Sir Alexander Korda and the British Film Industry'

Roger Owen (Fellow of St. Antony's College, Oxford, and Visiting Professor of Middle Eastern History), 'Reflections on the First Ten Years of Thatcherism'

Robert Hardgrave (Temple Centennial Professor of the Humanities), 'Celebrating Calcutta: The Solvyns Portraits'

Donatus Nwoga (Professor of English, University of Nigeria, Nsukka, and Fulbright Scholar-in-Residence, University of Kansas), 'The Intellectual Legacy of British Decolonization in Africa'

Francis Sitwell (Etonian, Seaman, and Literary Executor), 'Edith Sitwell: A Reappraisal'

Robert Vitalis (Assistant Professor of Government), 'The "New Deal" in Egypt: Britain, the United States, and the Egyptian Economy during World War II'

James Coote (Professor and Cass Gilbert Teaching Fellow, School of Architecture), 'Prince Charles and Architecture'

Harry Eckstein (Distinguished Professor of Political Science, University of California, Irvine), 'British Politics and the National Health Service'

Alfred David (Professor of English, Indiana University), 'Chaucer and King Arthur'

Ola Rotimi (African Playwright and Theater Director), 'African Literature and the British Tongue'

Derek Brewer (Professor of English and Master of Emmanuel College, Cambridge), 'An Anthropological Study of Literature'

Neil MacCormick (Regius Professor of Public Law and the Law of Nations, University of Edinburgh), 'Stands Scotland Where She Should?'

Janice Rossen (Senior Research Fellow, Harry Ransom Humanities Research Center), 'Toads and Melancholy: The Poetry of Philip Larkin'

Ronald Robinson (Beit Professor of the History of the British Commonwealth, Oxford, and Visiting Cline Professor, University of Texas), 'The Decolonization of British Imperialism'

*Fall Semester 1990*

'The Crisis in the Persian Gulf'—Round Table Discussion: Hafez
 Farmayan (Professor of History); Robert Fernea (Professor
 of Anthropology); Roger Louis (Kerr Chair in English His-
 tory and Culture); Robert Stookey (United States Foreign
 Service Officer, Retired, now Research Associate, Center for
 Middle Eastern Studies)
John Velz (Professor of English), 'Shakespeare and Some Surro-
 gates: An Account of the Anti-Stratfordian Heresy'
Michael H. Codd (Secretary, Department of the Prime Minister and
 Cabinet, Government of Australia), 'The Future of the Com-
 monwealth: An Australian View'
John Dawick (Senior Lecturer in English, Massey University, New
 Zealand), 'The Perils of Paula: Young Women and Older
 Men in Pinero's Plays'
Gloria Fromm (Professor of English, University of Illinios in Chi-
 cago), 'New Windows on Modernism: The Letters of Dor-
 othy Richardson'
David Braybrooke (Centennial Commission Professor in the Lib-
 eral Arts), 'The Canadian Constitutional Crisis'
Sidney Monas (Professor of History and Slavic Languages), 'Paul
 Fussell and World War II'
James Fishkin (Darrell Royal Regents Chair in Ethics and American
 Society), 'Thought Experiments in Recent Oxford Philoso-
 phy'
Joseph Hamburger (Pelatiah Perit Professor of Political and Social
 Science, Yale University), 'How Liberal Was John Stuart Mill?'
Richard W. Clement (Special Collections Librarian, Kenneth Spen-
 cer Research Library, University of Kansas), 'Thomas James
 and the Bodleian Library: The Foundations of Scholarship'
Michael Yeats (Former Chairman of the Irish Senate and only son
 of the poet William Butler Yeats), 'Ireland and Europe'
'William H. McNeill's *Arnold J. Toynbee: A Life*'—Round Table Dis-
 cussion: Standish Meacham (Dean of Liberal Arts); Peter
 Green (Dougherty Professor in Classics); Roger Louis (Kerr
 Chair in English History and Culture); Sidney Monas (Pro-
 fessor of History and Slavic Languages)
Jeffrey Meyers (Biographer and Professor of English, University of
 Colorado), 'Conrad and Jane Anderson'
Alan Frost (Professor of History, La Trobe University, Melbourne),
 'The Explorations of Captain Cook'

Sarvepalli Gopal (Professor of History, Jawaharlal Nehru University, and Fellow of St. Antony's College, Oxford), 'The First Ten Years of Indian Independence'

'The Best and Worst Books of 1990'—Round Table Discussion: Alessandra Lippucci (Lecturer in Government); Roger Louis (Kerr Chair in English History and Culture); Tom Staley (Director, Harry Ransom Humanities Research Center); Steve Weinberg (Welch Foundation Chair in Science Theory); and Paul Woodruff (Thompson Professor in the Humanities)

### Spring Semester 1991

David Hollway (Prime Minister's Office, Government of Australia), 'Australia and the Gulf Crisis'

Diane Kunz (Yale University), 'British Post-War Sterling Crises'

Miguel Gonzalez-Gerth (Spanish and Harry Ransom Humanities Research Center), 'T. E. Lawrence, Richard Aldington and the Death of Heroes'

Robert Twombly (Professor of English), 'Religious Encounters with the Flesh in English Literature'

Alan Ryan (Princeton University), 'Bertrand Russell's Politics'

Hugh Kenner (Andrew Mellon Professor of the Humanities, The Johns Hopkins University, and Visiting Harry Ransom Professor), 'The State of English Poetry'

Patricia Burnham (American Studies), 'Anglo-American Art and the Struggle for Artistic Independence'

'The Churchill Tradition'—Round Table Discussion: Lord Blake (former Provost of Queen's College, Oxford); Lord Jenkins (Chancellor, Oxford University); Field Marshal Lord Carver (former Chief of the Defence Staff); Sir Michael Howard (former Regius Professor, Oxford, present Lovett Professor of Military and Naval History, Yale University); with a concluding comment by Winston S. Churchill, M.P.

Woodruff Smith (Professor of History, University of Texas at San Antonio), 'Why Do the British Put Sugar in Their Tea?'

Peter Firchow (Professor of English, University of Minnesota), 'Aldous Huxley: The Poet as Centaur'

Irene Gendzier (Professor of History and Political Science, Boston University), 'British and American Middle Eastern Policies in the 1950s: Lebanon and Kuwait. Reflections on Past Experience and the Postwar Crisis in the Gulf'

John Train (Harvard Magazine and Wall Street Journal), 'Remark-
able Catchwords in the City of London and on Wall Street'
Alan Sisman (Independent Writer, London), 'A. J. P. Taylor'
Roger Louis (Kerr Professor), 'The Young Winston'
Adrian Mitchell (Professor of English, Melbourne University, and
Visiting Professor of English and Australian Studies), 'Claim-
ing a Voice: Recent Non-Fictional Writing in Australia'
Bruce Hevly (Professor of History, University of Washington),
'Stretching Things Out versus Letting Them Slide: The Natu-
ral Philosophy of Ice in Edinburgh and Cambridge in the
Nineteenth-Century'
Henry Dietz (Professor of Government), 'Foibles and Follies in
Sherlock's Great Game: Some Excesses of Holmesian Research'

*Summer Semester 1991*

Roger Louis (Kerr Professor) and Ronald Robinson (Beit Professor
of the History of the British Commonwealth, Oxford University, and Visiting Cline Professor), 'Harold Macmillan and
the Dissolution of the British Empire'
Robert Treu (Professor of English, University of Wisconsin, La-
crosse), 'D. H. Lawrence and Graham Greene in Mexico'
Thomas Pinney (Chairman, Department of English, Pomona Col-
lege), 'Kipling, India, and Imperialism'
Ronald Heiferman (Professor of History, Quinnipiac College), 'The
Odd Couple: Winston Churchill and Chiang Kai-shek'
John Harty (Professor of English, Alice Lloyd College, Kentucky),
'The Movie and the Book: J. G. Ballard's *Empire of the Sun*'
A. B. Assensoh (Ghanaian Journalist and Professor of History, South-
ern University, Baton Rouge), 'Nkrumah'
Victoria Carchidi (Professor of English, Emory and Henry College),
'Lawrence of Arabia on a Camel, Thank God!'
James Gump (Chairman, Department of History, University of Cali-
fornia at San Diego), 'The Zulu and the Sioux: The British
and American Comparative Experience with the "Noble Savage"'

*Fall Semester 1991*

Round Table Discussion on Noel Annan's *Our Age:* Peter Green
(Dougherty Professor in Classics), Robert D. King (Dean ad

interim and Rapoport Professor of Liberal Arts), Roger Louis (Kerr Professor of English History and Culture), and Thomas F. Staley (Director of the Harry Ransom Humanities Research Center)

Christopher Heywood (Okayama University, Japan), 'Slavery, Imagination, and the Brontës'

Harold L. Smith (University of Houston, Victoria), 'Winston Churchill and Women'

Krystyna Kujawinska-Courtney (University of Lodz), 'Shakespeare and Poland'

Ewell E. Murphy, Jr. (Baker & Botts, Houston), 'Cecil Rhodes and the Rhodes Scholarships'

I. N. Kimambo (University of Dar-es-Salaam), 'The District Officer in Tanganyika'

Hans Mark (Chancellor, University of Texas System), 'The Pax Britannica and the Inevitable Comparison: Is There a Pax Americana? Conclusions from the Gulf War'

Richard Clutterbuck (Major-General, British Army, Ret.), 'British and American Hostages in the Middle East: Negotiating with Terrorists'

Elizabeth Hedrick (Assistant Professor of English), 'Samuel Johnson and Linguistic Propriety'

The Hon. Denis McLean (New Zealand Ambassador to the United States), 'Australia and New Zealand: The Nuisance of Nationalism'

Elizabeth Richmond (Assistant Professor of English), 'Submitting a Trifle for a Degree: Dramatic Productions at Oxford and Cambridge in the Age of Shakespeare'

Kenneth Warren, M.D. (Director for Science, Maxwell Macmillan), 'Tropical Medicine: A British Invention'

Adolf Wood (Deputy-Editor of *The Times Literary Supplement*), 'The Golden Age of *The Times Literary Supplement*'

Eugene Walter (Poet and Novelist), 'Unofficial Poetry: Literary London in the 1940s and 1950s'

Sidney Monas (Professor of Slavic Languages and History), 'Images of Britain in the Poetry of World War II'

The St. Stephen's Madrigal Choir, 'Celebrating an English Christmas'


*Spring Semester 1992*

Jeremy Treglown (Critic and Author), 'Wartime Censorship and the Novel'

Toyin Falola (Professor of History), 'Nigerian Independence 1960'

Donald S. Lamm (President, W. W. Norton and Company), 'Publishing English History in America'

Colin Franklin (Publisher and Historian of the Book), 'The Pleasures of Eighteenth-Century Shakespeare'

Thomas F. Staley (Director, Harry Ransom Humanities Research Center), '*Fin de Siècle* Joyce: A Perspective on One Hundred Years'

Sarvepalli Gopal (Jawaharlal Nehru University), '"Drinking Tea with Treason": Halifax and Gandhi'

Michael Winship (Associate Professor of English), 'The History of the Book: Britain's Foreign Trade in Books in the 19th Century'

Richard Lariviere (Professor of Sanskrit and Director of the Center for Asian Studies), 'British Law and Lawyers in India'

Round Table Discussion on A. S. Byatt's *Possession*: Janice Rossen (Visiting Scholar, Humanities Research Center), John P. Farrell (Professor of English), and Roger Louis

William H. McNeill (University of Chicago and former President of the American Historical Association), 'Arnold Toynbee's Vision of World History'

Derek Brewer (Master of Emmanuel College, Cambridge), 'The Interpretation of Fairy Tales: The Implications for English Literature, Anthropology, and History'

David Bradshaw (Fellow of Worcester College, Oxford), 'Aldous Huxley: Eugenics and the Rational State'

Steven Weinberg (Josey Regental Professor of Science), 'The British Style in Physics'

Sir David Williams (Vice-Chancellor, Cambridge University), 'Northern Ireland'

## Summer Semester 1992

R. A. C. Parker (Fellow of Queen's College, Oxford), 'Neville Chamberlain and Appeasement'

Adrian Wooldridge (Fellow of All Souls College, Oxford, and Staff Writer for *The Economist*), 'Reforming British Education: How It Happened and What America Can Learn'

Chris Wrigley (Professor of Modern British History, Nottingham University), 'A. J. P. Taylor: An English Radical and Modern Europe'

*Fall Semester 1992*

Round Table Discussion on E. M. Forster's *Howards End:* The Movie and the Book. Robert D. King (Liberal Arts), Roger Louis (History), Alessandra Lippucci (Government), Thomas F. Staley (Humanities Research Center)

Lord Skidelsky (Warwick University), 'Keynes and the Origins of the "Special Relationship"'

Sir Samuel Falle (former British Ambassador), 'Britain and the Middle East in the 1950s'

Ian MacKillop (University of Sheffield), 'We Were That Cambridge: F. R. Leavis and *Scrutiny*'

Walter Dean Burnham (Frank G. Erwin, Jr. Centennial Chair in Government), 'The 1992 British Elections: Four-or-Five-More Tory Years?'

Don Graham (Professor of English), 'Modern Australian Literature and the Image of America'

Richard Woolcott (former Secretary of the Australian Department of Foreign Affairs), 'Australia and the Question of Cooperation or Contention in the Pacific'

Ian Willison (1992 Wiggins Lecturer, American Antiquarian Society), 'The History of the Book in Twentieth-Century Britain and America'

Iain Sproat (Member of Parliament), 'P. G. Wodehouse and the War'

Standish Meacham (Sheffield Professor of History), 'The Crystal Palace'

Field Marshal Lord Carver (former Chief of the British Defence Staff), 'Wavell: A Reassessment'

Lesley Hall (Wellcome Institute for the History of Medicine, London), 'For Fear of Frightening the Horses: Sexology in Britain since William Acton'

Michael Fry (Director of International Relations, University of Southern California), 'Britain, the United Nations, and the Lebanon Crisis of 1958'

Brian Holden Reid (King's College, London), 'J. F. C. Fuller and the Revolution in British Military Thought'

Neil Parsons (University of London), '"Clicko" or Franz Taaibosch: A Bushman Entertainer in Britain, Jamaica, and the United States c. 1919–40'

John Hargreaves (Burnett-Fletcher Professor of History, Aberdeen University), 'God's Advocate: Lewis Namier and the History of Modern Europe'

Round Table Discussion on Robert Harris's *Fatherland*. Henry Dietz
(Government), Robert D. King (Liberal Arts), Roger Louis
(History), and Walter Wetzels (Germanic Languages)
Kevin Tierney (University of California), 'Robert Graves: An Out-
sider Looking In, or an Insider Who Escaped?'


*Spring Semester 1993*


Round Table Discussion on 'The Trollope Mystique.' Janice Rossen
(author of *Philip Larkin* and *The University in Modern Fiction*),
Louise Weinberg (Angus G. Wynne Professor of Civil Juris-
prudence), and Paul Woodruff (Director of the Plan II Hon-
ors Program and Thompson Professor of Philosophy)
Bruce Hunt (Associate Professor of History), 'To Rule the Waves:
Cable Telegraphy and British Physics in the 19th Century'
Martin Wiener (Jones Professor of History, Rice University), 'The
Unloved State: Contemporary Political Attitudes in the Writ-
ing of Modern British History'
Elizabeth Dunn (Harry Ransom Humanities Research Center),
'Ralph Waldo Emerson and Ireland'
Jason Thompson (Western Kentucky University), 'Edward William
Lane's "Description of Egypt"'
Sir Michael Howard (former Regius Professor of Modern History,
Oxford University, present Lovett Professor of Military and
Naval History, Yale University), 'Strategic Deception in the
Second World War'
Gordon A. Craig (Sterling Professor of Humanities, Stanford Uni-
versity), 'Churchill'
Round Table Discussion on the Indian Mathematician Ramanujan:
Robert D. King (Rapoport Professor of Liberal Arts), James
W. Vick (Vice-President for Student Affairs and Professor of
Mathematics), and Steven Weinberg (Regental Professor and
Josey Chair in Physics)
Martha Merritt (Lecturer in Government), 'From Commonwealth
to Commonwealth, and from Vauxhall to *Vokzal:* Russian
Borrowing from Britain'
Sidney Monas (Professor of Slavic Languages and History), 'James
Joyce and Russia'
Peter Marshall (Professor of History, King's College, London), 'Im-
perial Britain and the Question of National Identity'
Michael Wheeler (Professor of English and Director of the Ruskin
Programme, Lancaster University), 'Ruskin and Gladstone'

Peter Marshall (Professor of History, King's College, London), 'Edmund Burke and India'

Anthony Low (Smuts Professor of Commonwealth History and President of Clare College, Cambridge University), 'Britain and India in the Early 1930s: The British, American, French, and Dutch Empires Compared'

*Summer Semester 1993*

Alexander Pettit (University of North Texas), 'Lord Bolingbroke's *Remarks on the History of England*'

Rose Marie Burwell (Northern Illinois University), 'The British Novel and Ernest Hemingway'

Richard Patteson (Mississippi State University), 'New Writing in the West Indies'

Richard Greene (Memorial University Newfoundland), 'The Moral Authority of Edith Sitwell'

*Fall Semester 1993*

Round Table Discussion on 'The British and the Shaping of the American Critical Mind: Edmund Wilson, Part II': Roger Louis (History), Elspeth Rostow (Stiles Professor in American Studies), Tom Staley (Director, Harry Ransom Center), and Robert Crunden (Professor of History and American Studies)

Roseanne Camacho (University of Rhode Island), 'Evelyn Scott: Towards an Intellectual Biography'

Christopher Heywood (Okayama University), 'The Brontës and Slavery'

Peter Gay (Sterling Professor of History, Yale University), 'The Cultivation of Hatred in England'

Linda Ferreira-Buckley, 'England's First English Department: Rhetoric and More Rhetoric'

Janice Rossen (Senior Research Fellow, Humanities Research Center), 'British University Novels'

Ian Hancock (O Yanko Le Redzosko) (Professor of Linguistics and English), 'The Gypsy Image in British Literature'

James Davies (University College of Swansea), 'Dylan Thomas'

Jeremy Lewis (London Writer and Editor), 'Who Cares about Cyril Connolly?'

Sam Jamot Brown (British Studies) and Robert D. King (Linguistics), 'Scott and the Antarctic'

Martin Trump (University of South Africa), 'Nadine Gordimer's Social and Political Vision'

Richard Clogg (Professor of Balkan History, University of London), 'Britain and the Origins of the Greek Civil War'

Herbert J. Spiro (United States Ambassador, Ret.), 'The Warburgs: Anglo-American and German-Jewish Bankers'

Colin Franklin (Publisher and Antiquarian Bookseller), 'Lord Chesterfield: Stylist, Connoisseur of Manners, and Specialist in Worldly Advice'

Jeffrey Segall (Charles University, Prague), 'The Making of James Joyce's Reputation'

Rhodri Jeffreys-Jones (University of Edinburgh), 'The Myth of the Iron Lady: Margaret Thatcher and World Stateswomen'

John Rumrich (Associate Professor of English), 'Milton and Science: Gravity and the Fall'

J. D. Alsop (McMaster University), 'British Propaganda, Espionage, and Political Intrigue'

'The Best and the Worst Books of 1993': David Edwards (Government), Creekmore Fath (Liberal Arts Foundation), Betty Sue Flowers (English), and Sidney Monas (History and Slavic Languages)

*Spring Semester 1994*

Thomas F. Staley (Director, Harry Ransom Humanities Research Center), 'John Rodker: Poet and Publisher of Modernism'

Martha Fehsenfeld and Lois More Overbeck (Emory University), 'The Correspondence of Samuel Beckett'

M. R. D. Foot (Historian and Editor), 'Lessons of War on War: The Influence of 1914–1918 on 1939–1945'

'Requiem for Canada?'—Round Table Discussion: David Braybrooke (Centennial Chair in Liberal Arts), Walter Dean Burnham (Frank Erwin Chair in Government), and Robert Crunden (Professor of American Studies)

Ross Terrill (Harvard University), 'Australia and Asia in Historical Perspective'

380 British Studies at The University of Texas, 1975–1998

Sir Samuel Falle (British Ambassador and High Commissioner), 'The Morning after Independence: the Legacy of the British Empire'

Deborah Lavin (Principal of Trevelyan College, University of Durham), 'Lionel Curtis: Prophet of the British Empire'

Robin W. Doughty (Professor of Geography), 'Eucalyptus: And Not a Koala in Sight'

Al Crosby (Professor of American Studies and History), 'Captain Cook and the Biological Impact on the Hawaiian Islands'

Gillian Adams (Editor, Children's Literature Association Quarterly), 'Beatrix Potter and Her Recent Critics'

Lord Amery, 'Churchill's Legacy'

Christa Jansohn (University of Bonn) and Peter Green (Dougherty Professor of Classics), '*Lady Chatterley's Lover*'

R. A. C. Parker (Fellow of Queen's College, Oxford), 'Neville Chamberlain and the Coming of the Second World War'

John Velz (Professor of English), 'King Lear in Iowa: Jane Smiley's *A Thousand Acres*'

Jan Schall (University of Florida), 'British Spirit Photography'

Daniel Woolf (Dalhousie University), 'The Revolution in Historical Consciousness in England'

*Fall Semester 1994*

Kenneth O. Morgan (Vice-Chancellor, University of Wales), 'Welsh Nationalism'

Round Table Discussion on Michael Shelden's *Graham Greene: The Man Within*—Peter Green (Dougherty Professor in Classics); Roger Louis (Kerr Chair in English History and Culture); and Thomas F. Staley (Director, Harry Ransom Humanities Research Center)

Robert D. King (Rapoport Regents Chair in Liberal Arts), 'The Secret War, 1939–1945'

Brian Bond (Professor of English, University of Auckland), 'The Evolution of Shakespearean Dramatic Structure'

Lord Weatherill (former Speaker of the House of Commons), 'Thirty Years in Parliament'

Hans Mark (Professor of Aerospace Engineering), 'Churchill's Scientists'

Steven Weinberg (Josey Regental Professor of Science), 'The Test of War: British Strengths and Weaknesses in World War II'

Dennis Welland (Professor of English Literature and American Studies, University of East Anglia), 'Wilfred Owen and the Poetry of War'

Alan Frost (Professor of History, La Trobe University), 'The Bounty Mutiny and the British Romantic Poets'

W. O. S. Sutherland (Professor of English), 'Sir Walter Scott'

Hazel Rowley (Lecturer in Literary Studies, Deakin University, Melbourne), 'Christina Stead's "Other Country"'

Herman Bakvis (Professor of Government, Dalhousie University), 'The Future of Democracy in Canada and Australia'

Peter Stansky (Professor of History, Stanford University), 'George Orwell and the Writing of 1984'

Henry Dietz (Associate Professor of Government), 'Sherlock Homes and Jack the Ripper'

James Coote (Professor of Architecture), 'Techniques of Illusion in British Architecture'

'The Best and Worst Books of 1994': Dean Burnham (Government), Alessandra Lippucci (Government), Roger Louis (History), Sidney Monas (Slavic Languages and History), and Janice Rossen (Humanities Research Center)

*Spring Semester 1995*

Elizabeth Butler Cullingford (Professor of English), 'Anti-Colonial Metaphors in Contemporary Irish Literature'

Thomas M. Hatfield (Dean of Continuing Education), 'British and American Deception of the Germans in Normandy'

Gary P. Freeman (Associate Professor of Government), 'The Politics of Race and Immigration in Britain'

Donald G. Davis, Jr. (Professor in the Graduate School of Library and Information Science), 'The Printed Word in Sunday Schools in Nineteenth-Century England and the United States'

Brian Bremen (Assistant Professor of English), 'Healing Words: The Literature of Medicine and the Medicine of Literature'

Frances Karttunen (Linguistic Research Center) and Alfred W. Crosby (American Studies and History), 'British Imperialism and Creole Languages'

Paul Lovejoy (Professor of History, York University, Canada), 'British Rule in Africa: A Reassessment of Nineteenth-Century Colonialism'

Carol MacKay (Associate Professor of English), 'Creative Negativity in the Life and Work of Elizabeth Robins'

John Brokaw (Professor of Drama), 'The Changing Stage in London, 1790–1832'

Linda Colley (Richard M. Colgate Professor of History, Yale University), 'The Frontier in British History'

Iwan Morus (University of California at San Diego), 'Manufacturing Nature: Science, Technology, and Victorian Consumer Culture'

Brian Parker (Professor of English, University of Toronto), 'Jacobean Law: The Dueling Code and "A Faire Quarrel" (1617)'

Kate Gartner Frost (Professor of English), '"Jack Donne the Rake": Fooling around in the 1590s'

Mark Kinkead-Weekes (Professor of English, University of Kent), 'Beyond Gossip: D. H. Lawrence's Writing Life'

## Summer Semester 1995

S. P. Rosenbaum (Professor of English, University of Toronto), 'Leonard and Virginia Woolf at the Hogarth Press'

Maria X. Wells (Curator of Italian Collections, Harry Ransom Humanities Research Center), 'A Delicate Balance: Trieste 1945'

Kevin Tierney (Professor of Law, University of California at Berkeley), 'Personae in Twentieth Century British Autobiography'

## Fall Semester 1995

Brian Levack (Professor of History), 'Witchcraft, Possession, and the Law in Jacobean England'

Janice Rossen (Senior Fellow, Harry Ransom Humanities Center), 'The Home Front: Anglo-American Women Novelists and World War II'

Dorothy Driver (Professor of English, University of Cape Town), 'Olive Schreiner's Novel *From Man to Man*'

Philip Ziegler (London), 'Mountbatten Revisited'

Joanna Hitchcock (Director, UT Press), 'British and American University Presses'

Samuel H. Beer (Eaton Professor of the Science of Government Emeritus, Harvard University), 'The Rise and Fall of Party Government in Britain and the United States, 1945–1995'

Richard Broinowski (Australian Ambassador to Mexico and Central America), 'Australia and Latin America'
John Grigg (London), 'Myths about the Approach to Indian Independence'
Round Table Discussion on *Measuring the Mind* (Adrian Wooldridge) and *The Bell Curve* (Richard J. Herrnstein and Charles Murray): David Edwards (Professor of Government), Sheldon Ekland-Olson (Dean of Liberal Arts), Joseph Horn (Professor of Psychology), and Robert D. King (Rapoport Chair in Liberal Arts)
Paul Addison (Professor of History, University of Edinburgh), 'British Politics in the Second World War'
John Sibley Butler (Professor of Sociology), 'Emigrants of the British Empire'
Round Table Discussion on the Movie 'Carrington': Peter Green (Dougherty Professor of Classics), Robin Kilson (Assistant Professor of History), Roger Louis (Kerr Professor of English History and Culture), Sidney Monas (Professor of History and Slavic Languages), and Elizabeth Richmond-Garza (Assistant Professor of English)

*Spring Semester 1996*

Kevin Kenny (Assistant Professor of History), 'Making Sense of the Molly Maguires'
Brigadier Michael Harbottle (British Army), 'British and American Security in the Post-Cold War'
Carol MacKay (Professor of English), 'The Singular Double Vision of Photographer Julia Margaret Cameron'
John Ramsden (Professor of History, University of London), '"That Will Depend on Who Writes the History": Winston Churchill as His Own Historian'
Jack P. Greene (Andrew W. Mellon Professor in the Humanities, The Johns Hopkins University), 'The *British* Revolution America'
Walter D. Wetzels (Professor of German), 'The Ideological Fallout in Germany of Two British Expeditions to Test Einstein's General Theory of Relativity'
Thomas Pinney (William M. Keck Distinguished Service Professor of English, Pomona College), 'In Praise of Kipling'
Michael Charlesworth (Assistant Professor of Art History), 'The English Landscape Garden'

Stephen Gray (South African Novelist), 'The Dilemma of Colonial
Writers with Dual Identities'

Jeremy Black (Professor of History, University of Durham), 'Could
the British Have Won the War of American Independence?'

Dagmar Hamilton (Professor of Public Affairs, LBJ School), 'Justice William O. Douglas and British Colonialism'

Gordon Peacock and Laura Worthen (Theater and Dance), 'Not
Always a Green and Pleasant Land: Tom Stoppard's *Arcadia*'

Bernard Crick (Professor of Politics, University of London), 'Orwell
and the Business of Biography'

Geoffrey Hartman (Sterling Professor of English, Yale University),
'The Sympathy Paradox: Poetry, Feeling, and Modern Cultural Morality'

Dave Oliphant (Harry Ransom Humanities Research Center), 'Jazz
and Its British Acolytes'

R. W. B. Lewis (Professor of English and American Studies, Yale
University), 'Henry James: The Victorian Scene'

Alan Spencer (Vice-President, Ford Motor Company), 'Balliol, Big
Business, and Mad Cows'

Peter Quinn (Novelist): A Discussion of His Novel, *Banished Children of Eve*

*Summer Semester 1996*

Martin Stannard (Professor of English, Leicester University), 'Biography and Textual Criticism'

Diane Kunz (Associate Professor of History, Yale University), 'British Withdrawal East of Suez'

John Cell (Professor of History, Duke University), 'Who Ran the
British Empire?'

Mark Jacobsen (U.S. Marine Corps Command and Staff College),
'The North-West Frontier'

Theodore Vestal (Professor of Political Science, Oklahoma State
University), 'Britain and Ethiopia'

Warren F. Kimball (Robert Treat Professor of History, Rutgers University), '"A Victorian Tory": Churchill, the Americans, and
Self-Determination'

Louise B. Williams (Assistant Professor of History, Lehman College,
The City University of New York), 'British Modernism and
Fascism'

## Fall Semester 1996

Elizabeth Richmond-Garza (Associate Professor of English and Comparative Literature), 'The New Gothic: Decadents for the 1990s'

Robin Kilson (Assistant Professor of History), 'The Politics of Captivity: The British State and Prisoners of War in World War I'

Sir Brian Fall (Principal of Lady Margaret Hall, Oxford), 'What does Britain Expect from the European Community, the United States, and the Commonwealth?'

Roger Louis (Kerr Professor of English History and Culture), 'Harold Macmillan and the Middle East Crisis of 1958'

Ian Willison (former head of the Rare Books Branch, British Museum, and Editor of the History of the Book in Britain), 'The History of the Book and the Cultural and Literary History of the English-Speaking World'

Walter L. Arnstein (Jubilee Professor of the Liberal Arts and Sciences, University of Illinois), 'Queen Victoria's Other Island'

Noel Annan (London), '*Our Age* Revisited'

Michael Cohen (Lazarus Philips Professor of History, Bar-Ilan University, Tel Aviv), 'The Middle East and the Cold War: Britain, the United States, and the Soviet Union'

Reba Soffer (Professor of History, California State University, Northridge), 'Catholicism in England: Was it Possible to be a Good Catholic, a Good Englishman, and a Good Historian?'

Wilson Harris (Poet and Novelist), 'The Mystery of Consciousness: Cross-Cultural Influences in the Caribbean, Britain, and the United States'

H. S. Barlow (Singapore), 'British Malaya in the late Nineteenth Century'

Donald G. Davis, Jr. (Professor of Library and Information Science), 'British Destruction of Chinese Books in the Peking Siege of 1900'

Round Table Discussion on the Film 'Michael Collins': Elizabeth Cullingford (Professor of English), Kevin Kenny (Assistant Professor of History), Robin Kilson (Assistant Professor of History), and Roger Louis (History)

A. G. Hopkins (Smuts Professor of Commonwealth History, University of Cambridge), 'From Africa to Empire'

The Austin Chapter of the Society for the Preservation and Encouragement of Barber Shop Quartet Singing in America

*Spring Semester 1997*

Round Table Discussion on 'T. S. Eliot and Anti-Semitism': Robert D. King (Rapoport Chair in Jewish Studies), Sidney Monas (Professor of History and Slavic Languages), and Thomas F. Staley (Director of the Harry Ransom Humanities Research Center)

Phillip Herring (Professor Emeritus of English, University of Wisconsin-Madison), 'Djuna Barnes and T. S. Eliot: The Story of a Friendship'

Bryan Roberts (Smith Chair in United States/Mexican Relations), 'British Sociology and British Society'

Andrew Roberts (London), 'The Captains and the Kings Depart: Lord Salisbury's Skeptical Imperialism'

Colin Franklin (London), 'In a Golden Age of Publishing, 1950–1970'

Susan Pedersen (Professor of History, Harvard University), 'Virginia Woolf, Eleanor Rathbone, and the Problem of Appeasement'

Andrew Seaman (Saint Mary's University, Halifax, Nova Scotia), 'Thomas Raddall: A Novelist's View of Nova Scotia during the American Revolution'

Gordon Peacock (Frank C. Erwin Professor of Drama), 'Noel Coward: A Master Playwright, a Talented Actor, a Novelist and Diarist: Or a Peter Pan for the Twentieth Century?'

Roland Oliver (Professor of African History, School of Oriental and African Studies, University of London), 'The Battle for African History, 1947–1966'

Alistair Horne (St. Antony's College, Oxford), 'Harold Macmillan's Fading Reputation'

Richard Begam (Professor of English, University of Wisconsin/Madison), 'Samuel Beckett and the Debate on Humanism'

Christopher Waters (Associate Professor of History, Williams College), 'Delinquents, Perverts, and the State: Psychiatry and the Homosexual Desire in the 1930s'

Sami Zubaida (University of London), 'Ernest Gellner and Islam'

Walter Dean Burnham (Frank C. Erwin Chair in Government), 'Britain Votes: The 1997 General Election and Its Implications'

*Fall Semester 1997*

Judith Brown (Beit Professor of the History of the British Commonwealth, Oxford University), 'Gandhi—A Victorian Gentleman'

Thomas Cable (Blumberg Professor of English), 'Hearing and Revising the History of the English Language'

Round Table Discussion on 'The Death of Princess Diana': Judith Brown (Oxford), David Edwards (Professor of Government), Elizabeth Richmond-Garza (Associate Professor of English), Anne Baade (British Studies), Sandy Lippucci (Instructor in Government), and Kevin Kenny (Associate Professor of History)

David Hunter (Music Librarian, Fine Arts Library), 'Handel and His Patrons'

Anne Kane (Assistant Professor of Sociology), 'The Current Situation in Ireland'

James S. Fishkin (Darrell K. Royal Regents Chair in Ethics in American Society), 'Power and the People: The Televised Deliberative Poll in the 1997 British General Election'

Howard D. Weinbrot (Vilas Research Professor of English, University of Wisconsin/Madison), 'Jacobitism in Eighteenth-Century Britain'

J. C. Baldwin, M.D. (Houston), 'The Abdication of King Edward VIII'

Kenneth E. Carpenter (Harvard University), 'Library Revolutions Past and Present'

Akira Iriye (Professor of History, Harvard University), 'Britain, Japan, and the International Order after World War I'

Anthony Hobson (London), 'Reminiscences of British Authors and the Collecting of Contemporary Manuscripts'

David Killingray (Professor of History, University of London), 'The British in the West Indies'

Alan Knight (Professor of Latin American History, Oxford University), 'British Imperialism in Latin America'

Round Table Discussion on King Lear in Iowa: The Movie *A Thousand Acres*—Linda Ferreira-Buckley (Associate Professor of English), Elizabeth Richmond-Garza (Associate Professor of English), Helena Woodard (Assistant Professor of English), and John Velz (Professor of English)

Timothy Lovelace (Assistant Professor of Music) and the Talisman Trio

*Spring Semester 1998*

Richard Ollard (London), 'A. L. Rowse: Epitome of the Twentieth-Century'

Round Table Discussion on Arundhati Roy's *The God of Small Things:* Phillip Herring (Harry Ransom Humanities Research Center), Brian Trinque (Economics), Kamala Visweswaran (Anthropology), and Robert Hardgrave (Government)

Jonathan Schneer (Georgia Institute of Technology), 'London in 1900: The Imperial Metropolis'

Trevor Burnard (University of Canterbury, New Zealand), 'Rioting in Goatish Embraces: Marriage and the Failure of White Settlement in British Jamaica'

Felipe Fernández-Armesto (Oxford University), 'British Traditions in Comparative Perspective'

Michael Mann (University of California at Los Angeles), 'The Broader Significance of Labour's Landslide Victory of 1997'

Dane Kennedy (University of Nebraska), 'White Settlers in Colonial Kenya and Rhodesia'

Round Table Discussion on 'Noel Annan, Keynes, and Bloomsbury': James Galbraith (LBJ School), Elspeth Rostow (LBJ School), and Walt Rostow (Economics and History)

Lisa Moore (Associate Professor of English), 'British Studies–Lesbian Studies: A Dangerous Intimacy?'

James Gibbs (University of the West of England), 'Wole Soyinka: The Making of a Playwright'

Marilyn Butler (Oxford University), 'About the House: Jane Austen's Anthropological Eye'

R. J. Q. Adams (Texas A&M University), 'Britain and Ireland, 1912–1922'

John M. Carroll (Asian Studies), 'Nationalism and Identity in Pre-1949 Hong Kong'

Round Table Discussion on the Irish Referendum: Anne Kane (Sociology), Kevin Kenny (History), Roger Louis (History), and Jennifer O'Connor (History)